Fielding's
MOTORING AND CAMPING EUROPE

Current Fielding Titles

Red Guides—updated annually

FIELDING'S BERMUDA AND THE BAHAMAS 1986
FIELDING'S CARIBBEAN 1986
FIELDING'S DISCOVER EUROPE: OFF THE BEATEN PATH 1986
FIELDING'S ECONOMY CARIBBEAN 1986
FIELDING'S ECONOMY EUROPE 1986
FIELDING'S EUROPE 1986
FIELDING'S MEXICO 1986
FIELDING'S SELECTIVE SHOPPING GUIDE TO EUROPE 1986

Blue Guides—updated as necessary

FIELDING'S ALL-ASIA BUDGET GUIDE
FIELDING'S EGYPT AND THE ARCHAEOLOGICAL SITES
FIELDING'S EUROPE WITH CHILDREN
FIELDING'S FAMILY VACATION GUIDE
FIELDING'S FAR EAST
FIELDING'S HAVENS AND HIDEAWAYS USA
FIELDING'S MOTORING AND CAMPING EUROPE
FIELDING'S WORLDWIDE CRUISES 2nd revised edition

Fielding's
MOTORING AND CAMPING EUROPE

by
Patricia and Robert Foulke

Fielding Travel Books
℅ William Morrow & Company, Inc.
105 Madison Avenue, New York, N.Y. 10016

Copyright © 1986 by Patricia N. Foulke and Robert D. Foulke

All rights reserved. No part of this book may be reproduced or utilized in any form or by any means, electronic or mechanical, including photocopying, recording or by any information storage and retrieval system, without permission in writing from the Publisher. Inquiries should be addressed to Permissions Department, William Morrow and Company, Inc., 105 Madison Ave., New York, N.Y. 10016.

Library of Congress Catalog Card Number: 85-70652

ISBN: 0-688-04807-2

Printed in the United States of America
First Edition
1 2 3 4 5 6 7 8 9 10

To
Robert William Foulke
who traveled with us in person and in memory
on each trip

Acknowledgments

We wish to thank those who contributed expertise, enthusiasm, time, and encouragement to this book.

England: Dorothy and Robert Blackburn, Anne and Paul Born, Martha Brown, Barbara and Donald Bush, Nancy and Peter Clarke, Pamela Clarke, Sue and Robert Gorton, Ian Harvey, Kay and Duncan Hodge, Jean and Geoffrey Hughes, DeAnne Julius, Nancy and John Kendall, Sue and Christopher Lee, Gillian and Thomas Lewis, Maggy and Ian Mills, Alicia Montagu-Johnson, Audrey and David Price, Margaret Smith, Gillian and John Taberner, Bettina and Robert Wessel.

France: Katherine Chaylade, Ardis and Herbert Ochsner, Richard Ochsner, Judith and James Potter.

Germany: Katherine and John Edstrom, Judith and David Ellingson.

Greece: Lynn Fragale, Andromachi Katsani, Andrew Kendall, Elizabeth McGrew, Virginia and Stephen Minot, Stella Nanos, Patricia and Robert Ochsner, Phebe Smith, Sally Vernon.

Holland: Jopie Been.

Italy: Anna Maria D'Amato, Catherine Feste, Margaret and Ancel Keys, Emilia and Enrico Notaro, Maria Grazia and Alessandro Notaro, Maria Scarano and Giovanni Notaro.

Portugal: Manuela and Antonio Leite.

Spain: Susanna and Michael Beer, Leslie Brown, Phillip Mitchell, Elizabeth and Adrian Montagu-Johnson, Mary and George Pegg, Luisa and Donn Pohren, Albert Smith, Nancy and Richard Winslow.

Sweden: Kerstin Andersson, Myrtle Edstrom, Susan Ellingson, A. Herbert Nelson, Ulla and Goran Printz-Pahlson, Veronica and Bo Rynningsjo, Carin and Goran Rynningsjo, Siv and Erik Rynningsjo, Ammy Stendahl.

Switzerland: Clemewell and Robert Young.

Wales: Eirlys Thomas, Morfudd and Thomas Thomas.

Yugoslavia: Valerie and Ken Allen, Pamela Kovacic.

To our children: David Foulke, Carolyn Foulke, and Deborah Waldbillig—who began winning "best traveler awards" at age three.

To Eunice Riedel and Randy Ladenheim for their helpful suggestions and scrupulous editorial advice.

CONTENTS

Introduction xi

Planning xv

Routes xxxvii
 Southwestern England **1**
 Central England, Wales, and the Lake District **29**
 Scotland **45**
 Scandinavia **53**
 The Low Countries, the Rhine, Bavaria, the Alps and the Black Forest **69**
 The Southeastern Mediterranean **85**
 France—The South and the West **131**
 The Iberian Peninsula **153**

Europe under Canvas (Campgrounds) 199

Camping Equipment 213

Camp Cooking 216

Driving Regulations 220

Conversion Tables 222

Index 225

LIST OF MAPS

Southwestern England   2

Central England, Wales, and the Lake District   28

Scotland   44

Scandinavia   52

Low Countries, the Rhine, Bavaria, the Alps, and the Black Forest   68

Southeastern Mediterranean   86

France   132

Iberian Peninsula   154

INTRODUCTION

AN OVERVIEW

Enjoy Europe! Yes, but how can a family, a couple, or a single person facing the giddy prospect of a week or a year in Europe make the most of it? Some people prefer to throw things into a suitcase and unravel threads of the trip as they go. Others carefully plan a crammed itinerary that leaves them exhausted and costs a mint. Over the last quarter of a century we have been lucky enough to live in Europe for four academic years, researching, writing, and traveling. During these years we tried a variety of approaches to travel and learned to develop those that worked best. Having pieced it all together for our own use, we decided to lay it out in a concise guide for other travelers in Europe.

The unique aspect of this book is a series of selected routes that we have followed through some of the most interesting parts of Europe. You may ask how we have selected them from the endless possibilities available. Our first trips were planned without experience but with unquenchable enthusiasm: We wanted to see and do everything. In the next round we explored new places in some depth through libraries and bookstores, streamlined former trips for repeat visits, and attacked the routes with a vigor somewhat tempered by reason and a sense of human endurance. Each set of trips was interspersed with six years at home, so we had time to savor the last sabbatical leave while planning the next. Our children appeared, traveled, grew, and traveled some more; over the years their ages and interests encouraged us to seek a variety of experiences. Frequent travel also made us pragmatic about the effort involved: As we went, we built on lists and records from previous trips that gave us a basis for realistic estimates of distance, cost, and time. Gradually, we learned to pace ourselves and to develop our own style of travel.

The first requisite for a memorable trip is openness to new experience and a bent for making personal discoveries. We want to pass on to you our enthusiasm and genuine feeling about places. To make them come alive, we have tried to paint visual images for you, to provide portraits of ordinary people in their daily lives, and to suggest the stark or subtle ambience of places you may wish to visit for yourself. One absorbs this by attending to sensations: listen to church bells or the human sounds of a village from a path above it, to strange bird songs, the cacaphony of a market square, the voices of a choir reverberating in the nave of a cathedral, or children playing familiar nursery-rhyme games in a foreign language; smell the incredible fishiness of an Italian harbor town, wild flowers growing in a Swiss meadow, the fragrance of an English herb garden, the aroma of moussaka wafting from Greek tavernas, or the pine scents of a Bavarian forest. You will want to taste the many wonderful culinary treats in store for you as you travel from country to country; let salt water tickle your tongue as you swim and float in the sea, lick an Italian gelato on a hot day, and try some "real ale" in Britain. Feel the soft, fine sand on a Mediterranean beach, the comfort of a light quilt or "puff" on a cold night, the roughness of cobblestones under your feet, the spray blown from the cold North Sea on your face, and the warmth of a pub fire. Above all, you will want to look at the immense variety of landscape and townscape that Europe offers—from Norwegian fjords to Riviera beaches, the valley of the Loire to Mont Blanc, as well as the history of architecture made manifest in cathedrals, castles, and chateaux.

We have tried to write for experienced travelers and those on their first trip. To formulate a style of travel is to be selective, to make choices from a vast array of possibilities. Our suggestions are meant to increase your range of choices without overcomplicating them by providing too much information or too many places. One can never "see" all of Europe, nor should one want to! We have given detailed, factual information about many well-known places and other virtually unknown places we know and enjoy.

Our routes are designed to include places of cultural interest, and we have provided archaeological, historical, literary, and legendary backgrounds for many of them. We have also tried to suggest a variety of things to see and do—museums, ruins, cathedrals, castles, chateaux, hiking trails, beaches, sports, and the simplest and most fascinating of all activities, people watching. Our routes should save you time and provide some focus for your further selection. You can make use of some of the information that has been tested by others without losing the zest of your own adventure. You can enjoy the humor of others' mistakes knowing that you will make your own, and your own discoveries as well. You can save time and effort by remembering to take along the crucial items we didn't think of. You can save the extraordinary amount of time it took us to travel some routes with miserable road conditions we hadn't known about until we endured them. It didn't usually take us more than one trip through a region to learn to allow more time for that 50-mile stretch of curvy, bumpy, narrow roads, but occasionally we had to learn our lesson twice because we were enticed by an equally unknown alternate route. For those who like to explore, lines on a map are irresistible temptations. If this book piques your interest and contributes to your travel pleasure, we will be content.

ATTITUDES TOWARD TOURISM

While visiting major ancient sites in Greece—Delphi, the Acropolis, the Temple of Poseidon at Sunion—we began to reflect on the nature of modern tourism. We had not realized that Greece in early May would be so filled with the hordes disgorged by tour buses; as independent travelers we were part of a small minority, just as the backpackers (not all young) were. So the dilemma of our reaction to tourism arose, as it had in Spain and Portugal during January.

It is easy to reject the whole enterprise of commercial tourism until one remembers all of the outer contexts, not just the money spent and the artificiality of a preplanned, fixed tour with no time or opportunity for random, personal discovery. "Canned," with all of its negative connotations, is the word that usually occurs to us when we think about the slick American and European packaged tours—overorganized, overextended, frenetically paced—that many of our friends have taken and even enjoyed. Although we, as independent travelers, can manage our use of time and space less mechanically, we do go to many of the same places and share many of the same experiences. So how can one cope with the idea of tourism or the feeling of being a "tourist"?

We start by remembering that tourism is only one part of the wider enterprise of travel, which has many aspects that cannot be entirely reduced to commercialism, such as exploration and discovery or understanding the customs and attitudes of other peoples. And at the heart of the urge to travel lies a fundamental desire for the freedom to move about the world as one chooses, to explore the strange, the remote, and the ancient aspects of civilization, to learn more about the past. Even the stereotypical boor (and bore) on a package tour, the man who loudly proclaims that he has no interest in art or history or culture and adds that he has been dragged along on this tour by his wife, will probably find a few sparks of interest as he views the uncanny symmetry of the columns of the Parthenon or wonders how the Mycenaean builders cut, moved, and placed such huge blocks of stone.

Tourism as big business is, of course, difficult to accept: a modern form of sheepherding. And the tourism that destroys the charm of old, impoverished villages with the concrete slabs of high-rise condominiums is an aesthetic anathema and an economic boon at the same time. Is the culture of a poor fishing village denuded of all its young, who have gone to the cities out of necessity, improved or destroyed by the tourism that brings new jobs and simultaneously removes the appeal of the old ones (fishing and farming)? Such questions are not easily answered, and our difficulty in coping with them should remind us to think more carefully about the implications of travel and tourism rather than falling back on an easy dismissal of the whole industry as just another example of tawdry commercialism in the modern world. When we remember its core value—the ability to move freely about the world and to enrich our lives with new experiences—travel, in whatever form, is worth preserving. In this book we strike for a mode of travel that lies somewhere between the rigidity of package tours and the waste of aimless wandering: planned but flexible routes that will encompass many of the delights and treasures of Europe but still allow you the freedom to discover more on your own.

PRAGMATICS

The next section will offer planning tips for before you go. As impecunious students and then teachers with young children, we were hooked on camping as the economical way to manage a trip without mounting guilt. Even at that time we splurged on one New Year's Eve in a French chateau, and stayed in hotels on special occasions. (During those years our children all won the "good camper's award" for being such good sports when the weather went bad.) It is possible to travel in Europe without blowing your children's or your own college fund. We discovered that 12 weeks of camping cost us no more than others spend on a 3-week package tour.

Now that we are traveling more than ever we have found that we can still keep our expenses at a reasonable level by searching out inexpensive accommodations and doing some camping, but occasionally splurging on paradores, pousadas, chateaux, and other historic places where the relative luxury is also interesting. In other words, we enjoy a variety of accommodations and will put up with something that is less than ideal for the sake of location or historic significance or even simple economy.

This guide also provides information about economic transportation, currency regulations, needed travel documents, camping equipment, organization of gear, packing, householding for a longer period of time, coping with emergencies, a planning countdown, and a variety of travel tips.

The major portion of the book is a series of carefully planned routes. At the beginning of each we have included a map of the route so you can visualize the whole. A list of estimated mileages (kilometers on the Continent) follows as a rough guide to planning (you will know how the mileage you have counted on your map differs from the actual mileage expended after you have gotten lost, retraced your route to go back to that little shop someone remembered, or whatever). The routes are meant to be flexible guides to planning with your own interests in mind. They are starting points to save you time and effort in planning your own trip.

We have included at the back of the book a list of campgrounds by itinerary, following each route. We have selected these from an endless list as those that are well established, have basic amenities, and are in a pleasant or satisfactory location. There are many others to choose from when you arrive in an area, including some "mom-and-pop" operations that may be excellent one year and closed the next. But if you are driving in late and need to look for a place in the dark, one of these will do. Also included are a list of necessary camping equipment and a section on efficient camp cooking in a European setting. If you camp in the U.S., you will probably cook much the same way in Europe, with the addition of local foods and the subtraction of barbecuing. Finally, you will find special driving regulations and conversion tables.

Planning

Getting the nerve to transform Sunday-afternoon fantasies into airline reservations is the hardest part. Once the choice has been made, you can begin to plan. If you really want to enjoy an adventure in Europe, you must be willing to work at planning. Experienced travelers tend to be precise and meticulous. The time available will determine the distance that can be covered with pleasure instead of panic. Cost estimates will be realistic only if they include a day-by-day listing of all known expenses and a slush fund for the unexpected opportunities that will crop up, as well as for inflation and fluctuating exchange rates. The focus of the trip—season, sports interests, cultural activities, and the proportion of time spent in large cities or in the country—will determine equipment and clothing needs, destinations, and routes.

ANTICIPATION Anticipating a trip abroad is great fun. If you are taking your children, you should share that planning with them—they may not realize what is in store for them. Collecting travel pamphlets with enticing photographs can stir up anyone's interest. Or you can plan evenings focused on each country to be visited. Such parties can include distinctive food, local costumes, typical pictures or decorations on the table and walls, and perhaps a unique product—smorbrod for Denmark, wooden shoes for Holland, brass rubbings for England. This kind of evening also provides a delightful aftermath of the trip; you can show slides or movies, wear clothing acquired abroad, use souvenir items as decorations, and perhaps have some conversation in the mother tongue of the country.

We took along a stack of photos of our life at home to show friends in Europe. Children may enjoy putting together a book showing special features of their area, school, friends, and general information about the United States. People we have met are always interested in what it is *really* like in the States. If you particularly want to meet people during your travels there are programs such as "Meet the Danes" available. Local tourist offices in each town often have information about such opportunities.

You may want to give friends a copy of addresses where mail can be received during the trip. It is always fun to get mail from home. You can arrange to pick up mail in American Express offices, if you are a card holder, or Poste Restante (general delivery).

TOURIST INFORMATION In the early stages of planning a trip, write to the national tourist office for each country you plan to visit. If you are taking children, put their names on your request for information, maps, brochures on festivals, sports features, castles, local crafts, zoos, and the like. This will give them the fun of receiving a deluge of mail. Reading done in anticipation of the adventures to come will enhance their enjoyment and learning during the trip. Apart from the pleasures of anticipation, you will receive much useful and up-to-date information on currency and customs regulations, regions of special interest, calendars of cultural events, lists of campgrounds and other accommodations, and maps. If you think you will visit certain places, or have an interest in specific activities be sure to name them in your request for information.

The following are New York addresses for national tourist offices.

Austrian State Tourist Department
545 Fifth Ave.
New York, NY 10017

Belgian Tourist Bureau
745 Fifth Ave.
New York, NY 10022

British Tourist Authority
40 W. 57th St.
New York, NY 10019

Box 504, Stn. F
Toronto, Ont. M4Y 2L8
Canada

Danish Travel Office
75 Rockefeller Plaza
New York, NY 10019

Finnish National Travel Office
75 Rockefeller Plaza
New York, NY 10019

French Government Tourist Offices
610 Fifth Ave.
New York, NY 10020

German Tourist Information Office
747 Third Ave.
New York, NY 10017

Greek National Tourist Office
645 Fifth Avenue
New York, NY 10022

Irish Tourist Office
590 Fifth Ave.
New York, NY 10036

Italian Government Tourist Office
630 Fifth Ave.
New York, NY 10111

Luxembourg Consulate General
801 Second Ave.
New York, NY 10017

Netherlands National Tourist Office
576 Fifth Ave.
New York, NY 10036

Norwegian National Tourist Office
75 Rockefeller Plaza
New York, NY 10019

Portuguese Tourist Office
548 Fifth Ave.
New York, NY 10036

Spanish Tourist Office
665 Fifth Ave.
New York, NY 10022

Introduction xvii

Swedish National Travel
75 Rockefeller Plaza
New York, NY 10019

Yugoslav Tourist Office
630 Fifth Ave.
New York, NY 10111

Swiss National Tourist Office
608 Fifth Ave.
New York, NY 10020

PLANNING YOUR ROUTE If you choose to follow a route that has been preplanned, you will know approximately where you will be on each day of your trip. If you want to work in a visit to see friends, enjoy a festival on a holiday, or visit Parliament when it is open, you will need to list these special interests and plan around them. We sketch out our specific priorities on a sheet of paper and then fill in the days between (with a supply of erasers handy as we study maps and guides to estimate just how long it might take to drive). We look at the directness of the proposed route, the kind of roads available, and terrain that might cause us undue delay; we think of possible side excursions and allow for days of relaxation. We erase and delete as choices are made and remade until we end up with (we hope) a manageable trip; then we neatly copy it onto an index card or two. On the card we list starting and stopping locations for each day, with the approximate mileage and estimated driving time. Useful planning maps can be obtained from AAA or map stores that carry European maps (especially Michelin or Hallweg).

Sample Route and Mileage Chart: Two Alternative Plans for a 22-Day Trip from England to Italy and Bavaria

		Plan 1		Plan 2	
Date		Place	Mileage	Place	Mileage
From Cambridge to:
April	3	Cologne	377	Cologne	377
	4	Basel	308	Lucerne	366
	5	Como	225	Venice	343
	6	Como/Milan	—	Venice	—
	7	Como	—	Florence	167
	8	Sorrento	550	Sorrento	288
	9	Sorrento/Vesuvius	—	Sorrento/Vesuvius	—
	10	Sorrento/Capri	—	Sorrento/Capri	—
	11	Amalfi/Pioppi	80	Amalfi/Pioppi	80
	12	Pioppi	—	Pioppi	—
	13	Pioppi	—	Pioppi	—
	14	Pioppi	—	Pioppi	—
	15	Florence	370	Rome	236
	16	Florence	—	Como	365
	17	Venice	167	Como/Milan	—

Sample Route and Mileage Chart: Two Alternative Plans for a 22-Day Trip from England to Italy and Bavaria *(continued)*

	Plan 1		Plan 2	
Date	Place	Mileage	Place	Mileage
18	Venice	—	Como	—
19	Grossweil	185	Grossweil	278
20	Grossweil/Innsbruck	—	Innsbruck	—
21	Garmisch	—	Garmisch	—
22	Grossweil	—	Grossweil	—
23	Brussels	542	Cologne	405
24	Cambridge	263	Cambridge	377
Total mileage:		3,067		3,282

We chose to follow Plan 1 knowing very well that we had planned to cover more distance than seemed quite reasonable in 22 days. We wanted to visit relatives in Pioppi (in southern Italy) and friends in Grossweil (in Bavaria) and therefore were fully aware of the reasons for our overplanning. We knew that if we did not want to give up any of our major stops we might have to drive long hours. Most of our choices were favorite locations from previous trips that we yearned to visit again. We went into the trip knowing that we might have to push a bit and enjoyed it in spite of a few stressful situations—detours, wet weather, arriving too late at campsites and pitching tents in the dark. All people traveling through Europe have to decide how much they will put up with to do what they want to do.

Before we start a trip such as this one, we search through many of the travel books on the market and find long lists of hotels, restaurants, sightseeing suggestions, and general information about currency, shopping, and local regulations. But we usually do not find what we want most—information on trips actually taken along certain routes and the difficulties that might be avoided. In the past we have wanted the kind of information that comes from experience. We wanted to know how much more it would cost to travel in Scandinavia than in England. We wanted to hear about what happens, for example, when people innocently choose Easter weekend (one of the busiest weekends of the year in Europe) for an adventure and get trapped in the center of a little Italian town on Good Friday while processions clog all available roads. We wanted to be reassured that camping can be a pleasure again—even after the misery of pitching tents at 1 a.m. in a torrential downpour. We wanted to be reminded that difficult situations could sometimes resolve themselves—like the time a chance encounter with some friendly people late one April night (when campgrounds had not yet opened for the season) led our family to a midnight spread of smorbrod, tenting in our hosts' garden, and a personal tour of Copenhagen the following day. We wanted to know what to do when seemingly impossible barriers were thrown our way—like the time in May we were due to catch a ferry and found that the mountain road leading to it hadn't been plowed! This is the kind of information that can come only from those who have driven the routes and encountered (or avoided) the difficulties.

ESTIMATING YOUR EXPENSES AND GETTING MONEY Once the route has been planned you can work up a cost estimate. We list all categories of expense such as accommodations, gasoline costs (based on the total mileage and the cost per liter in each country), highway tolls, ferries, tickets, entrance fees to museums or other entertainment, food costs (estimated on the cost per day in each country multiplied by the number of days there), meals out, launderettes, sports equipment rental, postcards, gifts, and a slush fund for miscellaneous expenses. Of course, no matter how careful you are there is no guarantee that your costs will actually match your estimates. After taking several trips during the same year, we learned to be wary of certain types of expenses that skyrocket—eating out, snacks, ferry costs in high season, sightseeing in cities—and could feel confident about those that tended to remain stable.

It is particularly important not to underestimate costs that can vary wildly from country to country—food costs in Scandinavia, for example, accommodation in Switzerland, gas and tolls in Italy, or ferries everywhere. In any case, you will feel more comfortable with a ballpark figure as you order traveler's checks and plan to make an emergency fund somehow available.

Getting money in a hurry in Europe is not easy. Years ago, as impecunious Fulbright scholars (or "halfbrights," because we were trying to support two people on the stipend of $156 a month), we started on a trip with the assurance that a check from the U.S. would be sent on when it arrived in our local bank in England. What we did not know was that the check had in fact arrived on schedule, but was sitting in another branch of the same bank in London. We spent many fruitless hours during the trip trying to obtain our own money and only succeeded when a kindly American Express clerk in Norway waived the rules and allowed us to charge cash to our account. Even with a bank account in one branch of an American bank in London, we found that it took three weeks to cash a check in another branch of the same bank; therefore we made advance arrangements to cash checks without waiting. A bank credit card is helpful as a guarantee; Visa and Mastercard (Access) are accepted throughout most of Europe.

In our years abroad we have learned more about beating the banking system in Europe—how to cope with problems that never occur to most Americans, who are offered more credit than they need. Before the last trip we made all sorts of advance arrangements and did achieve a smoothly running banking relationship with a British bank. We also armed ourselves with both British and American credit cards and knew where each might be acceptable. Even simple matters can be difficult. Banking hours vary a great deal and are likely to be sparse during holidays. In every case, it pays to think through your financial needs and plan how you are going to get the money in advance.

With the uncertain fluctuation of the dollar against other currencies it is often difficult to predict your costs accurately, but advance planning still helps you get the most pleasure for the least money. Cost differentials between countries seldom change radically in a short period of time, and they will affect your mode of travel and choice of accommodation if you have a limited budget. You might, for example, choose to stay in small hotels in Spain or Greece but camp or use hostels in Germany or Scandinavia. In addition to watching basic living costs, there are other economies that help to make a trip inexpensive as well as enjoyable. The fares to Europe have now dropped enough to offset higher prices for food and goods. You can plan shorter visits in countries that are the most expensive, staying just over the border in a less expensive country. You can buy small things to remember pleasant days instead of stocking up on sweaters and other items that are no longer much of a bargain in Europe. You can plan to take advantage of the free sightseeing available almost everywhere: There is a great deal of natural beauty to enjoy, including hiking through the countryside on public footpaths; narrow streets lined with open-air shops, festivals, cathedrals, and walks through little villages with half-timbered buildings are all free.

CURRENCY REGULATIONS Be sure to check special currency regulations as you cross borders, especially when entering Yugoslavia and Portugal. Both countries prohibit the export of any significant amount of currency, even what you could carry in your wallet for several days' food and incidentals. You may want to buy Yugoslav dinar checks rather than dinars as you enter so you can change back any unused checks as you leave. You will not be allowed to exchange *any* note over 100 dinars outside Yugoslavia under current regulations. We drove out of Portugal at night, after the bank exchange was closed, and had great difficulty changing our Portuguese escudos into Spanish pesetas: It was possible to change only small amounts at any one time, after completing a long bureaucratic process. Plan to make the exchange at the border if you can.

GAS COUPONS As you cross into both Italy and Yugoslavia, be sure to buy gas coupons, especially in Italy, where the discount helps offset extraordinarily high prices. (In Italy coupons are not available on rental cars—only on your own car.) If you are following our route through Italy we recommend that you buy the large package of coupons for both northern and southern Italy. You will use up the autostrada coupons quickly and you can always turn back any leftover gas coupons as you leave the country. The saving in Yugoslavia is less but still worth the trouble.

Accommodation

Through years of travel we have run the gamut of accommodation from camping to well-appointed inns and castles; we now find flexibility within a modest range of price levels is most satisfactory for us. We remember the nights we said to each other that we *would* camp even while setting up quite unhappily in pouring rain. There were other times when the experience of living in a historic castle was the right choice. Large, modern hotels leave us cold, and we do object to paying their inflated prices, or the astronomic prices of the old but pretentious grand hotels. On a rainy night a bed and breakfast place at moderate cost is usually worth it for campers, and a night or two of roughing it in less than satisfactory rooms will not hurt those who choose small hotels as their basic kind of accommodation.

CAMPING There are many reasons for deliberately choosing to camp. Cost is the most obvious one. We know that a family can camp for a fraction of the cost of a hotel trip with all meals out. But there are other advantages as well. Camping can also provide freedom from the meal schedules and dress restrictions of hotels, from constant tips and railroad timetables. It can let you explore villages and beaches and mountains where there are no hotels, or it can bring you to the periphery of Europe's most interesting cities. People working together making camp, cooking, and relaxing by their tents create a special kind of intimacy. There is a sense of adventure involved in picking a campsite with a gorgeous view in a mountain wilderness, or one with historic interest near an ancient Roman wall or within an old castle enclosure. Camping allows you to travel more while paying less, to be free to live by weather and impulse rather than by one of those intricate itineraries that makes work out of fun.

Before you make such a choice, think about the length of time you have available to travel. If you will be in Europe for less than two or three weeks, it probably will not make sense for you to transport or even rent all of the equipment you will need to camp. If you will be traveling for a longer period of time and will have a car available, then camping makes perfect sense. And there are middle positions: Backpackers often camp at night but eat most of their meals out, thus avoiding the necessity of carrying much cooking equipment.

Those who have not camped before may be appalled by the prospect of uncertainty or discomfort, thinking that such travel is only for young students trying to find themselves by hitchhiking around. And those who roll into a city campground at 10 p.m. in August may well be put off by a crowded site, noise, and the prospect of setting up camp hurriedly—perhaps with tired children. But many European families camp whenever they travel, and when you meet them you will notice that they are generally well equipped, well organized, and comfortable. Ordinarily you can set and meet personal priorities all over Europe in the form of hot showers, lovely views, attractive sites, and quiet neighbors. As you travel, these priorities will shift, depending upon the weather, the number of days planned in each area, the activities and sights nearby, and individual preferences.

PENSIONS, BED-AND-BREAKFAST PLACES, GUEST HOUSES Accommodation in these places can be delightful or barely satisfactory for one night only. You never know what to expect until you get there, and we cannot make a general statement that will be of any use to you. Throughout Europe we have found a number of interesting and helpful proprietors willing to provide us with clean, comfortable lodging for a night when we were tired and ready to stop. If you start looking before the end of the afternoon, it is a challenge to roll into a new town wondering where you will sleep that night.

HOSTELS Hostels are not restricted to young people, in spite of the titles of the associations that run them. Although hostels vary in architecture and range of accommodation, many of them are placed in interesting buildings—castles, boathouses, mansions, farmhouses, or old mills. The first hostel was opened in a castle, Burg Altena, in Germany in 1910; the first hostel in Britain was opened in 1930. They appeal to hikers, cyclists, and other travelers who want inexpensive lodging without carrying camping equipment. Meals are available at low cost, or you can cook your own. There are rules on hours, as well as restrictions on smoking and drinking. Some hostels are in beautiful locations; we looked at one in Salcombe, South Devon, England, housed in a former mansion within a lovely garden, offering a beautiful view of the harbor below ringed with cliffs. For more information, write to American Youth Hostels, Delaplane, VA 22025, Canadian Hosteling Association, 33 River Road, Vanier, Ont. K1L 8H9, or Youth Hostels Association, Trevelyan House, 8 St. Stephens Hill, St. Albans, Herts AL1 2DY, England.

PARADORES, POUSADAS, CHATEAUX, NATIONAL TRUST INNS Staying in historic buildings can add an exciting dimension to your trip. Each has its own history, period furnishings, public rooms to explore, and, perhaps, ghosts. The range of amenities runs from a standard bedroom with private bath to an elegant suite with a panoramic view, since castles and monasteries are situated on the tops of hills. Those that are owned by a state government (Spanish paradores and Portuguese pousadas) tend to have comfortable facilities and carefully selected regional cooking at reasonable prices. You can book your stay in paradores and pousadas through a central office rather than contacting each one. Others (especially in France and England) may be run as independent hotels or as parts of a chain of luxury hotels; some are absolutely elegant . . . and expensive.

For paradores, write to the Spanish National Tourist Office, 665 Fifth Ave., New York, NY 10022; for pousadas, to the Portuguese National Tourist Office, 548 Fifth Ave., New York, NY 10036; for French chateaux to the French Government Tourist Office, 610 Fifth Avenue, New York, NY 10020; and for National Trust Inns to the British Tourist Authority, 40 West 57th St., New York, NY 10019.

If you are traveling to northeastern Portugal, you may want to investigate solares, which are manor houses opened by Portuguese families for tours and for accommodation. Write to the Portuguese National Tourist Office.

Transportation

Choosing your mode of transportation for a trip is reasonably complicated because it depends upon the answers to a number of preliminary questions. How many are there in your party? How much space do you and your traveling companions need while driving? Will you want to sleep in hotels, motels, paradores, pousadas, chateaux, pensiones, b & b's, inns, hostels, or campgrounds? What is your minimum acceptable level of comfort? What sort of terrain will your trip cover? How long will it last? The right choice of vehicle will probably be a compromise of some sort, balancing comfort, space, cost, gasoline consumption, ease of handling, ruggedness, the convenience of pickup and dropoff points, and possible future use of the vehicle either abroad or back home. In any case, you will want to consider the advantages and disadvantages of four possible ways of acquiring a vehicle: rental, leasing, purchasing and reselling, and purchasing to ship home.

AUTOMOBILE RENTAL, LEASE, OR PURCHASE Renting a car often can be the most economical way to travel, as well as the most convenient. The breakeven point between public and private transportation is usually reached when you have more than one or two persons traveling together; and for camping ventures the convenience of having your own vehicle is almost always worth the extra money because it frees you from timetables and gives you access to places not easily reached in any other way. Rental cars are available in all major European cities. Information on cars, caravans, or campmobiles can be obtained from:

Europe by Car, Inc.
1 Rockefeller Plaza
New York, NY 10020

Nemet Auto International
153-12 Hillside Avenue
Jamaica, NY 11432

France Auto Vacances
420 Lexington Ave.
New York, NY 10017

Avis, Hertz, and other American rental agents can also make these arrangements. Be aware of the fact that rates differ from country to country. Sometimes you can do better by waiting until you arrive to strike a bargain. In high season, this may not be worth the risk.

We have always chosen to purchase a car in Europe, timing the sale of our cars here carefully to mesh with years spent abroad. For long stays or long trips, this is still a good plan, though it saves less than it did a decade ago. The European delivery price is usually significantly less ($1000–3000) than the American price for the same car because it includes no European or American taxes or transatlantic shipping costs. (You *must* export the car within 12 months of delivery to avoid these taxes.) You save further by paying U.S. import duty and state sales taxes on the *used* car value when you return, and you do not have to pay extra for your transportation while traveling abroad. At one point a camper was perfect for our family of young children, with a tent as a supplement. Later we found that a small station wagon was adequate for our needs. The purchase, delivery documentation, insurance, and financing can be arranged in advance by a dealer at home so that the car is waiting upon your arrival in Europe. Some local dealers do not have the expertise to handle delivery abroad, so you may want to choose a major city dealer or a company that specializes in such delivery.

Buying used cars in Europe usually does not make much sense because initial purchase taxes (as high as 50% of the price of the car) are included in their resale values, thus jacking up the price toward new car export prices. But you can arrange to lease a car, which may be cheaper than renting because there is no mileage charge. It is also possible to buy a car with the understanding that it may be sold back to the selling agency, sometimes at a guaranteed price.

CAR SHIPMENT HOME Some companies (SAAB and Volvo, for example) still include free car shipment home in the cost of the car. Otherwise, there are a number of agencies available. North Sea ports (Antwerp, Rotterdam, Bremen, and Hamburg) provide more sailings and cheaper prices than most other ports. E. H. Harms and Company, Hansestrasse 5, Bremen, Germany, has offices in a number of ports. AAA or other automobile clubs can also make arrangements for you. The *Queen Elizabeth 2* allows you to bring a car home free as part of your passage (up to the capacity of the car deck). Check to find out which passage plans include this feature.

CARAVAN RENTAL Rental caravans are very popular and easily available in England through International Caravan Holidays, 292 Lower High St., Watford, Hertfordshire, England. You can reach other agencies by contacting the AAA in the U.S., the Automobile Association or Royal Automobile Club in England, or the Yellow Pages for the city in which you will begin your tour. The national automobile clubs in each country can make arrangements or send you the name and address of the appropriate agency. The British Tourist Authority publishes a book, *Camping and Caravan Sites,* that has a list of caravan rental companies.

FERRY TRANSPORTATION There are wild variations in the costs of ferries depending upon the time of year. The prices during high season are much higher than during low season, and the rates also skyrocket on certain days just before and just after holidays during the rest of the year. At times it is imperative to book ahead to avoid long lines and the frustration of missing one sailing after another. Europeans travel a great deal on holidays and they have learned to plan ahead.

There are a number of possible ferry links between the Continent and Britain, varying in length of sailing time, cost, and convenience. It takes a bit of studying to figure out the best possible route to fit in with your total itinerary. You can obtain information on ferries from automobile clubs and travel agents.

Travel Details

PASSPORTS AND CUSTOMS Before you leave for your European trip, you will need to allow enough time to get passports, which are available from any federal or state court authorized by law to naturalize aliens or at passport agencies of the U.S. Department of State in large cities. Each application requires two passport photos (2½ x 2½ to 3 x 3 inches), proof of citizenship such as a birth certificate or expired passport, and identification, which may be your driver's license or expired passport. There is a fee for each passport—$35 at this time. Your passport is good for 10 years. Visas are not necessary for most western European countries (with the exception of Yugoslavia).

For information on current customs regulations, write for *Customs Hints for Returning U.S. Residents,* available from the U.S. Government Printing Office, Washington, DC 20402. It's a good idea to bring sales slips along for previously purchased European cameras, clothing, watches, and jewelry to avoid paying duty again.

CAMPING CARNET Many campgrounds offer a discount for those carrying **camping carnets**. The other reason to carry a camping carnet is even more important: The campground manager will usually hold it instead of your passport until you check out and pay your bill. We did not feel completely easy about giving up a passport to a campsite clerk and sometimes needed it during the day to cash traveler's checks.

INSURANCE We recommend checking with your insurance agent before you go to be sure you are covered for theft, accident, or cancellation of a flight. Comprehensive travel insurance can be purchased from a variety of sources here (automobile clubs, credit card companies, travel clubs, etc.) but it is usually not as broad in coverage as the policies you can purchase through automobile clubs and camping organizations in Europe (for example, AA, RAC, or Caravan Club in England). Then take reasonable precautions, especially in large cities.

Although we have locked most of our belongings, including the manuscript for this book, xeroxed copies of our passports, car papers, and other documents out of sight in the trunk for safekeeping, it would still be a nuisance to replace a car window after a break-in. You should not leave anything of value in your car; try to fit everything in the trunk, leaving the interior of the car clear. Even then, thieves can easily force the trunk open and make off with your possessions. We have heard enough stories of smashed windows in Paris, Rome, and London—even in daylight—to encourage us to travel lightly. Several years ago we traveled in a station wagon with gear exposed and had no trouble, but would rather not have a first experience. (Incidentally, the paradores in Spain and many hotels elsewhere have enclosed parking spaces or a garage. And when you are camping your car is right there with you.)

We purchased insurance for our camping gear and clothing for one trip because we had heard the usual tales about the prevalence of thievery in Italy. Young men on motorscooters are notorious for snatching purses and disappearing in a flash. The campground we chose outside Venice was barely open, with just a few campers around. We felt reasonably safe there until the next morning at 7 a.m. when a crew of workers appeared at the hotel next to the campground. We had thought it was not open and had purposely pitched our tents in the corner right next to it, away from other campers, for privacy as well as a superb view of the sea. There was nothing we could do except take the ferry into Venice, leaving our camping equipment zipped in the tents (which of course one can't lock) and try to keep our minds on other things all day. When we drove in that night, we were all on the edges of our seats, straining to see if our tents were in fact still there, then hurriedly unzipping each tent to see if it had been cleaned out—fortunately, nothing had been touched. Camping insurance is probably worth the small cost to save you worry about an unlikely (though possible) heist of your gear.

Packing

When all these segments of a total plan are reasonably firm, it is time to develop a packing list. Everyone seems to take too much the first time and trims the list more ruthlessly on each successive trip. If there is any question about needing an item on your list, leave it home. Fewer possessions are easier on the arms that carry them, the tempers of those who fit them into an intricate jigsaw puzzle in limited car space, and the patience of those who want to find things quickly in an orderly duffel bag. After a few days of struggling with too much stuff, most of us end up wearing the same thing over and over, wishing that the rest had been left at home. Like Thoreau's man of property weighed down by all his possessions, we begin to curse ourselves for bringing them in the first place.

CLOTHING Before each trip we have collected booklets and packing lists from many airlines, luggage companies, and travel agents. Then, with a list of the clothing we have used on previous trips in hand, we check through new lists and add whatever makes sense for us. We read travel columns in newspapers and magazines, watching for the occasional new idea that may turn out to be tremendously useful. Then we go into reverse with our old lists, culling out any items that were infrequently used to reduce the weight, clutter, and annoyance of too much baggage. Finally, we type out and make copies of a list of basic clothing for the entire family and hand each person one to adjust to his or her own needs and check off as items are packed.

The goal is to take only what will actually be worn or used. Otherwise you will return resenting the gear that took up space without paying its way.

Coordinate colors so that no item requires a specific match with another to cut down on duplication. We have found that packing interchangeable blazers (lightweight and washable), slacks, skirts, and shirts provides variety in our wardrobes. We scrutinize every item to be sure it would look presentable with hand washing and no ironing. A sensible packing list for an average trip of 2–6 weeks in warm weather (May–September) might look like this:

WOMEN	MEN
2 slacks, 2 skirts	2 slacks
2 blazers	2 blazers
7 shirts, blouses, tops	7 shirts
7 sets underwear	7 sets underwear
7 pairs socks or hose	7 pairs socks
2 nightgowns	2 pajamas
1 robe, slippers	1 robe, slippers
2 sweaters	2 sweaters

WOMEN	MEN
light jacket	light jacket
raincoat, hat	raincoat, hat
bathing suit	bathing suit
2 shorts	2 shorts
sunhat	sunhat
2 pair walking shoes	2 pair walking shoes
1 pair dress shoes	1 pair dress shoes
1 dress	ties
2 dressy blouses, skirt	2 dress shirts

MISCELLANEOUS: washcloth, soap, Woolite, laundry bag, stretch clothesline, cosmetic or dop kit, medications and supplies, sunglasses, safety pins, tissues, sewing kit, first-aid kit. Add heavier sweaters and a wool blazer if you anticipate colder weather.

If you are camping, you may wish to add: heavy socks, turtleneck tops, hiking boots, towels, another jacket to layer, rain outfit, gloves, cap, scarf, long underwear, jogging suit.

LUGGAGE Choose the best type of luggage for the style of transportation you will use. If you travel by train, one suitcase with wheels may be all you can manage maneuvering down those endless platforms. Some people like to stack two smaller suitcases on a cart with wheels because it is easier to bump up and down stairs in the train station. If you will be traveling by car, consider soft luggage that can change its shape in a tightly packed vehicle. We have found marvelous sets of cordura nylon suitcases that are completely soft, without frames, yet take suitcases shape when packed. They have several zippers and compartments, plus a shoulder carrying strap. They adapt to space requirements and somehow always expand to enclose extra items. We have traveled for almost three months with the largest size, which we left in the trunk of the car, and the smallest size, which we refilled with several days' worth of clothing to take in at night. In addition, we each used a strong carry bag to swoop up current reading materials, a bottle of wine with corkscrew, and odds and ends needed for the night. We also brought several empty duffel bags for carrying purchases made enroute.

Each piece of luggage should have an identification card on the outside as well as on the inside. We also make a design with tape on all pieces; this helps to identify them as they tumble into the baggage claim area. Luggage locks and keys help to keep the contents intact, and a complete list of the entire contents of each piece is immediately useful if one gets lost.

When packing, we place all shoes in separate plastic bags, underwear in one bag, other small items in bags, tucking in several more for future use. Plastic bags make it easier to slip things in and out and help you find what you want more quickly.

Children will find a small backpack very useful as a carryon bag and they can use it later as a car bag and for hikes. Toys, paperbacks, an extra sweater or jacket, slippers, cards or games, journal, pen, extra film, handwork such as needlepoint or a leather project can be slipped in.

You may want to carry camera gear and film in a special bag, but make sure that it does not go through the X-ray machine at airports. A large purse is a convenient carrier for important documents such as passports and traveler's checks, tickets, and your itinerary. You can even make a liner with several zippers for greater security and ease in finding things.

If you are camping, you may want to consider packing cooking gear, tents, air mattresses, and sleeping bags in sea bags or very large duffels. Check current airline restrictions on weight or size of bags. Frankly, taking a great deal of camping equipment can be a hassle. (See "Camping Equipment" for more information and a suggested packing list.)

Householding

For those who are lucky enough to spend six months or a year abroad, finding a home in a village or an apartment in a city can be an unnerving experience. But there are effective ways to make a good start before leaving home. Some academic communities offer help through organizations like the Society for Visiting Scholars in Cambridge or the Newcomers in Oxford. Sometimes it is possible to live in university or college housing temporarily while you are house-hunting. Advance inquiries will result in an exchange of letters with such societies and with realtors (called estate agents in England) to help locate specific houses. British Tourist Authority offers a booklet entitled *Holiday Homes* with details on renting in Britain. You can also answer ads in foreign newspapers, in the *International Herald Tribune,* in the newsletters of agencies promoting foreign exchanges, or in the catalogues of house-swapping networks. Some college alumni magazines include listings of flats and homes available for rent abroad, and friends or acquaintances may be able to suggest realtors to contact in a specific area.

Some people hesitate to take a place sight unseen and prefer to make a concentrated search after arrival. Others, especially those with young families, prefer the convenience of a smooth entry to life abroad. Finding a temporary flat for a week or two in advance is a middle way. You will have to be honest about your own (and your children's, if you are taking them) anxiety levels and adaptability when making this choice.

There are a number of home-exchange organizations in existence. They can help you rent your home while you are gone and rent the home of someone abroad during the same period. In some cases a direct swap is arranged that can even include cars and pets. When such arrangements work smoothly, they save a great deal of time and effort, and they can solve problems (for example, the long quarantine for pets) that are otherwise difficult. *A partial list of home-exchange brokers includes:*

Loan-A-Home
2 Park Lane
Mount Vernon, NY 10552

Interchange
213 W. 38th St.
New York, NY 10016

The Vacation Exchange Club
12006 111th Ave.
Youngtown, AZ 85363

There is a fair amount of extra planning to be done when you will be away for an extended period of time. One of our adventures in Europe lasted for a year, with 12 weeks of travel during that time. We chose to rent a home by mail, which allowed us to have things sent ahead. Also, we then had an address to use for arranging various business affairs such as insurance, banking, and professional correspondence.

We began making lists of things to do here and things to do over there and organized them by weeks, both to avoid slipping up on something important and to get some sense of progress in accomplishing the necessary miscellaneous chores. Checking off many items in one week was a cause for celebration. Four weeks before we left our list included: update house inventory and take to safety deposit box; compile income tax information necessary for computing and filing from overseas; arrange to pay all insurance premiums once for the year; collect health records from the doctor; call in address changes for utilities, banks, and other services; get international driver's license from AAA; type Christmas card list; and call car rental agencies to reserve cars in New York, Luxembourg, and Dover. Three weeks before departure the list looked like this: get student identity cards for the children; send change-of-address cards to friends and relatives; mark all luggage with name tags and a special design in tape; buy film; set up banking arrangements in Europe by letters from banks and employers here. Two weeks before departure: settle *final* arrangements for purchase of a car to be picked up in London on the second day after arrival in Luxembourg; find a recent currency converter; order dog tags with the name of friends who will keep the dogs; have extra house keys made for renters; diagram garden so renters will know where not to spade; make a list of appliance repair numbers and household information for renters; clear drawers and closets. The last week is always hectic and by then it is too late for lists—you simply hope you haven't forgotten anything.

After farewell parties, cleaning the house, and inevitable last-minute details to attend to, we always look forward to the moment of relief that comes as we settle down into our airline seats. It is nice to relax, sleep a lot, and enjoy the feeling of being in between two parts of your life.

You will want to settle into your new home for a week or two before planning the focus of your first trip. We have always had thoughtful neighbors who have helped us learn the ropes of shopping, early closing hours, utilities, and other routines in the village or area. As you meet people you will hear about the holiday they took recently or where they would like to go, and you will find yourself becoming interested in planning your first trip.

Countdown

In order to aid your planning, we have organized a countdown list by months before departure. The deadlines are not precise for every trip, but they can help you to prevent missing something you want to do and avoid unneeded flurry and raw nerves during the last weeks before departure.

Six months before departure (or when you know you are going)
- Write to national tourist offices for information and maps.
- Write to airlines and shipping companies for schedules and fares.
- Write to car rental and purchase companies, both in the United States and abroad.
- Begin clipping and collecting articles and information on the places you want to visit.
- Organize all the incoming material by category or country.
- Keep information obtained by phone in a folder or notebook.
- Check your library for books on the countries and regions you plan to visit.
- Brush up on your previous foreign language skills.
- Plan an itinerary within Europe.
- Make travel reservations (earlier during peak summer periods of transatlantic travel).

Four months before departure
- Make the arrangements for car purchase, including shipment home.
- Apply for passports.
- Make ferry reservations within Europe if you will be traveling during holiday periods.
- Make arrangements for rental of your home (if you will be away long enough to make this feasible and desirable).

Two months before departure
- Obtain camping carnet and International Driver's License.

Get International Medical Assistance card and information.
Collect health records from doctors.
Make arrangements for house utilities and other services during absence.
Purchase needed clothing and equipment.
Make reservations for car rental (both in United States and abroad).

One month before departure
Get letter of credit from your bank.
Buy film.
Buy gifts for friends in Europe.
Prepare your itinerary with addresses for mail to be received in Europe.
Make final arrangements for home and pets in your absence.

One week before departure
Buy traveler's checks.
Pack as much as possible.
Make arrangements for your mail at home.
Check to make sure you have all tickets and documents.

We have found that when some of these things-to-be-done slip down from week to week on the list, the final week can be horrendous. With all the last-minute excitement and fatigue we always wish we had begun earlier.

Emergencies

Although we have not yet had to seek emergency help in our travels, an emergency situation can happen at any time. Problems encountered by a traveler can be upsetting, but inconvenience should not ruin the trip. There may be different kinds of solutions in various countries, but in any case, there *are* solutions.

State Department officials suggest that travelers take some precautions, such as carrying extra money in the form of traveler's checks, leaving a copy of your itinerary with a relative or friend, and carrying an identification card for any health insurance coverage that embraces foreign travel. We also carry photocopies of our passports (and all other important travel documents) in separate pieces of luggage to avoid the inconvenience of having to reconstruct the information for replacements.

LOSING YOUR PASSPORT Report the loss of your passport to the local police. Then contact the nearest American embassy or consulate, which will issue a replacement. It is helpful to carry two extra passport photos, the number, date, and place of issue of your passport, and some other form of identification separately. If you cannot adequately establish your identity and citizenship, the embassy or consulate will have to cable or telex the State Department for instructions, which may cause some delay.

LOSING YOUR TRAVELER'S CHECKS Either the nearest office or bank that deals with the issuing authority of your traveler's checks can reimburse you with checks for those you've lost. It pays to keep the purchase information and numbers of your checks in a separate, safe place while traveling. Most major credit card companies (American Express, Diner's Club, Visa, Mastercard) have systems for getting you cash through the use of the card directly or as a guarantee for a personal check.

If you need further help, the nearest American embassy or consulate can advise you on the procedure to follow. They can also help you, *in a real emergency,* to get in touch with bankers, employers, or friends in order to get needed funds. Someone at home can cable money abroad in 24 to 48 hours.

GETTING BUMPED FROM A FLIGHT To avoid getting bumped, plan to arrive at the airport early. Allow plenty of time to check in and get to the gate. On flights originating in the United States, airlines must pay "denied boarding compensation" to anyone who is bumped provided you have checked-in on time and hold a confirmed reservation. The carrier must immediately furnish you with a written explanation of the terms, conditions, and limitations of the compensation. And the carrier must schedule you on a flight to arrive at your destination within four hours of your scheduled arrival.

Before you go, write to the Consumer Information Center, Pueblo, Colorado, for two publications entitled *Air Travelers' Fly-Rights* and *Consumer Guide to International Air Travel.*

RESOLVING MEDICAL PROBLEMS The American embassy or consulate will help you find appropriate medical services, including English-speaking physicians. We have found that people on the spot have been able to advise us when we needed quick medical service. A sprained ankle in Zermatt turned into a more pleasant experience than we had expected, with several days of going about in a horse-drawn sleigh to visit a jovial Swiss doctor who laughed and joked during each heat treatment, and rides up in the chairlift (with crutches instead of skis) to enjoy a gorgeous view. In England we signed on at the local surgery (National Health Service), and were seen quickly when necessary. Write to International Association for Medical Assistance to Travelers (IAMAT), 350 Fifth Ave., New York, NY 10001 for a list of English-speaking doctors, a world immunization chart, and information on various other medical services.

ENCOUNTERING THE LAW You should know that most European countries strictly enforce traffic laws, especially the stiff penalties for drunk driving. One of the real advantages of belonging to an automobile club is the service it will render if you do get into trouble. In case of an accident, follow the same procedure that you would at home, beginning with getting medical aid for the injured. In most countries you must carry and display a warning triangle to warn traffic of an obstruction. You must notify the police, if it is a statutory requirement of the country, if someone is injured or dead, or if there is no one present to represent the injured.

Carry with you the detailed instructions for each country you plan to drive in, and be sure that you have the necessary bail bond if you are going to drive in Spain. Under Spanish law, if you are involved in a car accident, you may be detained and your car may be impounded. Automobile Clubs can make the necessary arrangements, and many of the European clubs (the Royal Automobile Club or Automobile Association in England, for example) will provide you with all the information you need.

Enjoying

WITH CHILDREN Some children hate a trip that is heavily loaded with art galleries, cathedrals, and museums and vow not to enjoy any of it. Involving them in some of the conversations before the plan is established and letting them help choose among desirable options can go a long way toward ensuring their enjoyment of the trip. Without too much effort you can do a little research on the countries you will visit and the attractions you might choose to see. There are endless literary works to enjoy before going. Some families choose to seek out a special interest, such as visiting every Van Gogh museum in Holland. The British Museum has enough variety to reach some special interest your child has developed in school, whether it be Egyptian mummies or ancient coins. Those with marine interests will find famous ships and many kinds of boats preserved in maritime museums scattered throughout European ports. There is a wealth of music to listen to in especially interesting surroundings, like the King's College Choir in Cambridge or the Vienna Boys' Choir, as well as many concerts and performances of opera and ballet in major cities. Famous ancient buildings and ruins can be enjoyed in depth by anyone, and country houses, castles, and cathedrals abound.

COLLECTING Many people enjoy collecting something while they travel. The range is limitless: postcards, maps, decals, recipes, foreign stamps, fabric badges to sew on backpacks, demitasse spoons, recipe books, traditional costumes, tiles to make into a coffee table at home, and other souvenir items. Usually everyone in our family is collecting something different on a trip. As long as the items are not too bulky or too hard to procure, collecting can be fun—and if there are children in your party, you'll find that the collecting impulse can even make that perennial adult interest—shopping—more tolerable for them.

KEEPING A JOURNAL It's easy to acquire the habit of writing in a journal every day on a trip. Children can develop their own styles and fresh points of view, which often differ remarkably from those of their parents. Wherever we have traveled we have bought several postcards to paste in the journals opposite the narrative, adding zip and interest to the books. As our children walked through art galleries for example, they thought about their favorite works and hoped to find postcards of those for their books. We have enjoyed seeing Europe through their eyes and we have all read and reread their journals as well as our own to recapture an exciting part of past travels. Through journals, parents can pick up clues to their children's enjoyment of activities during the trip. You may not have known that your child had always wanted to see the Mona Lisa and was delighted to take her picture home to hang on a bedroom wall. We have enjoyed reading a description of the details learned while exploring the *Wasa,* a ship raised from the bottom of Stockholm harbor, from the eyes of one of our children.

BALANCING TOURISM AND SPORTS Breaking the customary pattern of sightseeing can boost travelers' morale. You can intersperse touring with sports having a special appeal, such as glacier walking in Norway or Switzerland, hiking in the English Lake District, or cycling in Holland. Swimming is available in lakes and in pools, as well as fjords (sometimes cold) and fine ocean beaches. You can charter a sailboat for a day on a beautiful lake or along the coast. You can go to an English game of soccer or cricket, watch the regatta at Henley, lawn tennis at Wimbledon, or horse racing at Ascot. Most national tourist bureaus can send you a detailed schedule of special sports events in advance.

CHOOSING WHAT TO DO Lists of museums, art galleries, castles, and cathedrals are available from tourist offices and from guidebooks as well. Some of these attractions are free, some ask a modest admission fee or a donation, and a few are more expensive. On the whole, admission fees are not a major cost on a trip and they do help to support the maintenance of what you came to see. You will need to decide which to visit with the interests of your group in mind. It is not easy to choose when so much is offered, but some of what you might do can always be saved for another trip. The rule of thumb is not to be compulsive about seeing *everything.*

FINDING LOCAL SIGHTS Save time for attractions that you hear about when you are actually there. Local people always know about something the rest of the world has not heard about. You may find a little church that has a collection of paintings of ships done by the men who sailed them long ago, as we did in Italy. You may meet someone who wants to show you a building that means a great deal to his family. You may have a friend who can show you a little town not yet on the tourist trial where the inhabitants wear their traditional dress all the time. You may encounter another hiker who has found a trail off the beaten path with a gorgeous view. Sometimes local surprises mean a great deal more than following the customary tourist route to "major" attractions.

RELAXING Compulsiveness is a demon that is very hard to lick. Most people overplan because they cannot bear to give up even part of what they might do. The more places we read about, the more we want to experience. The more we meet people and talk about their interests and impressions, the more we want to share those too. We *know* we will be tired and cranky if we drive too many hours, traipse through too many long hallways, and go at a rapid pace from one thing to another all day long. The problem then is to choose—to choose what will be pleasing to us and yet not too arduous. The rule is never too much or too long.

TIME OUT FOR EVERYONE There will be times on a trip when you won't want to go along on an outing that the other member or members of your group are eager to try. You shouldn't have to. Perhaps you have some letterwriting to do, or want a chance to sit and do needlepoint while absorbing the sunshine and the view. If you are bored by too much shopping, you can choose something else you want to do while the others plough through the Straw Market in Florence. You may want to continue looking at favorite paintings while the other has "had it," so you can separate and regroup later. Everyone needs relief from togetherness on a trip; if you get some time alone you can rejoin the group later, refreshed.

DISCOVERING A MEDITERRANEAN SENSE OF TIME Relax and enjoy. The people who live around and near the Mediterranean have a beautiful life. They live in spectacular settings and they know how to relax and enjoy each day. They can work hard building their stone fences for their children and grandchildren; they can be outside all day cultivating and improving their land. But on a special day when the mood is right, they put a sign on the door of their business and take a young son out fishing. They can sit in the square in midmorning, drinking coffee and enjoying their friends. They can drop everything when you come to call and offer an aperitif or coffee for an hour of conversation. We have vowed that we will try to remember and relax when we return to the United States, but it is not easy to import this style of living into the American culture.

A trip can be a perfect time to relax and enjoy your family. No one has to set an alarm and get to a job on time. No one has routine tasks to perform. You can take time out for a child, a view, a new friend, a new experience—if you will.

Routes

The following trips will bring travelers into some of the most interesting areas of Europe; each has variety in terrain and activity. All have been designed for travelers who want to balance the greatest possible enjoyment with economy. Every itinerary includes a suggested pattern for the trip, details of routing, mileage, a map, sightseeing tips, and sources of information on the areas to be visited. Each plan outlines a specific trip that has worked well for families, but the locality, length, and pattern of activity can easily be modified to plan trips for singles, couples, or other small groups.

The **Southwestern Circuit in England** includes exploration along the south and southwest coasts, with plenty of exposure to Britain's great maritime tradition, early Roman civilization, and some of the wildest moors in the country. A number of splendid cathedrals lie on or near the route, and there is plenty of opportunity for walking along rugged coasts and through lovely villages and college towns.

The **Central Circuit in England and Wales** will appeal especially to hikers and climbers, although it also offers short strolls at historic sites or amid scenes of extraordinary natural beauty. Those with a compelling interest in Shakespeare or in castles will have more than enough to explore. The wild terrain of the Snowdonia region of Wales is matched by the meshing of water and mountains in the Lake District of England. Oxford and Cambridge, ancient university towns, lie at the beginning and end of this trip.

Scotland has a fascination all its own in rich historical and romantic legends and a bold landscape full of sharp contrasts. Sportsmen will find excellent fishing, hiking, and climbing, as well as swimming and boating in resort areas.

Scandinavia offers a spectacular collage of land and water with natural beauty everywhere. Scenery in Denmark, Sweden, and Norway ranges from mountains, glaciers, and fjords to the rolling hills and farmland near the lakes. Cities are full of interesting modern and ancient architecture, with superb shopping an added attraction. Local traditions, crafts, and festivals abound in every region.

Central and Southern Europe is by far the most ambitious adventure. The range of possible layovers, cultural attractions, natural beauty, and opportunities for special interests or sports is wide. Unless you have a great deal of time you will probably choose to travel through one route, rather than three in central and southern Europe, or in one or two countries. There are links from section to section to enable you to do this. The first route, **The Low Countries, the Rhine, Bavaria, the Black Forest, and the Alps,** begins in Holland, with its new lands reclaimed from the sea, then heads south along the Rhine through Bavaria and the Black Forest in Germany to the Alps of Austria and Switzerland and returns through medieval towns in Belgium. The second route, **Southeast Mediterranean,** begins in Venice, continues south along the starkly beautiful Dalmation coast through Yugoslavia, takes a ferry around forbidden Albania to Greece for a tour of ancient sites in Delphi, Athens, the Peloponnese, and the islands, continues by ferry to southern Italy, and then works north through the marvelous cities and hill towns of Roman and medieval civilizations back to Venice. The third route, **France,** begins in Paris, heads south to the varied landscape of Provence, moves through two valleys, the idyllic Dordogne and the Loire, and continues on to the wild coastline of Brittany and the once-embattled beaches of Normandy before it returns to Paris.

The **Iberian Peninsula** offers a holiday in both Spain and Portugal. It circles the peninsula along varied coastlines, turns inland to high mountains, and visits archaeological treasures spanning several thousand years and the artistic heritage of successive cultures.

Fielding's
MOTORING AND CAMPING EUROPE

SOUTHWESTERN ENGLAND

London to Chichester	82 miles
Lymington to Salcombe	167 miles
Salcombe to Bath	125 miles
Bath to Oxford	71 miles
Oxford to London	57 miles
Salcombe to Plymouth	28 miles
Plymouth to Truro	43 miles
Plymouth to Land's End	90 miles
Land's End to Boscastle	75 miles

From London: (Surrey) Dorking; (Sussex) Chichester; (Hampshire) Portsmouth, Silchester; (Isle of Wight); (Devon) Salcombe, Hallsands Village, Slapton Sands, Dartmouth, Exeter, Plymouth, Dartmoor; (Cornwall) Polperro, Fowey, Falmouth, Gweek, Lizard Point, Mousehole, Land's End, St. Ives, Tintagel; (Wiltshire) Stonehenge, Avebury Circle; (Oxfordshire) Oxford; (Berkshire) Reading.
(14 days: 737 miles)

This trip provides a balance between the exploration of history and the sheer relaxation and pleasure of enjoying life in seaside towns, with many evenings spent amidst quiet scenes of beauty rather than in the noise and excitement of large cities. The route has been planned to allow brief stopovers at points of interest on the way to a destination and longer stays for more intensive exploration in areas of special beauty or interest. There are a number of side trips and hikes you can take without moving. Children will enjoy Lord Nelson's flagship, the H.M.S. *Victory*, and the Maritime Museum in **Exeter**. The ferry to the **Isle of Wight** gives marvelous views of all sorts of ships and yachts in the harbors. In **Salcombe** you can hike along spectacular cliffs or enjoy beaches. **Stonehenge** will fascinate those who wonder about the ordeal of moving such huge stones and the reason for the symmetrical arrangement.

The itinerary includes a number of England's most interesting cathedrals, with their soaring spires and stained-glass windows. Both the

BRISTOL CHANNEL
Ilfracombe
Blackmoor
Gate
Dunster
Bridgwater
Braunton
Wheddon Cross
Croyde
Barnstaple
Bideford
Bude
Okehampton
Exeter
Lyme Regis
Boscastle
Tintagel
DEVON
Port Issac
Padstow
CORNWALL
Newquay
Perranporth
St. Austell
Looe
Plymouth
Portwreath
Fowey
Polperro
Mevagissey
Kingsbridge
Salcombe
St. Ives
St. Just
Chysauster
Penzance
Helston
Gweek
Falmouth
Mousehole
Land's End
Lizard Point

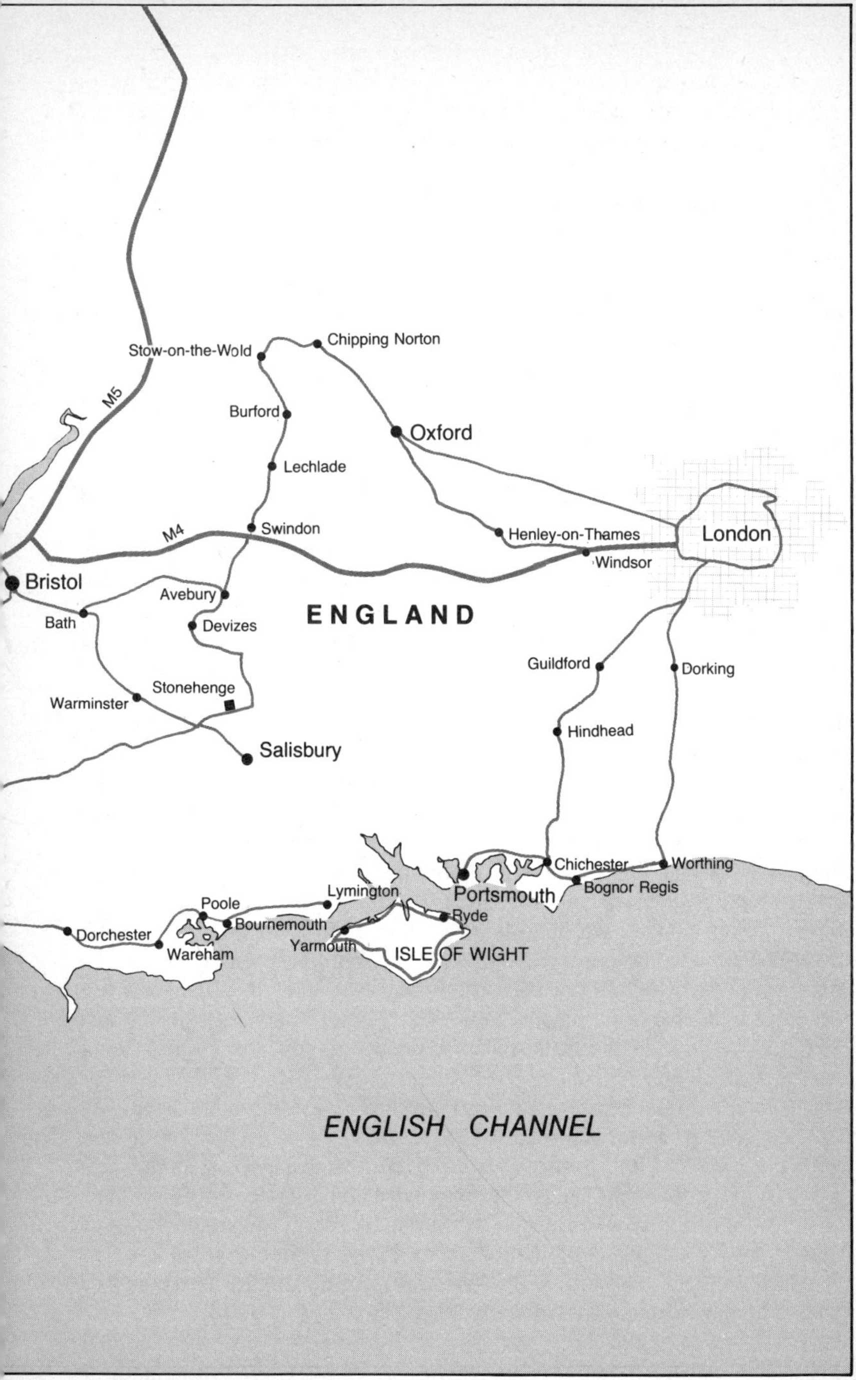
Stow-on-the-Wold
Chipping Norton
M5
Burford
Oxford
Lechlade
Swindon
M4
Henley-on-Thames
London
Windsor
Bristol
Avebury
Bath
Devizes
ENGLAND
Guildford
Dorking
Stonehenge
Warminster
Hindhead
Salisbury
Chichester
Worthing
Lymington
Portsmouth
Bognor Regis
Poole
Bournemouth
Ryde
Dorchester
Wareham
Yarmouth
ISLE OF WIGHT
ENGLISH CHANNEL

sad-eyed ponies and the prison on **Dartmoor** impart a gloom that sets off the expanse and isolation of the moor. There are a number of Roman villas in varying stages of excavation; one in the **Chichester** area has exquisite mosaic floors. Chichester is a marvelous area for sailors; you can charter cruising boats or daysailers for poking around harbors. **Salisbury** and **Winchester** cathedrals are within easy reach of this area. The rolling **Cotswolds,** dotted with sheep, unfold the lives of the wool merchants who lived there. Memorials to them can be found in churches in the form of brass plates elaborately engraved with figures, sheep, dogs, epigraphs, and ornate canopies. The imprint from brasses can be rubbed on paper with a wax crayon and taken home to be framed. You'll find that **Oxford,** with its many enclosed colleges and pleasant gardens, requires a day of exploration on foot in order to fully discover its charms. Those who follow this itinerary have many choices of activity and will find it difficult to leave something for the next trip.

The cost of this trip is not excessive for several reasons. Mileage is limited by the fact that the same roads that provide striking views are often narrow and curvy and do not encourage one to drive much over 30 miles per hour. Some of the roads have only one lane, some are also footpaths for sheep, and some have high hedgerows loaded with primroses. Beauty is abundant, and travelers are relaxed and cordial about backing up to a passing place (a widening of the road) on one-lane roads.

Food costs can be kept low by shopping as the British do. Most housewives shop every day, buying fresh fruits, vegetables, and meats in small quantities. You can stock up on canned goods and staples in a supermarket and then enjoy the fun of buying fresh provisions in smaller shops or in open markets. You will discover the specialties of each region from the people who live there as well as from fellow campers. Word passes fast when crab is available in Salcombe; you can often get fresh bread still warm and fragrant from a village bakery, or fish and chips piping hot and wrapped in newspaper. Most English towns have a market day at least once a week, and it is fun to wander among the open stalls savoring special cheeses, fruits, and vegetables, and looking for household bargains of all kinds. The vendors hawking their wares add good humor to the atmosphere, as long as you don't mind being called "ducky" or "love."

Campground costs vary. Sites may contain elaborate facilities or they may be quite primitive. However, there is some appeal in sharing ground with the ghosts of the past near a partly ruined castle, or sleeping in a meadow with cows and sheep that may occasionally peer into your tent. On the other hand, when a hot shower/sparkling-clean sink/hair dryer outlet/laundry facility combination seems like a dream, you can find it.

Entrance fees for castles and museums are not high—a worthwhile cost. There are three kinds of control over the many magnificent historic properties in England: the Department of the Environment, the National Trust, and private ownership. Travelers who expect to be in England for some time may save money by purchasing admission cards from the Historic Buildings and Monuments Commission for England. Membership is available at any of the historic sites or from Fortress House, 25 Savile Row, London, W.1. The National Trust also offers membership; write to the National Trust Membership Department, Box 30, Beckenham, Kent BR3 4TL. A brochure listing all the country houses, abbeys, castles, and gardens that may be enjoyed by showing the card contains other useful information about opening and closing dates and times. In addition, a guide entitled *Historic Houses, Castles, and Gardens* (ABC Historic Publications, Oldhill, London Road, Dunstable, Bedfordshire), available in most book shops, also lists those properties that are privately owned but open to the public.

Other expenses will probably include some meals out. A delicious pub lunch usually costs a bit over $1.00 and can be enjoyed in a setting of polished paneling, surrounded by collections of brass and copper hanging from the ceiling. Menu selections range from a hearty "plowman's lunch," chicken, shrimp or fish with chips, salads, and scotch eggs, to a complete buffet. Fish and chips, bought hot and shared in a park or on a beach, are a treat for children, while a selection of English cheeses, some nutty, crunchy granary bread, and a bottle of wine will warm the hearts of adults. River pubs, complete with lovely rose gardens, have great appeal in nice weather. For campers, lunches are cheaper and more efficient than dinners out on this trip because most of the good campsites are on beaches or moors at some distance from town.

London/Chichester

Proceed south to **Dorking**, via route A24, passing **Box Hill** just to the north. You may be interested in reading for a little taste of the area before you go. George Meredith lived on Box Hill, where he wrote *The Egoist, The Tragic Comedians,* and *The Adventures of Harry Richmond*. The crucial picnic scene that resolves the action of Jane Austen's *Emma* is set on Box Hill. Dorking is a lovely town located between chalk downs and a sandstone ridge. **Leith Hill,** just south of Dorking, is the highest point in southeastern England. From the tower on top you can see into 13 counties. **Leith Hill Place** has been in the Wedgwood family for generations and contains a marvelous collection of original jasperware. If you stop at the house in spring or summer, be sure to see and sniff the magnificent rhododendron and azalea wood on the grounds.

Continue south on A24 to **Horsham,** an old market town, then on to the south coast. **Worthing** is a resort town, warm and sunny because it is sheltered by the downs, leading to a shingle beach. Turn west on route A259 to **Bognor Regis,** which has a sandy beach.

CHICHESTER Continue on to Chichester, which is laid out in the pattern of a Roman walled town. The walls were built about A.D. 200 and the *City Museum* includes displays of prehistoric, Roman, and medieval periods. *Chichester Cathedral* is Norman in style but has many later additions; the campanile is detached, which is unusual in England. *Goodwood House,* 4 miles from Chichester, is the home of the Duke of Richmond and Gordon; it is three-sided and is noted for its Sussex flintwork. The *Roman palace,* 1 mile west at **Fishbourne,** was discovered only in 1960 and is especially remarkable for its fine mosaic floor. For sailors, nearby **Bosham** has all types of boats and yachts perched at various angles in the mud at low tide; from mid- to high-tide, the estuary is one of the most active yachting centers on the south coast. Camp in the Chichester area or drive west a few miles to **Fishbourne, Bosham,** or **Hayling Island** (which has a number of campgrounds).

PORTSMOUTH is 20 miles west of Chichester on A27 and A3. Visitors to the H.M.S. *Victory* (in drydock) will see the spot where Lord Nelson died during the Battle of Trafalgar in 1805. Young seamen, some with elaborate tattoos on their arms, deliver spirited and interesting accounts of life on board this well-preserved flagship of one of England's greatest fleets.

The *Mary Rose,* raised in 1982, is also on display in Portsmouth. She was the first British warship designed with a huge load of heavy guns between decks, an experiment to increase firepower at some risk to stability. In a post-launching disaster very much like the one that overtook the *Wasa* in the next century, the *Mary Rose* sank in Portsmouth Harbour in July 1545. King Henry VIII probably watched this disaster from *Southsea Castle,* where there are exhibits about the sinking. In 1979 the Mary Rose Trust was formed; plans were made to raise her and preserve both the hull and everything inside. At this writing, she is undergoing modern preservation treatments in the *Royal Dockyard,* where you can look down on the process from a footbridge above the dry dock. After 437 years on the bottom, there is much restoration work to be done.

ISLE OF WIGHT After this visit, take a ferry to the Isle of Wight, which takes about 30 minutes. The island is 18 miles (north to south) by 22 miles (east to west) and contains a remarkable variety of landscape and many historical sites. Pick a campsite nestled into the cliffs along the rugged southern coast and plan to stay for two nights. (The area called *Undercliff* is especially nice for camping. In addition to Undercliff there are campgrounds at **Sandown, Cowes,** and **Ryde.**)

There is much to explore by car and by foot. *Carisbrooke Castle,* situated high above the sea near the center of the island, is of Norman origin. King Charles I, his son, and his daughter were all kept prisoner there by Cromwellian forces during the Civil War. It is possible to walk completely around the castle on the ramparts, if you are not faint of heart, while looking down into moats. There is a well house complete with a donkey on a treadmill to bring up heavy buckets.

Farther south, **Appuldurcombe House** is the shell of a once magnificent Georgian country house. It belonged to the Worsley family, which once owned most of the island. The curator has interesting stories to tell as you explore the museum, and there is a fascination in wandering through roofless rooms that once were lived in; plaques on the walls indicate the original use of each room.

On the north shore near the Solent lies **Osborne House,** built by Queen Victoria, which contains a large collection of furnishings from her era. She used this huge, rambling house as a summer residence until her death in 1901. You can visit Queen Victoria's private apartment as well as the state apartments. The furnishings are authentic "Victoriana"!

The coastline of the Isle of Wight has many natural beauties such as **The Needles,** three large chalk rocks just offshore rising vertically to 100 feet, and Undercliff, a chalk and limestone plateau that reminds us of the Riviera. Tennyson used to take walks in the woods along this coast near his home, **Farringford House** (to avoid admiring fans).

On the other side of the island, Cowes is a major sailing center, the home of the Royal Yacht Squadron, which manages Britain's most famous regatta, Cowes Week, each August. The schooner *America* received the cup that bears her name in international yachting competition by winning a race around the Isle of Wight in 1851, with Queen Victoria and Prince Albert watching from the royal yacht. For variety, take the ferry from **Yarmouth,** at the western end of the island, back to the mainland at **Lymington,** which has a harbor packed with boats.

Also in the area
   Beaulieu Abbey and Palace House (14 miles south of Southampton)

Lymington/Salcombe

Some may prefer to poke along this coast, on A337 to **Bournemouth,** A35 to **Poole,** A351 to **Wareham,** A352 to **Dorchester,** A35 to **Lyme Regis,** A3052 to **Exeter** and **Kingsbridge,** and A381 to **Salcombe.** If you want to fully appreciate this section of Dorset, you might want to stop for lunch in Lyme Regis, where you can walk the quay John Fowles described in *The French Lieutenant's Woman.* Jane Austen also summered there, and set *Persuasion* in Lyme Regis. Others may prefer to proceed west on A337 North to **Cadnam,** then left on A31 to Dorchester. This is Thomas Hardy country. You may want to read *The Mayor of Casterbridge, Far from the Madding Crowd, The Return of* *the Native,* or *Tess of the D'Urbervilles* before you go. Then take A35 to Exeter, A38 to the exit for **Ugborough** on B3196 to Kingsbridge, and A381 to Salcombe. This trip will take around 5 hours, not counting the many stops you may be tempted to make. Allow some time in the Salcombe area to find the perfect campsite for at least a 3-day stay. We found a campground with large, flat sites and a view of the sea. The beach far below was accessible. Facilities were among the best we found anywhere in England. In that area many campsites are bound to be sloping and rocky, which can be difficult with tents. There are also campgrounds in Kingsbridge. You will find small campgrounds all over England, run by families on their fields. In some cases amenities are minimal. Campgrounds can be spotted by signs on the roads.

SALCOMBE is a very picturesque seaside resort village. Oriented toward its dramatic harbor, you'll find high hills on both sides leading into an estuary that winds all the way to Kingsbridge. After first visiting Salcombe years ago, we chose to live there for 10 weeks—writing most of the day, clearing our heads with late afternoon walks along the cliffs, enjoying the quiet village streets in off season, and gazing at the ever-changing sea at the mouth of the estuary. We lived high up on the terraced hillside, above ***The Moult,*** once the marine house of the Earl of Devon before it was sold to the distinguished Oxford historian, James Anthony Froude. Alfred, Lord Tennyson stayed there with his friend and was inspired (not without reason) to write about the impressive and dangerous Salcombe harbor bar, which is wild with rollers, at low tide— waves that "gave forth a surfy, slow, deep, mellow voice, and with a hollow moan crossed the bar on their way to the harbor." Crossing the bar came to symbolize the passage from life to death in the poem, just as it had in reality for the many sailors who have drowned there.

We can recommend this idyllic spot enthusiastically. Froude commented, "The winter at Salcombe is winter only in name—only the sea is wild. The climate resembles Spain or Italy." Many people retire here; the weather is Mediterranean, so winters are not as arduous as they are elsewhere in England. People walk up and down the steep hills in the village, taking their dogs out along the cliffs; year-round exercise is possible.

Tidal creeks in the estuary, which look like the fingers of a hand on the chart, empty completely at low tide and leave boats tilting at all angles in the mud (the range is 14–17 feet). Salcombe harbor has always been a center for marine activity; years ago sailing ships were built in local boatyards noted for their exceptionally fast fruit schooners, and trading was brisk, with vessels coming in from the West Indies, America, and the Mediterranean laden with all kinds of goods. Today the harbor, one of the finest on the southern coast, is a mecca for yachtsmen as well as a center for the active local fishing fleet.

Cliff walks: From the center of town, take Fore Street and Cliff Walk along the estuary toward the sea, past the ruins of **Salcombe Castle,** built during the reign of Henry VIII as a deterrent to Spanish and French privateers. In 1643, during the Civil War, Sir Edmund Fortescue of Fallapit, Royalist High Sheriff of Devon, refortified the old castle so that it was strong enough to survive a 4-month seige in 1646, when it became the last bastion of the Royalist cause in Devon to surrender to Parliamentary forces. Renamed **Fort Charles** by Fortescue, the ruin perches on a rock at the narrowest point of the harbor entrance. Recently an adjacent house, also known as Fort Charles, went up for sale; the ruin goes along with it unless a rightful heir of Sir Edmund turns up to claim it.

When you have passed the ruins, continue on to the first beautiful cove with a fine sand beach, **North Sands,** climb the hill on the other side, where you can look down on Froude's Moult End, and walk down another steep hill to the second cove, **South Sands;** along the way, look to the right for views of the jagged tor atop **Bolt Head** and to the left for the cliff-lined coast leading toward **Prawle Point.**

Our favorite walk in this area—hard as it is to choose one among the many magnificent sections of the 500-mile-long Southwest Peninsula Coastal Path—begins either at South Sands or up the hill beyond, at the edge of the National Trust property. Go through the "kissing-gate" and follow Courtenay Walk, a corniche path cut into the bluffs along the coast, until you are below **Sharp Tor,** a jagged, towering pinnacle; then go up the steps, around the bend, and pause for the view down into **Starehole Bay.** In 1936 the four-masted Finnish barque *Herzogin Cecille* crunched onto the rocks here, and the corn in her hold rotted, polluting the air for miles around.

Continue along the perimeter of the bay to the slight depression where a bridge crosses a small brook. This is **Starehole Bottom;** brass coins found here date back to the days of a Danish encampment, and there is a local legend that a cave extends from it all the way to Malborough Church, two miles away. At the bottom, where you will find clear signposts, keep to the left, cross over a stile, and head up toward Bolt Head. After a long climb you'll find a bench on top; the magnificent view in all directions is well worth the climb. Fifty yards beyond the bench you will come to an old lookout post used during the invasion scares of World War II; from it you can look down nearly 400 feet to the sea churning on the rocks below or gaze along the coastline toward **Bolt Tail.** Just beyond the lookout, up a steep meadow (where you may find Dartmoor ponies grazing), you will come to another stile; take the path to the right, along a hedge, which will lead you down through a higher section of Starhole Bottom and back up on the downs to the top of Sharp Tor. Look for the mounted direction plaque that gives you the distance to Cherbourg, Exeter Cathedral, the Eddystone Lighthouse, Kingsbridge, Malborough, Hay Tor (Dartmoor), and The Needles (Isle of Wight). If you would like a walk with less uphill mileage, park your car in the Overbeck parking lot and walk this route in reverse.

By following this upper path along the edge of the downs back toward Salcombe, you will come to **Sharpitor Gardens,** a National Trust property containing an exotic collection of plants and trees, many of them subtropical in origin. Be sure to bring your camera if you are there when the enormous magnolia tree, planted in 1901, is in bloom. The house, **Overbeck,** is operated as a youth hostel; school groups use it during the school year for the study of marine biology and other subjects. There are several rooms inside that are a museum on local history and seafaring. The garden and house are just above your starting point, closing a circuit of something less than four miles. Longer walks may be taken by continuing on from Bolt Head to **Soar Mill Cove,** then turning inland to return by road, or walking the whole six miles of the coastal path along the cliff edge of the downs to Bolt Tail and **Hope Cove.**

From Salcombe, you can take a short ferry across to the **East Portlemouth** side of the estuary to reach another rugged and more isolated section of the coastal path. Walk along the estuary past **Mill Bay,** with its beautiful sand beach, and **Rickham Sands** (also called Leeke Cove, where the sailing ship *Meirion* foundered) to the Gara Rock Hotel, where you can turn inland and walk on the road to East Portlemouth or on a marked footpath across fields and woods back down to Mill Bay and then to the ferry, all circuits of less than four miles. A longer walk involves continuing on the coast path past **Deckler's Cliff, Pig's Nose, Ham Stone,** and **Ball Rock** to the memorable rock formations of **Gammon Head;** after the Armada was defeated, two Spanish galleons sank here in the great gales that finally dispersed and destroyed the Spanish fleet. For some really spectacular views, go around the bend to look down on beautifully secluded **Macely Cove** and **Elender Cove** to the coast-guard lookout on **Prawle Point,** which is the most southerly point in Devon. Turning inland, you will pass coast-guard cottages that were the scene of violence in 1872 when survivors of an Italian brig wrecked nearby got into a fight, stabbing each other and coast-guard officers. Where the road forks, take the left turning and walk to **East Prawle,** then onto the road back to the ferry at East Portlemouth.

There are a number of excursions you can take from Salcombe. If you are really energetic, you can continue the coast walk from Prawle Point to **Start Point,** where there is a lighthouse dating from 1836. Aside from its magnificent view, Start Point is also famous as the first landfall of butterflies migrating northward. Yachtsmen and fishermen know that the steep chop of Start Race, just off the point, can be especially dangerous in southerly gales when the current is running against the waves.

Around the bend from Start Point is the tragic ruin of **Hallsands Village.** Once a thriving fishing community of 37 houses built in two rows on a narrow ledge tucked under a cliff, the village was swept out to sea after human error undermined its foundations. At one point 128 people lived there; the village supported a tailor, carpenter, shipbuilder, grocery, post office, inn, and many fishermen. Tourists came by steamer from Torquay for the local white ale. Because the village overlooked the sea at such close range, its fishermen could easily spot shoals of fish, launch their boats, and draw the fish into seine nets. Crabs were collected from local pots and kept fresh in boats with wells in their bottoms. In bad weather the fishermen used Newfoundland dogs to retrieve the lines on nearby pots.

In 1897 contractors from Plymouth began dredging sand and gravel from the bed of the sea below the low-water mark. Although fishermen objected—because the dredging interfered with their livelihood—the work continued. Local inhabitants noticed the pebble ridge on which their houses were built beginning to shift; sea walls were undermined, and the high-water mark of the spring tides reached 30 feet from the ledge instead of the usual 70–80 feet. Storms in 1903–1904 caused the sea wall in front of the inn to collapse, with the subsequent washing away of other material beneath, and several houses were declared uninhabitable. By 1904 all of the houses on the front had been damaged, and the sea continued to erode them, especially when storms and high tides coincided; to prevent this, a very large sea wall was built, and it held for some years. However, in January 1917, during a terrific storm, the houses fell, one by one. Twenty-nine homes, with the lifetime belongings of the owners, were washed away. All the townspeople moved away, except Miss Elizabeth Prettejohn, who stayed in her home until she died in 1964. Her house is still standing, but the rest of the structures are total ruins. In 1924 a government report belatedly recognized the plight of the town: "By the manner in which they have endured undeserved ill-fortune the inhabitants of Hallsands have earned the respect of all who have been associated with them."

After leaving Hallsands, head back to A379 and drive north to **Slapton Sands,** the site of practice landings by U.S. forces in 1943 as they prepared for D Day. This area was chosen because it has a configuration similar to the landing beach on the Cherbourg peninsula codenamed Utah Beach. A necessary but painful episode in the life of the community began in the village hall on November 13, 1943. The inhabitants were told that they would have to evacuate their homes by December 20. Because many of the younger people were away in the armed forces, the burden fell heavily on the shoulders of the elderly. Moving a lifetime's possessions must have been almost more than they could bear. Two information centers were set up by volunteers to offer accommodation and help. In all, 750 families, which included 3000 persons, were moved. They took with them everything that could be moved, including their cattle and their harvested crops. Only empty churches, shops, and farmhouses remained. The area affected was centered on Slapton Sands, and included the surrounding villages of Torcross, Stokenham, Chillington, Sherford, East Allington, Blackawton, Strete, and Slapton.

American troops were also quartered in Salcombe, Dartmouth, and Brixham, but their civilians were not evacuated.

As the exercises continued, there were some disasters. In April 1944, German U-boats slipped through the screen and attacked American vessels, killing 700 American soldiers. In 1984 South Devon newspapers carried stories about the possibility of a mass grave near Blackawton. A local woman claimed that she saw American bodies stacked in the back of a lorry in 1944 and that she watched as they were taken to a field for burial. Other local residents came forth with further eye-witness accounts. Yet the present owner of the site, now farmland, maintained that there was no evidence of a mass grave on his land.

The sacrifice made by these South Hams people was not just the inconvenience: To simulate the reality of the Normandy landings, the shellfire was real and the invading troops were opposed. The result was a shell-scarred landscape. After the war, rehabilitation began by removing mines, repairing homes, and clearing fields. It must have been very difficult for people to return to find their homes in ruins and their land untended. As Americans, we wondered how people really felt about the U.S. forces at that time. A necessary occupation, yes, but were there grumbles? Apparently not, unless memory has effaced them. The people we met had nothing but praise for their visitors; in a large group meeting about "Old Salcombe," we heard only expressions of gratitude interspersed with funny anecdotes. In 1984, the 40th anniversary of the occupation, one newspaper article carried the headline: GOOD GUYS, THOSE GIS. Read Leslie Thomas's novel, *The Magic Army,* to appreciate the atmosphere of this strange "occupation" by friendly forces.

From Slapton, continue north on A379, the coast road, through the lovely villages of **Strete** and **Stoke Fleming** (you may want to stop in either) to **Dartmouth,** an old and famous port. The town tumbles down steep hills to the harbor. Boat trips are available up the River Dart, in the harbor, and out to the coast. Birdwatchers will find cormorants, kingfishers, and osprey in the Dart estuary. The ***Brittania Royal Naval College,*** located on the hill overlooking the harbor, was designed by Aston Webb and opened in 1905.

Dartmouth Castle, built in the 15th century, guards the entrance to the harbor. **St. Petrock's church** is adjacent to the castle; there are several memorial brasses inside. ***Gallants Bower,*** a wooded hill behind the castle, is the site of a Civil-War earthwork dating from 1645, marking the struggle of the Royalists to hold the town. (Dartmouth fell to the Parliamentarians in January 1646.) Walk along the ***Butterwalk,*** a row of four shops arcaded by overhanging rooms and supported by 11 granite piers, which dates from 1630. The ***Dartmouth Town Museum,*** located in a former merchant's house built in 1640 on the Butterwalk, contains the original paneling and ceilings. The collection includes both historic and maritime displays and 140 ship models. If you want to explore the surrounding area, one of the most interesting in South Devon, stop in the tourist office and ask for the official guide, which contains a section on rambles around Dartmouth.

Take either the upper or lower ferry from Dartmouth across the river, then continue heading north on A379, A302, A380, A38, and A30 to Exeter. (This sequence is much easier than it sounds.) The *Maritime Museum* flanks both sides of the river and has vintage boats of all kinds displayed indoors and out, with the distinction of allowing children (and adults) to climb through them. The 12th century *cathedral* was built in perfect symmetry with matching pillars, aisles, canopies, chapels, and tombs. It has an unusually bright interior. Look for the Bishop's Throne, dating from 1312, and a large clock with all its mechanisms in view. There are underground passages to explore near the town information center; these were once a medieval aqueduct designed to solve the town's water shortage.

The Exeter area figures largely in the literary imagination. Dickens found a model for the original "Fat Boy" of *Pickwick Papers* in The Turk's Head in High Street, Exeter. Chatteris, in Thackeray's *Pendennis,* is really Exeter, and several crucial scenes in Fowles's *The French Lieutenant's Woman* are set there. Richard Blackmore, who wrote *Lorna Doone,* grew up in Exmoor, north of Exeter, and drew upon the region for the ambience of his romance.

From Salcombe, you can also drive west on A379 over massive swells of down used mostly for grazing to **Plymouth,** whose name has been adopted by 40 other cities around the world. The history of this famous port city is rich, stretching from an Iron Age and Roman past through medieval prosperity; it has been the scene of many important and calamitous events, including a raid by a French force that burned 600 houses in 1403. Plymouth was the source of ships and men who stopped the Armada in 1588, and it saw the sailing of the *Mayflower* in 1620 and withstood bombing by Hitler's Luftwafte in the early stages of World War II, which devastated most of the city center. New, wide streets were laid out after the war so the shopping area is well designed and easy to navigate.

If you want to get your bearings on the city as a whole, try the view from the 13th floor of the *Civic Center.* Armada Way rises up to the **Hoe,** an elevated promenade overlooking the sea. Also on the Hoe are the Naval War Memorial and the National Armada Memorial. A Statue of Sir Francis Drake stands on the spot where he was playing bowls when the news of the sighting of the Armada was brought to him; at that moment he is supposed to have uttered the legendary boast, "Time enough to finish our game, and beat the Spaniards." If you have the time and inclination, swim in the gigantic open-air seawater pool below Armada Way, or lounge on the terraces beside it. And don't miss the **Barbican,** the old section of Plymouth, with its narrow, crooked lanes.

From Plymouth, drive north on A386 to **Yelverton** to see **Buckland Abbey.** Built in 1278, it passed to Henry VIII after his split with the pope and was purchased by Sir Francis Drake a few years after he returned from his voyage around the world, perhaps with the spoils of that venture. In the Great Hall you will see Drake's drum, which traveled with him at sea (drums were used for calling muster rolls and battle stations) and was brought back to Buckland in 1596, at his death. Deeds and documents signed by Drake are also on display. The chapel houses a large collection of exquisite English church silverware, some from the 16th century. Banners said to have been flown on the *Golden Hind* are hung in the gallery. Marine paintings and displays continue up the stairs and into the gallery on the top floor. The adjoining tithe barn, built in the 14th century, was the storehouse for goods given as one-tenth of the worth of local parishioners. It now houses an interesting collection of vehicles, ranging from fire engines to coaches, dating back to the 18th century—and a noisy colony of pigeons roosting in the rafters.

For an excursion into nearby **Dartmoor,** follow B3212; when you pass a cattle grid on the road you are inside the moor proper, where sheep, cattle, and wild ponies graze at will, even on the road shoulders. (We noticed a sign with a pun, DRIVE WITH MOOR CARE, as we entered.) This bleak and desolate wilderness remains just as it was many, many years ago; we wouldn't want to be lost in a blizzard on the moor, either now or centuries ago.

It is possible to explore some of the **Dartmoor National Park** by driving; much more is accessible on foot or horseback. Hikers should beware of adders, treacherous peat bogs, and mist. On a sunny day we found that a walk of several miles on the open moor was very pleasant; even in these favorable conditions, though, a compass is recommended. We parked by the information board at Venford Reservoir, where you can study suggested walks. We chose to walk along the reservoir, up the sloping moor through the bracken to a Celtic Cross, one of many that serve as landmarks in an area where there are no other distinguishing features, and past a large grouping of rocks forming a natural tor. These tors (derived from the word *tower*) are outcrops of granite which the erosion of ages has molded into shapes that are anthropomorphized by names such as "Bowerman's Nose." Wild ponies graze amongst the tors, with sheep as their companions.

Conan Doyle set *The Hound of the Baskervilles* in Dartmoor. Eden Phillpotts wrote *The Secret Woman, Children of the Mist,* and *Children of Men* depicting this area. And R. D. Blackmore used Dartmoor as the setting for *Christowell: a Dartmoor Tale.*

CORNWALL, the wildest part of the West Country, is surrounded by water on three sides; this peninsula is attached to Devon on its northeastern border. Cornwall has something for everyone—beautiful sandy beaches pounded by surf, rock outcroppings and giddy cliffs, fishing villages and an abundance of dramatic landscapes for the artist or photographer. Hikers can follow the Cornish Coast Path completely around the peninsula; there are no roads other than the coast path between some villages. In addition, Cornwall has a fascinating Celtic culture and more than a touch of legend and myth.

The south coast is varied, with estuaries penetrating inland through a maze of boats high and dry at low tide, and cliffs and headlands interspersed with coves and bays. The north coast is by far the more rugged, beginning with the rock outcroppings of Land's End and leading up to 700-foot cliffs near Tintagel Castle in North Cornwall. Because the coasts are so exhilarating, the inland region may go unnoticed. Yet the open moorland, busy market towns, forested river valleys, and a wealth of Celtic monuments are there to be enjoyed as an alternative to the attractions of the coast.

Cornwall has been called the land of legend. Not too many years ago, one of the highlights of life in the isolated homes and small villages was the arrival of the wandering story-teller. He stayed one night in each house; in exchange for bed and board, he would entertain the family with ballads sung to a fiddle accompaniment, relate legends, and provide the latest news and gossip.

Historically, the Cornish people were unusually superstitious; they believed in the legends of elves and gremlins. The Cornish "piskey" was about the size of a mouse, a little old man dressed in white weskit, green stockings, brown coat, and breeches, wearing diamond dewdrops in his buckled shoes. As the good spirits of Cornwall, piskeys helped the sick and elderly with their work. Who wouldn't like to wake in the morning to find that the piskeys had threshed their corn during the night? They could also be mischievous, playing tricks and kicking up their heels. "Spriggans" were the bad elves: they were known to conjure up sudden storms, flatten corn fields with hail, and steal children from their beds. They haunted and protected treasure hidden in granite cairns and burial mounds.

The most mysterious of the little elves were the "knackers" or "knockers" who lived in the mines. These sprites were ugly, with thin limbs, large hooked noses, and a penchant for making faces, crossing their eyes, and thumbing their noses at the miners. Most of the men respected them, leaving a little bit of dinner for them as insurance against evil. A man who took pains to annoy them was sure to come to harm.

Salcombe/Cornwall

Take A379 from the Salcombe/Kingsbridge area to Plymouth, then A374 signed to **Torpoint,** crossing on the Torpoint ferry. Continue on A374 until you meet the A387, which you take past **Looe** to **Polperro.** Once a small fishing village wedged into a gap in the cliffs, this is still one of the most picturesque spots in Cornwall. Park your car in the lot on the edge of town and explore the narrow streets with their shops and historic houses. *Couch House* still belongs to Dr. Arthur Couch, grandson of the writer, Sir Arthur Quiller-Couch; look for *House on the Props* and *Crumplehorn Mill.*

Retrace 2½ miles to the sign for **Fowey**, where you will follow B3359, a one-lane road leading to the ferry to Fowey. A haven for yachtsmen with its landlocked harbor, it is also the port for large vessels laden with china clay from St. Austell. You can get a list of walks around Fowey from the information office. We had a picnic lunch on the quay within sight of *St. Catherine's Castle,* which was built in the 16th century. The *Noah's Ark Folk Museum* is located in the oldest house in town, also dating from the 16th century. Daphne du Maurier lives in Fowey. If you loved *Frenchman's Creek, Rebecca,* and *Jamaica Inn*, all set in this area, you can find a huge stack of her other novels in the local bookstore. We enjoyed reading her *Vanishing Cornwall* while traveling through the county; it contains good descriptions of the areas we find most appealing.

From Fowey, find your way back to A3082, pass the "china alps" (heaps of china clay) in the **St. Austell** area, and head off on B3273 to **Mevagissey,** another charming fishing village. Once renowned for pilchard fishing and smuggling, Mevagissey is still a pleasant place; you can watch the fishing-boat activity from the seats in the inner harbor. By the way, the navy christened the pilchards they were served too often for dinner "Mevagissey ducks."

Go back to the A390 until it joins the A39 into **Falmouth,** an important center for shipping and for yachting. Because of its strategic location at the western approach to the English Channel, this large natural harbor has a maritime tradition going back to the days of commercial sail, when ships went to "Falmouth for orders." Many homewardbound vessels sailed into Falmouth after months at sea either to discharge their cargoes or, more frequently, to await new instructions from owners or charterers. No matter what the level of the tide or wind direction, ships could get out to sea here without the use of a tug, making it even more attractive for commercial shipping. But its virtues for mariners were discovered long before there were tugs to use. Phoenicians sailed to Falmouth searching for Cornish tin, and the Romans also used it as a base during their colonization of southwestern Britain.

Henry VIII built the castles of *Pendennis* and *St. Mawes* here to protect the estuary, with one on each side. Pendennis Castle was begun in 1542 on the site of a prehistoric fort. The granite central keep has two semicircular bastions enclosed by gun positions. We noticed that these gun emplacements were constructed with a crescent-shaped track so that the guns could be swiveled to advantage. The finest hour in the history of Pendennis came in 1646 when Sir John Arundel, at 80 years of age, held out against the forces of Parliament for many months. He would not surrender the castle even when food supplies became low, water was severely rationed, and the inhabitants were forced to dine on their horses, dogs, and cats. When he finally did negotiate, he won concessions from Parliament, including an immediate supply of food. Then he, with his retinue of supporters, marched out of the castle with colors flying, trumpets blaring, and drums beating. His courageous fight did not go unnoticed.

From Falmouth, take B3291 to **Gweek** and follow signs to the ***Cornish Seal Sanctuary.*** If you are as fascinated by these gentle creatures as we are, this is a good time to see them close at hand. Leave your car in the adjacent car park and walk 400 yards through the woods along the Helford River to the Seal Sanctuary. Ken Jones, its founder, met his first "orphan of the sea" in 1958 when a newborn baby seal washed up on the beach at St. Agnes. From then on his life was devoted to caring for sick and injured seals. As word of the sanctuary spread, he was notified of injured seals and would try to save them from batterings on the rocks, often climbing down the cliff on a stormy winter night. The rate of survival is often in direct proportion to the time treatment is begun. His hospital contains a number of seal pens for those who are quite ill; when somewhat recovered, they graduate to a series of five outdoor pools, where they can convalesce and begin to cavort with their mates again. Most of the seals are released when they are well; some will never be able to fend for themselves and are kept at the sanctuary. We met one seal, Lucky, who has a cleft palate and harelip; he is a permanent and contented resident. We were touched by the care and devotion of Mr. Jones and his staff. Bring your camera to record the seals playing with balls and life rings; the surrounding countryside in this lovely river setting provides a pleasant background and if you have children, they will love it.

When you are able to tear yourself away from the very appealing seals, head toward **Lizard Point** on B3291 to A3083. You will pass through the **Goonhilly Downs,** barren except for gorse and heather. Visit the lighthouse on this most southerly tip of Britain to see the machinery inside. The light contains 5¼ million candle-power, one of the most powerful in the world. We can attest to the fact that it flashes once every three seconds; when you are sleeping out there your body becomes attuned to that interval. In *Vanishing Cornwall,* Daphne du Maurier recalls that she could not sleep under the sweep of the lighthouse beam. She also writes about the lack of a beacon 200 years ago, when unlucky sailors waited on board, listening to the crash of the surf on reefs that might destroy their ships. The supposedly unsinkable *Titanic* underwent her sea trials here; one writer remembered seeing her at that time, before she sailed off to Southampton to begin her first and only transatlantic voyage. The rocks off the Lizard have claimed a tremendous number of ships, including the *Mohegan,* which foundered on **Manacle Point** on her second voyage to America in October 1898. It is possible that there may be a magnetic influence in the rocks that can disturb the accuracy of a ship's compass, particularly after a strong east wind. As a result of this shipwreck, 106 persons lie in a mass grave in **St. Keverne** churchyard under a monument with a single name carved in granite: MOHEGAN. In 1911 the *Hansy* of Sundsvall, Sweden, ran up against the cliffs in Housel Bay, within sight of the modern lighthouse. Local inhabitants felt their good fortune (or "God's Grace") as they gathered flotsam and jetsam from her hold. A salvage group came upon a pig helping himself to potatoes in the hold and two goats happily ensconsed in the crew's bunks.

There are many spectacular walks near the Lizard, to places like the **Devil's Frying Pan,** north of **Church Cove; Kennack Sands,** north of **Ruan Minor** and **Kuggar; Housel Bay Cove,** east of Lizard Point; and **Kynance Cove,** a few miles northwest of Lizard Point. The serpentine rock will dazzle you with its varied hues of green, red, and black. This rock is of igneous origin, but metamorphism has changed it into serpentine. Pressure on the rock caused the colored crystals to appear as beads in a string; they look like a serpent's skin. On the Lizard, lava flows created schist, which is a black and dark green rock with some yellow veins. Kynance Cove is a painter's dream; we saw a couple perched on the rocks capturing the essence of **Steeple Rock, Bishop's Rock,** the **Devil's Letter Box,** and the **Bellows.** They said that the contrast of color tones provided by green moss and grass set against black, red, and green rocks are enhanced by misty weather; colors are particularly deep in the spring.

When your bag is full of enough rocks to supply your family with paper weights for years to come, head back to the main road, A3083, through **Helston,** to A394 to **Marazion,** where you can stop to see **St. Michael's Mount,** an island not far from shore that resembles and is historically connected with Mont-St-Michel, off the coast of Brittany. Some say this island was King Arthur's lost land of Lyonesse; you may even hear the bells of the churches ringing under water. **Chevy Chase Hall** was once the refectory of this 11th-century monastery. During restoration in 1720 a man's skeleton was found on the other side of a hidden doorway, perhaps that of Sir John Arundel. You can walk out to the island across a sandy causeway when the tide is low. On the way you will see **Chapel Rock,** associated with a legend of the giants. The giant, Cormoran, and his wife, Cormelian, were building a stronghold of white granite. One day, when her husband was asleep, Cormelian brought green rock instead, which could be found nearer than the white rock. Her husband was annoyed when he woke, kicked her, and the rock fell to the ground and remained there.

From St. Michael's Mount, continue on A30 to signs for **Gulval** and **New Mill;** at New Mill look for signs to the ancient settlement of **Chysauster,** which is reached by a footpath from the site carpark. Dating from the first four centuries A.D., this ancient village is the largest among those found in Cornwall. There are eight houses in a group and several others located nearby. Most of the houses have been excavated and include hearths, stone-covered drains, stones with sockets in them to hold upright timbers that supported roofs, and some paved areas. The entrances face east or northeast, away from the prevailing southwest wind. From the entrance you emerge into an inner courtyard 25 to 30 feet wide. House 5 should be visited first because its plan is the most basic; House 6 is the most complex. A *fougou* (Cornish for cave) is located southeast of House 7. This underground chamber is 6 feet below ground level, and two large lintel-stones from its roof are intact.

Return to **Penzance,** then follow the coast road south out of town to **Mousehole** (pronounced "Mowzell"), a fishing village of granite houses overlooking a large, protected harbor. Follow signs to **Lamorna,** an old smuggling village that is beyond **Trewoofe.** As you drive along B3315, look carefully for an ancient stone circle now referred to as the *Merry Maidens,* 19 upright stones that, in local legend, represent girls who were changed to stone for dancing on the Sabbath. In the field before the one containing the maidens you may spot two taller stones that are supposed to be the *Pipers* for the dance. This ancient group is very difficult to find from the north, but it is about one mile from Lamorna and easy to spot from the road when approaching from the south. The Cornish name for the group is Dans Maen (Stone Dance). Each maiden is about a meter high; the pipers are over four meters high. We shared this scene with a number of cows who came over for a nuzzle, apparently quite used to strangers in their field.

A little farther on the same road you will come to the *Tregiffian Barrow Burial Chamber,* a megalithic chambered tomb built during the Neolithic period. As you continue, look for the Celtic crosses, one on the left and then another farther along on the right.

Continue on B3315 to A30 and follow signs for **Land's End,** the most westerly tip of Britain. The Cornish name for Land's End is *Pen-Von-Las* (End of the Earth). There is legend that it once might have extended a little farther; there are those who have stood on the cliffs at Land's End and sworn they saw the tips of towers, spires, and battlements near *Seven Stones Reef,* which is on the way to the Isles of Scilly. This version of the location of the vanished Lyonesse is one among many. One writer goes on to say that the earthquake in Portugal in 1755 (the one that destroyed Lisbon) caused the ocean to rise ten feet along the coast of Cornwall; a similar occurrence could have swallowed Lyonesse. Despite a number of lighthouses in the area—such as *Longships* off the End, *Pendeen* to the north, *Wolf Rock* to the southwest, and *Seven Stones* lightship—there have been many shipwrecks. Some of them may have been caused by the greed of a few who walked donkeys along the cliffs carrying false lights to simulate the way to safety; more certainly, plundering wrecks aroused the greed of whole towns. In writing about the innumerable wrecks off the nearby Isles of Scilly (in an excellent brief book called *Shipwreck*), novelist John Fowles notes that both a current and a repeated chart error have been partly responsible for the deservedly evil reputation of these isles among mariners. Even modern aids to navigation cannot save this area of Cornwall from more than its share of maritime disasters, including the stranding of the *Torrey Canyon* in 1967, with its aftermath of a massive oil spill.

If you visit Land's End on a wild day you will get some sensation of what it must have been like for those whose ships foundered there. Madgy Figgy, a witch who lived at Tol-Pedn, used to sit in her chair-shaped rock scanning the sea for ships in trouble. Once the ship had struck she would fly down on her imitation broomstick, a stalk of ragwort, and be first on hand to claim the spoils. Local villagers surmised that she had something to do with luring ships to her chair.

From Land's End heading north, B3306 is the **Penwith Coast Road,** with some interesting views followed by an area of closed mines and desolate stretches with only a gray stone house here and there as reminders of the lonely, hard life of the miners. D. H. Lawrence lived in Zennor for several years (1914–1917) while he worked on *Women in Love*.

You will soon come to **St. Ives,** once a little fishing village, now an artists' paradise and seaside resort. The town has narrow, cobbled streets, palm trees, and sand beaches. There are craft shops, galleries, and artist's studios to visit. Don't miss the **Barbara Hepworth Museum** in her home. On the ground floor there is a striking sequence of photographs taken throughout her career, personal memorabilia, letters, and medals and honors she has received. Upstairs in her studio is a fine collection of both sculpture and paintings. The garden is filled with a variety of plants, trees, and a remarkable collection of her sculpture. There are paths to walk on so you can see her work from all angles; chairs and tables invite visitors to relax. Her workshops were left as they were when she died. As you look at her work you will understand how the ancient stone monuments in Cornwall might have served as inspiration for her shapes.

Virginia Woolf spent summers here at Talland House, the summer home of her father, Leslie Stephen; **Godrevy Lighthouse** was the inspiration for *To The Lighthouse,* although the novel's setting was switched to the Isle of Skye in Scotland.

From St. Ives, drive along A30 to signs for **Perranporth,** where you will find three miles of sand beach noted as a good place for surfing. It is said that the oldest chapel in Britain disappeared here in shifting sand in the 10th century, then reappeared in 1835 when the sands shifted again. Three headless skeletons were found inside.

Unless you want to poke along small coast roads, return to the A30 and follow it to **Fraddon,** then take A39 to the turn for **Port Isaac,** an old lobster port. Drive on to **Port Gaverne,** formerly a port for coal coming in and slate going out. Take the coast road up the hill for views of the sea and rejoin B3314 on top of the down. You can ramble around the country on one-lane roads with fairly steep grades and pretty countryside through **Delabole** and **Trebarwith** to **Tintagel,** or you can take B3314 and B3263 to Tintagel. There are some particularly nice stone walls constructed in a herringbone pattern along the former route. These are called Cornish hedges, reflecting an ancient art still preserved by countrymen. The diagonal herringbone pattern is chinked in with earth, and sod is placed on top to protect the wall from rain.

King Arthur's Country is beautiful, whether or not you believe the legends. It is said that here the baby Arthur was washed up on the shore and into the waiting arms of Merlin the magician.

Alfred Lord Tennyson wrote about Arthurian legends throughout much of his life. His *Idylls of the King* (1859) continues an identification of **Tintagel Castle** as King Arthur's seat begun by Geoffrey of Monmouth's *History of the Britains* in the 12th century, and later works like *Merlin and the Gleam* (1889) reinforce that association. Tennyson's diaries contain references to his travels throughout Cornwall. Charles Dickens also writes about "clambering up the goat path to King Arthur's Castle at Tintagel," and Algernon Swinburne describes the "double ruin of Tintagel Castle" in a letter of 1864, written during a two-month visit to Tintagel. He also tells of his escape from a rising tide at Tintagel as a boy.

Originally, there was a Celtic monastery on the site. In the 12th century Reginald, Earl of Cornwall, built a castle over the ruins. During the 14th century it was used as a prison; it then began falling into the ruin you see today. To reach Tintagel Castle, park your car in town and head down the hill toward the ruin on the well-marked path. The sea has been eroding this land, so the castle is now in two sections. The mainland site consists of the upper and lower wards and the prison. Walk 115 steps down and then 100 steps up on the island side. The gateway leads into the Great Hall, the monastery, rooms probably once containing sauna baths, up to a plateau, through the garden area, and into a group of 12 rooms and a 15th-century chapel. On your way back look for Merlin's Cave, which is right on the edge of the water. At low tide you can walk through and emerge on a beach; be careful to note the level of the tide so you can return safely.

Thomas Hardy lived in **St. Juliot,** near Boscastle; as an architect, he restored the 15th-century parish church there.

Follow B3263 to **Boscastle** for one last cliff walk before leaving Cornwall. Drive up behind the church in the upper town to park your car and walk to the *Coast-Guard Lookout,* which is visible from the church. There are lovely views both ways from this headland, including caves to peer at through your field glasses. We were entranced by a number of paired gulls nesting up and down the cliffs. One intruder tried to attract the attention of a female on her nest until her mate chased him away. Undaunted, he flew across the chasm to try his luck with another female, to no avail. This is an area of especially high cliffs, 700 feet in some cases, which drop right down to the sea. If you are continuing on to North Devon, there is more coastal scenery to hike in and enjoy.

To continue north, take B3263 to A39, which will take you to **Barnstaple**. One can either spend some time exploring North Devon (beaches, dunes, or a cliff walk at **Croyde**) via A361 and B3231 to **Ilfracombe**, A399 to **Blackmore Gate**, B3358 and B3224 through **Exmoor** to **Whedden Cross**, A396 to **Dunster**, A39 to **Bridgewater**, A38 to **Bristol**, and A4 to **Bath**. For those who want to loaf, there are virtues in having time to take an unplanned side excursion or arriving early enough to pick out one of the best campsites, bed and breakfast spots, or hotels.

Bath

Bath possesses the only natural hot springs in England. It has been a fashionable watering place since the 18th century. Although the old baths are no longer in use and the papers carry stories about closing the new baths, there is still much for visitors to enjoy. Bath is built of Bath stone, on a series of terraces rising to 600 feet. With baths, churches, parks, and museums available, there is more than enough to fill a day. Many writers focused on the area in and around Bath. You may want to read some of the following before you go: Jane Austen's *Persuasion* and *Northanger Abbey;* Henry Fielding's *Tom Jones;* Tobias Smollet's *Humphrey Clinker;* Richard Brinsley Sheridan's *The Rival* and *The School for Scandal;* and Charles Dickens's *Pickwick Papers.*

Also in the area
  Longleat House (4 miles southwest of Warminster)

Stonehenge/Avebury Circle

Leave Bath on A36 to A303, then turn East to A344. Stonehenge has fascinated people for ages and continues to puzzle those who are searching for the answers to its design. Guidebooks and scientific papers promote various theories, but no one is quite certain who built Stonehenge or why. Some feel that it was constructed as a temple of worship, possibly to celebrate the winter solstice; others see it as an astronomical observatory. In any case, admiration is due. As you stand by such giant monoliths you cannot help but feel awed by the enormous task of completing such a project. Some of the stones are from only 25 miles away, others from 135 miles away at least; some may have come by sea, others were dragged on rollers. There are also many burial barrows in the area that yield interesting artifacts.

Those who are fascinated by Stonehenge will want to drive on A360 to Devizes and A361 to **Avebury**. Avebury Circle is the largest stone circle in Britain and probably dates back to the early Bronze Age. It consists of three concentric circles (incomplete in places). The stones are shaped as obelisks. There is also a museum detailing the discovery of a large burial barrow a short distance away.

Bath/Oxford

A route can be planned through the **Cotswolds** on the way to Oxford. Picture-postcard villages are dotted through the Cotswold hills. Many of the houses are built of an oolitic stone, contain mullioned windows, and have steep stone roofs. If this kind of scenery is to your taste, take A4 from Bath to Avebury. From Avebury take A361 to **Swindon, Lechlade,** and **Burford,** then A424 to **Stow-on-the-Wold.** In nearby **Bourton on the Water** there is a miniature village to delight children as well as adults. Nearby **Moreton-in-Marsh, Little Compton,** and **Chipping Norton** also have antique village charm. For those interested in brass rubbing, some of the finest brasses of wool merchants are available in **Northleach.** From the Cotswolds, continue east to Oxford on A34 or plan a stop at **Blenheim Palace** (see page 34, The Central Circuit) on the way.

As you drive into Oxford, you will be struck visually by the multitude of spires from churches and colleges, and you will probably enjoy driving down some of the narrow streets along college walls—until you try to park and begin to walk, as you must, for all the real treasures are within those walls. Head for the large multistory car park near **Carfax,** the center of Oxford, unless you are prepared to drive around behind some of the colleges; then you have to be lucky to find a space on a little side street. When you have unloaded your car, the information office on High Street is a good place to start. There you can collect detailed information on the colleges, maps, theater bookings, the schedule for sound and light performances (summer outdoor shows based on the history of the city), boating on the Cherwell, museums, and libraries. In addition, you may want to buy one or more of a series of pamphlets on the history and attractions of Oxford.

Oxford University dates back to the 12th century. Many of the 23 colleges are built right on High Street and contain traditional quadrangles with chapels, halls, libraries, and gardens. Favorite colleges for visitors to stroll through include **Christ Church, Magdalen,** and **Trinity.**

Christ Church, also known as The House, was founded in 1525 by Cardinal Wolsey as Cardinal College; it was renamed King Henry VIII College when Wolsey fell out of favor and it was given its present name in 1546. The entrance is on St. Aldgate's. Look for Wren's Tom Tower to see and hear the 7½ ton bell called Great Tom. The cathedral dates from the eighth century; it contains exquisite stained-glass windows. Thomas More studied Greek there from 1492 to 1494. Richard Hakluyt, who collected accounts of voyages in *Hakluyt's Voyages,* was in residence in the mid-16th century. John Locke was expelled from the college for his part in the Shaftesbury's plot; he had already received a degree in 1658 and had returned to live in the college in 1680. John Ruskin lived in Peckwater Quad, writing *The Stones of Venice* while in residence, and graduated in 1842. He fought with the authorities to get permission to build the **Oxford Museum;** the controversy centered upon the contention that science was "adverse to religion," so he promised there would be prayers held at the beginning of each day. The pen name Lewis Carroll, in reality Charles Dodgson, is well known to most people; he wrote *Alice's Adventures in Wonderland* after punting with the little daughter of the Dean, Alice Liddell.

Magdalen College, located in a lovely spot on the River Cherwell, was founded in 1458. You can enter from the High Street and visit the chapel and dining hall with its oak paneling, stroll through the deer park, which our children loved when they were small, and along the river walk. John Fox studied there as an undergraduate in the 1530s; he later resigned from his post as a Fellow over religious disagreements. **Addison's Walk** was named after Joseph Addison, who wrote poems in Latin, as well as the better-known *Spectator* papers. R. S. Hawker arrived in 1824; his "The Song of the Western Men" was written the next year and he won the Newdigate Prize for "Pompeii" in 1827. Oscar Wilde, a student from 1874 to 1878, also won the Newdigate Prize for "Ravenna." C. S. Lewis, who was a Fellow from 1924 to 1954, wrote literary criticism and religious philosophy as well as books for children, including *The Lion, the Witch and the Wardrobe.*

Trinity College, on Broad Street, was founded in 1554. Don't miss the 15th-century chapel and the Lime Walk in the gardens. Look in the Old Library for the portrait painted by Sir Joshua Reynolds of Thomas Warton, who is buried in the antechapel. Warton was a prolific writer of works including "The Triumphs of Isis" in 1749, a satire on guide books, "A Companion to the Guide" in 1760, and *Observations on the Faerie Queene of Spenser* in 1754. There is a bust of J. H. Newman, a student from 1816 to 1820, in the college garden. Sir Arthur Quiller-Couch, who spent his undergraduate years here from 1882 to 1886, edited *The Oxford Book of English Verse* in 1900. Joyce Cary was an undergraduate from 1909 to 1912. His novels include *Charlie is My Darling, The Horse's Mouth,* and *Not Honour More.*

It is delightful to stroll through the gardens and enjoy the meticulously tended displays of seasonal flowers. In the spring and summer students and visitors alike enjoy punting on the river in flat-bottomed boats that are poled with consummate skill or utter abandon—there are many styles on the river. More serious college crews rowing shells compete in various regattas throughout the year, climaxing in June with Eights Week, and the Henley Regatta not far down the Thames.

In addition to the colleges, many university buildings in Oxford have treasures that should not be missed. The **Bodleian Library** contains one of the world's most impressive collections of books and manuscripts. It was started with a bequest of manuscripts from Duke Humphrey of Gloucester, who died in 1447. Thomas Bodley left his personal collection to the library after working all of his life to acquire volumes for the Bodleian. Among other pursuits, he arranged for a copy of every book printed in England to be given free to the library. Look for the plaque on the stairs that lists other benefactors.

The **Ashmolean Museum** houses artifacts from all over the world as well as Britain. Located on Beaumont Street, it was founded in 1677.

The **Museum of Oxford,** on St. Aldgate's, contains objects and displays of the history of Oxford and of the university. There is a bookshop there as well.

When you need refreshment, we suggest one of our favorite pubs, the *Turf Tavern* (Bath Place, off Holywell) for a great lunch; it is reached through narrow and not obviously marked passageways beginning near the Bodleian's Ratcliffe Camera. You can turn onto New College Lane, then into St. Helen's Passage, or, from the other direction, turn off Holywell into Bath Place. Jude, in Thomas Hardy's novel, *Jude the Obscure,* courted the barmaid there. One more suggestion for pulling it all together: End your day with an hour or two in a river pub, surrounded by roses and quiet waters. We have enjoyed these gardens in the late afternoon or early evening, visiting with friends over a beer while our children played among the rosebushes or fed the fish in the river. The Trout and the Perch are old favorites in the outskirts.

For those especially interested in literary history, a great number of writers lived and worked in Oxford. Geoffrey of Monmouth, who chronicled the adventures of King Arthur, studied there in 1129. Chaucer uses Oxford as a setting in *The Canterbury Tales,* and Shakespeare stayed at the Crown Inn in Cornmarket Street. Jane Austen describes Oxford in several of her novels. There is a marble memorial in the quad of University College honoring Percy Bysshe Shelley. Thomas Hardy named Oxford "Christminster" in *Jude the Obscure,* and Henry James set scenes in a number of Oxford colleges. Algernon Swinburne wrote *Rosamond* while studying at Balliol College and Yeats lived near Balliol at one time. There is a plaque in the cloisters in New College honoring John Galsworthy. If you have enjoyed the Tolkien stories you should know that some of them were conceived in Oxford. Dylan Thomas spent much of 1946 at Holywell Ford and Matthew Arnold and Robert Graves wrote major works in nearby Boar's Hill. If you visited Oxford via the TV series "Brideshead Revisited," remember that Evelyn Waugh was an undergraduate at Hertford College in the 1920s.

Also in the area

The Roman town of *Cavella Atrebatum* is located in **Silchester,** southwest of London. Take the M4 to **Reading,** a university town in the heart of the Thames valley. As a cultural center, Reading offers drama at the *Hexagon,* concerts at the *university,* and a thriving *museum* and *art gallery.* The museum has a fine collection of artifacts from the Silchester excavation. Rosemary Sutcliffe wrote *Eagle of the Ninth,* inspired by the Silchester Eagle, which is on display in the museum.

To get to the site from Reading, take the A33 toward **Basingstoke.** Get off at the first circle and head toward **Mortimer,** follow signs to Mortimer West End, and then to Silchester. (Or, if you want an interesting side trip on the way, you can continue on A33 until you see signs for *Stratfield Saye House,* built in 1630 and bought by the nation in 1817 as a reward for the Duke of Wellington. The house contains elegantly furnished rooms, a Wellington exhibition, and, on the grounds, the grave of Copenhagen, the Iron Duke's horse at the Battle of Waterloo. Nearby, **Wellington Country Park** offers boating, fishing, nature trails, animals to pet, and a miniature steam railway. Return to Cavella Atrebatum through the village of Stratfield Saye, then follow signs to Silchester.)

First visit the small *Calleva Museum,* which is in the grounds of Silchester Rectory—a little blue building signposted from the road. Exhibits include a description of the plan of the town, development of excavation sites within it, and a number of artifacts from those excavations. (Most of the artifacts are in the Reading Museum.) You can buy a guide there by putting money into the box; the museum is unattended and supported only by contributions. As you read that guide, you may be tempted to believe that King Arthur was crowned here by Dubricius, Archbishop of the City of the Legions when he was 15 years old.

Ancient writers described this "woodland town" of the Atrebates, one of the Belgic tribes of north Gaul, who arrived around 57 B.C. and founded the town. However, what you will see is of Roman origin, after A.D. 43. When the crops are ripe on this 107 acres of farmland, you can see the Roman grid street patterns, which show as light or dark bands in the crop; there are no buildings standing, but you can walk around the earthworks, which are well preserved in some sections. The town wall is the most complete of any Roman wall in Britain. The South Gate is the best preserved, and it can be visited with permission from Manor Farm. The amphitheater is located between the inner and outer earthworks toward the northeastern corner of the site, with entrance through a field across a paved road. To get to this area of the site and the best sections of the Roman wall, follow the Drove, an ancient right-of-way running from the museum past some current excavations to a very interesting 12th-century parish church, *St. Mary the Virgin,* just inside the wall. Alternatively, you can get a fine view of the wall by following a path around its perimeter (south semicircle) all the way to the church.

Oxford/London

Take M40 for speed or A423 along the Thames for pleasure through **Wallingford, Henley,** and **Maidenhead.** A stop at Henley can be very pleasant, during racing season or not (see page 34). You can also take A308 to *Windsor Castle,* which is the largest inhabited castle in the world. The State Apartments house many historic treasures, and Queen Mary's doll house will fascinate the whole family. The grounds are pleasant to roam around and you might be lucky enough to catch a changing of the guard (see page 34). Nearby, *Eton College* is also worth a visit if you want to catch the flavor of a British "public" school.

This trip can be expanded or condensed. It can take 14 days or more, and you will still not run out of things to do. Without reservations to lock one into a pattern, it is possible to change plans with the weather or as new discoveries appear. This trip has been completed enjoyably by a family with two teenaged children at one time; part of the trip was taken earlier with younger children very successfully. Smaller children are delighted with beaches, boats, miniature villages, ponies, parts of some museums, and small doses of cathedrals. Older children (as well as adults) enjoy in more depth special interests such as maritime history, the different architectural styles found in cathedrals and other historic buildings, art museums, Roman antiquity, prehistoric monoliths, hiking, sailing, and making a personal collection of brass rubbings.

Keswick
Grasmere
Ambleside
Windermere
Coniston
Kendal
Lancaster
M6
Skipton
Harrogate
York
IRISH SEA
Colwyn Bay
Caernarvon
Llanberis
Capel Curig
Chester
Betws-y-coed
Beddgelert
Ffestiniog
Llangollen
Trawsfynydd
Bala
Druid
Harlech
Dolgellau
Penrhyndeudraeth
ENGLAND
Shrewsbury
A1
Cardigan Bay
Bridgnorth
WALES
Kidderminster
Studley
Kenilworth
Warwick
Alcester
Stratford-Upon-Avon
Huntingdon
Cambridge
Royston
Baldock
Chipping Norton
Woodstock
Oxford
London
Henley-on-Thames
Maidenhead
Windsor
BRISTOL CHANNEL
N
ISLE OF WIGHT
ENGLISH CHANNEL

CENTRAL ENGLAND, WALES, AND THE LAKE DISTRICT

London to Oxford	57 miles	
Oxford to Stratford	27 miles	
Stratford to Warwick	8 miles	
Warwick to Kenilworth	4 miles	
Stratford to Bala	108 miles	
Bala to Snowdonia	31 miles	
Betws-y-Coed to Windermere		157 miles
Windermere to Cambridge		247 miles
Cambridge to London	60 miles	

From London: (Warwickshire) Stratford-upon-Avon, Warwick; (Wales) Bala, Snowdonia; (Lake District) Windermere, Grasmere, Keswick, Coniston Water; (Cambridgeshire) Cambridge.

 This trip includes a variety of pleasures, beginning with the exploration of the intricate college courtyards in **Oxford,** as long as your feet hold out. A few miles north is a stately home on the grand scale, **Blenheim Palace,** the birthplace of Winston Churchill, where you can imagine living in the midst of elegance. Shakespeare country in the **Stratford** area is full of carefully preserved half-timbered houses; a day of exploring Elizabethan memorabilia can be topped by a performance in the *Shakespeare Theatre* (but be sure to order your tickets months in advance). A few miles northeast lie two of England's most interesting castles, **Kenilworth,** in ruins, and **Warwick,** which is very much intact and full of carefully planned displays.

 The next section of the trip includes some of the most beautiful, rugged scenery in **Northern Wales,** with a great variety of hiking and backpacking available in **Snowdonia National Park,** for both serious climbers and those who prefer gentler walks with gorgeous views. After a brief stop in **Chester,** an ancient and interesting city, you will return to mountains and lakes.

 The *Lake District* abounds with winding roads and unexpected views of a distinctive landscape. Shopping is a delight in towns and villages. There are a number of well-marked trails available for hiking, and tourist centers can offer advice for longer treks into the more remote regions.

The return south takes you through or near some of the most interesting cathedral towns of England (York, Lincoln, Ely), each worth a half-day stop, on the way to **Cambridge.** Cambridge matches Oxford in many ways, but it is more rural at the edges and more compact in the center. As is true of Oxford, Cambridge is best explored on foot. Colleges are scattered all over town, with many fronting on the main streets and ending in plowed fields, but they are not far from each other. If your timing is lucky, you might hear the choir as you visit the chapels in King's College or St. John's. In nice weather it is fun to go punting on the Cam, renting a flat-bottomed boat that is propelled by a pole (not an easy feat). This is one of the best ways to get superb perspective on the large number of colleges lining the banks; students tend to congregate on the banks of the Cam to study, relax, and watch inexpert punters lose their poles and topple into the river. As it began in Oxford, this itinerary ends in Cambridge, with just a short drive taking you back to London.

London

London, a city we know better than most other large cities in Europe, is nevertheless very difficult to write about because of its size and complexity. It covers the heart of southeastern England like a great sprawling monster, has the intricacy of a labyrinth for anyone unfamiliar with its byways and mews and alleys, yet remains (apart from IRA bombings) one of the safest major cities in the world. Visiting London is always like coming home for us, and we suspect that you will want to stay longer, too. On our last trip we had an unexpectedly relaxing day there with absolutely nothing that we had to do. The car and our baggage had gone and we felt free to stroll and savor the city at will. We emerged from the train, began walking along streets, over bridges, through parks, chose a place for lunch, watched people, meandered through shops, and let ourselves be guided by whim. We can highly recommend this unscheduled and unharried sort of day as a way to capture the essence of a city.

On the other hand, London has some special features that you will not find anywhere else in the world. If your itinerary allows more than a day or two in London, you will probably want to buy a detailed guidebook and make a careful selection of sights and activities based on your own interests. If you are making a first visit, you can choose to take an escourted bus tour of a few hours' duration that will help you get your bearings in this sprawling metropolis. If you are driving into London be advised that the driver may find his knuckles turning white while passengers try to keep a couple of blocks ahead on the map so turns are made onto one-way streets appropriately. (There is a map showing one-way streets that is almost a necessity.) We suggest parking your car and continuing on foot, on the underground (called the tube), by taxi, a boat on the Thames, or the most fun of all—riding in the front seat on the upper level of a red double-decker bus. Careening around corners when you may have momentarily forgotten about driving on the left, even though you are leaving the driving to the bus driver, can be startling.

Although we cannot play the "don't miss" game here amongst such a plenitude of things to do, we will suggest some of the more familiar sights. **Parliament,** or the **Palace of Westminster,** is a stunning building to view from across the river and well worth a tour inside. Be sure to get information on opening hours and the time of the last tour of the day. The historical anecdotes given during the tour make this scene of centuries of intrigue and tradition fascinating, and the furnishings and galleries are elegant. We hardly need add "don't miss **Big Ben'';** you have probably heard its chimes on New Year's Eve as well as on state occasions. **Westminster Abbey** is right across the street and you can expect to lose a couple of hours inside locating innumerable famous persons who are buried there. Memorials, statues, brass markers, and paintings are everywhere. The building itself, with its graceful vaulting and lovely windows, is appropriately majestic without being ponderous.

If you are fortunate in the timing of your visit, you may get a glimpse of regal London on one of its state occasions, like the opening of Parliament (early November) or the Queen's birthday (June). We recall being in England for Princess Margaret's wedding in 1960, when we spent the day before wandering around photographing the elaborate floral displays along the processional route and in parks. We watched the Queen's Jubilee ceremony in Westminster Abbey on TV during an interlude in a camping/sailing trip. The most fun of all was seeing the displays people created for the event outside their homes in every little village as well as in cities. Perhaps you also got up in the early dawn to watch the televised wedding procession to St. Paul's Cathedral of Prince Charles and Lady Diana. Birdcage Walk leads to **Buckingham Palace,** the scene of crowds waiting outside the gates for the notice to be put up of a new prince or princess's arrival into the world, for a wedding procession to start, or simply for watching someone interesting drive in or out. London, perhaps more than any capital in Europe, offers many such occasions for confirmed Anglophiles.

You can choose to walk along **Whitehall** from Westminster Abbey past the **Horse Guards,** where you can see the daily changing of the guard, a ceremony incomparably seen through the eyes of Alice and Christopher Robin in A. A. Milne's *Winnie the Pooh.* At the end of Whitehall you will come to **Trafalgar Square** with its spate of fountains, lions, and Admiral Nelson himself high on his pedestal. The square is always crowded with people feeding the pigeons and basking in the sun. The **National Gallery** is on the high side of Trafalgar Square; it contains more works than you can view in many days, so select the periods that interest you most. **Piccadilly Circus** is a couple of blocks away; the statue in the center is "Eros," and the name Piccadilly derives from a tailor's shop there that once featured a new kind of lacy neck ruff called a pickadil. From the top of the Circus, walk up around the graceful curve of **Regent Street** past some of the most elegant shops in London.

From Westminster, you can take a boat to the Tower Bridge stop, which is great fun on a nice day. This trip takes about 20 minutes; you will pass the county hall, Victoria embankment, **South Bank Arts Centre, St. Paul's Cathedral** in the distance, **London Bridge,** and Southwark. The **Tower of London** fascinates visitors of all ages, and all of the stories you have heard about some of the darker moments in English history come alive as you walk through these gates. We find the collection of armor on the third floor of the White Tower particularly interesting, and we really mean "don't miss" the Crown Jewels!

English literature is full of references to London because most writers were drawn to the center of their culture at some time in their lives. Beginning with Chaucer (1340–1400), London is described in vivid detail as a vibrant, noisy city. John Donne (1571–1631), the poet, was one of a group including Christopher Marlowe, Ben Jonson, and Shakespeare who frequently visited the Mermaid Tavern at the corner of Wood Street and Cheapside. Shakespeare arrived from Stratford in 1588 and the Globe Theatre, which produced his plays, was built in 1599. You can see a brass plaque posted on a building on Park Street that proclaims it to be the site of the original Globe. Henry Fielding (1707–1754) studied at Middle Temple in London, was called to the bar in 1740, and wrote a number of his novels while living in London. Dr. Samuel Johnson (1709–1784) lived in a number of areas of London; if you have lunch in the Cheshire Cheese, located in Wine Office Court off Fleet Street, you will be dining in the place where Jonson and Boswell conducted many of their discussions. Look for his portrait over the head table. His house is located nearby in Gough Square; you can visit the house to see the attic room where he worked on his dictionary. Thomas Carlyle (1795–1881) lived in Chelsea at 24 Cheyne Row; you can visit this Victorian house to see his manuscripts and furnishings as he left them. William Makepeace Thackeray (1811–1863) studied at Middle Temple, lived in Bloomsbury and later in Kensington. Charles Dickens (1812–1870) worked in solicitors' offices in Holborn Court and Gray's Inn, gathering material to use in his novels. He may have been fascinated by prisons such as Newgate, Fleet, Horsemonger Lane Gaol, and the King's Bench because his father was once imprisoned in Marshalsea Prison. You can visit his house and library on Douty Street. George Bernard Shaw (1856–1950) lived in Bloomsbury; his plays were produced at the Royal Court Theatre on Sloane Square. Oscar Wilde (1854–1900), playwright, poet, and creator of fairy tales, lived in Chelsea on Tite Street. Sir Arthur Conan Doyle (1859–1930) lived at 2 Devonshire Place in Marylebone; the creator of Sherlock Holmes was also a physician. The address of Sherlock Holmes is 221B Baker Street. (If you are a Holmes fan, check the Marylebone Library for Sherlock Holmes collections.) Virginia Woolf (1882–1941) lived and wrote in Bloomsbury, associating with a group of writers and scholars who gathered to talk and enjoy intellectual pursuits.

We could go on and on telling you about London—the parks are very pleasant in nice weather, offering boat rides, a zoo, and ducks to watch and feed from a picnic lunch. The arts are there to be enjoyed at the **Royal Festival Hall** built right on the Thames in 1951, the **Barbican,** built by the City on 60 acres as a redevelopment over bombed ruins from the last war, contains the **Barbican Theatre,** the **Royal Albert Hall** opened by Queen Victoria, which holds 8000 persons for a variety of concerts, ballet and boxing matches, and the **National Theatre,** built next to the Royal Festival Hall on the South Bank of the Thames. London has many small theaters; you can enjoy a different one every night for a couple of weeks. If you are interested in getting discount tickets, you can join the queue at Leicester Square for real bargains. We often drove in on Saturday mornings, parked the car, stood in the queue for a time, had lunch, and went either to a matinee or evening performance. **Covent Garden** is not far from the theater district; although the vegetable market is long gone there are lots of shops and boutiques to wander through. If you have time to kill before a performance, you can find one bookstore after another on Charing Cross Road. Also nearby is **Soho,** an area teaming with restaurants and shops featuring a variety of ethnic foods and goods, which once had a bad reputation but is not considered dangerous anymore.

Among the wealth of museums in London, the **British Museum** is an education in itself; one could not see everything there in a lifetime. Parliament opened the museum in 1759 after collecting gifts that needed to be housed together for a couple of hundred years. As acquisitions were received, extensions were constructed to house them. You will want to pick up a diagram of the rooms and floors as you enter this marvelous museum. A concentration of museums are in Kensington, including the **Victoria and Albert,** which has 7 miles of artistic masterpieces divided into two parts. The Primary Collection contains art arranged by period, style, and country. The Study Collection contains sculpture, ceramics, and metals. The **Natural History Museum** has a section and a library for each division: botany, mineralogy, zoology, palaeontology, and entomology. The **Geological Museum** includes the Story of the Earth, regional geography of Great Britain, and collections of diamonds, precious gems, and fossils. The **Science Museum** contains all sorts of exhibits to push, pull, ponder, and explore.

Whatever you choose to enjoy in London, be assured that there will always be plenty left for another time. This city's pleasures are almost inexhaustible.

London/Oxford

Proceed west toward Oxford on M40 for speed or M4 for a more leisurely trip. Get off at **Maidenhead** and watch for signs to *Windsor Castle.*

WINDSOR is open all year long and contains a wealth of royal exhibits. (When the Queen is in residence, the flag is flying; the State Apartments are open most of the year except for six weeks during the Easter period and three weeks for Ascot.) Windsor Castle is bound to be crowded in the summer, and you may have to queue to see the doll house. When the guards' uniforms change to a deep purple in the winter, they stamp around trying to keep warm, or so our children thought. As students in the fifties, we were fascinated by descriptions of the funeral cortege for King George VI, who had died a few months before, and the coronation of his daughter, then Princess Elizabeth. Most British citizens love and respect the royal family and are deeply interested in their lives. As we noticed during the time Princess Margaret was married, when Queen Elizabeth delivered one of her sons, and again during the Jubilee, each royal family occasion grows into a public pageant. Dedicated Anglophiles will not want to roar by Windsor on the motorway.

Windsor Castle itself dates from the 12th and 13th centuries. *St. George's Chapel* has a beautiful collection of stained-glass windows, as well as statues of royal figures, banners, and crests displayed in niches and corners. The doll house, which was given to Queen Mary in 1924, fascinates children and adults alike. From the towers one can catch a glimpse of *Eton College,* one of the most famous English public schools, which is worth a visit if you have time. Shakespeare used *Frogmore,* a country house adjacent to Windsor Great Park, as the setting for *The Merry Wives of Windsor.*

When you leave Windsor, take A423 to **Henley** and wander along the towpath that flanks the Henley Regatta Course, by the various university and rowing clubs that are used by practicing oarsmen much of the year. Henley is a lovely old town to stroll through and has some interesting shops and galleries. It would make a fine luncheon stop.

OXFORD See pages 23–25, The Southwestern Circuit (England).

BLENHEIM Take the A34 to *Blenheim Palace* near **Woodstock.** The palace exhibits a fine collection of portraits, tapestries, furniture, and china. The baroque-style building was constructed in the early 18th century. Capability (Lancelot) Brown laid out the gardens, park, and lake. Blenheim is the seat of the Duke of Marlborough, who lives in one wing. Because of its magnitude, proportion, and detail, Blenheim is one of our favorite stately homes in all of England. (You can appreciate these qualities better if you visit Blenheim on a weekday.)

STRATFORD-UPON-AVON Proceed through **Chipping Norton** to Stratford-upon-Avon. We have found campsites on meadows bordering the River Avon to be very convenient and pleasant—in spite of the forward swans. (There are also campgrounds at **Broadway** and **Weir Meadow** in the Vale of Evasham.) Our daughter, when she was three, extended her hand to a very large swan roaming up from the river and he nipped it, expecting some morsel to eat, then hissed at her for not providing a treat for him. Many English campsites provide such extra inhabitants, whether they be swans, ducks, geese, sheep, or cows. Children love what adults learn to tolerate. You can also rent a boat and go rowing among the swans opposite the *Shakespeare Theatre.*

If you would like to get tickets for the Royal Shakespeare Theatre you *must* write in advance. The performances are booked ahead for months and sometimes it is impossible to get tickets at all. There is always the chance that a few will be available on the day of the performance, but you cannot count on it. Any that are available can be purchased after 10:30 a.m.; it is often easier to get standing-room tickets, but they are obviously not as comfortable for long performances.

One highlight of our stay in Stratford was always a walk through the fields out to *Ann Hathaway's Cottage* in the early morning when the dew and mist were still lifting and everything was fresh. Those less romantically inclined can also drive the short distance out there, or take a tour bus. *Shakespeare's Birthplace* and *New Place* are also attractions worth seeing, as well as the *Shakespeare Centre,* which opened in the mid-1960s.

WARWICK When you have satisfied your appetite for Shakespeariana and half-timbered houses, take the A46 for 8 miles to Warwick to tour *Warwick Castle.* Standing on a steep rock cliff beside the River Avon, this is one of the finest inhabited medieval castles in England. The routes, displays, and descriptions throughout the towers and apartments are beautifully designed to introduce the visitor to medieval life. The castle was fortified over 1000 years ago by Ethelfleda, daughter of King Alfred, complete with dungeons and towers, one of which now houses a fine display of armor. Children particularly enjoy climbing the narrow, circular staircases to the tops of towers, where they may imagine themselves in all sorts of heroic roles. The first Lord Brooke turned the inside of the castle into a magnificent residence in the 17th century, and it is now the seat of the Earl of Warwick. The state apartments house a fine collection of paintings by Rubens, Van Dyck, and others.

Capability Brown landscaped the 12 acres of grounds inside and around the castle walls, and it shows in varied elevations, sudden vistas, and a mixture of formal gardens and rural parkland. Once we were lucky enough to happen upon a group of Morris dancers on the grounds. These are men who dress in traditional costume and dance, usually to celebrate the harvest. Their dancing is full of knee-slapping, whoops, and hollers that appeal greatly to children. The gardens are inhabited not only by live peacocks but also by a collection of sculptured peacocks in the hedges. Once we were treated to the mating dance of a peacock who tried in vain to interest a female; she showed utter disdain for him no matter how widely he fanned his beautiful turquoise feathers.

KENILWORTH From Warwick it is only a little over 4 miles to Kenilworth on the A46. Henry I gave Kenilworth to his chamberlain, Geoffrey de Clinton, in 1122. The keep, which is the first masonry building in England, was built between 1150 and 1175. In 1362 John of Gaunt added the Banquet Hall, the White Hall, and the Strong Tower. Elaborate entertaining went on over the centuries in this magnificent castle until it fell into ruin. Do read *Kenilworth* by Sir Walter Scott before you go.

Stratford/Wales

Take A422 to **Alcester,** A435 to **Studley,** A448 to **Bromsgrove** through **Kidderminster,** A442 to **Bridgnorth,** and A458 to **Shrewsbury.** Shrewsbury, the county town of Shropshire, is full of lovely Tudor buildings. It makes a nice lunch stop, with plenty of interesting things to see. To get a sense of what rural life once was like in this hilly corner of England, you may want to read "A Shropshire Lad" by A. E. Housman before your trip.

BALA Continue on the A5 into Wales through **Llangollen** to **Druid** and then take the A494 to Bala, which is set in rolling hills leading down to the largest natural lake and one of the finest sailing centers in Wales. (Bala has fascinated us because our ancestors left a farm on the hillside there in 1698 to settle in Bala Cynwd, Pennsylvania, when persecution of Quakers drove them out of this beautiful land.) Look for a campsite near the lake or up on the hill on the road (B440) leading to **Llandrillo.** In town, the shopping district (look for Welsh tapestry woolens) is several blocks long, and it is pleasant to stroll the length of it without meeting the crowds of some resort towns. Once we were lucky enough to be there during an October fair; vendors brought Welsh crafts from all over Wales, so we almost completed our Christmas shopping. The main business of the fair was a day-long auction of Welsh black cattle and sheep, attended by men dressed in sport coats and ties, mostly in somber earth colors, and there were also rides and food stalls that delighted our children.

Bala/Snowdonia

Bala is one natural gateway to the *Snowdonia National Park*. Driving in that direction is breathtakingly beautiful, with rugged scenery on all sides. From Bala take the A494 to **Dolgellau** (where you will find more wool shops) and the A470 to **Ffestiniog**. A lonely but spectacular alternate route is the A4212 over the high moors (be sure to close the sheep gates) to **Trawsfynydd** and the A470 to Ffestiniog. Then take the A487 to **Penrhyndeudraeth.** At this point you may want to take a short side trip south on the A496 to *Harlech Castle,* one of the most rugged in a series of castles built by Edward I. Though once directly on the sea, it now lies half a mile inland with sand flats below, yet still perches over all the countryside with commanding views on all sides.

After returning to Penrhyndeudraeth, take the A4085 to **Beddgelert,** where you may want to camp in the state park or in nearby private campgrounds. For alternative bases in Snowdonia, you may choose to take a scenic mountain road that skirts the east flank of the mountain for 8 more miles northeast until you reach the A4086. If you turn left toward **Llanberis** you will find a number of campgrounds that are very primitive in alpine meadows (mountain tents are advised). If you prefer more amenities, turn right onto the A4086, through **Capel Curig,** and continue on the A5 to **Betws-y-Coed,** a beautiful and comfortable resort town 17 miles from Beddgelert. Welsh woolen and craft shops abound here.

SNOWDONIA For serious mountaineering, get contour maps that are available for planning trips. For less strenuous hiking and walking, drive to the height of the pass on A4086 toward Llanberis and walk in to **Llydaw,** near the center of the group of peaks making up Mount Snowdon. There is a lovely lake there, and the walk is not difficult. In Llanberis there is a railway that climbs to the top of the mountain complex.

You can also take a trip to *Caernarvon Castle* by continuing on through Llanberis. Set where the river joins the sea, it is considered the most important of Edward I's castles, and Prince Charles's Investiture was here in 1969. The outer walls are 8–14 feet thick and you can climb up into many towers and look over the ramparts, continuing along the perimeter on walkways between them. (Some views downward might not appeal to the fainthearted.) This castle really looks like the castles we imagine as children, with dark, winding staircases, small, damp stone chambers with a single window looking out beyond the castle walls, and plenty of secret passageways. There are also some very fine exhibits on the castle's role in history, including displays on the Investiture.

Betws-y-Coed/Windermere

Take the A470 north to **Colwyn Bay** and the A55 to **Chester,** which is a fascinating old town that would make a good lunch stop. You may enjoy a walk around the walls that follow the line of the Roman city walls and also include the castle. Chester is one of the most medieval-looking cities in England. The timbered houses are beautifully preserved. Take the A56 to **Hapsford,** the M56 east, and the M6 north (possibly getting off at **Lancaster** for a side excursion to the cathedral and town rich in the history of the War of the Roses). Continue on the M6 until exit 36, take the A65 to **Kendal** and the A591 to Windermere.

LAKE DISTRICT Windermere, a town on the largest lake in England and an old resort and touring center, is a good spot to begin exploring this famous corner of England. The Lake District is a national park that lies within the boundaries of the three northern counties of Westmorland, Cumberland, and Lancashire. The terrain here is full of contrasts between high mountains and deep lakes. The many lakes, lined with woods and overshadowed by craggy rocks, are interspersed with green valleys containing gentle streams and lush pastures. *Scafell Pike* is the highest peak in England at 3210 feet. The terrain for hiking in this area (the *Langdale Pikes*) is more rugged and barren, but leads to spectacular views. Boats may be rented on the lakes, pony trekking is a popular way to see the more remote regions, and good fishing is available in both lakes and rivers. Here you must make choices. There is more than enough to keep you enjoying your days and wishing you had more time to explore this extraordinary landscape. Suggestions include climbing in the Langdale Pikes region, hiking in the **Grasmere** area, climbing the *Old Man of Coniston,* taking the National Trust walk on the ridge near *Ullswater* (including **Glencoyne Park** and a hike up *Airaforce*), taking boat trips on the lakes, shopping **Keswick,** Grasmere, Windermere, and other villages, driving the tortuous but rewarding roads over *Wyrnose Pass, Styhead Pass, Knott Pass,* or *Eskdale Pass.* Favorite areas for serious climbers include **Wasdale Head, Great Langdale, Borrowdale, Ennerdale, Coniston, Great Gable, Pillar Rock, Dow Crag,** and *Scafell.* (Note: The Lake District gets a great deal of rain, but wet weather need not hinder the enjoyment of campers who come prepared with good, light waterproofs—both jackets and trousers—and, above all, Wellingtons or a pair of similar heavy rubber boots.)

There are many local crafts available in the district, some found in the workshops where they are made. Look especially for sweaters, scarves, woven shawls, and blankets.

For those interested in literary history, the area abounds with artifacts and memorabilia. William Wordsworth lived at *Dove Cottage* in

Grasmere from 1799 to 1808. The house contains mementos of the Wordsworths as well as literary documents. Wordsworth later lived at **Rydal Mount,** located between Ambleside and Grasmere, from 1813 until his death in 1850. This house contains first editions of his work, furniture belonging to the family, and portraits; the garden here was landscaped by Wordsworth himself. The house on Main Street in **Cockermouth,** which was his birthplace, is now a museum containing china collections and a Turner painting. Wordsworth used "spots of time," or experiences he had in certain places, in his poetry. These topographical references to place are particularly frequent in "The Prelude." The daffodil field in "Dora's Field" is in Rydal, that in "Gowbarrow Park" in Ullswater.

Samuel Taylor Coleridge visited Wordsworth at Dove Cottage. He settled at Greta Hall, Keswick before returning to London in 1803. Robert Southey shared Greta Hall with Coleridge in 1802 and stayed on in the house when Coleridge left. In 1811 Percy Bysshe Shelley came to stay, then returned to Keswick in 1813.

John Ruskin lived in **Brantwood,** on the east bank of **Coniston Water** from 1872 to 1900. This home contains his library, paintings, furniture, boat, and coach; there are also gardens and nature trails to enjoy. In Coniston the *Ruskin Museum* contains Ruskin memorabilia and displays on local history.

Beatrix Potter, while visiting Keswick, sketched **St. Herbert's Island,** which she called Owl Island in *The Tale of Squirrel Nutkin.* You can visit the island by boat from Keswick. You can also visit her home, *Hill Top Farm,* which is located in **Sawrey,** south of **Ambleside,** on the road to **Hawkshead.** Six of her stories were set there. Inside the house, look for the chest by the door; you can almost see Aunt Maria there with her plate of dough. Outside, you can see the garden where Jemima Puddleduck, wearing her bonnet and shawl, looked for a nesting place.

Camping areas are often primitive but beautiful. Check your camping guide, and get as much information as you can from the tourist offices in towns. We have enjoyed camping at Grasmere in a sloping meadow on the northwest side of the lake with village and mountain before us. There are more rugged campsites in the Langdale Pikes and some with more amenities at Keswick on **Derwent Water** and on **Lake Windermere.** Our favorite was the area near the head of **Lake Coniston,** situated just below the Old Man of Coniston peak and across the lake from John Ruskin's house. Almost 20 years ago there were no amenities except toilets and sinks in one part of an old ruin, and we discovered that the lights were turned off at 8:30 p.m., just as we were approaching, toothbrushes in hand. We shared a grassy meadow with sheep and cows (and a few bulls that kicked over our very hastily vacated camp chairs), and we were mesmerized by the conjunction of mountain and calm water in one of the most idyllic views possible. This campground, located just east of the village of Coniston, is not listed in any of the guide books but we had heard about it from campers the night before.

Windermere/Cambridge

When you have done all you can in the Lake District, take the A591 to Kendal, the A65 to **Skipton,** and the A59 through **Harrogate** to **York** for a lunch stop. The cathedral here is the largest medieval church in England and there is also a castle, as well as several museums. (You may wish to linger and add an extra day to the itinerary.) Then take the A64 toward **Leeds,** meet the A1 at **Thorne,** and continue south to **Huntingdon,** where you will take the A604 to Cambridge. Alternatively, if your family has developed a strong interest in cathedrals, take the extra time to leave the A1 via the A57 and visit **Lincoln,** or leave at **Huntingdon** via the A1123 until it joins the A10, turning north for **Ely.** (If you do this, do not plan to reach Cambridge in one day from Windermere.) Camp in one of the many pleasant villages surrounding Cambridge, where there are grounds, such as **Comberton, Coton,** or **Trumpington**; there is no camping in the city itself. There is a campground east of Huntingdon (which is northwest of Cambridge) and one southwest of **Newmarket** (which is northeast of Cambridge).

Cambridge

We lived in Cambridge for 10 months and have a special fondness for the city. Cambridge began life as a Roman camp and grew through commerce by road and river; it became the market town for much of the region between London and East Anglia. In 1068 a castle was built as the center of royal power in the region. In 1209, when scholars in Oxford had to leave following trouble with the townspeople, some came to Cambridge and slowly developed a sister university by founding colleges, beginning with Peterhouse in 1284. There are now 23 separate colleges affiliated with the university, each with its own Master, Fellows, and Scholars. All the colleges are built around courtyards, bright with flowers in season; all have chapels, halls (for dining), common rooms, and libraries. The university consists of a ruling body, the Regent House, composed of all officeholders in the university and the colleges. The Council of the Senate includes four heads of colleges, four professors, and eight members of Regent House. The university sets examinations and awards degrees; the colleges prepare students through tutorials and provide a congenial residence for them. Most of the students live in their colleges and study a single subject for three years.

Among the many special things one can choose to do in Cambridge, we suggest this college tour: Park on the backs (the backs of the colleges, as opposed to the front entrances on the city streets) on Queens Road or on Silver Street. Walk through the old sections of Queens College, where in June you may be lucky enough to attend a Shakespearean performance against the backdrop of the lovely old half-timbered buildings dating from the 16th century, and red brick from 1448. This is one of the most interesting grouping of old college buildings in Cambridge. Walk across the street into Corpus Christi College, which was founded in 1352. There is a memorial tablet in the old courtyard for Christopher Marlowe, who was a student there in the 16th century.

Continue along King's Parade to King's College, founded in 1441 by Henry VI; it has a magnificent chapel walled with glorious windows, built with the help of Henry VIII. They were created by English and Flemish craftsmen and portray scenes from both the New Testament and the Old Testament. The carved screen was added in 1533 and contains the initials of Henry VIII and Anne Boleyn. At the far end stands the "Adoration of the Magi" by Rubens. You may have heard the King's College Choir during a Christmas service on radio or television. On December 24 we walked by a long line of people who had been waiting since the previous afternoon to get a seat inside for the Christmas concert; they had provided themselves with sleeping bags, blankets, lawn chairs, food, and wine for the long wait.

Clare College is next, with an old courtyard in perfect proportions and beautiful gardens stretching down to the river. After leaving Clare, walk north on Trinity Lane to Senate House Passage and dip into Gonville and Caius (pronounced *Keys*) College to see the clock tower. Head back through the college to Trinity Street and enter the main gate of Trinity College, which was founded by Henry VIII in 1546 and is the largest college in the university. There is an ornate fountain in the center of the Great Court, and a clock tower (also known as the **Edward III Gate**). Christopher Wren designed the library, which was built in 1676; it contains many valuable books and manuscripts, which may be seen between the hours of 1 and 4 p.m. on weekdays.

Trinity Street then becomes St. John's Street, where you may walk into St. John's College, continuing through its many courtyards, each in a different architectural style, over the imitation of Venice's Bridge of Sighs (with its barred windows to keep undergraduates in), and into the New Court and out onto Magdalene Street (see the row of 16th- and 17th-century houses in this section). Across the street is Magdalene College, founded in 1428 as a home for Benedictine monks from abbeys in the region who were studying in Cambridge. The library of Samuel Pepys is located there.

When you leave Magdalene, walk back down Bridge Street to St. John's Street, Trinity Street, and King's Parade to **St. Mary's Church**, where you can climb the tower and look over all the colleges you have been through. You may want to replenish your fresh fruits, vegetables, cheeses, or almost anything else you need in the open market located next to the church before heading down King's Parade to your car.

Literary connections are exciting to discover in Cambridge because they are so manifold. Christopher Marlowe was an undergraduate at Corpus Christi College. John Milton wrote "Hymn on the Morning of Christ's Nativity" while a student at Christ's College. Samuel Pepys wrote in his diary about a drunken revel following his graduation in 1653. Many writers studied at Trinity College, including Francis Bacon, Andrew Marvell, John Dryden, Lord Byron, William Makepeace Thackeray, Alfred Lord Tennyson, A. E. Housman, and G. M. Trevelyan. In 1820 Charles Lamb wrote "Oxford in the Vacation" while in Cambridge; it is a comparison of memories of both Cambridge and Oxford. E. M. Forster studied classics at King's College while living in "A" stairwell during a period described in *The Longest Journey,* and returned to live in college rooms for the latter part of his life. Scenes from Cambridge are described in Anthony Trollope's *John Caldigate,* written in 1879. As you stroll along the backs, think of Henry James, who wrote glowingly of them. Rose Macauley grew up on Grange Road and used her experiences there when writing her novels. You will discover much more of the history of English literature as you poke through the memorabilia displayed in various college halls and libraries.

For those who can stay longer, there are many activities ranging from rubbing the brass of Roger de Trumpington—the second oldest and one of the best-preserved brasses in England—in the nearby village of **Trumpington** to visiting country houses and cathedrals in the surrounding area. To the north we especially enjoyed visiting **Burghley House,** a 16th-century mansion built by Elizabeth I's Lord High Treasurer, William Cecil, and loaded with art treasures (located near **Stamford**); the cathedral in **Peterborough** where Katherine of Aragon is buried; and the beautifully proportioned cathedral in Ely, which dates from the 12th century and dominates the countryside for miles around. To the southeast, **Audley End Mansion,** near **Saffron Walden,** is a lovely Jacobean country house dating from 1603. Also to the southeast are the charming medieval wool towns of **Cavendish** and **Lavenham,** which are filled with picturesque half-timbered buildings leaning at all angles. To the south is *Hatfield House,* another Jacobean house built in 1611 to replace an older home in which Elizabeth I grew up. To the west is **Woburn Abbey,** an 18th-century mansion containing various fine art and china collections, but unfortunately a little overdone by the addition of "tourist" attractions (go off season).

Cambridge/London

Return to London by the M11 for the *City* (financial district), or take the A10 to **Royston,** the A505 by **Baldock,** the A1 (M) and the A1 for the *West End* (theaters and shopping).

This trip can be expanded or condensed, and you can plan time in London before the trip begins or afterward. We enjoyed this trip with teen-aged children once, and part of it again with relatives up to the age of 90. We felt that 14 days were not enough to linger very long anywhere, but it was possible to follow the itinerary without feeling rushed. Some travelers may choose to spend more time in Oxford or Cambridge; climbers or hikers might prefer a longer stay in Snowdonia. We have spent time in the Lake District on three separate trips, mostly in soggy weather, but that choice would not appeal to everyone.

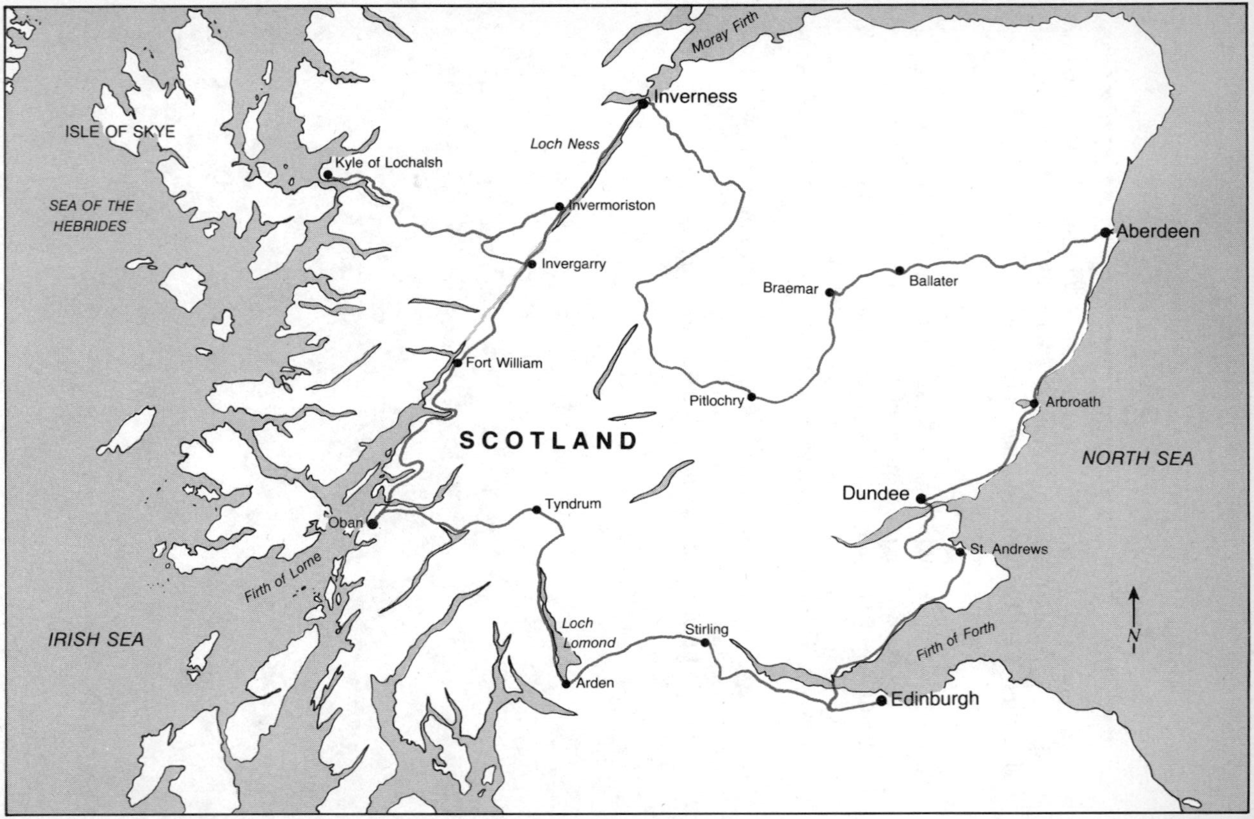
Moray Firth
Inverness
ISLE OF SKYE
Loch Ness
Kyle of Lochalsh
SEA OF THE HEBRIDES
Invermoriston
Aberdeen
Invergarry
Braemar
Ballater
Fort William
Pitlochry
Arbroath
SCOTLAND
NORTH SEA
Dundee
Tyndrum
Oban
St. Andrews
Firth of Lorne
Loch Lomond
Stirling
IRISH SEA
Firth of Forth
N
Arden
Edinburgh

SCOTLAND

Edinburgh to Aberdeen	133 miles
Aberdeen to Pitlochry	105 miles
Pitlochry to Inverness	85 miles
Inverness to Isle of Skye	82 miles
Isle of Skye to Fort William	73 miles
Fort William to Oban	64 miles
Oban to Stirling	102 miles
Stirling to Edinburgh	32 miles

From Edinburgh: (Grampian) Aberdeen; (Highlands) Ballater, Braemar, Inverness; (Hebrides) Isles of Skye; (Western Highlands) Fort William; (Seaside) Oban; (Central) Stirling.
(14 days: 676 miles)

Caledonia, as Scotland was called long ago, was inhabited by the Picts (who lived north of the Firth of Forth and Clyde) and the Celts (who occupied the land south into England) until the Roman invasion in A.D. 82. The enmity dating from those ancient times has continued through the ages as southerners sought to grasp Scotland. Although the Romans left in A.D. 410, Scotland battled with Norsemen as well as their English neighbors, finally declaring war on England in 1542. In 1603 the accession of James VI of Scotland to the throne of England as James I signified the first union of Scotland and England. A series of rebellions and invasions followed, including the attempt of Bonnie Prince Charlie to take over the throne in 1746. The spirit of the Scots continues to be strong (as evidenced by the home rule controversy in recent years), and although Scotland and England cooperate, the Scots take great pride in Caledonian traditions and history.

Visitors to Scotland often become intrigued by the legends and the romance as they walk through the haunts of Mary Queen of Scots, Bonnie Prince Charlie, Sir Walter Scott, or Robert Burns. The traditions of the clans, with their colorful kilts and Highland dances fascinate; the haunting music of bagpipes, perhaps heard on a clear starlit night at the **Tattoo** in front of **Edinburgh Castle,** stays with you forever.

The land itself includes a surprising variety of contour and color ranging from green glens, purple heather on moors and heaths, brown bogs and flatlands, craggy rocks on mountains, and blue alpine lakes and fjords. The natural features of this beautiful country lend themselves to sports enthusiasts. You can fish for trout and salmon, play golf on the famous **St. Andrews** course, ski in the **Cairngorm** area, sail on the lakes, climb and go pony trekking in the **Highlands.** Much of Scotland is rugged, wild, and lonely, appealing to those who seek solitude rather than crowds and cafes.

This trip begins with a day in Edinburgh. (You may want to add another day there, or perhaps part of a day at the end of the trip.) A drive up the coast, stopping in **St. Andrews** and some of the little fishing villages on the way, leads you to **Aberdeen.** There are a number of castles to visit between Aberdeen and **Pitlochry,** as well as the church the royal family attends in **Crathie,** near **Balmoral.** Pitlochry, **Braemar,** or **Aviemore** can be jumping-off places for climbing in the Highlands. **Inverness** is steeped in history and is also a convenient base for a day trip along the coast or the shores of Loch Ness, where you may hope to see the monster. To the west, the **Isle of Skye** is the largest and most romantic of the **Inner Hebrides.** The *Cuillins* are mountains that attract experienced climbers, *Dunvegan Castle* reminds us of the original purpose of castles, and the rugged terrain of the island opens up startling prospects for those who can appreciate the beauties of barren land. Back on the mainland, *Ben Nevis,* the tallest mountain in the British Isles, overlooks the town of **Fort William.** Continuing along the coast to **Oban,** you can pause to enjoy the pleasures of this resort area, then dip inland to enjoy the lush shores of Loch Lomond. Finally, *Stirling Castle* reminds you of the embattled history of Scotland.

Edinburgh

The center of Edinburgh is Princes Street, which is approximately 1 mile long and runs from east to west. On the north side are shops of all kinds, many of which sell tartans, bagpipes, and other symbols of Scottish tradition, as well as beautiful woolen sweaters and blankets. The views from the street are extraordinary, especially the panorama of the over-hanging castle and the intricacies of the *Old Town,* seen from the Princes Street Gardens. People have lived on this ridge, which runs from **Castle Rock** to *Holyrood Palace,* for many centuries. When the street and surrounding Old Town could hold no more inhabitants, the *New Town* was developed. The *Mound* was made with earth dug from the foundations of the New Town and now separates East and West Princes Street Gardens. The *Castle,* occupied by both Scottish and English forces at various times, dates from the 11th century. If you are there in late August or early September during the Edinburgh Festival, you can enjoy the famous *Tattoo.* We enjoyed this thrilling performance on a crisp, clear, starlit night, shivering from the cold but moved by the Scotsmen dancing and marching to bagpipe music with kilts swirling. The music is haunting and the pride and honor of the country are evident in the performance. While touring the castle during the day, you may walk through the *Royal Apartments,* the museum of armor, and see the *Scottish Regalia* or *Honors of Scotland* in the *Crown Chamber.* Near the chapel is *Mons Meg,* a 15th-century cannon and a newer 25-pound howitzer that fires over the city at one o'clock each day. *St. Margaret's Chapel* itself was built in 1076 by the daughter-in-law of King Duncan, who is in *Macbeth.*

Continue down the *Royal Mile,* dipping into the *High Kirk of St. Giles,* which is the principal church of Edinburgh. The *Chapel of the Thistle* has beautiful stained glass heraldic windows and elaborately carved stalls. Then you will pass *Parliament House,* the *City Chambers, John Knox's House,* built in the 16th century, and *Canongate Tolbooth,* once a jail and now a museum.

At the end of the street you will find Holyrood Palace, which is the official residence of the Queen when she is in Scotland. The palace was built as a guest house for the abbey in the 12th century, and Bonnie Prince Charlie lived there in 1745 during his attempt to seize the castle and win the crown. Mary Queen of Scots lived there from 1561 to 1567; in her apartments is a brass tablet that marks the spot where her alleged lover, David Rizzio, was murdered by her husband, Lord Darnley, and other nobles. Nearby are the ruins of *Holyrood Abbey,* which was built by King David I, as one legend goes, in gratitude for his deliverance from the attack of a wild stag by the appearance of a Holy Cross or Rood. Others say that the abbey was named after the True Cross belonging to St. Margaret, his mother. The *King's Park,* located southeast of the palace, contains *Arthur's Seat,* an 823-foot chunk of volcanic rock that provides an excellent view of Edinburgh.

Those who would like to follow a literary tour can visit *Lady Stair's House,* which has a collection of the memorabilia of Robert Burns, Robert Louis Stevenson, and Sir Walter Scott. The Robert Louis Stevenson house is at 8 Howard Place; Sir Walter Scott's is at 39 Castle Street.

There is a large campground in north Edinburgh that is fully equipped with facilities. There are also campgrounds located in **Kinross, Kirkcaldy, Kinghorn, Comrie, Newbridge,** and **Haddington.**

Aberdeen

Cross the graceful, much-photographed *Firth of Forth Bridge* on A90, take A92 to Kirkcaldy, and A915 to **St. Andrews,** the site of the oldest university in Scotland (started in 1412), a ruined cathedral, a castle, and a number of medieval churches, as well as the famed golf course.

(Golfers may want to spend more time here.) Next take the A91 and A919, then A92 to **Dundee,** which was known in the 18th century as a whaling port, and for its marmalade, then as the center of the jute industry in the 19th century. Continue on A92 to **Arbroath,** a pleasant fishing port containing the ruins of a 12th-century cathedral. *Dunnottar Castle,* a 14th-century fortress, is almost completely surrounded by the sea just south of **Stonehaven.** Continue on the A92 to Aberdeen, where there is a 2-mile-long beach, a thriving fishing industry, a leading university, and some grim relics of the past, like the tolbooth and the guillotine. Aberdeen is also within easy range of a large number of castles located between the coast and the Grampian Mountains.

There is a campground in the city, plus one at **Nigg** (2 miles away), **Skene** (10 miles west), and at **Inverbervie** (south of Aberdeen). There are many campgrounds north of Aberdeen in **Fraserburgh** and **Peterhead.** Most of these are on the sea, with beaches, but campgrounds listing a beach do not guarantee that they are suitable for swimming.

Aberdeen/Pitlochry

Take A93 along the River Dee into the *eastern Highlands.* Fourteen miles west of Aberdeen is *Crathes Castle.* Then **Ballater,** near *Balmoral Castle,* the residence of the royal family, which is not open to the public but can be glimpsed from the road on a curve of the River Dee. *Crathie Church,* where the royal family attends services while in residence, is nearby. As students, we waited for hours to see the Queen there on a beautiful Sunday morning in late August. We went into the church early in the morning and found it peaceful and rich with the colors of the stained-glass windows and the velvet on the pews and kneeling cushions. Back along the road leading up to the church, we decided on a spot for waiting, along with the other people who had gathered there. At 11:30 the royal procession began moving up the hill to the church. First came a bagpipe followed by the Black Watch Guard, next, in cars, the Duke of Gloucester and the Duke of Kent and the royal staff, and another car bearing Princess Margaret and the Queen Mother, and at the end another with Queen Elizabeth and Prince Phillip. A nearly perfect morning closed with a walk up the hill to get a view of Balmoral Castle, nestled in a stand of pine near the river.

Continue on A93 to **Braemar,** the site of the Highland Games in September, continue to the *Bridge of Cally,* then take A924 to **Pitlochry.** This is a very popular resort area and there are a number of campgrounds in Pitlochry as well as in **Kenmore, Aberfeldy, Dunkeld,** and **Blair Atholl.**

Alternate Route

Hikers who want to climb the Cairngorms may prefer to camp near Braemar or continue on the A9 to **Aviemore** (on the way to **Inverness**).

A chairlift located near Aviemore runs both winter and summer. Aviemore may well be the ideal location to camp for a day or two. The problem is covering the distance from Aberdeen in one day over mountain passes. You may want to stay longer in Braemar and then drive to Aviemore in one day.

Pitlochry/Inverness

Take the A9 to Inverness. Macbeth's castle once stood in the center of Inverness; the city is now the leading shopping and tourist center of the area. In this capital of the Highlands, traditional Highland dancers perform throughout the summer, and there are special Highland Games in July. You can enjoy the multiplying legends and fanfare about the *Loch Ness Monster,* which has been sighted for hundreds of years. The site of the **Battle of Culloden,** where Bonnie Prince Charlie was defeated by the Duke of Cumberland in 1746, is marked by a tall cairn (rock) and scattered headstones. East of Inverness, you may drive along the coast of the *Moray Firth.* Resorts such as **Nairn, Elgin, Findhorn,** and **Lossiemouth** offer wide beaches and various sports such as golf and sailing. Boats for longer cruises on Loch Ness and the rest of the Caledonian Canal are available. The Inverness area contains several campgrounds. There is one in **Beauly** that is 12 miles west and one in **Kessock** on the shore that is accessible by car ferry.

Inverness/Isle of Skye

Take A82 along beautiful Loch Ness to **Invermoriston** and A887 and A87 to the ferry at **Kyle of Lochalsh** for the Isle of Skye. On the way you will pass *Eileen Donan Castle* in **Dornie,** set beautifully on an islet connected to the mainland by a narrow causeway. We have camped without benefit of a campground on the Isle of Skye for one night but there is a campground at **Broadford** that has a beach.

Alternate Route
Those who have days to spare and the desire to explore one of the most rugged seacoasts in the world may wish to circle north on A9 and A838 to the **Pentland Firth,** which separates the mainland and the **Orkney Islands.** The seas encountered between *Duncansby Head* and *Cape Wrath* are reputed to be among the wildest in the oceanic world.

ISLE OF SKYE Portree, a town with a sheltered harbor, is the capital of the Isle of Skye. It is a good center for touring, as are Broadford and **Sligachan.** The island is beautiful, wild, lonely, and quite primitive. The Cuillins are the most memorable mountains in Britain; the pinnacles are precipitous and often shrouded in mist. Most of the climbs will appeal only to experienced climbers. John MacLeod, the present clan chief, occupies **Dunvegan Castle** for several months each year with his family. At one time the castle was only accessible by the sea through a small gateway with an opening on the rocks; there is now a bridge across a ravine that was originally a moat. Among the objects preserved in the castle you can see the *Fairy Flag,* which has twice saved the clan on the battlefield. Flora Macdonald is a name well known to all Skye residents. In 1746 she disguised Prince Charles as her maid, Betty Burke, and rowed him to Skye to hide from the royal forces.

Fort William

Take A87 to **Invergarry,** A82 to Fort William. Highland Games are held here in August and there is a *West Highland Museum* to visit. The most striking feature of this area is Ben Nevis, the tallest mountain in the British Isles (4406 feet). This mountain, a towering granite mass, does not show a cone or peak. *Glen Nevis* is one of the finest glens in Scotland, ascending the left bank of the Nevis and passing the site of a medieval fort, a waterfall, and a spectacular gorge.

Spean Bridge, northeast of Fort William, has a number of campgrounds. There is one in Fort William, a short distance toward Glen Nevis along A82. Others may be found in **Ballachulish, Glencoe, Kinlochleven,** and **Archaracis.**

FORT WILLIAM AND BEN NEVIS Climbers may want to reach the top of Ben Nevis; some have suggested that it usually takes four hours to climb up and three to come down. Experienced climbers may try the hazardous north faces; others may enjoy the 5-mile trail that begins on the bank of the River Nevis. You may wish to visit Glencoe (glen of weeping in Gaelic), the scene of a massacre in 1692. The MacDonald of Glencoe had refused to take the oath of allegiance to the king until the very last minute, and then when he tried to do so found no magistrate available in Fort William and had to travel to Inverary. When the papers finally arrived in Edinburgh they were hidden and the clan was outlawed. Cambell of Glenlyon and 128 soldiers attacked the inhabitants at dawn, killing more than 40 of 200 inhabitants.

Oban

Take A82 and A828 to Oban. Campgrounds with beaches may be found at **Scammadale,** 13 miles south; and at **Benderloch,** 10 miles north of Oban, a resort area enjoyed by yachtsmen, fishermen, and other vacationers. Steamers carry visitors to islands in the Inner Hebrides such as **Mull** and **Staffa.** An uninhabited island, Staffa was once the scene of a volcanic action in which liquid basalt was spewed to the surface. The cooling and coagulating of these masses produced a series of curious rock columns. *Fingal's Cave,* which looks like a cathedral of rock, is 227 feet long, and the depth of the water at mid-tide is 66 feet. It is possible to go in by boat. Mull, "a mass of hill," has cliffs, beaches, lakes, and a network of sealochs and creeks on the west side that remind one of an archipelago. In 1588 the *Florencia,* a galleon of the Spanish Armada, was blown up and sunk in the harbor of **Tobermory.** Since the 17th century, divers have explored the hulk searching for treasure.

Oban/Stirling

Take A85 to **Tyndrum** and A82 to **Arden,** along the beautiful shores of Loch Lomond, where you may want to stop for a picnic or swim. Then take A811 to **Stirling.** There are several campgrounds in or near Stirling; two have beaches. Stirling lies in the center of Scotland and has played an important part in its history; it is situated between two famous battlefields. Southeast of Stirling is **Bannockburn,** where Robert the Bruce defeated King Edward's army in 1314. To the northeast, on *Abbey Craig,* is a tower marking the site where Sir William Wallace defeated an English army in 1297. *Stirling Castle* stands on a precipitous cliff overlooking the town. Alexander I died in the castle in 1124 and William the Lion in 1214; four of Scotland's six Jameses lived here, including James VI, the son of Mary Queen of Scots, who spent his boyhood here. During the reign of the Stuarts, James I of England turned the castle into a luxurious residence. Nearby *Doune Castle,* a restored fortress from the 15th century, was built by Robert, Duke of Albany, and his son, Murdoch. When Murdoch was executed in 1425 the Crown seized the castle. In 1745 the hero of Scott's *Waverley* was detained there.

Stirling/Edinburgh

Take M9 to Edinburgh.

Scotland has enough beauty and serenity to entice travelers to linger. There are many spots that will appeal to people for longer stays. However, it would be difficult to compress this trip easily because driving can be slow. For travelers with very limited time, we suggest omitting an entire area, such as the trip to Aberdeen, Inverness, the Isle of Skye, or Oban.

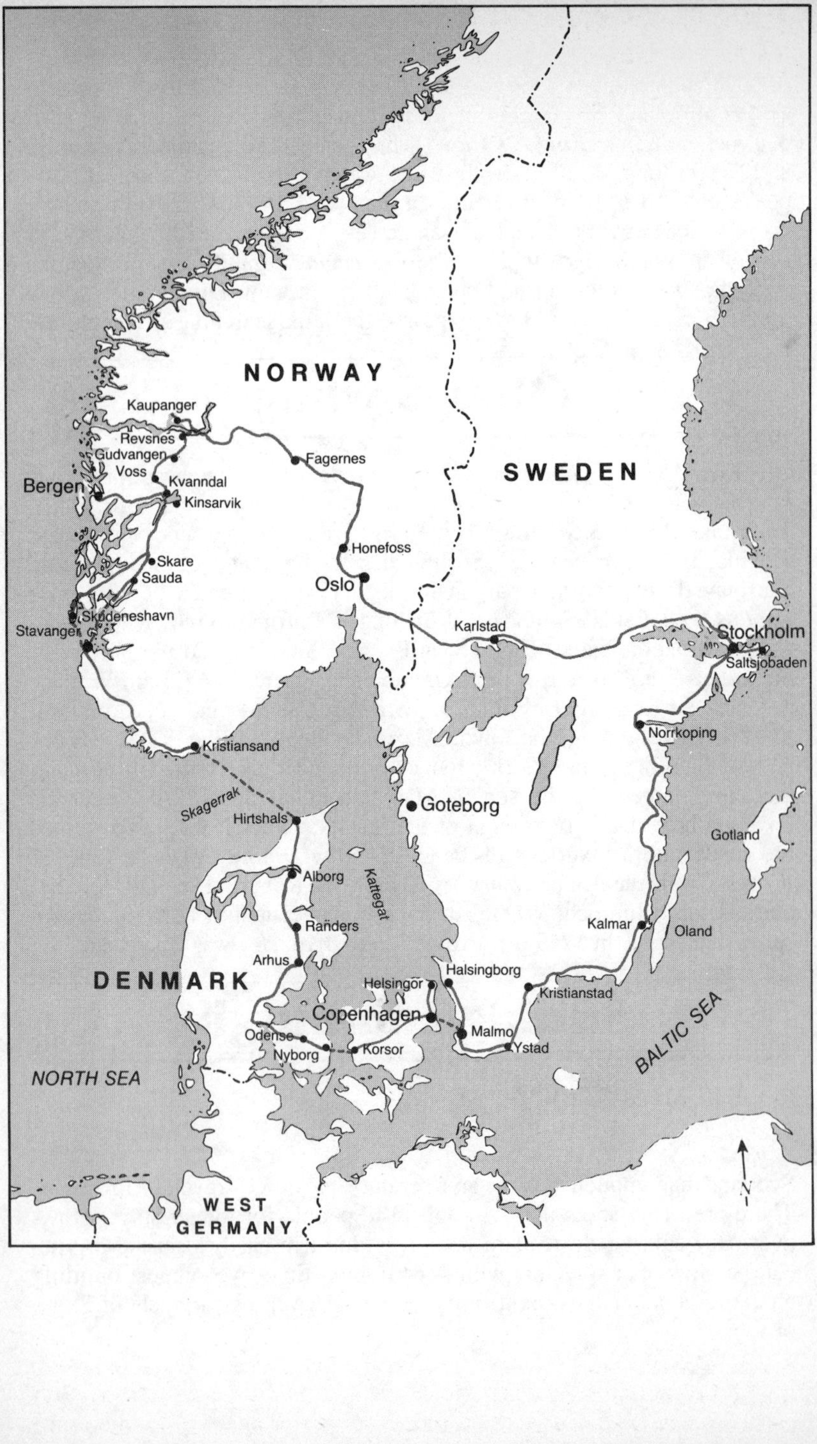
NORWAY
Kaupanger
Revsnes
Gudvangen
Voss
Kvanndal
Bergen
Kinsarvik
Fagernes
Honefoss
Skare
Sauda
Oslo
Skudeneshavn
Stavanger
SWEDEN
Karlstad
Stockholm
Saltsjobaden
Norrkoping
Kristiansand
Skagerrak
Hirtshals
Goteborg
Gotland
Alborg
Kattegat
Randers
Arhus
Kalmar
Oland
DENMARK
Helsingor
Halsingborg
Kristianstad
Copenhagen
Malmo
Odense
Nyborg
Korsor
Ystad
BALTIC SEA
NORTH SEA
N
WEST
GERMANY

SCANDINAVIA

Copenhagen to Oland, Sweden	378 kilometers
Oland to Stockholm	378 kilometers
Stockholm to Oslo, Norway	427 kilometers
Oslo to Sogne Fjord	323 kilometers
Sogne Fjord to Hardanger Fjord	82 kilometers (excluding ferry to Gudvangen)
Kvanndal to Bergen	114 kilometers
Kvanndal to Stavanger	171 kilometers
Stavanger to Kristiansand	259 kilometers
Kristiansand to Arhus, Denmark	162 kilometers (excluding ferry)
Arhus to Odense	118 kilometers
Odense to Copenhagen	133 kilometers

From Copenhagen: Helsingor, Oland, Stockholm, Oslo, Sogne Fjord, Jostedal Glacier, Hardanger Fjord, Bergen, Stavanger, Kristiansand, Arhus, Odense, Copenhagen
(24 days: 2544 kilometers)

    Scandinavia is made up of five countries, each with a different though related language and varied topography, but with a common history of alternating strife and cooperation. The countries have developed alongside one another, exchanged pieces of land and sometimes kings, fought and negotiated peace, traded with one another—all while maintaining independence and yet sharing many common elements in a recognizable culture. Norway and Sweden are contained in a large peninsula extending to the North Cape and separating the Baltic from the Atlantic. Finland meets the base of this peninsula and lies a short distance across the Baltic from Sweden, which has encouraged interaction through trade. Denmark, although completely separate geographically on another peninsula and a series of islands, was linked to Sweden in earlier times when part of the peninsula belonged to Denmark. Remote and isolated Iceland once belonged to Denmark, and shares its culture. (Those who are particularly interested in Scandinavia may want to make one trans-

53

atlantic crossing via Icelandic Airlines with a layover for several days or a week to explore its magnificent landscape.) In 1953 Norway, Sweden, Denmark, and Iceland formed a Nordic Union that Finland later joined.

The topography of Scandinavia was shaped during the Ice Age by giant glaciers that chiseled their way down valleys to the ocean, leaving fjords and islands. All of northern Scandinavia was covered with ice until 10,000 years ago. This heavy ice caused the land to sink and then rise again when the ice melted. The land is still rising, perhaps 15 inches in each century, which necessitates changes in harbor use and facilities.

Human beings entered Scandinavia between 10,000 and 5000 B.C., during the Epipalaeolithic Period, as a race of fishermen. During the Neolithic and Bronze Periods, the people in the remote inland areas remained primitive much longer than those living in more populated coastal regions. In the eighth century A.D., the Viking Period, Scandinavian society was well organized enough so that people undertook long sea voyages for conquest and colonization.

One of the best approaches to understanding Nordic culture is through its mythology. Scandinavian legends and sagas were passed down through the ages from one generation to the next by word of mouth. The first recorded writing in Scandinavia, that of runic inscriptions, appeared around the ninth century. Sagas detailed the lives of leaders, feuds between families, courtships, the deeds of brave warriors, chivalrous and courageous behavior, and historical events. Snorri Sturluson, who lived from 1179–1241, chronicled the kings of Norway in his "Heimskringla."

We do not know where the original Scandinavian creation legend came from; some scholars feel that the basis may be Oriental, passed along trade routes in the first several centuries A.D. Others date the origination of this legend to long before the birth of Christ, passed on by Teutonic travelers to Scandinavia. Snorri Sturluson's version of the creation appears in his "Prose Edda." In essence, life was created by the melding of ice from the north and fire from the south. The first being was Ymir, and the first animal was a cow, Audumla. The cow licked the ice and Buri, a man, appeared. He had three grandsons: Odin, Vili, and Ve.

Thomas Carlyle claimed that Scandinavian paganism continued well into the 11th century, when Odin was still worshiped as a god. Odin learned from wise giants such as Vafthrudnir, and used his knowledge intelligently. He was the most important of all the gods because his powers included controlling the outcome of battle. Odin had one eye, wore a hat with a wide brim to disguise his identity, swung a blue cape over his shoulders upon which perched the ravens Huginn, who represents thought, and Muninn, who represents memory. He carried a magic spear called Gungnir.

The three grandsons of Odin hated Ymir and finally killed him; then they created the world from his body. His flesh provided the earth, his bones the mountains; his teeth were made into rocks, and his blood formed the sea and lakes. They fashioned the sky from his skull and placed dwarfs by each corner, named East, West, North, and South.

Odin and Earth had a son—Thor, a god who was loved by the people. He supported farmers instead of the kings Odin favored, and stood for order rather than Odin's penchant for battle. Thor was a large god, had a quick temper to go with his red beard, and possessed a large appetite. His chariot wheels made the sound we know as thunder; lightning was produced by chips of whetstone within his head. Thor was in charge of weather, so we can blame him to this day.

Loki, a sometimes evil giant, was unpredictable and hostile. His character was unstable, cruel, and treacherous. Sturluson describes him as "handsome and fair of face, but [he] has an evil disposition and is very changeable of mood. He excelled all men in the art of cunning, and he always cheats."

There are other gods to read about; also goddesses, dwarfs, and elves. "Scaldic" poems provide sources for some of the legends. They were eulogies composed to honor contemporary figures, but they make use of metaphors developed from legend.

The fascination with elves and dwarfs is certainly visible in everyday Scandinavian life. If you buy anything to bring home, you can hardly avoid the "little people." We have decorated our home with Scandinavian elves every Christmas, no matter how inappropriately; they appear on the tree, on table linen, and can even be seen tiptoeing across the mantel.

The visitor of today can expect to find some of the most beautiful scenery in the world, ranging from the mountains, glaciers, and fjords to the flat farmland and rolling hills near the lakes. Almost any venture will bring you near water in a lovely setting. The geological development and history of each region are detailed in many fine museums, where the traditions, costumes, and crafts of the people are also exhibited. The Scandinavian peoples love hiking, sailing, skiing, cycling, fishing, and the outdoor life in general. They have developed a very high standard of living, efficient transportation systems, and excellent medical and recreational facilities for everyone. The prices may be high (particularly in Sweden, less so in Norway, and moderate in Denmark) but by camping the traveler can afford to enjoy this beautiful part of the world. Scandinavia is not as jammed with tourists as the countries in central Europe; it is still unspoiled, peaceful, and full of natural beauty.

The national tourist offices in each country are trying to encourage visitors to camp because that is one of the best ways to enjoy the landscape and meet the people. A letter will bring you maps, a list of camping sites, pamphlets with all sorts of information about museums, shopping, seasonal events, and a collection of beautiful photographs to whet your appetite. Camping sites are clean, pleasant, and have more than the usual number of amenities. Camping fees are reasonable, and Scandinavian campers are often friendly and very likely to speak English. Mountain roads are usually open from late May or early June until October. When you find an area you like especially, you may want to stay longer.

Ideally, the itinerary that follows could be spread over a longer period of time; it could be extended by several weeks to include the more remote regions of northern Norway and Sweden. You may prefer to omit some sections and spend more time in others; we discourage one-night stands and suggest that you plan to stay for several days in each campsite, relaxing and enjoying the munificence of natural beauty.

Copenhagen

Copenhagen is a city to have fun in, apart from remembering those fairytales heard in childhood. *Tivoli,* an amusement park located in the center of Copenhagen, is like a child's dream world. It is also the biggest bargain in Europe. For the price of admission you can spend all day and all evening until midnight enjoying performances or sitting and watching the world go by. Despite the fact that 40,000 persons stroll through the gates every day, the grounds look fresh and green, with fountains spraying and flowers blooming. You can enjoy concerts every evening, traditional pantomime, ballet with internationally renowned performers in the open-air theater, a marionette theater, and fireworks. The Tivoli Boy's Guard, similar to the King's Royal Guard, marches through the park with its own band. There are a number of restaurants on the grounds, not inexpensive but loaded with atmosphere. (Tivoli is open from May 1 through mid-September.)

The **National Museum,** on Fredericksholms Kanal, has archaeological collections ranging from the Stone Age to historic times, including Viking ships, folklore exhibits, and coin collections. **Christiansborg Palace** houses the Danish Parliament, the Ministry of Foreign Affairs, and the Royal Reception Rooms. Bishop Absalom, who was well known for his ingenuity in fighting pirates, built the first castle as a fortress in 1167. It is likely that Absalom would have been pleased to know that during World War II his castle housed explosives used by the resistance fighters to hinder the occupation by Germans. At one point in 1940, when the general supply of explosives ran out, this well-hidden cache came to good use. You can tour the cellar ruins of Absalom's Castle as well as the royal reception rooms. Christiansborg Palace has other historic associations of some interest. "My Sorrow" was written in the Blue Tower by Leonora Christine, who lived there for 22 years as a prisoner of her brother. Leonora and her husband, Corfitz Ulfeldt, tried to remove her brother, Frederick III, from the throne because they thought he was a poor ruler. As a result, this talented 17th-century lady spent her days embroidering, writing poetry, and playing the piano until she was finally set free by her nephew.

Adjacent to the palace is the **Theatre History Museum** in the **Royal Court Theatre,** where you can see ballet slippers and costumes of Anna Pavlova as well as displays about the history of Danish theater for the last three centuries. Hans Christian Andersen became a writer only after unsuccessful attempts to become a singer (his soprano voice changed) and then a troll in the ballet. As an enterprising youth of fourteen, he left Odense with his belongings on his back, arrived at the theater, somehow wangled an interview with a ballerina, and gained a walk-on roll. Apparently his performance was enough to discourage him from seeking a future in dance.

The changing of the guard takes place every day at noon at **Amalienborg Palace. Rosenborg Palace,** near the **Botanical Gardens,** houses the Danish crown jewels, as well as tapestries and china. You can take a canal and harbor tour from **Gammel Strand,** a marketplace, to **Langelinie** to see the statue of the **Little Mermaid** from Hans Christian Andersen's fairytale. We almost always buy smorbrod and walk to the Little Mermaid for lunch as we did on our first visit with Danish friends. In 1964 someone stole the head of the mermaid; sailors believe that kissing her brings good luck, so perhaps someone wanted her for all time. In any case, she had a new head within a few months. Again, in July 1984, her right arm was spirited away, but quickly restored the next month.

The **Arsenal Museum** houses a collection of armor, weapons, uniforms, and battle flags. The *zoo and zoological gardens* contain a play zoo and a structure that looks like a Chinese pagoda; you can ride up in it for a fine view from the top.

For excursions out of Copenhagen, try **Dyrehaven,** a deer park near **Klampenborg** (you can also swim there). At **Lyngby** you will find an open-air museum in a 40-acre park called **Frilandmuseet,** where Danish farms have been reconstructed and are fully furnished with authentic pieces; there are also folk-dancing demonstrations. We particularly recommend **Louisiana,** a lovely modern art gallery with much sculpture outside in beautifully landscaped settings. It is north of the city near Klampenborg, along the pleasant coast road to **Helsingor** (Elsinore). Here you will find **Kronborg Castle,** famous as the setting for *Hamlet,* which lives up to its reputation; it also contains the **Mercantile and Maritime Museum.**

In our opinion, shopping in Copenhagen is unrivaled. The main shopping street, **Stroget,** is closed to traffic, so you can wander back and forth with great pleasure. We always wish we had more time for shopping there. Everyone on our gift list has received either silver jewelry, wooden candlesticks, bowls, or trays purchased from small shops along Stroget.

Camping sites in Denmark are pleasant and easy to locate. There are 511 sites approved by the National Camping Committee of Denmark, six of which are in the Copenhagen area.

Copenhagen/Oland, Sweden

Drive from Copenhagen on E4 to Helsingor and take one of the ferries to **Halsingborg,** Sweden, or take a longer ferry directly from Copenhagen to **Malmo.** If you are interested in visiting **Lund,** take 66 (Swedish NR15) from the ring road around Malmo. Lund was founded by King Knut the Great in 1020 and flourished as a major cultural, religious, and political center in Scandinavia during the Middle Ages. The cathedral, *Domkyrka,* dates from the 12th century; it has a 14th-century astronomic clock, a mosaic of Christ in the apse, and beautifully carved choir stalls. The *University of Lund* was founded in 1668; adjacent to the church is a 16th-century red brick royal residence that was the original university center. You will enjoy walking the winding old streets of Lund, especially with a stop in the market in *Martenstorget.*

Take E6 through Malmo, E14 to **Ystad,** 20 to **Kristianstad,** and 15 to **Kalmar** for the bridge to Oland. This route takes you along the Baltic coast of southern Sweden through fishing villages and small resorts, with many half-timbered houses in Ystad and a castle in Kalmar.

Ystad features at least 300 half-timbered houses from the 16th century. You can visit **Backakra,** the old farm renovated by Dag Hammarskjold, several miles to the east.

If you enjoyed reading any of Vilhelm Moberg's novels, such as *The Immigrants* or *Unto a Good Land,* you will recognize the land around Kalmar. During the Middle Ages the power that ruled Kalmar also controlled Sweden. The castle was begun in the 12th century, then enlarged by Gustavus Vasa in the 16th century. There is a legend that during a wild celebration in Kalmar Castle, Eric XIV hit his head on a beam as he was being tossed about in a blanket . . . and so became insane.

You can easily park near one of the old squares, such as **Larmtorget,** and stroll around amongst the shops and historic buildings. Kalmar Lans Hemslojdsforening on Larmgatan 26, just steps from the square, is a shop that displays handicrafts from every area of Sweden.

Another treat is in store if you are interested in visiting world-famous glass factories. Take NR25 and NR31 to the northwest from Kalmar, then continue on NR31 when it branches right from NR25 to **Orrefors.** You can tour the *Orrefors Glass Museum* as well as watch glassblowers at work. And there is a "seconds" shop adjacent, where you can purchase glassware to send or carry home with you. Orrefors maintains three other shops in the region.

Alternate Route
For those who want to push on to **Stockholm** in one full day of driving, the main line is E4 from Halsingborg through **Jonkoping** on **Lake Vattern** and **Norrkoping**.

OLAND accessible from Kalmar via the longest bridge in Europe, is a thin strip of an island with 300 kilometers of coastline. It appeals to sailors, windsurfers, cyclists, and horseback riders, as well as those who enjoy swimming or sunning on the beach. There are 5 youth hostels and 27 camping areas; you can also rent a cabin or mobile home at campsites. Staffs in four tourist offices on the island will help you find a room in a private home if you wish. The tourist office can also supply information on the rather fascinating history, geology, and botany of Oland, which has rock formations, flora, and fauna not found elsewhere in Sweden. Principal historic sites include the *Borgholm Slottet,* built as a medieval castle and now in ruins; *Solliden,* the summer residence of the royal family, where you can tour the gardens; *Gardslosa,* the best-preserved medieval church on the island, with frescoes from the late medieval period; and *Eketorp,* site of a pre-Viking ring-fort now under reconstruction, as well as bronze and Iron-Age burial mounds and graves. There are over 400 windmills on Oland, some of them lined up, providing a photographer's dream.

You can take a ferry to **Gotland** and explore **Visby**, known as "The City of Ruins and Roses," following years of rich trade, subsequent ruin, and rediscovery. There are relics and ruins all over the island.

Oland/Stockholm

Leave Oland via the bridge to Kalmar and take 15 to Norrkoping, then E4 into Stockholm. There are several campgrounds in Stockholm, all run by the municipality. You can camp outside the city in pleasant suburbs such as **Sollentuna** or **Bromme;** in **Eskilstuna** to the west; **Vasteras,** northwest of Stockholm, or **Uppsala,** to the north on the large lakes (**Malaren**) just west of the city, or on the Baltic coast to the east. Of the more than 500 campgrounds in Sweden, more are listed as first class than in any other Scandinavian country.

Stockholm and Area

Stockholm, the "Venice of the North," is an expensive city to live in but worth the price for the treasures you can enjoy as a visitor. It developed from a fortress on an island at the junction of Lake Malaren and the Baltic, became a town in 1250, and later expanded to the present city of 14 islands. The **Old Town,** also known as the "City Between the Bridges" or **Gamla Stan,** centers on the **Stortorget** (Great Square), which is near the **Royal Palace.** The Stockholm Massacre took place here in 1520 when 94 Swedish noblemen were arrested by the king and beheaded; their heads were piled in a pyramid in the middle of Stortorget. There is a changing of the guard at the Royal Palace every day at noon and some of the rooms in the palace are open to the public. Inside the **Storkyrka** (Great Church) you will find a painted woodcarving of St. George with the dragon, given to the church in 1489.

Across the inner harbor, the **Stadshuset** (City Hall) is a beautiful example of modern architecture with lovely mosaic walls in gold inside. Joining a guided tour at the appointed time is well worth the trouble. You will enjoy a perfect view of Stockholm if you are willing to undertake the long but interesting climb through various stages leading to the top of the tower.

You can take an elevator up to the top of the 508-foot telecommunications tower, **Kahnastornet.** There is a glassed-in observation platform with panoramic photographs placed to help you identify areas of the city below. Don't worry about the safety of the tower in high winds; it is anchored to bedrock by 72 steel rods sunk to 26 feet below the surface. It will sway a maximum of 2⅓ inches at the top in winds of 45 miles per hour—a comforting thought.

Djurgarden (Deer Park) is situated on an island that is 2¼ miles long and ½ mile wide. Originally an enclosure for deer, the park now contains a wealth of interesting places to visit. **Skansen** is a favorite. As an open-air museum, it represents all of Sweden through reconstructed houses and shops, churches, farmhouses, rune stones, and a number of buildings from estates. Crafts are demonstrated, including glassblowing, weaving, spinning, and bookbinding. Entertainment includes folk-dancing in traditional costumes, folk operas, fireworks, and a Punch and Judy show. You can wander by a Lapp camp and see the reindeer, or sit and watch the peacocks strutting about on the grass. There is also a zoo on the grounds. The **Nordic Museum,** by the north gate of Skansen, has collections that illustrate the development of Swedish civilization from the 16th century.

Nearby is the *Wasa,* a Swedish man-of-war sunk in the harbor by a freak squall just after she had been commissioned in 1628. This oldest intact ship of the 17th century, loaded with elaborate carvings, is in the process of being restored and preserved. She was raised from the harbor mud in 1961 and has since been bathed in preservative liquids to keep her from drying out and falling to pieces; the humidity is decreased slowly year by year. There is a marvelous museum with all sorts of details about the raising and preserving process. This was as fascinating to our son at 6 as it was when he was 16, and is interesting to adults as well. A film is also shown. We have visited the *Wasa* three times at 7-year intervals since she was first raised. Each time we eagerly explore the new displays and note the addition of more carved sections to the hull. By 1988 she will be housed in a much larger new museum with a copper roof; the masts will be in place and the bowsprit will be extended to its original length, which is ten meters longer than it is now. For those interested in ships and the sea, the **National Maritime Museum** is also interesting.

Outside Stockholm you can visit **Drottningholm,** the favorite winter palace of the royal family, located on an island in Lake Malaren. The ceiling paintings are impressive, as are the tapestries. **Drottningholm Court Theater** is next to the palace; 18th-century plays are performed here.

Just across the water from Stockholm lies the island of **Lidingo** and the home of the famous Swedish sculptor Carl Milles. **Millesgarden** was purchased in 1906 and developed into a beautiful studio and home, which have been given to the Swedish nation. Milles's statues are placed inside, as well as in the carefully terraced garden leading down to the water. Milles was also a collector of sculpture and paintings, so both the wealth of fine work and the magnificent setting make this a memorable spot to visit.

Saltsjobaden is one of the most popular year-round resort areas; tennis, swimming, sailing, horseback riding, and golf are available. It is located on a lovely Baltic fjord **(Baggensfjord)** southeast of Stockholm. It is also possible to take boat trips out into the archipelago to visit some of the 25,000 pine-covered, rocky islands that sprawl eastward from the city proper. Here the water is warm and has so little salt that one can almost drink it. City dwellers take to their boats and may camp anywhere on private property as long as they remain a reasonable distance from summer houses. **Sandhamn,** on the eastern edge of the archipelago, is one major center of Swedish yachting on the Baltic. The Royal Swedish Yacht Club arranges international races there in the summer.

There are also many more museums, castles, and cathedrals to visit in the area surrounding Stockholm. Uppsala was the center of Sweden until the late 13th century. In 1273 the archbishop settled there and the king moved to Stockholm; *Uppsala Cathedral* was begun around 1285 and finished in 1435; the university was founded in 1477. **Old Uppsala** is 2 miles north of the present city; the huge burial mounds there (dating from A.D. 500) may contain the bones of pre-Christian kings.

Stockholm/Oslo, Norway

Take E18 all the way to Oslo, passing through **Varmland,** the province that is the setting of Selma Lagerlof's books (*The Wonderful World of Nils* and *The Saga of Gosta Berling*), through **Karlstad** on huge **Lake Vanern,** part of Sweden's inland waterway, and through the rugged timbering country on the Swedish-Norwegian border.

If you enjoyed *Wild Strawberries,* Ingmar Bergman's film, you may want to take a side trip to the ***Dalarna*** area northwest of Stockholm. Our Swedish relatives vacation there and participate in the Midsummer Day festivities held in late June. This festival includes processions of decorated boats from various parishes sailing by on **Lake Siljan,** folk dancing in regional dress, and the raising of the maypole.

To get to Dalarna from Stockholm, take E18 to **Enkoping,** and NR70 to **Mora.** Resort areas in Dalarna include **Rattvik, Leksand,** and Mora. Painters and writers have long treasured the beauty of the lakes and hills of this region, just as the Lake District has had a special place in the artistic life of England. Shop in the Hemslojd shops for traditional handicrafts, including wooden horses in bright colors *(dalahast,)* bowls, plates, spoons, and all sorts of woven items.

We had a friend who began training for the famed *Wasaloppet,* a cross-country ski race from Mora to Salen, many months before the start. The route was originally taken by Gustavus Vasa in the 16th century and runs 85 kilometers northwest to **Salen.** Gustavus Vasa tried in vain to get the inhabitants of Mora to band together against the king of Norway and Denmark, Christian II, who had massacred a large group of Swedish noblemen in Stockholm as he proclaimed himself king of Sweden. Because Vasa was not able to convince his neighbors to join with him, he began skiing toward the Norwegian border, where he planned to gain support for a rebellion. The two fastest skiers from Mora caught up with him near Salen, calling his name in his local dialect to identify themselves. The people of Mora had reconsidered and wanted him back as their leader, so he returned and eventually became the first king of Sweden.

To return to the main route toward Oslo, take NR70 to Leksand and **Borlange,** then NR60 to **Ljusnarsberg** and NR63 to Karlstad.

We have stayed several times in a large campground located west of the city on a lake. Many facilities are provided. There are several others in the Oslo vicinity. If you don't mind a drive, there are any number of campgrounds on both sides of the Oslo Fjord and to the west of the city in **Kongsberg, Drammen,** and **Svelvik.**

Oslo

Oslo is situated in a spectacular location at the end of the 60-mile-long Oslo Fjord, with mountains rising on both sides. The natural beauty of Oslo and all of Norway never ceases to entice those who love mountains and the sea. Water is never far away and people whose livelihood depends indirectly on the ships in the harbor can also enjoy the beauty of the fjord, swim in it, sail on it, and eat its delicacies. You can buy a bag of freshly cooked shrimp on the waterfront in Oslo or as you wait for ferries to cross the many fjords that make car travel through Norway slow but delightful.

For those who enjoy the sea, Oslo is full of maritime exhibits. In the *Viking Ship Museum* there are three long ships that were apparently used as burial chambers. The *Gokstad Ship,* 76 feet long, was a seagoing ship and is less ornate than the others. Warriors' shields were displayed over the gunwales as the ship was sailed or rowed on voyages in the Baltic, the North Sea, and the Atlantic. The *Oseberg Ship,* 70 feet long, originally contained the remains of a Viking queen, horses, dogs, a bed, a loom, clothing, cooking equipment, and a young servant girl buried alive. The *Tune Ship* consists of only a few pieces of the ship's bottom. *Kon-Tiki,* the balsa-wood raft sailed by Thor Heyerdahl from Peru to Polynesia in 1947, is on display with diaries and records of the trip. The ship's complement included five other men and one parrot. The *Fram,* the ship that carried Nansen to the Arctic in 1893 and Amundsen to the South Pole in 1910, is preserved with equipment and rigging intact.

The *Norwegian Folk Museum* includes an open-air collection of 150 wooden buildings arranged in courtyard groupings representing various provinces of Norway. The 12th-century stave church from Gol, beautifully carved, is there. Henrik Ibsen's study is on exhibit, along with other Norwegian cultural collections. **Frogner Park,** located in the northwestern edge of Oslo, houses **Vigeland Sculpture Park and Museum.** Gustav Vigeland contracted with the city of Oslo to create a sculpture garden in the park. In 40 years he completed 1650 sculptures with the aid of assistants and workers. The results are very controversial but impressive because he tried to create the cycle of human life in bronze and stone. Pathos, joy, agony, and other emotions are depicted in the nude figures. During the year of his death (1943), a gigantic monolith over 50 feet high and comprising 121 intertwined human figures was completed. The **Radhuset** (City Hall) is a large red brick building with two towers. Both modern and lavish, it is decorated with paintings and sculpture done by contemporary Norwegian artists. The city also offers a number of art museums including the **National Gallery,** the **Munch Museum,** and the **Henie-Onstad Museum.**

There are several spots for a panoramic view of the Oslo Fjord and the city. One is **Holmenkollen Tower,** which was used in the 1952 Winter Olympic Games and is the most famous ski jump in Europe; a sports museum adjoins the tower. **Tryvannstarnet Tower** has the highest elevation in Oslo and overlooks many square miles of fjords and towns. One may also enjoy the view looking up at the mountains by taking boat trips on the Oslo Fjord.

Oslo/Sogne Fjord

Take E68 through **Honefuss, Fagernes,** and **Laerdal** to **Revsnes.** There are spectacular views all along this route. Then take a ferry to **Kaupanger** and choose a campground in the area. Campgrounds are dotted along the fjord from **Skjolden, Gaupne, Hoyheimsvik, Luster,** and **Sogndal** on the *Luste Fjord,* which is an arm of the Sogne Fjord. To the west there are campgrounds at **Viksdalen, Balestrand,** and **Vangsnes.** Along the edge of the fjords the roads are narrow and curvy; in the mountains they are often steep. Visitors towing trailers should get a copy of *Motoring in Norway,* available from the Norwegian National Travel Office, which gives information on road conditions.

SOGNE FJORD, the longest fjord in Norway, stretches from the sea 125 miles inland to the foot of the *Jotunheimen* mountains. In places the mountains rise as much as 2000 feet straight up from the water, and the fjord is as deep as 4000 feet in some spots. The mountains northeast of the Sogne Fjord were christened Jotunheimen (home of the giants) by the poet Vinje; they are the highest mountains in Norway. *Jostedal Glacier,* the largest ice and snow area in Europe, can be compared with the gigantic icecap in Greenland. The top is 6686 feet above sea level, the ice is between 1300 and 1600 feet thick, and it covers an area of 385 square miles. Twenty-six glaciers lead down into the valleys. Take the road to **Jostedal** and continue on to **Kroken** to a toll road leading to **Nigardsbre,** where you can play on the glacier. If you have time, go on over the highland tundra to **Lom** and turn west toward **Loen.** On the north side of Jostedal Glacier you can reach the *Briksdalbre Glacier* by turning at Loen. The walk in is about a mile, but worth it for the spectacular view. The glacier rises from an ice-blue lake with small icebergs floating in it. Or, as an alternate expedition, take a ferry to **Flam** across the Sogne Fjord and ride the *Flamsbane,* said to be the most expensively constructed electric railway in the world. Within 12 miles it ascends 3000 feet with a gradient of 1 in 18. There are spectacular views, tunnels, loops, and waterfalls to enjoy.

Sogne Fjord/Hardanger Fjord

Take the ferry from Kaupanger to **Gudvangen** for a magnificent crossing. Gudvangen is at the end of the *Naeroy Fjord,* a branch of the *Aurlands Fjord,* which is in turn a branch of the Sogne Fjord. The approach to Gudvangen is increasingly shadowy and dark as the mountains become higher and closer together. Sheer drops provide more waterfalls than one can count easily; sometimes in the winter the sun is not visible in the fjord. As you leave Gudvangen, upon reaching the top of the gorge, look back at the view of the hairpin turns and amazing drops you have just navigated. Take E68 to **Voss,** an ancient town rich in peasant culture. The oldest standing house in Norway, *Finneloftet,* was built here in 1250. You might be lucky enough to see a wedding procession lining up outside the 13th-century church, with everyone in traditional dress. Northwest of the town there is a ski lift, and the lake provides swimming and sailing. Continue on E68 to **Kvanndal,** where it is very pleasant to camp on the Hardanger Fjord or one of its branches. Campgrounds are located in **Ringoy, Ovre, Eidfjord, Kinsarvik,** and **Lofthus.** (To reach those on the southern shore of the fjord, take the ferry from Kvanndal to Kinsarvik.) Most have marvelous views of the mountains along the fjords. Here you must decide whether you wish to spend more time hiking and exploring the fjords or would prefer city time in **Bergen.** You can reach Bergen for day trips from fjord campsites, or you can find campsites closer to the city on E68.

Kvanndal/Bergen

King Olaf Kyrre founded Bergen in 1070, Germans inhabited it starting in 1236, and commercial development began after 1343 with the rise of the Hanseatic League. Fishing and trade have been the sources of prosperity in Bergen. Artistic talent brought fame to Bergen through Ole Bull and Edvard Grieg in music and Bjornstjerne Bjornson and Henrik Ibsen in literature.

The funicular leading almost straight up the mountain to **Floyen** will give you a marvelous view of the city and the waterfront. The panoramic view must be one of the most beautiful anywhere; it is a perfect spot for lunch. **Bryggen** is composed of wooden warehouses built 250 years ago along the wharf. The houses are long, narrow, timbered, and gabled, all jammed together so that daylight barely has a chance to enter. *Torget* is a fish market at the end of the quay. The *Hanseatic Museum* is also in the same vicinity, with exhibits about the merchants from the 14th to the 17th centuries on display. (You can see a set of scales used when a merchant bought goods and a separate one used when he sold goods.) *Gamle Bergen,* an open-air museum at **Sandviken,** has a number of old houses that had been removed from Bergen proper before a series of fires devastated the city.

Kvanndal/Stavanger

Take the ferry from Kvanndal to Kinsarvik. Drive on 47 to **Skare,** on E76 to **Haugesund,** and on 14 to **Skudeneshavn,** where you can take the ferry to Stavanger. Alternatively, take E76 from Skare to **Roldal** and 520 to **Sauda,** where you can take a longer ferry to Stavanger. (In choosing which route to take, decide how much you want to drive and how much you want to go by sea down the fjords. It is also possible, although more expensive, to take the ferry all the way from Bergen to Stavanger.) You will find a campground in Stavanger and another in **Sandnes,** to the southwest. Others are located farther south on the shore.

STAVANGER, the "Sardine Capital of the World," is one of the oldest towns in Norway. The old town, dating from the ninth century, is a fine collection of gabled houses, cobblestone streets, winding alleys, and busy markets. *Stavanger Museum* houses antiques, exhibits on the natural history of the area, and a nautical museum. *Ledaal Manor,* once the Kielland estate (named for a novelist who died in 1906), is now a royal residence. The *cathedral,* built in the 11th century, is one of two medieval churches in Norway (the other is in **Trondheim**). You can take a boat trip into the *Lyse Fjord* to *The Pulpit* (1800 feet above the fjord) for a spectacular view. Near **Viste** there are cave dwellings from the Stone Age.

Stavanger/Kristiansand

Drive through the plain of **Jaeren,** one of the few flat areas in Norway, on E18 to Kristiansand. King Christian of Denmark founded Kristiansand in 1641. *St. Olov's Cathedral, Christiansholm Fort, Gimle Castle, Mollevann,* a folk museum, and *Kongsgard,* a royal manor turned into a school, are of interest. There are also excellent trout streams in the area. There is a campground in the southeastern part of the city that has fine facilities. Many others are available all along this popular resort shore.

Kristiansand/Arhus

Take the ferry, a 5-hour trip, from Kristiansand to **Hirtshals, Denmark.** Drive on A14 through **Alborg** to **Randers,** then A10 to **Arhus.** There are many campgrounds in Jutland, along the sea as well as in the interior. The sand beaches of Jutland are among the finest in Europe.

ARHUS *Den Gamle By* (the old town) is an open-air museum containing old town houses and shops grouped together to form a village. The shops have trade signs and are equipped with tools of the period. Weekly concerts are given during the summer in the *Cathedral of St. Clement,* which was founded in 1201. This is Scandinavia's longest church and is visible for miles. The *Town Hall,* which opened in 1941, provides a sharp contrast with its unusual architecture, a 200-foot tower, and a great deal of glass. The *University,* founded in 1928, has a 37-acre campus and is interesting architecturally. At **Moresgaard,** south of Arhus, you can see the 1600-year-old Grauballe Man, who was discovered in a peat bog, as well as other exhibits of prehistoric culture. There are also fine beaches nearby for a day of relaxation.

Arhus/Odense

Drive from Arhus to Odense via E3, E67, E66 and A1. Hans Christian Andersen was born in Odense in 1805. Besides visiting the bronze statue in the *Hans Christian Andersen Park* you can visit his birthplace at Hans Jensenstraede 39; this is now a *museum* housing his sketches, correspondence, school notebooks, furniture, clothing, and manuscripts of his fairytales. His childhood home on Munkemollestraed is also open to the public. There is a monument to King Canute in the market square. His bones were interred in a crypt in *St. Knud's Church* after he was murdered by pagans in 1086.

North of Odense, in **Ladby,** is a 1100-year-old Viking ship (72 feet long) that was discovered in 1935. A Viking chief was buried in this ship around A.D. 900 with all his possessions, including 4 dogs, 11 horses, and many jewels. *Den Fynske Landsby,* south of Odense, is an open-air museum containing 19 buildings including an inn, a weaver's house, mill, farm, hospital, and a theater that presents Andersen plays for children in the summer.

Many campgrounds can be found on the island of **Fyn,** all close enough to enjoy Odense.

Odense/Copenhagen

Take E66, a ferry from **Nyborg** to **Korsor,** A1 and A4 into Copenhagen. You may enjoy finishing your tour in a familiar city. There are sure to be pleasures you did not have time for before you left the city, and you may want more time for shopping there.

Our family completed this trip once as a whole and two or three times in sections. We found that 24 days allowed us to finish the entire route, but we spent more time driving than we prefer. As we traveled, we stored memories for more leisurely future trips in our favorite areas. Those who like to explore more slowly would find it pleasant to spend several weeks in one country or region.

Enkhuizen
Volendam
Lelystad
Amsterdam
Den Haag
NETHERLANDS
Utrecht
Arnhem
Bruge
Gent
Antwerpen
Bruxelles
Köln
WEST
GERMANY
BELGIUM
Koblenz
LUXEMBOURG
Bingen
N
Metz
Heidelberg
FRANCE
Heilbronn
Rothenburg
Baden-Baden
Strasbourg
Dinkelsbühl
Freiburg
Konstanz
München
Bern
Zürich
Lausanne
Luzern
Thun
SWITZERLAND
Feldkirch
Garmisch
Genève
Montreux
Interlaken
Chamonix
Lech
Innsbruck
Martigny
Brig
Andermatt
Chur
St. Anton
Salzburg
Verbier
Zermatt
AUSTRIA
ITALY

THE LOW COUNTRIES, THE RHINE, BAVARIA, THE ALPS, AND THE BLACK FOREST

Amsterdam to Koln	270 kilometers
Koln to Koblenz	115 kilometers
Koblenz to Heidelberg	162 kilometers
Heidelberg to Rothenburg	160 kilometers
Rothenburg to Dinkelsbuhl	39 kilometers
Dinkelsbuhl to Munchen	159 kilometers
Munchen to Salzburg	134 kilometers
Munchen to Garmisch	90 kilometers
Garmisch to Innsbruck	49 kilometers
Innsbruck to St. Anton	92 kilometers
St. Anton to Chamonix	256 kilometers
Chamonix to Geneve	83 kilometers
Geneve to Lausanne	63 kilometers
Montreux to Berne	130 kilometers
Berne to Interlachen	55 kilometers
Interlachen to Luzerne	70 kilometers
Luzerne to Zurich	56 kilometers
Zurich to Konstanz	56 kilometers
Konstanz to Baden-Baden	219 kilometers
Baden-Baden to Luxembourg	226 kilometers
Luxembourg to Bruxelles	300 kilometers
Bruxelles to Gent	50 kilometers
Gent to Bruge	43 kilometers
Bruxelles to Anterwerpen	54 kilometers
Anterwerpen to Den Haag	129 kilometers
Den Haag to Amsterdam	43 kilometers

70 The Low Countries, the Rhine, Bavaria, the Alps, and the Black Forest

From Amsterdam: Koln (Cologne), Koblenz, Heidelberg, Rothenburg, Dinkelsbuhl, Munchen, Salzburg, Garmisch-Partenkirchen, Innsbruck, St. Anton, Zermatt, Verbier, Chamonix, Mont Blanc, Geneve, Lausanne, Montreux, Berne, Interlachen, Luzern, Zurich, Konstanz, Schwarzwald, Baden-Baden, Luxembourg, Bruxelles, Gent, Bruge, Antwerpen, Den Haag, Amsterdam.

This trip, beginning in the Low Countries, moving along the Rhine, through Bavaria, and into the Alps before circling back through the Black Forest, has been planned to include a variety of terrain and activity. It covers a lot of ground, but the countries visited are close together and interlaced with motorways for quick, easy travel. Those who wish to explore some areas further or to stop for special interests or sports will find a slower pace particularly rewarding. This itinerary includes several of the most noted cathedrals and universities in Europe, almost undisturbed medieval walled towns, the heart of the Bavarian, Austrian, and Swiss Alps, including ski resorts, climbing and hiking centers, and lakeside cities, touring and walking routes within the Black Forest, one of the oldest spas, and the old cities of the low countries that developed commerce as the western world knows it today. All of this can be circumscribed in a tour of 2876 kilometers in two to three weeks.

Since you cannot expect to become fluent in several languages all at once as you prepare for this trip, take along phrasebooks (or cassettes, if you will have access to a player in your car). If you do speak some German or French, either will serve as a backup language in most regions. Enjoy!

Amsterdam

A city of canals, can be seen and enjoyed best by boat. As the city developed outward, circular canals were added so that cargo could be brought from the Indies into the center of Amsterdam. Most of the tall, slender row houses have a beam extending from just above a large door in the top floor, where a block and tackle was once hooked to haul up goods from the barges below. These gabled houses have a variety of interesting roof shapes, some of them resembling stairsteps, that individualize them; don't forget to look up. Four hundred bridges link the narrow roads between the canals, but traffic is slow and congested.

Amsterdam is really a city for cyclists. Everyone—businesspeople, students, nuns, mothers with babies—cycles. There are special rooms set aside for the storage of bicycles throughout the city, and bikes can be taken on trains and into houses.

In 1204 a castle was built on the site of Amsterdam. In 1578 the city gained its freedom from Spanish domination and began to grow as Gent and Antwerpen declined, doubling its size within a century as trade with the Dutch East Indies grew. From the middle of the 17th to the middle of the 18th centuries, Amsterdam was the center of European commerce until the vast resources of the British Empire shifted power to London. More than a century later, the North Sea Canal (built in 1875) and the Merwede Canal, which connected Amsterdam with the Rhine (completed in 1892), reinforced Amsterdam's advantageous position for trade in modern Europe.

The name *Amsterdam* came from the dam built at the junction of two rivers, the Amstel and the Ij. In one of the wettest places anywhere, a dam was successfully constructed and the main square, called the Dam, was laid out on top of it. The city center is still called the Dam. The **National Monument** to the Dutch victims of World War II is in the center; soil from the 11 provinces of the Netherlands and from Indonesia was placed in 12 urns that stand there. On the west side of the square lies the **Royal Palace,** built in 1665. It is used only for receptions several times a year; the royal family lives in *Soestdijk* near **Utrecht,** a residence that was given to Queen Juliana as a wedding present. In the northwest corner of the Dam is the *Nieuwe Kerk* (New Church), which dates from the 15th century.

In East Amsterdam you will find **Rembrandt's house,** built in 1606, which holds a collection of his drawings and etchings. The **Rijksmuseum,** founded in 1808, contains a collection of old Dutch masters, led by Rembrandt, Steen, de Hooch, Van Dyck, Ruisdal, Hals, and Vermeer. There you may see "The Night Watch," one of the most famous paintings in the world, which Rembrandt completed in 1642. There are also collections of porcelain, earthenware, sculpture, engravings, furniture, stained glass, and much more in the Rijksmuseum. In 1973 the **Van Gogh Museum** opened in a nearby, modern building; it houses an outstanding collection of his work. In an old residential section of Amsterdam, the **Anne Frank House** has been preserved. You can see the bookcase that could be moved out to reveal a tiny stairway leading up to the rooms where Anne Frank wrote her diary while she and her family, Dutch Jews, lived in hiding.

In 1971, after the Royal Dutch Navy had abandoned the ancient arsenal of the Amsterdam Admiralty, which was originally built in 1656, the **Netherlands Maritime Museum (Sheepvaart Museum)** moved in. It is located at Kattenburgerplein 1, right on the water. In the old days the arsenal was used to supply ships under construction in the nearby shipyard with line and sails, navigational instruments, and weapons, as well as food and clothing for the crews. Exhibits trace the notable history of Dutch maritime enterprise in fishing, whaling, overseas commerce, battles at sea, and the evolution of sailing ships and navigation, instruments, and charts. This collection, one of the finest in the world, includes three ships moored below the museum. You may become so engrossed that you lose track of time, as we did, emerging into 20th-century maritime activity on the canal half a day later.

There are many interesting side trips from Amsterdam. The **Kroller-**

Muller Museum, located in *Hoge Veluwe National Park* north of **Arnhem**, is famous for the Van Gogh paintings and drawings on display there; other artists whose works are displayed include Picasso, Mondrian, Seurat, and Braque. There is a modern gallery indoors and a lovely English garden that displays sculpture outdoors.

The world's largest open-air flower exhibition, *De Keukenhof,* is located at **Lisse** (southwest of Amsterdam and south of **Haarlem**). It is open from the end of March until mid-May; displays by bulb-growers cover 70 acres attractively arranged with pools containing black swans, sculptures, a windmill, and many greenhouses on an old estate in a natural woodland setting. There are other bulb fields to be seen all over Holland throughout the spring.

Near **Den Haag** (the Hague) you can visit *Madurodam,* a Holland-in-miniature that contains buildings constructed on a scale of 1 to 25. This fascinating place includes many houses, a harbor with a lighthouse, canals, railroads, an airport, an amusement park with merry-go-rounds and Ferris wheels, windmills, churches, and an opera house. The walking route is 2 miles long and all buildings are numbered.

Authentic old Dutch villages where the townspeople may wear their traditional clothing daily and maintain most of the customs of their forefathers include **Spakenburg, Giethoorn,** and **Staphorst.** Visitors are not as welcome on Sundays in Staphorst because the townspeople are very pious and do not want others to stare as they walk in two separate files to church.

We suggest a circle tour from Amsterdam through the new lands reclaimed from the sea by diking and draining. Begin on A1 to **Muiderberg,** A6 across the bridge to *Muiderstrand,* then turn left to the dike directly on the edge of the water and follow it around to *Oostvaardersdijk.* You will pass *Oostvaardersplassen,* a sanctuary where a variety of birds float in the water and live in the vegetation. When you come to **Lelystad,** stop at the information center, which is located at the edge of the dock area. Continue along the Ijsselmeerdijk until you reach **Kamperhoek,** where you will drive on Ketelmeerdijk to **Ketelhaven.** There you will find the *Museum Voor Scheeps Archeologie,* where there is a continually expanding collection of artifacts brought up during the process of reclaiming land from the old Zuiderzee. Some of the wrecks were brought up with their household inventories intact, largely because the bottom mud of the Zuiderzee is an excellent preservative. You can walk around the wreck of a merchant ship of nearly 30 meters that sank in the middle of the 17th century. You can also learn about modern conservation methods; wrecks are preserved with Polyethyleenglycol after being cleaned with water.

Drive back along Ketelmeerdijk to the bridge across the Ketelbrug, turn right, and drive along the dike on the north side of the Ketelmeer until you see signs for *Schokland Museum.* This museum displays pictures of the area when it was an island, and also describes the process of forming new land.

To the west is the town of **Urk,** once an island in the Zuiderzee and now a port on the edge of the Ijsselmeer, the new "lake" formed from remnants of the old sea. This old fishing harbor has a lighthouse, a fish auction, and a ferry running to **Enkhuizen** across the Ijsselmeer to the west. You can also get to Enkhuizen via the dike from Lelystad.

Enkhuizen has two Gothic churches, a town hall from the 17th century, and the *Zuiderzee Museum.* Inside the museum is a collection of 130 houses and other buildings depicting life and labor in that area dating from 1880. The *Binnenmuseum* nearby exhibits fishing boats, furniture, and decorative pieces. A friend told us the story of the wealthy, miserly lady who ruled this area with an iron hand. When her people were starving and asked her for food, she replied by throwing her ring into the sea, telling them that they would not receive food from her until the ring was retrieved. But the ungenerous never win in fairy tales; in due course a fish was caught, and of course the ring was inside.

From Enkhuizen, continue southwest along the shore of the Merkermeer to **Hoorn,** an ancient shipping center, then to **Volendam,** which may once have been an authentic representation of old Dutch village life, but is now a tourist mecca overlaid with the usual extraneous trappings.

Links

A2 to Utrecht, A12 to Arnhem, A3 to Koln; A2 to Utrecht, A27 and E10 to Antwerpen and Bruxelles, E10, A2, and A1 to Paris; A1 to Bremen, Hamburg, and Puttgarden, ferry to Rodbyhavn, Denmark; **Scheveningen** or **Hoek van Holland** or **Rotterdam** or **Vlissengen** for ferries to England.

KOLN *Koln-Cathedral,* generally regarded as one of the finest in Europe, took 600 years to build. In a few years during World War II it was hit by so many bombs that only the shell remained, but it has now been completely restored. Its 515-foot-high towers completely dominate the entire region and can be seen as you approach from most directions. You can climb up 500 steps to the top of one of the spires for a view of the countryside and the city. Inside, look for the Shrine of the Three Magi, which is a striking gold and silver 12th-century work kept in a glass case behind the altar. The best view of the cathedral can be had from *Rhine Park,* accessible by cablecar as well as by road. Driving in at night on one occasion, tired from travel, we found ourselves wakened and inspired by the sight of this magnificent cathedral looming over the city, with its illuminated towers clearly visible for many miles.

From Koln, you can either drive A3, E5, and A48 to **Koblenz** or choose one of several routes on the west side of the Rhine River to Koblenz. Located at the junction of the Mosel River and the Rhine, this attractive port town has been our choice for a stop several times. It is definitely picturesque, with spires soaring above the town and several gigantic rocky outcroppings enhancing its natural beauty. There are a number of Rhine castles to visit nearby, including **Marksburg**, a castle that looks and feels as a castle should. The dark rooms and sparse, heavy furnishings enclosed in cold rock gave us an immediate sense of the rugged quality of life in hilltop fortresses. While in the area between Koblenz and **Mainz,** you may want to take a steamer trip on the Rhine (leaving your car and returning by train), or at least cross on one of the little car ferries that link east and west banks. The vineyards, rocks, castles, and wooded hills between Koblenz and **Bingen** make this stretch one of the most interesting. You can take 9 along the river on the west bank, or 42 on the east bank to Bingen. You will pass **Lorelei Rock,** where the river narrows and boats encounter whirlpools; perhaps the captains are bewitched by an enchantress who tries to lure them to their doom. From Bingen, continue south on A61 until signs for **Heidelberg.**

HEIDELBERG has a medieval town (enclosed in a larger modern city) with an enormous castle and Germany's oldest university. The castle, which rises above the town and the river, is now in ruins, and there is a rose-tinted cast to the stone; it could be the scene of a romantic operetta and, in fact, *is* during the summer. The castle was first built in the 13th century but was destroyed along with the town in 1689 during the Orleans War. Then, in 1764, the rebuilt castle was struck by lightning and has remained a ruin ever since, but a large part still stands with many interesting rooms, terraces, towers, and gardens to visit. You can also see the **Heidelberg Tun,** a gigantic cask dating from the 18th century. According to legend, its guardian, a dwarf named Perkeo, had a tremendous capacity for wine and was able to drain it to the last drop. In the town you can visit the **Studentenkarzer** (Student's Jail), where rowdy students carved inscriptions, their silhouettes, and coats of arms on the walls. The **Universitatsbibliothek** (Library) contains rare manuscripts, and there is also a beautiful old lecture hall with frescoes and carving preserved in the university.

ROTHENBURG OB DER TAUBER From Heidelberg, either drive the scenic route 37 east to **Heilbronn** or the fast route south on E4 (A5), then east on E12 (A6) to Heilbronn. Continue on E12 to signs for Rothenburg ob der Tauber (A7 may be finished when you get there, otherwise 25 will take you). Rothenburg is one of the favorite "romantic" places to visit in Europe. You may have seen the photograph of the junction of two picturesque streets with their half-timbered buildings and clock tower, called **Plonlein;** now you can take your own photograph. For some of the best views, especially of secluded courtyards, walk around the city on the old wall and climb up into the 197-foot belfry. This small city, with its cramped quarters and crooked streets, will transport you back to town life in the 14th century.

From Rothenburg, head south on 25 to **Dinkelsbuhl,** another charming medieval town that merits an hour or two of strolling on the wide, cobbled streets, climbing the Romanesque tower, and viewing the dungeons in the town hall. Since the 19th century, artists have descended to capture the painted oriel windows that hover over the streets from upper stories, gilt and wrought-iron signs, half-timbered buildings, and gabled roofs. This town is also a photographer's dream.

Continue south on 25 to 2, and AB to **Munchen,** and on to **Salzburg** on the E11 (A8) if you have time for a fascinating side trip, especially for connoisseurs of music.

SALZBURG lies in a beautiful setting on the banks of the Salzach River, with a profile overtopped by huge castle walls. It is also the home of the renowned *Salzburg Music Festival,* which runs from the last week in July through August. Wolfgang Amadeus Mozart was born in Salzburg in 1756; Mozart's *Geburtshaus* at 9 Getreidegasse contains his violins, spinet, letters, and manuscripts.

Hohensalzburg, the 12th-century fortress above Salzburg, provides a fine view of the town. Dancing the Viennese Waltz on the terrace of the Cafe Winkler can be romantic for anyone young at heart. There are many churches to visit in Salzburg, as well as the *Archbishop's Residence* and the *Glockenspiel,* with 17th-century bells, on Residensplatz. Six miles away is *Schloss Hellbrunn,* the summer residence of Archbishop Marcus Sitticus, who, with a delicious sense of humor, created hidden water jets all over the garden to surprise the unwary.

While you are in Bavaria you will undoubtedly see some men wearing the regional costume: leather shorts, a short jacket with horn buttons, and a green hat with a tuft. Some Bavarian women wear dirndl skirts, peasant blouses with puffed sleeves, and an apron. You can bring home these garments for gifts or to wear on special occasions.

GARMISCH-PARTENKIRCHEN From Munchen, take A95 to Garmisch-Partenkirchen, an Alpine sports area; your eye will be immediately struck by the large Bavarian murals painted on houses and hotels. From town, you can take an electric railway and cablecar to the top of the *Zugspitze* for a spectacular view of the Alps and for skiing (winter or spring) or hiking and climbing on a variety of trails on the glacier (summer and fall). The *Olympic Stadiums,* built for the 1936 Olympics, are worth a visit. The *Skistadion,* or ski stadium, has facilities for training as well as competition. *Olympia-Eisstadion* contains three skating rinks and seats 12,000 spectators. Adjacent to that you will find five indoor and one outdoor swimming pool, as well as a solarium. Garmisch has a special charm, whether snow crunches under your feet or the hills are ablaze with wild flowers. In the surrounding forests and hills there are many good walks on well-kept and well-marked trails, where you will almost always find local residents displaying their passion for brisk walking. This is a good place for an extended pause in your travels.

When you do decide to move on, follow signs to **Innsbruck**, around the Zugspitze on one side or the other, either 2 to **Scharnitz** and 313 to Innsbruck or 24, 187, and E6 toward **Seefeld** and Innsbruck.

INNSBRUCK (Bridge over the Inn River), capital of the Tyrol, remains one of our favorite cities anywhere. The beautiful mountains rise straight up from the city, to the north the Alps and to the south the mountains of the Tuxer range. In winter you can ski or ride chairlifts up for the view from a number of locations, including **Seegrube** to **Hafelekar, Igls** to **Patscherkofel, Seefelt,** and **Mutters.** In the summer hiking is available in big doses or small, in combination with the funicular or chairlifts.

At some point you will find youself strolling along the ***Maria-Theresien Strasse,*** the main street. Look toward the north for a striking view of the ***Nordkette,*** which is the Northern Karwendel mountain range. At the southern end of the street is the ***Triumphal Arch,*** built in 1767 by Maria Theresia to commemorate the marriage of Archduke Leopold to Maria Ludovica and the death of Franz I, husband of Maria Theresia, events that occurred at the same time. ***Annesaule*** (St. Anne's Column) is a monument halfway down the street, commemorating the birthday of St. Anne; the Tyrol was liberated from the Bavarians on that day in 1703. At the end of Maria-Theresien Strasse, continue on down Herzog Friedrich Strasse to the end, where you will see ***Goldenes Dachl*** (Little Golden Roof), built by Maximilian with golden coins. He used the balcony as a "royal box" when watching performances or tournaments below. ***Hofburg Palace,*** built by Maria Theresia on the site of an earlier 15th-century palace, contains paintings and ornate furniture. There is a lovely park there patterned after an English garden.

Links

St. Anton–Zurich or Cortina–Venice.

THE ARLBURG To continue along the itinerary, take E17, (A12), and 316 to **St. Anton,** a good base for mountain activities at all seasons. The Arlberg area is known worldwide as the birthplace of modern alpine skiing and the source of the Arlberg technique, which dominated the sport for decades. A system of cablecars interlinks the villages of St. Anton, **Zurs,** and **Lech,** making the area ideal for skiers who want an extended system of runs from a single base, or for hikers and climbers in the summer. There is one run over a very spectacular gorge for half a mile. The open fields at very high altitude are almost completely above the tree line. We enjoyed beautiful spring skiing in bright sun (bring very dark glasses for the flat light); you may need chains on your car (a requirement to drive over some of the passes).

Riding the cablecars, including one that crosses between two peaks high above an intervening valley, can provide a day's entertainment in itself, as well as a moving platform for photographing a mountain panorama. The villages themselves are busy but pleasant, and they are surrounded by chalets scattered about the lower mountainsides that provide a perfect base for exploring the beauties of this whole region.

From the village of St. Anton, cross the Arlberg Pass by road (or take the tunnel) and follow 316 and E17 to **Feldkirch**, 191 and N13 to **Maienfeld**, where you can make a stop if you loved Johanna Spyri's *Heidi*. The Tourist Office in Maienfeld developed "Heidi Wanderweg"—the red Heidi Weg is a short, 1½-hour walk and the green Heidi Weg takes 3 hours to complete. Both routes begin in Maienfeld, then go to **Rofels** (which is "Dorfli" in the book), **Ober Rofels** (where you may recognize the "Heidi House" where Heidi stayed in the winter, now privately owned), **Bofel**, then make a right turn on the green trail up to the goatherd Peter's hut, and finally to the grandfather's hut. The meadows, the pines, and the clear, crisp mountain air will make *Heidi* live on in your imagination. In **Jenins** there is a *Heidi Fountain* that was built with funds collected from Swiss children to commemorate the 125th anniversary of Johanna Spyri's birth.

Continue on N13 past **Chur**, 19 to **Andermatt** and **Brig**, 9 to **Sion** and **Martigny**—a drive along the valley bottom overhung by giants among the Alps. There are many, many beautiful mountain resorts accessible from this route—including **Davos, Zermatt, Verbier**, and **Chamonix**.

ZERMATT (SWITZERLAND): Spectacular views of the *Matterhorn;* three different areas, serviced by lifts, ranging from sunny, open snowfields facing the Matterhorn to skiing under the base of it; a very picturesque village with only sleigh or foot traffic, remote from the noise and confusion of the 20th century; you will leave your car below Zermatt (in an area that is plowed and easy to drive to) and take a cog railway up to Zermatt; doing without a car is worth it when you gaze at that amazing hunk of rock in all weather and from various angles.

VERBIER (SWITZERLAND): a huge high bowl facing in three directions, with the village at the bottom so it is possible to follow the sun throughout the ski day; many convenient lifts with frequent bus service free with your lift ticket; intermediate skiing in a high bowl at high altitude; expert skiing in many sections of the bowl; fine beginners' slopes at the edge of the village; *Mt. Zele,* an area for experts, serviced by a cablecar up to what seems like the top of the world; you can see into Italy and France from the station perched on a cliff, as well as ski into those countries.

From Martigny, take N9 to **Montreaux.** On the way, you can visit the **Chateau de Chillon,** where Francois Bonivard, who displeased the Duke of Savoy, was cast into the dungeons and lived chained to a pillar for four years. Byron visited the castle in 1816 and wrote the lyrical poem about Bonivard that made the castle famous.

Chamonix, located along N506 southwest from Martigny is another in the spring of renowned mountain resorts along this itinerary. One of the most cosmopolitan resorts in Europe, Chamonix lies at an altitude of 1037 meters in a high mountain valley. There are a number of cablecars to ride all over this spectacular area under the shadow of **Mont Blanc;** one of them, the **Aigle du Midi,** will take you 2800 meters to the top of Mont Blanc in the most touted cablecar ride in Europe, a ride so high that a jet once hit the cable by mistake! From here, B41 will take you to **Geneve** and N1 or 1 along the north shore of **Lac Leman** will rejoin the itinerary at Montreux.

GENEVE Lake dwellers chose the site of **Geneve** for their home as early as 4000 to 5000 B.C. The left bank of the River Rhone became the center of the town. In the fifth century, Geneve became a bishopric, the **Cathedral of St. Pierre** was built between the 10th and 13th centuries. John Calvin arrived in 1536, turning the city away from entertainment to rigid austerity during the Reformation. Geneve is now the home of the International Red Cross, the International Labor Office, and the World Health Organization. It is a cosmopolitan and international center of world renown.

In a lovely setting on Lac Leman is the **Palais des Nations,** which was originally the home of the League of Nations; notice the beautifully sculptured sphere in front. You may want to wander around the cobblestone streets of the **Old Town.** It surrounds the Cathedral of St. Pierre, which is plain but impressive. You can climb the north tower for a view of the entire region—Geneve, the **Jura Mountains,** Lac Leman, and the Alps. During the summer, concerts and plays are performed in the courtyard of the **Hotel de Ville,** a 16th-century building. You can also take boat trips to **Nyon,** a lovely town with a medieval castle, or to the Chateau de Chillon.

From Montreux, continue around Lac Leman on N1, the fast road, or 1, beside the lake, to **Vevey,** then take N12 to **Bern,** the city of bears. Don't miss a visit to **Barengraben** to see some live symbols of this city. During the 11th century, the Duke of Zahringen agreed to name the new town after the first wild animal captured during a hunt, so a bear now graces the coat of arms of the city.

From Bern, drive south on N6 to **Thun,** which commands a lovely view of the Bernese Alps. You can take a boat trip on this lake surrounded by mountain meadows and perhaps climb the **Niederhorn** for a panoramic view. Drive on to **Interlaken,** the town filling the isthmus between **Thuner See** and **Brienzer See,** which is one of the most popular summer resorts in Switzerland. Follow 6 or N8 northeast to **Luzern.**

LUZERN's old town charms us with its many painted buildings, squares, and ancient walking bridges, including two with painted triangular panels under the roof. Since the city center is on a small scale, park your car in Bahnhofparking, where there is a large underground lot, and enjoy the day on foot. As you leave the parking area and cross the street toward the river, you will come upon a fine view of a covered bridge with a water tower to photograph. Take time to enjoy the bird sanctuary built into the corner of the road, bridge, and quay. It has a large wire cage that birds can fly into and out of at will; stone arches, houses, and roosts have been built for their pleasure. Farther along the quay there are floating pens for paddling and diving and a walkway with more houses to shelter them. We saw quite a variety of ducks and swans happily splashing about. Also along this quay is a flower, fruit, and vegetable market that is held on several days each week. Stroll along farther to see the *Jesuits' Church,* which can be identified by two towers with domed belfries. Inside, the effect of red marble pillars and painted frescoes on walls and ceiling against a white background is quite dramatic. The church was completed in 1663 and renovated in 1980.

Cross the river on *Spreuerbruck,* a covered bridge also known as Mills Bridge. Panels that represent the Dance of Death march down the bridge in the V of the roof. These skeletal figures interact with citizens of the city in each panel. As you wander around the old town you will spot the *Muhlenplatz,* dating from the 16th century, which was the site of markets. The *Weinmarkt,* with a Gothic fountain in the center, features St. Maurice, the patron saint of soldiers. Buildings around the square are decorated with paintings representing the guilds they once housed.

After wandering around in the old town you can cross the river again on the *Kapellbrucke,* (Chapel Bridge), another covered bridge built in 1800; it is supposed to be the oldest covered bridge in the world still in daily use. The paintings depict scenes from Swiss history and the life of St. Leodegar, who is the patron saint of Luzern. There is a 13th-century octagonal water tower beside this bridge, *Wasserturm,* to lend the perfect touch for photographic composition. As you enjoy the views, you will catch glimpses of the *Musegg Wall,* built in the 12th century, and the Town Hall, *Altes Rathaus,* built around 1600; the latter overlooks the Kornmarkt. If you are so inclined, stop for a fondue lunch in one of the many restaurants.

Mount Pilatus overlooks Luzern; you can take a cog railway or an aerial lift to the top of the 7000-foot summit. The panoramic view is lovely, whether or not you believe the local proverb: "When Pilate hides his head, sunshine below will spread; when Pilate's head is bare, of rain beware."

Mark Twain wrote of the *Lowendenkmal,* "the Dying Lion of Lucerne," as "the saddest and most poignant piece of rock in the world." It was erected in 1819 to honor the Swiss guardsmen who died in Paris during the French Revolution. The inscription above the 9-meter lion, poignantly simple, reads: "Dedicated to Swiss loyalty and courage."

The *Gletschergarten* (Garden of Glaciers), was discovered in 1872; it represents 20 million years of geological history from the time when Luzern was covered by a layer of ice. There are 32 "giants' potholes" hollowed out and polished by water falling through the ages. One of them is 29 feet deep. The museum contains prehistoric artifacts, a model of Luzern in 1792, antique furniture and furnishings, and a variety of changing exhibits.

The *Swiss Transport Museum* contains many original vehicles, models, dioramas, and exhibits, including early railway locomotives, carriages, motorcycles, bicycles, vintage airplanes, and boats. And the *Longines Planetarium* offers an interesting program of astronomical demonstrations.

When you have enjoyed the city's sights and museums, follow the shore road, 2, northeast around the lake to **Kussnacht,** where you will see signs to *Astridkapelle,* a chapel that marks the place where Queen Astrid of Belgium was killed in an automobile accident in 1935. The queen, who was very much loved by the Belgians, met her death when the royal car plunged into an orchard.

From Kussnacht, take the north shore road, 21, to **Greppen** and **Weggis,** a quiet resort village wedged between lake and mountain meadows. While taking an early morning walk here, we chanced upon a plaque with this inscription quoting Mark Twain: "This is the most charming place I have ever lived." It is indeed beautiful, a landscape meadowed with fruit and walnut trees, marked by chalets and set off by the azure blue of the lake and the mountains all around. It is a perfect place for early morning walks or jogs up into the meadows and down through a village just coming to life.

There are a number of attractive villages tucked under the mountain along this shore including **Vitznau, Gersau,** and **Brunnen.** At Vitznau you can take the rack-railway up to climb the *Rigi-Kulm.* Built in 1871, this railway was the first mountain railway constructed in Europe. There is also a modern cablecar to the top of the range at Weggis. Another interesting landmark is a large rock called *Obere Nase,* or "nose," which is located between Vitznau and Gersau.

At the end of the lake you can visit *Tellskapelle,* the William Tell chapel. After the dramatic scene with the apple, William Tell was taken by boat onto the lake. When a violent storm swooped down on the lake the bailiff needed the help of his captive; William Tell took this opportunity to steer the boat to shore, jump out, and shove the boat back into the lake.

From Brunnen, continue the itinerary by taking N4 and 4 to Zurich.

ZURICH, located between wooded slopes at the end of the Zurich See, is the largest commercial and industrial center in Switzerland. Modern buildings and banks line the *Bahnhofstrasse,* which is the business center of Zurich. You can stroll along the quays by the water and through lovely gardens set against a backdrop of boats. The *cathedral,* dating from the 11th century, was originally founded by Charlemagne as a collegiate church, and it contains his statue in the south tower. Don't miss the stained-glass windows by Augusto Giacometti. The *Fraumunster,* built in the 12th century, has stained-glass windows by Marc Chagall. The most exciting museum is the *Swiss National Museum,* a gigantic building housing collections of prehistoric and Roman artifacts as well as tapestries and frescoes, altarpieces, and fine furniture. The Treasury displays a wealth of silver and gold. Each canton in Switzerland is represented by an exhibit of local costumes. Entire rooms patterned after 16th- and 17th-century life have been developed, complete with stained-glass windows, paneled ceilings, tapestries, and painted walls. The fine arts museum, *Kunsthaus,* contains works by Picasso, Matisse, Utrillo, Degas, Cezanne, Renoir, and Toulouse-Lautrec. There is also a large collection by Marc Chagall. Another exhibit features the work of Alberto Giacometti.

There are a number of pleasant excursions into the country from Zurich. Head to **Uetliberg,** on the steepest standard-gauge adhesion railway in Europe from Selnau station for a view of the Zurich area from the belvedere tower, up 167 steps. On a clear day you can see the *Jura Mountains* to the west, the *Vosges* to the northwest, the *Jungfrau* to the southwest, and the *Santis* to the east. Or you can take a train from **Uetliberg** to **Adlisuil** and an aerial cableway to **Felsenegg.** If you head to **Kilchberg,** west of Zurich, you will pass through an elegant residential area. Thomas Mann, who died in 1955, is buried in the cemetery there. Boat trips of varying lengths are available on the lake; you can go out for several hours, half a day, or an evening excursion. Inquire at the landing at Burkliplatz. A funicular, the Polybahn, runs from the square near the main station to the Poly terrace, where there is a view of the city and the Alps. This is used by students at the Federal Institute of Technology and the University of Zurich.

LAKE OF KONSTANZ From Zurich, N1 and N7 will take you almost all the way to Konstanz (perhaps the new road will be completed soon). The **Bodensee,** or Lake of Konstanz, is 64 kilometers long and 13 across at its widest point. It is bordered by three German-speaking countries: Switzerland, West Germany, and Austria. Lunch along the promenade beside the lake in Konstanz is pleasant. Originally a fishing hamlet, it became a fortress in Roman times, and then a center for the Holy Roman Empire. The *Rosgartenmuseum,* on Rosgartenstrasse, was built by the butcher's guild in the 15th century. The building itself is interesting, with paneling and leaded glass windows, and the art collection includes pewter, silver, wooden carvings, engravings, and pottery. The *Munster* has a single spire with a baroque pulpit inside. The Isle of Mainau, *Insel Mainau,* is a tropical garden containing a baroque palace and church, owned and operated by the Swedish Bernadotte family. The botanical garden contains an array of flowering shrubs, exotic trees, and flowers.

You can take a ferry from Konstanz to *Meersburg,* West Germany, a little village that combines the medieval, renaissance, and baroque. The ancient streets, with their half-timbered buildings, are enhanced by the *Marktplatz,* the *Rathaus,* and the *Obertor,* which is a tall gate. There are two castles to visit. The Old Castle, *Asltes Schloss,* dating from the seventh century, has a moat, dungeons, and a collection of arms. The New Castle, *Barockschloss,* was built in rococo style, designed by Balthasaar Neumann. You can attend concerts there in the summer.

Take the coast road along the Bodensee, E121, which winds through rolling hills and connects with 31 to **Neustadt** and **Titisee.**

SCHWARZWALD This area is a good choice for establishing a base in the Schwarzwald (Black Forest). You can hike in the mountains and enjoy watersports on the lake, or cycle on the well-paved hilly roads. The landscape is spotlessly neat, the meadows look manicured, and there is not a scrap of paper lying around anywhere. The Black Forest is a lovely, peaceful place for a true vacation. We chose to drive on secondary roads, including 500, which meanders up into the rolling meadows, past pine forests, grazing sheep, houses and barns all in one, with gigantic sloping roofs (called Alemannian houses), tiny chapels, and tiny villages like **St. Margen** and *St. Peter.* Inside the buildings we found a variety of folk art, especially paintings on furniture and walls done during the long winter months. We emerged from the forest near **Freiburg,** which was founded by the Zahrign family in the early 12th century. This trading center specialized in the mining of silver and bronze. Marie Antoinette was the recipient of lovely garnet jewelry mined from this spot. The *cathedral,* with its twin spires, dates from 1200. Inside, the choir is full of beautiful art treasures, including stained-glass windows. After finishing your visit, continue on to the *Augustinermuseum,* which is one of the finest art museums in all of Germany. Don't miss the chapel, with its wooden carvings and paintings. From Freiburg, E4 will take you north to **Baden-Baden,** one of the most fashionable spas in Europe.

BADEN-BADEN The Romans named it *Aqua Aurelia,* from the mineral springs they enjoyed. Caracalla, who had developed baths in Rome as well, was the last Roman emperor to rule Aqua Aurelia. In the third century local Germans, the Alemanni, reigned. During the early Middle Ages, the Christian Franks conquered the town, built the first castle there, and renamed it Baden-Baden. The Dukes of Zahringer, rulers of Freiburg, seized control and moved into the castle. While the golden era was in full swing in the 17th century in Bath, England, Baden-Baden was being reconstructed after the devastating Thirty Years' War. It came into its full glory early in the 19th century as a popular watering place, with the added attraction of a casino. Visitors came from all over Europe, the arts flourished with the music of Brahms, who lived in town, and Dostoyevsky, who came to write and to gamble. People still enjoy coming to this elegant resort set in a lush, green valley at the edge of the Black Forest.

The *casino,* designed by Charles Sechan, is in the neoclassic style of the early 19th century with tall, white columns. Inside, the rooms will make you think you are in a French palace, with styles ranging from Louis XIII through the Napoleonic era. Don't miss the Louis XIII Hall of a Thousand Candles, an ornate room done in gold.

If you are interested in the thermal baths, the *Trinkhalle* is right next door to the casino. There you can drink the waters, or grape juice, to make you feel rejuvenated. At the other extreme is the modern *Augustabad,* built in 1966, which offers underwater jet baths, mudpacks, a sauna, and a sun terrace on the roof.

There are museums to visit, including two housed in the *New Palace* (new that is, as compared to the old one, now in ruins). The *Zahringer Museum* is one you shouldn't miss. It has a fine collection of portraits, porcelain, silver, crystal, and furniture. The house Brahms lived in for 10 summers, beginning in 1865, is located at Maximilianstrasse 5. Nearby is the convent, *Kloster Lichtenthal;* you can visit the *Klosterkirche* and look around in the retail shop run by the sisters, where they sell items they have made, including liqueurs.

There are two castles to visit nearby. *Schloss Favorite,* northeast of Baden-Baden, is an 18th-century baroque palace. Don't miss the porcelain collection and the hall of mirrors. Concerts are given there in the summer; you can have lunch in the restaurant. *Schloss Neuweier,* southwest of Baden-Baden, contains a collection of shields, armor, and weapons.

If you have time, take the 40-mile scenic tour into the Black Forest, going out on the high route along the ridge, *Schwarzwald-Hochstgrasses* (Route 500) and returning in the valley on the *Schwarzwaldtalerstrasse* (Route 462). You can stop to take a walk to picturesque overlooks, enjoy a swim in a pool, and have lunch in one of the fine restaurants to complete your excursion. If you have a meal, try some of the local wine: The white wines produced in the Baden area are fresh and light.

LUXEMBOURG From Baden-Baden, head south on E4 to E11 to **Strasbourg,** then take A4 to **Metz** and A3 to Luxembourg. Encircled by France, Germany, and Belgium, this tiny country looks like something out of a fairy tale, with its medieval castles and quaint villages.

In 963 Count Siegfroid of Ardennes seized control of the ruins of a Roman fort, a prime position for defense on a cliff overlooking the Alzette River. The fortress was restored; city and country expanded around it. This "Gibraltar of the North" has consciously sought to remain independent rather than becoming a province of any surrounding country.

If you're hooked on sports, you can find superb fishing as well as boating, hiking, riding, and bicycling here. The city makes a fine base for traveling to the surrounding countryside, and provides gastronomic treats with a variety of cuisines from the adjoining countries.

A new road is being constructed between Luxembourg and Bruxelles; check your map for the latest progress on A4 and E40. The E5 road from Bruxelles will take you to **Gent,** a lovely old Belgian city with medieval architecture and narrow streets. Located on a number of islands in the Lys and Scheldt Rivers, Gent contains several castles, a seventh-century *abbey,* and many museums. Boat trips are available from Vleeshuisbridge and Korenlei.

Farther along E5 is another picturesque medieval city: **Bruges.** The special appeal of this city lies in its handsome gabled buildings, canals that are attractively flood-lit at night, a market, churches, and a number of galleries and museums. I remember the canals as a romantic place to stroll under the stars from a trip 32 years ago; the lace industry was thriving then and women wearing tall lace hats added to the scene.

The N617 road (partially completed at this writing), will take you on to Antwerpen, E10 and A16 to Rotterdam, and A13 to the government center of **Den Haag** and its adjoining beach resort of **Scheveningen.** You may be ready for some time on a beach; this resort has a promenade along beautiful, fine sand. When you've had enough sun and surf you can return to Amsterdam on A4.

We have traveled this basic route in 21 days with young children; with two teenagers, we traversed a similar route in 22 days; in our youth we stretched it out to 35 days, including a fair amount of seasonal sports. You may find it reasonable to plan more activity in some areas, cutting out others. On the other hand, for a once-in-a-lifetime trip, you may choose to see and do as much as possible. This route resembles part of the "Grand Tour" of days gone by—fun to read about before you go and exhilarating to travel.

THE SOUTHEAST MEDITERRANEAN

YUGOSLAVIA	
Venezia to Trieste	146 kilometers
Trieste to Opatija	77 kilometers
Rijecka to Zadar	225 kilometers
Zadar to Split	161 kilometers
Split to Dubrovnik	221 kilometers
GREECE	
Igoumenitsa to Delfi	383 kilometers
Delfi to Athine	142 kilometers
Athine to Korinthos	86 kilometers
ITALY	
Brindisi to Napoli	380 kilometers
Napoli to Roma	220 kilometers
Roma to Assisi	149 kilometers
Assisi to Siena	150 kilometers
Siena to Firenze	68 kilometers
Firenze to Pisa	93 kilometers
Pisa to Rapallo	157 kilometers
Rapallo to Milano	169 kilometers
Milano to Verona	160 kilometers
Verona to Venezia	110 kilometers

From Venezia: Trieste; Yugoslavia's Dalmatian Coast: Opatija, Zadar, Trogir, Split, Dubrovnik; Greece: Corfu, Delfi, Athine, Peloponissos, Crete, Santorini, Paros; Italy: Brindisi, Paestum, Amalfi, Sorrento, Capri, Pompei, Napoli, Roma, Spoleto, Assisi, Siena, Firenze, Pisa, Rapallo, Portofino, Milano, Verona, Ravenna, Venezia

We chose to begin the Southeast Mediterranean Circuit in Venezia because it is convenient to reach from any of the adjoining countries. However, you may prefer to begin this circle route somewhere else, or

Milano
Verona
Trieste
Venezia
Rijeka
Opatija
Krk
Cres
Genoa
Parma
Rapallo
Bologna
Zadar
YUGOSLAVIA
Pisa
Firenze
Trogir
Split
Siena
Hvar
Assisi
Todi
Spoleto
Terni
ADRIATIC SEA
Dubrovnik
Roma
ITALY
Igoumenitsa
Kerkira
AEGEAN SEA
GREECE
Napoli
Bari
Salerno
Alberobello
Fasano
Ostuni
Brindisi
Capri
Sorrento
Potenza
Battipaglia
TYRRHENIAN SEA
Delfi
Patras
Athine
Piraeaus
Korinthos
Nafplion
ICNIAN SEA
Paros
Thira
Rethimnon
Iraklion
Kritsa
Agios Nikolaos

to limit yourself to a convenient section of the trip. You might want to spend more time in Yugoslavia, traveling inland to Mostar and Sarajevo, for example. You could easily spend several more weeks exploring the Greek islands and the Peloponnese. We found a car useful even in touring the islands we chose to visit, but to arrange this you must allow extra time to fit your car into ferry schedules, which can be done if you don't mind an extra day or two on a gorgeous island. There are many possibilities for variation in traveling through Italy. We have chosen a route that takes you to our favorite places, but you can make other selections and cross the boot easily.

VENEZIA Although the early history of Venezia is obscure, the earliest settlers may have been Romans seeking refuge from their Lombardian conquerors in the islands of the lagoons. The first doge was probably Paulucius Anafestus in the eighth century A.D. In A.D. 809 King Pepin, the son of Charlemagne, sailed up into the lagoons but was repulsed. By 819 Angelus Participotius, the doge at that time, was living on the site of the present Palace of the Doges. Venezia was growing and developing as a link between the Byzantine and Franconian empires to the east and west. In 828 the body of St. Mark was brought to Venezia; his symbol, the winged lion, was taken over, and St. Mark became the protector of the town. During the Crusades, Venezia made many conquests and became one of the most important of Italian powers. Marco Polo returned from his travels with riches in the late 13th century. Venezia was at its height of naval and mercantile power in the 15th century until the discovery of America and new sea routes to India changed the pattern of world trade and brought decline to sea routes in the Mediterranean.

The relationship between Oriental commerce and the art of Venezia is evident. **St. Mark's Cathedral** is an example of Byzantine style, and mosaics throughout the city reveal that influence. From the 11th century to the 13th century, the architecture developed from closer Lombard-Romanesque sources, and from Gothic styles during the 14th and 15th centuries. In the last half of the 15th century the famous school of Venetian painting began to develop with Bellini, Giorgione, and Carpaccio. During the later Renaissance Titan, Veronese, and Tintoretto flourished there.

Venezia lies almost 3 miles from the mainland in a lagoon protected from the sea by long sand-hills or *lidi*. Much as we might wish it otherwise, the sea is gradually destroying Venezia; there are floods every year and Venezia is slowly sinking. It used to be the custom to recognize this dependence on the sea. Every year on Ascension Day the doge, elaborately dressed in gold, would sail out and throw a ring into the sea, saying, "We wed thee, Sea, in token of our perpetual rule." Voltaire commented that the marriage was not valid without the consent of the bride.

The most interesting and efficient way to explore Venezia is by water. You can take a *vaporetto* (water bus), a ferry, a water taxi, or a gondola, depending on where you want to go. You can have a fine tour of the **Grand Canal** at little cost by taking Line 1 of the *vaporetto*. In a gondola, you can poke into narrow back canals, with or without the romantic trappings of commentary or serenade by the gondolier. (Be sure to bargain for your gondola hire before you step in, and hold to it when you pay. Then relax and enjoy your trip in one of the most graceful and efficient boats ever designed.)

Most visitors spend some time in **Piazza San Marco,** a gigantic square bordered by elaborate arcades sheltering shops and cafes on three sides, facing the **Basilica San Marco.** You may want to pick up mail at American Express just off the square, collect some tourist guides and information, and settle down for a leisurely cup of espresso in an open-air cafe while enjoying the view. The Basilica, or Church of Gold, was originally built to hold the remains of St. Mark. In the Byzantine style, St. Mark's is a dazzling example of mosaic and marble combined. The facade is built around five doorways with a number of columns in between them, a gallery above, and one gigantic dome and four smaller ones on top. Inside, the mosaic work glitters with gold and brilliant colors. The famous **Pala d'Oro** (gold altarpiece), made in 976 in Constantinople, contains diamonds, emeralds, rubies, and topaz. The **Treasury** contains the spoils of the Crusades and relics such as bones, skulls, goblets, and chalices. Up in the gallery is the **Marciano Museum,** which exhibits mosaics and tapestries. Outside, you can have a close-up view of the Bronze Horses, taken to Paris by Napoleon and returned after the fall of the French Empire. Climb (or ride an elevator) up the adjoining **campanile** for a panoramic view of Venezia.

The **Palazzo Ducale** (Doges' Palace), built with pink and white marble in a geometric pattern above a Gothic gallery, looks like a gigantic birthday cake. It has a horseshoe shape around a courtyard adorned with sculpture. Inside, you will see treasures of painting and sculpture, including works by Bellini, Titian, Veronese, and Tintoretto. The full tour of all the reception rooms, halls, and courts used in the administration of this city-kingdom is well worth the time. The **Bridge of Sighs** unites the palace with the prison, and gave prisoners a last glimpse of the Grand Canal as they passed over it to incarceration or death.

The much-photographed **Clock Tower** on the piazza features two Moors, carved in bronze, who have been striking the hour for 500 years. Below them on the tower stands the winged lion, the emblem of Venezia, and below the lion, the Virgin and Child in copper. You can also climb this tower for an unobstructed view of the city.

There are many churches, schools, museums, and bridges to see, but you may prefer to just wander at will. It is easy and pleasant to be lost in Venezia, even with map in hand. Each alley and square brings new discoveries, and some of the finest palazzi can be seen only from the canals. The most ardent shoppers will find more to look at than they can manage or afford, and world watchers will enjoy the small cafes overlooking squares and canals. You may also want to spend time on the beaches of **Lido,** or take a boat trip to **Murano** to see glassblowers at work, to **Burano,** famous for lacemaking, or to **Torcello.**

Among the literary works about Venezia are Goethe's *Italian Journey,* Ruskin's *The Stones of Venice,* Henry James's *The Aspern Papers,* and Thomas Mann's *Death in Venice.*

Yugoslavia

From Venezia, take A4 and S202 to **Trieste.** Although the road to Yugoslavia is not well signed, if you follow signs to **Basovizza,** you will eventually come to the border. *American citizens need a visa to enter Yugoslavia;* we chose to get our visas in advance to avoid any delay in case the border office was closed for any reason. As you cross the border, read the current regulations on foreign currency carefully; in some cases, it is not possible to exchange dinars as you leave the country unless you buy convertible Yugo checks. As you estimate the amount of money you will need in Yugoslavia, remember that food, accommodation, and many other items are unbelievably inexpensive. After our first trip through a supermarket we refigured our conversion, thinking we had made a mistake, because our bill was so small. We considered with glee the choice of saving much more on our travel budget than we had estimated by camping and cooking, or living it up by eating out and staying in hotels; we compromised and chose to enjoy both a little pampering and a considerable saving for a future adventure. You can buy gasoline coupons for your car at the border; although the saving is much smaller than it is in Italy, where coupons are essential, they are worth purchasing. Because English is taught as a second language in schools, most Yugoslavians (other than some of the elderly) speak English.

We were fascinated by the distinctive geological features of the Dalmation coast including, in the northern section, many vegetable gardens located in the bottoms of circles. The karstic (irregular limestone) rock is porous, allowing water to sink through crevices leading to underground caves and rivers. When some of the caves collapse, they leave circular depressions (called dolines or polje), which then fill up with the runoff from scanty topsoil, making them very fertile. Rivers also flow into certain holes, called ponori, and out on the other side, depositing soil. These become lakes in times of heavy precipitation, so the farmers need to be careful to get their crops out before flooding begins. Most of the rivers along this mountainous coast do not reach the sea above ground, but rather as underground rivers and springs. The **Dinaric Mountain Range** has always been a barrier sealing off the coast from inland Yugoslavia. As you drive farther south you will notice more "naked" karstic rock. As forests were demolished, the rock was exposed and the topsoil washed down the slopes, revealing the white limestone underneath. This is a desolate, but fascinating barren coastline, with its striking white rock set against the blue sea. Obviously agriculture is limited here; the inhabitants derive their living from the more fertile sea.

From the border, take E63 (M12) to **Opatija**. The city and the coast heading southwest, called the *Opatija Riviera,* extends for 30 kilometers, linking Opatija with several smaller towns from **Moscenicka Draga** to **Volosko**. This area is sheltered from the cold north winds prevalent along the coast by *Mount Ucka;* the foliage is subtropical, green, and lush. In 1844 a wealthy businessman from **Rijeka**, named Scarpa, built a vacation villa there, the *Villa Angiolina.* Nobles from the Austrian and Hungarian courts were attracted by the climate and beauty. In 1860 the Austrian Empress Maria Anna came to stay in Scarpa's villa to take a sea cure. Viennese doctors recommended this area, with its "high concentration of ozone," as a beneficial health spa. The Villa Angiolina is located in a botanical garden, where you can see trees and plants from all over the world.

Opatija offers boating, tennis, and magnificent walking on the 12-kilometer-long coastal path built on the sea side of old coastal villas. The beaches are shingle because the coastline contains enormous slabs of rock; in the center of town there is a beach of imported sand, which is crowded in the summer. Many cultural events, including folk dancing, concerts, ballet, and opera, take place in season.

After dallying in Opatija as long as you can, drive past Rijeka, Yugoslavia's largest shipping center. The road takes you around a horseshoe bend that gives you a clear view looking down on many ships being repaired in dry dock. Unhappily, there is also an oil refinery to pollute the seascape. Along this section of coast there are many almost totally barren islands, stark piles of rock in the azure sea. The islands **Krk**, near the shore, and **Cres**, farther out and large, can be visited by ferry; another island farther south, **Rab**, can be reached by ferry from **Senj**.

Senj is one of the most interesting mainland towns along this northern section of the Dalmation coast. In 1615 the citizens of Senj caused a war between Venezia and Austria. They had been involved in piracy for many years, threatening Venetian maritime interests, so the Venetians solved the problem by transporting them inland. By 1617 all of the pirates had been rounded up and taken to the center of Croatia to begin a new life as farmers.

Most of the historic buildings in Senj were destroyed during World War II, but the *cathedral,* dating from the 11th century, was restored in 1947. There is a 15th-century stone tabernacle inside. The *Vukasovic Palace* was built in the 15th century, as well; there is an exhibit of the history of Senj in the museum there. Don't miss *Nehaj Castle,* on the hill, which was built in 1558 by General Ivan Lenkovic, and nicknamed "Fear Not." One of the interesting meteorological phenomena of this coast is the bora, a violent mountain wind that can be wild in this section, especially during the winter months. Driving along the coastal road under those conditions would be unpleasant.

As you drive in this region, you will be struck by the cracked and dry limestone rock that lends a moonlike quality to the landscape. There is almost no vegetation to soften the majesty of rock spires tilting toward the sea. The building of the coastal highway in the 1960s must have been a courageous engineering feat. Much of the road is lined with rock walls, built of small rocks, holding up the edge of the highway and preventing erosion; the number of man hours it took to build these must have been staggering. There are no shoulders—just the sharp edge of the pavement and a drop on the sea side, but the road is well designed and surfaced; with reasonable care you will not come anywhere near the edge.

Continue on to **Zadar,** an old seaport city enclosed by walls; park your car outside the walls in one of the parking lots and go into the old town on foot. Zadar was first inhabited during the Neolithic period, later the Illyrians used it as an important seaport; it has been a Roman municipium, a Byzantine capital, a Croation city, a Venetian port, and a part of Napoleon's Illyrian province. It was controlled by the Austro-Hungarian Empire until 1920, when it was ceded to Italy. In 1943 and 1944 it was occupied by German troops until October, when Partisan (National Liberation Army) forces arrived.

A number of Roman ruins are visible as you walk around town. We were told that during the cleanup after World War II, the houses that had been destroyed had covered many of these ruins. Southwest of the cathedral are the remains of the *Roman forum.* There is a tall column still standing; apparently, it was used as a pillory during medieval times. Nearby is the *Square of Five Wells.*

The *cathedral* dates from the 12th century; it is considered to be the most beautiful and the largest church in Dalmatia. It is an example of pure Romanesque architecture; there are five Roman arches in the main door and two Romanesque marble thrones in the chancel. Saint Anastasia, the patroness of weavers and a patron saint of Zadar, was martyred in the fourth century. It is thought that she was persecuted by Diocletian; her stone sarcophagus is to the left of the high altar.

Sveti Donat (St. Donatus's Church) dates from the ninth century. A number of Roman fragments can be seen in this remarkable building. Saint Donatos was an Irishman who went to Fiesole when the old bishop died and became known as Donatus of Fiesole. This circular church has three semicircular apses that contain blind arches and some small windows. There is a museum inside.

From the old town, drive across the river and continue past **Sibenik,** which is an industrial area, to **Primosten,** once an island but now connected to the mainland by bridge. The church and the red-roofed buildings in town provide a photographer's dream. This old fishing harbor is now an attractive resort area; the beaches are shingle and rock, with some imported sand. Yachtsmen are attracted by a marina in a sheltered bay, with a good location near excellent cruising waters in the Kornat archipelago. Vineyards in the area also provide very pleasant wine.

One of our favorite places, **Trogir,** is several hours farther south along the coast road. We have returned several times to explore this ancient town. It is located on an island connected by bridge to the mainland on one side and to the island of **Ciovo** on the other. It is a popular place for yachtsmen to gather; we saw yachts from Italy, France, Germany, and Sweden tied up at the quay. Never needing an excuse to peruse handsome vessels, we spent some time looking at the latest roller-reefing gear inside the boom on a French boat. One of the crews wore matching royal blue jackets and pants, ready to sail in the ocean racing circuit.

Trogir was inhabited over 50,000 years ago by Neanderthal Man; his tools were found in the ***Mujima Cave,*** located nearby in the Trapina Valley. Other prehistoric artifacts have been found in the fields and hills around Trogir. Inside Trogir, excavation has produced remnants from prehistoric Greek and Illyrian civilizations. You can see a famous piece of art in the ***Benedictine Convent:*** a relief of the Kairos God of Luck, which was found in the attic of a house belonging to the Statileo family. The figure is a young man who looks as if he is running with his hair blowing in the wind. The sisters of the convent will show you the other items in their interesting art collection as well.

Trogir is one of those fascinating medieval towns that invites you to stroll through it, then have a cup of espresso at an outdoor cafe in one of the squares. The main square contains the cathedral, palace, and a clock tower. ***St. Sebastian's Church*** was built in 1477 in thankfulness for salvation from the plague. Nicholas of Florence designed the statue of St. Sebastian on the facade. On the southern side of the square is the loggia, which has been used through the ages as a courtroom and a palace, where important announcements were made. When we were there, three little girls were playing a jump-rope game beneath the painted ceiling. ***St. Lawrence's Cathedral,*** called St. John's by the local people, has three apses and a tall belfry. You can climb up to the belfry for a great view of the city and the Adriatic. Inside the cathedral, you will notice many sculptured pieces done by Radovanus. The benches in the choir were carved by Ivan Budislavic in the 15th century. Look for the painting "St. John saves the shipwrecked."

During Roman times, Trogir was eclipsed by nearby **Salona,** which became a thriving metropolis. The Romans developed a series of land lots and paths in the area that are still in use today. There are some remains of villas where country paths cross.

Just beyond Trogir, you will come to ***Kastel Riviera,*** a series of seven fortresses built by the nobility of Trogir and Split as defenses against the Turks. Take side roads down toward the sea to catch glimpses of them. We found **Kastel Stari** and **Kastel Novi** interesting. The area has been built up so that you cannot see all of the seven fortifications but the ambience and the sea provide pleasant settings.

Split is a university city, an international port, and a commercial center. Park down along the quay and walk into the old town for a day of exploration. The city dates from early Greek settlements in the fourth century B.C. in nearby **Solin**. Emperor Diocletian built his palace near Salona, on the site of the present Split in A.D. 295. Use one of the gates to walk through thick walls into the old town, which is full of the flavor of the past, with its maze of winding streets. The *Emperor's Apartments* have all been destroyed, but there is much else to see inside the walls. *Diocletian's Mausoleum,* which was converted into a *cathedral* in the seventh century, no longer contains his body. The cathedral has elegantly carved doors depicting the life of Christ in 28 scenes. Inside, the hexagonal pulpit, from the 13th century, and the choir stalls, both with intricate carving, are among the oldest in Dalmatia. Take a look at the black granite Egyptian Sphinx at the entrance to the cathedral and, nearby, the two Romanesque lions. You can climb the tower for a fine view of the palace. Walk up to the *Golden Gate* in the north wall. Just outside the gate is a gigantic statue of Bishop Gregory of Nin, created by Ivan Mestrovic. Notice his grotesque fingers and highly polished toe, touched by many visitors. Several thousand persons now live inside the gates, so there is a lot of modern activity in ancient Split.

You can take ferries from Split to **Brac, Korcula, Vis,** or **Hvar,** the latter an island first inhabited 3000 years ago. We have heard from friends that this lovely archipelago should not be missed; however, like us, you may have to save it for the next trip.

Continue on the coast road from Split to **Omis,** a port located where a river emerges from a gorge—formerly the lair of pirates. In 1221 the pope launched a holy war against the pirates because they were destroying the crusaders' ships. The Venetians also tried to annihilate them; some pirates relocated in Senj and continued their exploits for another couple of hundred years. You can imagine pirates lying in wait for passing ships in Omis, at the base of enormous rocks towering up several hundred feet, which form natural hiding places. The *River Cetina* emerges through a gorge there; look up and you will see the remains of fortifications on the mountain behind the town. There is also a ruined castle, *Starigrad,* to complete the romantic picture of a pirate's nest. We spent several nights camping under the bluffs and caves in the only campground open off season in the Split area. On Easter Sunday, two little German girls searched for eggs in the grass in this now peaceful setting.

As you continue south from Omis, you will again see the spectacular *Dinaric Alps* on your left. They are enormous, sloping steeply toward the sea. There is some terracing, with vineyards, above the rocky shore. Near **Makarska,** the landscape changes to one of green pines and olive and fig trees, as well as vineyards. This would be a pleasant region for a pause in your travels, and there are accommodations of all types available, as well as ferries to the islands of Brac and Hvar. Narrow roads lead down from the corniche road to recently built villages on the shore. From ancient times to the 19th century, villages were built up high for protection from the Turks and from the pirates of the sea. Look up at the **Biokava Masef,** a mountain range that is bare and foreboding; you can climb up there if you wish to look down on appealing, red-roofed towns and sand beaches.

As you pass **Podgora,** you will notice a large monument called the *Gull's Wings* standing against the mountain outline; it soars up for about a hundred feet to serve as a memorial to the partisans who liberated Yugoslavia during World War II.

Although there are few rivers leading down to the sea in Yugoslavia because the karstic rock absorbs so much water (there are also not many passes over the mountains, which has meant little access to Dalmatia except from the sea), there is one wide river valley, that of the *River Neretva.* You can't miss the only low, flat area with its "little Venice" of orchards, crops, and rice fields. Here we suggest that you turn inland to **Pocitelj,** which is located above the sandy banks of the river. This village has a castle, a mosque, and ancient buildings for you to see. Painters have gravitated to Pocitelj to capture the essence of this 16th-century Turkish museum of a town.

Continue on to **Mostar,** located farther up on the banks of the River Neretva. Here there are buildings dating from the Ottoman Empire of the east, which, when meeting western culture, provided a mixture of Oriental, Byzantine, and western influences. Although the Turks departed in 1877, the town retains its strong Turkish quality. Almost half of the population is Moslem and 10 of the original 14 mosques are still in use. The area produces grapes; visitors enjoy Blatina, a red wine, and Zilauka, a white. The *Stari Most,* or Old Bridge, arches across the river with elegance and beauty. Walk along the *Stara Carsija,* the business street also known as Kujundziluk, to see towers, mosques, and Oriental shops. During the summer, boys make money by diving from the 65-foot-high bridge into the river. Sportsmen can fish for salmon, and hunters can seek both large and small game in the *Hercegovina hunting grounds.* An ideal setting for a stay is in **Buna,** or **Blagaj,** located 12 kilometers from Mostar. The castle named *Stjepan Grad* is in Blagaj. When you have finished your excursion inland, retrace your route down the river to the sea and continue southeast on the coast road to **Dubrovnik.**

Dubrovnik is striking, with the sea on one side and high city walls on the other, built into the hill during the 10th century to provide protection from maurauding predators. The first settlers in Dubrovnik were survivors, fleeing the destruction of their former city, Epidaurum (now called **Cavtat**), which is east of Dubrovnik. They settled on this rocky promontory in the seventh century. Their small, rocky island was separated from the mainland by a narrow channel; on the mainland side, fresh-water springs and thick, oak woods provided them with a means of life. In the Slavic language *dub* is the word for oak, and *dubrava* means oak forest; the name Dubrava turned into Dubrovnik. There is some speculation that people lived on the rocky islet much earlier; artifacts have been found that indicate the first settlement may have been before the sixth century. A rich cultural heritage developed from the mixture of Slavic and Mediterranean influences, and this is still evident today. Through shipping and trading, Dubrovnik rose in both importance and prosperity. Caravans led by Dubrovnik merchants traveled throughout the Balkans; its sea fleets expanded, then developed their range and strength.

The city walls were built carefully, the shape of the walls adapted to the curvature of the existing rocky landscape. The city is completely enclosed by these towering walls, with their bastions, and the fortress. **Molo-Sveti Ivan** encloses the old city harbor. In the high northwestern corner of the city stands the large, round tower of **Minceta**. There are four city gates, two facing landward and two facing the sea; the landward gates now have wooden drawbridges for entry. Another gate, **Vrata odd Buze,** which faces north, was added during the time of the Austro-Hungarian rule. Be sure to take time to walk along the 1940-meter length of the walls for splendid views of the roofs of the old town, the harbor, and the sea. We suggest buying the small guidebook, *Dubrovnik and its Surroundings,* which will help you make choices for your visit. When we were there, several of the historic buildings were being restored, but there were others to enjoy. It is pleasant to wander along the wide center shopping street, or to climb the steps up the hill to the next street for more shops and restaurants. A walking city of such distinction is a rare treat to enjoy. You should be tired but satisfied at day's end.

If you are planning on continuing through Greece you must either drive around Albania, a long, ardous trip, or take a ferry from Dubrovnik to **Corfu** (or to the mainland at **Igoumenitsa**). (Citizens of western democracies are not allowed to enter Albania, a tiny, rugged corner of the Soviet bloc.) There are also ferries to several cities in Italy, including Venezia, Ancona, and Bari, if you plan to tour Italy next.

Greece

Visions of Greece have danced in our heads during each of the four years that we have lived in other parts of Europe. Three times our plans to visit this enchanted country had been frustrated—first by finances, then by the colonels' coup, and finally by several earthquakes. On the fourth try we made it, and we haven't stopped talking and thinking about Greece since. The feel of Greece is even better than the travel posters suggest—

that vision of beautiful vistas of white, cubed houses set against an azure sea, with the Doric columns of a ruined temple in the foreground is real. But posters cannot convey the perfumed air from flowers and herbs, the silence of ancient sites such as Delfi and Mycenae, the heart-pumping pace of Greek folk dancing, the taste of moussaka, Greek salad with feta cheese, and wine, the feel of swimming in crystalline water, or sailing into rocky coves.

The overnight ferry from Dubrovnik will take you to the town of **Corfu (Kerkira),** on the island of the same name. This lovely, lush, emerald island has mountains to the north and to the south beyond a central plain. Geologists believe that the island was once connected to Albania, just a few miles away, and that it is really a mountain range only partly exposed, with the rest remaining under water like an iceberg. Because of heavier rainfall from the west, Corfu has more vegetation than any other part of Greece, ranging from tropical, olive, orange, and lemon trees, oleander, and wisteria to a variety of blooming shrubs and flowers. It is laced with back roads connecting remote villages; some of the roads are bumpy with hairpin turns, but the views are worth it. "Local color" is inescapable, provided by black-clothed and wrinkled old women working in the olive groves with their donkeys, herds of sheep and goats reaching up to nab the young olive leaves, and village families sitting by the road to watch the world go by. You will enjoy good beaches all around the island, sailing, walking, cycling, or simply sitting in tavernas sampling local foods and wines.

If you drive north along the eastern shore from the town of Corfu, you will pass many hotels, restaurants, and campgrounds. **Kassiopi,** farther up the shore at the northeast corner of the island, is a particularly pleasant objective for an excursion. The village has a fortress dating from medieval days, many little tavernas, and swimming available off the rocks or from a shingle beach. We can attest to the gastronomic pleasure of being on hand when fresh bread came out of the oven in the bakery there (and admit to some snacking on our breakfast loaf on the way home).

We recommend another excursion into the interior that begins by leaving the east coast road at **Pirgi.** You will drive up a series of hairpin turns with sea views becoming increasingly more spectacular as you ascend, passing the villages of **Spartilas, Sqourades,** and **Strinilas** on the way up. Views of *Mount Pandokrator,* at 906 meters, are around every bend. The drive is full of anticipation as you crane your neck to catch the next vista. Silvery olive leaves shimmer above knarled old trunks that are often so hollow you can see through them; black netting is laid under the trees to catch the olives. Watch for people shaking boxes hanging from a limb; they are screening out the olives from the leaves. Patient donkeys wait for bags of olives to be loaded onto their backs, then plod along with someone riding sideways, swinging his or her legs. When we were there, spring flowers bloomed everywhere—we were told that Greece has more varieties of wild flowers than anywhere else in the world—presenting a riot of color to complement the succession of views. We meandered up the mountain with pleasure, finally heading down from **Episkepsis**, where we gave a lift to a young girl who was on her way home to **Acharavi**, on the northwest coast. The scenery along the north coast is beautiful, and the road will lead you back to Kassiopi.

Another excursion begins just south of **Ipsos**, where you will turn toward **Korakiana**. You may want to stop for wine-tasting at *Kepkypaikh Notonoiia*, where you can sample the local kumquat liqueur, either sweet or dry, various wines, and other local drinks. Continue on the road signed to **Paleokastritsa**, to visit the legendary scene of Odysseus's meeting with Nausicaa in the cove below her father's palace. Drive up to the 16th-century monastery on the cliff overlooking the sea, where you can look over the edge to see *Kolovri*, a rock that looks just like a ship. In fact, local legend tells us that Poseidon was so enraged when he heard that the Phaeacians had given Odysseus a ship that he turned it into stone on that spot. Walk through the pure silence of the monastery, with its graceful white arches lined in brilliant blue, past icons and into a chapel filled with paintings and silver-filagree hanging lights. For swimming and snorkeling there are a number of coves with clear aquamarine water, where you can enjoy sand and shingle beaches and explore a grotto or two.

Upon leaving Paleokastritsa, head for **Liapades**. We made one wrong turn and drove up a track that grew too narrow for cars, then craned our necks to back down again until one very nice woman opened her gate, after moving her donkey, so we could back in and turn around. We tried another road and ended up circling around a well at the top, to the amusement of a number of men sitting in the afternoon sun; apparently, we weren't the first carful of tourists to do so. As we finally headed down on the right road, we noticed a group of women wearing flat hats tied under their chins, which provided a base for bags of greens or groceries or whatever. They wore black skirts, a blouse or sweater, and heavy stockings with comfortable shoes. To complete your tour, continue south through the *Plain of Ropa* to the *Kaiser's Throne* at **Pelekas**. The kaiser enjoyed driving to this spot above the village in order to watch the sunset.

When you decide which day you would like to take the ferry to **Igoumenitsa** on the mainland, be sure to book a day or two in advance; ferries are crowded. The ferry trip is an experience to remember—tourists and Greeks are jammed into a lounge where people smoke right next to no smoking signs until the place is blue and heavy, families have a meal or play cards, and everybody seems to be having a good time with some singing and lots of laughter.

There are several ways to reach **Delfi** from Igoumenitsa. We suggest driving 480 for a scenic route to **Ioannina**, where there is a fortress containing a folk museum and a fine view across the lake to the snowcapped *Pindos Mountains*. You can also take a boat trip to the island where Ali Pasha sought refuge in the monastery of **St. Panteleimon;** in fact, he was shot through the floor of his room there. Ali Pasha was born in 1741 in Albania, came to power under Turkish patronage, and seized Ioannina in 1788. Once considered an "heroic rebel," Ali Pasha became notorious for his outrageous cruelty. At one point, enraged by the refusal of his mistress to receive him, he tied and weighted her, along with 17 other women, and tossed them into the lake to drown. Lord Byron visited Ali Pasha in 1809; he was impressed with his power, in spite of his knowledge of the barbaric nature that was its source. (Byron wrote about this meeting in "Childe Harold.") Ali's death was ironic because he had lied and used tricks all his life; he was lured to the Monastery of Pantaleimon by an offer of pardon from the sultan and was shot there. The bullet holes remain in the floor for all to see.

From Ioannina, turn south to **Arta, Amfilohia, Agrinion,** past the signs for **Messolongi,** through **Nafpaktos,** which has a fortress and an interesting harbor with fishing boats and yachts riding at anchor, and on through **Galaxidi,** where you will see the red bauxite mined for aluminum and a number of tankers and cargo vessels "rafted" together in the water, waiting to be turned into next year's razor blades. From **Itea,** follow signs to Delfi.

Trying to describe ancient Delfi leaves one at a loss for the right words to capture the amalgram of impressions that make a visit memorable. The setting is beautiful, with varying shades of green in the olive trees and cypresses and wild flowers among the ruins, all cradled in a valley protected by a crescent of soaring rock behind Delfi. The mountains all around on the other sides complete a perfect circle; this "center of the earth" is magnificent. The entire scene looks like a giant amphitheater, with Delfi isolated from the rest of the world; a perfect shrine. Variations in light change the intensity of the red color in the rock throughout the day. **Mount Kirfis** stands behind with the two red cliffs, **Rodina** and **Flambouko,** and the valley, filled with olive trees. Below all is the pure blue of the **Gulf of Itea.**

From early times, a number of deities were worshiped at Delfi, including the Earth Goddess, Gea, Themis, Demeter, Poseidon, Python (the son of Gea), Apollo, and Pythius. Pythius, through the Priestess Pythia, gave cryptic prophecies to those who came to seek wisdom from the Oracle. Heads of state respected the reputation of the Oracle, and by the sixth century B.C., Delfi had become an international diplomatic center, which led to the building of many temples and treasuries.

We spent a day of pure delight slowly exploring the archaeological sites and the museum. The delight came from the warm, clear day, the shapes of the trees, the abundance of blossoming flowers, and the uncanny quiet—all despite the arrival of many loaded tour buses. They were all there—Germans, Dutch, Italians, Austrians, English, Americans, and Japanese—but the hillside of ruins seemed to contain them easily and noiselessly. Novelist John Fowles is right: There is a special, absolute quality to the silence one encounters at certain times and places in Greece, one which can absorb the noise of people and even of machines. Part of this effect is pure hillside acoustics, part the imaginative perception of older civilizations that lasted far longer than ours probably will. So, in spite of the trappings of tourism in modern Delfi—all the hotels, shops, restaurants, and tour buses—the magic of the hill of the Oracle seems to survive, at least on beautiful spring days.

If at all possible, visit Delfi before the high season (in April, May, or early June) or after it; we have heard that the summer months bring more tourists than the site can bear, producing long lines. In April there were times when we were the only ones admiring a part of the site. In more crowded times you would be advised either to arrive early and walk all of the way up to the stadium, then take your time on the way down, or to start up in mid-morning, when the tour groups have already reached the top. In any case, there is a great deal of room and more than enough beauty to go around. Be sure to bring more film than you think you will need; temptation is strong to capture many angles around the *Sanctuary of Apollo,* the *theater,* the *stadium,* the *Temple of the Pronaia Athena,* and the *Palestra.* Wear comfortable shoes for the climb; the trails are rough and uneven.

In terms of planning your time, you can reach the top section of the ruins in about 20 minutes, with a few stops to catch your breath. We spent several hours up there, then walked down slowly to explore, and had lunch outdoors in a taverna in the modern village of Delfi. After lunch we returned to spend most of the afternoon in the museum, which contains many of the artifacts recovered from the site. Most of the descriptions are written in Greek or French, rather than English. There are statues and fragments displayed in each room, leading up to the exquisite bronze charioteer in the last room. He was created in 478 B.C. and has magnificent detail in his eyelashes and facial features. The spell of Delfi may lead you to extend your stay and explore the region dominated by the enormity of **Mount Parnassus,** home of the muses, or take the many opportunities for hiking and skiing, even as late as the end of April.

Leave Delfi on the only road heading east and drive to **Arahova,** a little mountain village that has many textile shops filled with bedspreads, rugs, table linen, carry bags, blouses, and handmade sweaters. At **Thive** (ancient Thebes), you have a choice of roads to Athens. You can drive south to **Erithre, Mandra,** and **Elefsis** (ancient Elouisis), or head east on a faster road that later swings around south to Athens.

Athens

We hardly know where to begin with Athens (Athine), a modern city of 2½ million people, with priceless ruins of the ancient world dotted on hills in or near the center of town. Ruins are also nestled in between buildings in this bustling metropolis. Yet our introduction to these treasures was mildly distressing. The euphoria of haunted Delfi gradually disintegrated on our drive to Athens. Modern Thebes was crowded, dusty, and totally undistinguished, and ancient Elouisis is buried in an ugly industrial city. The closer you get to Athens, the deeper the smog. Not without appropriate irony, the seaside campsite we selected in **Voula** (in every other respect excellent) was under the main landing pattern for Glifada Airport, so for four nights we were treated to 747s and L1011s screaming down the last part of their approach. In spite of this quite realistic introduction to the noise, confusion, and clutter of modern Athens, reinforced a few days later by a large dose of Monday morning traffic in the city proper, we found that our time spent at the principal sites (Acropolis Agora, parts of the Plaka, and the temple of Poseidon at Sounion) was pleasant and we went largely unmolested by the throngs of tourists.

Originally a fortified citadel and home of the Mycenaean kings who built a palace inside, the *Acropolis* has contained many temples over the centuries. Settled since Neolithic times, this hill was easily defended except from the west. As it was devastated by fire and invasion, new buildings were constructed over old. Built on a high platform of rock, the Acropolis served well as the focus of the city, which expanded down the hill and across the countryside. You will see the magnificent *Parthenon* from a long way off as you drive into the city toward the Acropolis by day or by night (when it is lit). The Parthenon was built between 447 and 432 B.C., then the *Propylaia, Athena Nike,* and *Erechtheion.* Artisans collected from all over Greece to work on these structures during the fifth century B.C., the "golden age" in the construction of these monuments.

As you look to the left at the foot of the hill, you will see a gate flanked by two towers. The construction is irregular; porous stones and marble from older Greek buildings were used to build the *Beule Gate.* As you head up the hill to the Parthenon, the Temple of Athena Nike is located on your right, the Propylaia on your left. Continue up the *Sacred Way* to the Parthenon; you can walk all around, but not inside. This masterpiece of white Pentelic marble has 8 columns on the ends and 17 on the sides. Each column is 34 feet high and has a diameter of 6 feet at the base. There are 20 flutings around the column and an outward curve in the middle. As you see columns in various temples, you will be able to visually distinguish Doric columns, which are more massive and swell in the middle from Ionic columns, which appear to be straighter and smaller and stand on a base. Look left from the Doric columns of the Parthenon toward the *Erechtheion* to compare the Ionic columns there. This building was constructed on a sacred spot, where Poseidon's trident made salt water spout and where Athena struck the rock with her lance and caused an olive tree to sprout. Carytids (young, slender, female forms) support part of this building on their heads.

There is much more to explore in the Acropolis; wear comfortable shoes (we saw women in spike heels gingerly picking their way, hardly looking at the monuments). The museum has one of the best collections in Greece, including much of the treasure originally displayed on and in buildings of the Acropolis. Part of the Parthenon frieze is in this museum; a larger portion resides in the British Museum (the Elgin Marbles). You can get permission to photograph there (as well as in many other sites and museums in Greece) by paying for one extra admission ticket.

Walk down from the Acropolis through the *Agora,* the ancient market area that was once the hub of the city. The ruins are a little confusing, dating anywhere from the sixth century B.C. to the fifth century A.D. Begin in the museum to get your bearings before walking around the site. The Agora museum is located in the restored *Stoa of Attalus,* originally built by King Attalus and given to the city of Athens. There are artifacts from the Neolithic Age through the Geometric Period. Visitors will have a chance to learn about the ancient Athenian system of government as well as the commerical uses of the area.

The small *Temple of Hephaestus and Athena,* also called the *Theseion,* is noted for being the best preserved temple in Greece. The Theseion, built in 449 B.C., was saved from destruction by its conversion into a Christian church. Set up on a hillock overlooking the Agora, it is complete and enclosed; you can walk into it to get the sense of interior space that it is only possible to imagine in the ruins of larger temples. The Doric columns, Ionic friezes on the facades, metopes (friezes in triangular shape), and coffered ceiling (one with recessed panels) are in good condition.

The *National Archaeological Museum* is the most exciting and most valuable collection in all of Greece. Don't miss it! There is more to see in this enormous museum than visitors can reasonably expect to cover; look over the offerings available in each of the rooms and set your priorities before you begin. It is helpful to begin on the left side in order to follow the evolution of Greek civilizations in chronological order. The collections include Neolithic, Mycenaean, and Cycladic periods. You will see bronzes, sculpture, jewelry, and vases. Highlights include frescoes excavated in the 20th century and in excellent condition from **Thera,** the island of **Santorini,** which was destroyed by a volcanic explosion around 1500 B.C.; the burial mask of Agamemnon (however, late research has indicated that this may not be his); a bronze Poseidon; the Marathon Boy; and the Horse and Jockey of Artemision.

For another excursion into the ancient world drive 60 kilometers southeast of Athens along a lovely stretch of rocky promontories and sandy beaches to **Sounion,** also known as the *Cape of Columns.* Those who come by sea can see the soaring columns of the *Temple of Poseidon,* high on a hill; they are a treat to view by land as well. Poseidon was quite naturally associated with the promontory at Sounion, the sea gateway to Athens; in fact, he was worshiped there before the temple was built in the fifth century; the present temple was built on the site of another ancient sanctuary. At one time a fortress enclosed the temple, but not much remains of it. This Doric temple originally had 13 columns on the long sides and 6 on the short sides. You can see Lord Byron's name engraved on one of the columns; as a frequent visitor, he immortalized Sounion in "Don Juan." Unhappily, this lovely site can be jammed with hordes of tourists because it is so close to Athens. Although tours advertise the lovely sunsets, we noticed most of the tour buses pulling out in the late afternoon.

When you are ready to leave Athens, drive to **Korinthos** on a toll road that seems especially hazardous in sections because traffic runs in the break-down lane, with one wheel over the white line, to make a four-lane road. We made this trip six times and eventually felt more comfortable with the road, but were still extremely watchful. The Korinthos Canal was built between 1882 and 1899, completing a plan developed in Roman times. It's easy to understand the delay when looking down a narrow chasm cut through solid rock; the canal has walls 80 meters high and is only 25 meters wide. Ships up to 10,000 tons can navigate its 26-foot depth. As you cross, stop and walk back to the bridge to peer down at the large vessels navigating this extraordinary canal.

Anticipating the rich cultural heritage of the Peloponnese is half the fun of going there. On the trip down through the Argolid from **Korinthos** to **Argos** and **Nafplion,** scan each hilltop with sharp eyes for signs of ancient acropoli or medieval fortresses, most often the latter built on the former, with Roman works built in between. Those hilltops are plenteous: ancient Corinth, Mycenae, Argos, Tiryns (a small hump on the coastal plain of the Argives), and Nafplion—all within sight from the main road. And there are many more off in the hills. You can trace prehistoric legends, including that of the god of healing, Asclepius, who was born at Epidavros; Io, the daughter of Inachus at Argos; Perseus, who decapitated Medusa at Argos; Bellerophon, a Corinthian hero who tamed Pegasus, the winged horse, at Acro-Corinth, Heracles, who conquered the invulnerable nine-headed lion, the Hydra, and the Stymphalian birds; and Agamemnon, the King of Mycenae, who led the Greeks against the Trojans. Sagas of the historical period followed, as writers were inspired by the lives and deeds in this center of Greece. Homer, Hesiod, Pindar, Aeschylus, Sophocles, and Euripides all drew material from this area.

From Korinthos, follow signs to **Patras** until another road turns left to Argos. Then watch for signs to **Mikine (Mycenae).** From the many sites to visit in this area, we chose to begin with Mycenae, the hub of ancient civilization. Although Mycenaean culture evolved from the Minoan civilization on Crete, the Mycenaeans became more powerful as Crete dwindled in power. The royal house of Mycenae was both rich and powerful; and the Mycenaean period of the Late Helladic Era was the time of its greatest strength. The violence and passion of this family figures in many Greek tragedies—including Atreus's hatred for his brother, Thyestes; Clytemnestra's murder of her husband, Agamemnon; Orestes's murder of both his mother, Clytemestra, and her lover, Aegisthus. Orestes became king of Mycenae, then his son, Tisamenus, ruled until the great fire of 1100 B.C., which destroyed the citadel. Mycenae is one of Schlieman's three greatest archaeological finds (Troy and Knossos being the others); all have provided a spatial context for the legendary figures of the epics.

Mycenaen ruins are most impressive by virtue of their massive building blocks, carefully chosen hill sites, and sense of isolation. Mycenae itself brings the works of Homer and the Greek tragedies to life through its palace, fortifications, vaulted tombs, and proportions. Situated on a small hilltop backed by steep, barren mountains and overlooking the plain stretching down to Argos and *Tiryns,* it represents physically the precariousness of late-Bronze Age life, as well as the need for communication with the sea. The smallness of the palace rooms, the largest of which barely exceeds the size of a living room in a large modern home, suggests the compression of daily living and the inevitability of the dark deeds dramatized in the tragedies—a palace version of cabin fever. There was for us a special sense of spring in the ancient ruins, with the eternal recurrence of flowers amidst the rock. And, once again, a deep silence.

Before you reach the main site you will come to the **Treasury of Atreus,** one of the famous tholos (round house tombs). Look at the extraordinary construction of this large monument; the huge rectangular blocks of stone are in excellent condition, and one wonders at the difficulty of raising them and placing them in position so precisely. The entrance passageway is 36 meters long and 6 meters wide, leading to a doorway topped by great slabs of stone. Inside, the shape is that of a beehive made without mortar. There is a smaller chamber to the right of the central room. (Be sure to bring a flashlight to light your way.)

Back on the road, continue to the **Citadel** and enter through the **Lion Gate,** a 3-meter-high structure that narrows at the top. The lions face each other in profile; unfortunately, their heads have disappeared. Inside, you will come upon **Grave Circle,** where tombs have been excavated inside a double circle. Continue up to the **palace,** which is sketchy in outline because the **Temple of Athena** was built on top of it. Past the **House of Columns** you will find the area that is most fun to explore and romanticize because, again, it suggests the precariousness of life inside the palace; the intrigue of palace life is illustrated by the sally port, an exit toward the plain of Argos and the sea, and, near by, the entry to a secret underground well.

Mycenae has one very nice feature; there is no visible habitation within immediate sight. When you are up there wandering around the ruins you can imagine what it might have been like in the second millennium B.C. There is nothing to disturb your thoughts as you overlook rounded mountains, gray rock, olive groves, tall standing cypress, surrounded by bright red poppies, the white, yellow, and purple blooms of various wild flowers, the sweet scent of orange trees, and the song of birds punctuating the stillness.

From Mycenae continue to Argos, then to **Naflion,** on the Gulf of Argolis, under the spectacular rock, *Akronafplia.* Nauplios, the son of Poseidon and Amymone, founded the town, according to mythology. Because of his interest in the sea, the town became a strong naval center, possibly participating in the Argonaut campaign. Drive or walk up to see the *Palamidi Fort,* which contains seven batteries; look for the Lion of St. Mark, the symbol of Venice, used as decoration. The offshore island of **Bourdzi** is a picturesque place just 500 meters away. Take time to wander around the harbor, perhaps stopping for a drink or a meal in one of the outdoor tavernas.

Tiryns is a Mycenaean acropolis located on a small hill 5 kilometers from Naflion, visible from the main road. According to mythology, Tiryns was built by the Cyclops, with their extraordinary strength. Artifacts indicate that it was fortified two generations before that of Mycenae. A great fire destroyed Tiryns at the end of the Mycenaean Period. Homer mentioned this "wall-girt Tiryns" and the walls are indeed 8–17 meters thick, some built with corridors inside. The main gate is similar to the Lion Gate at Mycenae. Walk up to the palace; frescoes from this elegant palace are housed in the National Archaeological Museum in Athens. Here is another site you can enjoy in the peace and quiet of a country setting.

Nearby **Tolon** is a resort area with 15 campgrounds listed on signs as you approach the village. Most are in town, unattractively situated between buildings; we found one first-class campground located beside the ruins of Asine, right on Kastracki Beach. There are also many hotels and rooms available in Tolon. *Asine,* lovely to visit in early morning before the town wakes, with the dew still on the flowers, is a ruin that is really a ruin. It requires some trial and error to find the trail to the top through weeds and fallen stones. The view from the top of this rocky promontory jutting out to the sea is worth the exploration.

We enjoyed staying in the Argolid region a number of days and came to recognize some of the people who live there. We noticed a number of women, many of them wearing black, sitting beside railroad crossings doing handwork as they waited for the train to pass. People in the shops were very helpful as we searched for flashlight batteries; ours must have been switched on inside our rucksacks all day; they were constantly wearing out. We had several good meals in local restaurants, always, according to Greek custom, being invited to look at the offerings in the kitchen before they were prepared.

Epidavros, 25 kilometers east of Nafplion, is noted for having the best-preserved theater of the ancient world. It is magnificent and well worth visiting; in fact, performances are still given there. The acoustics are so remarkable that visitors can stand in the center of the stage and speak in normal voices that will be heard clearly in the last row. A coin dropped on stage can also be heard at the top of the 54 rows of seats. Besides perfect acoustics, every seat also has perfect vision. The adjoining **Sanctuary of Asclepios,** the god of healing, was very popular toward the end of the fifth century B.C., when a temple was built to contain a statue of Asclepios, as well as other buildings in his honor. In 86 B.C. the Roman general, Sulla, destroyed much of the sanctuary; in the second century A.D. the Roman senator, Antonius, gave money to rebuild it. In the fourth century A.D. this sanctuary, as well as others, was ordered closed by the Christian Emperor Theodosius. It was ruined further by earthquakes in A.D. 522 and 551. In the same complex, the **Tholos of Pausanias** is a circular structure with exterior and interior colonnades; scholars are still debating the use of this building. Some sources claim that the labyrinth was used as a snakepit, shock therapy for patients. The setting of Epidavros, in a lovely valley heady with the scent of pine and thyme, is memorable.

If you are planning on making trips to some of the islands, you will probably want to journey back to **Piraeaus** to catch your ferry. Return along the **Saronic Gulf** from the Peloponnese, past Korinthos. This is a pleasant, scenic drive, with views of islands dotting the sea. As you come around the bend overlooking the harbor of Elefsis, you can't help but see the many, many vessels moored there, lying like great rusting hulks waiting to be broken up because of the worldwide shipping depression.

On this drive, as on others, we noticed the number of buildings that have been left unfinished. Often sand, stone, and other building materials are lying around, waiting for the right time to finish the structure. When another floor is planned for some time in the future, the steel rods that reinforce pillars for each layer are left sticking up around the edges. (They can be lethal at times, as attested to by a friend who was dancing on the top of an unfinished house when she gashed her leg on an upright wire rod.) Cement steps are cast, going up the outside of the house one or two stories to nowhere, with a graceful curve but no handrails. Those with acrophobia will find these stairs unnerving. As you pass through the industrial areas of Elefsis and Piraeaus, the magic of the ancient world fades into the smog-laden dreariness of modern cities, but Piraeaus is the starting point for another excursion into the Greece that was—the islands of the Aegean.

Greek Islands

From Piraeaus and many other coastal cities, ferries fan out to the most fabled (if not fabulous) island groups in the world. Where to go?

To the nearby islands in the Saronic Gulf, to the Sporades, to the Cyclades, to the Dodecanese, to Crete or Rhodes, or to the Ionian islands? With this choice you can't be comprehensive and you can't lose. Each group of islands offers its own special pleasures and discoveries, but no one can find them all in anything short of a lifetime of exploration. What we suggest is an extremely small sampling for those who have limited time—one of the major islands and two smaller islands of different character. The choice will vary with the individual and the availability of convenient ferries.

We chose **Crete** first because of the wealth of archaeological finds to explore. You can fly to Crete or take a ferry and hire a rental car for use on the island. Unless you are in a hurry, you should probably take a Greek ferry at least once. Like no other ferries in Europe, they have their own character: difficult to find and book, irregular in schedule, sometimes dirty and crowded, but supremely competent and confident in their navigation and seamanship. When it comes to providing information about ferries, shipping agents or travel agents are very likely to provide misinformation or tell you your voyage is impossible. The modern Greek sense of truth seems to have no relation to degrees of certitude—all information is given definitively, without qualification or reference to authority—and the Greek sense of time is thoroughly Mediterranean. Only Northern Europeans or Americans ask when the ship will arrive or sail. The whole experience (apart from the seamanship, which, without fanfare, is superb) belongs to the world before timetables.

Finding a ship in the Aegean islands is an adventure in itself, more like searching for a sailing centuries ago than booking through a modern travel agency. Having our own car with us presented some difficulty because most ferries take only passengers, not cars, to our next choice, **Santorini.** The car is useful on many of the islands, especially when toting along camping gear, but if you have one with you, allow for some flexibility in getting from one island to another. Getting to an island from Piraeus is not difficult, but because Greek ferries run on erratic schedules, travel agencies will not book interisland travel on some car ferries in advance. They will advise calling the day before departure to get an approximate time, then rechecking several hours before that time, since ferries can be delayed for several hours or more. Much as we enjoy a full night's sleep, often we had no choice but to sail on a ferry that was a number of hours late. And we chose **Paros** rather than **Mykonos** (with the trip to ancient Delos) because our car could not get to Mykonos easily, if at all. So the car was both a help and a burden: it made remote parts of even small islands accessible, but it also limited the range of islands we could reach.

We usually book all ferries in advance, and we had hoped to have our tickets in hand before we arrived in Greece. This is easier said than done! You must either stick to a rigidly preplanned schedule or relax and accept Poseidan's will. (Odysseus did!)

CRETE is wonderful! Located in the sea between Asia, Africa, and Europe, it is the most southerly Greek island and the largest. The landscape varies from snowcapped peaks to sandy beaches lined with palm trees. There are three mountain ranges, wooded on the western side and barren on the east. Because much of Crete has been deforested, the rivers have become almost dry. The ocean dashes against craggy rocks and laps on sandy beaches all around the island. This is a great place to visit at any time of year, with much to enjoy.

We have planned several routes that include fine scenery, the major archaeological sites, old churches, and good beaches. We have described each route as beginning from **Iraklion,** the major port for ferries. Since this is the least attractive of Cretan cities, you may want to stay elsewhere, as we did.

For the first excursion, drive west out of Iraklion on the new road through unattractive flat land laden with hotels and clutter, past the smokestacks of a power plant and an oil tank farm until you emerge suddenly into beautiful mountains. These mountains have few trees, red earth, lots of rocks, pink flowering shrubs, yellow gorse growing on long stems, goats munching along the road . . . and striking glimpses of snowcapped peaks, including that of *Mount Ida* in the distance. The new east–west road is high above the sea and there is another view just around each bend. You will pass the sign for **Fodele,** the birthplace of El Greco, which is 8 kilometers from this modern highway. Olive groves march up and down the terraces. Villages in these mountains look like collections of white cubes with red roofs. Stop a minute as you take a photograph, and listen to the sounds from a village: roosters, birds, babies, and a horn honking through town. We stopped for an overview of a lovely village, **Sisae.** There are orange stands all along the road, with women in black sitting patiently by their fruit with needlework in their hands.

The next stretch of road is uninhabited until you reach **Panormos,** another pretty village on the shore. The coastal plain is next, with lots of apartments and greenhouses. The city of **Rethimnon** has Venetian ruins along the harbor and pleasant tavernas to stop in for a drink or lunch; have a swim at the beach, along with topless females, or stroll in the gardens that are cool and inviting on a hot day. As a reward for good campers who had put up with ants crawling on and in the tent, we treated ourselves to lunch on the lovely terrace of the Panorama Hotel (just west of the city), complete with a view that matched the name.

Perhaps the most essential excursion is a trip to *Knossos,* a site we had been dreaming about for years; it is located a few kilometers south of Iraklion on a well-signed road. Situated on a small hill with larger barren hills as a backdrop and smaller hills strewn with olive trees below, Knossos is in the perfect spot. Having read some of the arguments about too much restoration in Knossos, we were prepared to be skeptical, yet we found it helpful to see this intricate palace partially restored so that visitors can better visualize daily life in ancient times. So many ancient ruins are ankle- or knee-high at most; here is one that will give you more perspective for understanding others that are "pure," i.e., unreconstructed, like Phaestos.

This once elegant Minoan-Mycenean palace dates back to the seventh millennium B.C., with a turbulent history. The first palace was constructed over ruins from Neolithic times; it perished in 1700 B.C. from a cause as yet unknown. The next palace was built and subsequently damaged by earthquakes in 1600 B.C., 1500 B.C., and finally during the explosion at Santorini in 1450 B.C. It was rebuilt and used between 1400 and 1200 B.C. by Mycenean rulers. Although the site was discovered in 1878 by Minos Kalakairinos, it was not excavated until Sir Arthur Evans, an English archaeologist, took over in 1900. He reconstructed it, using ingenuity to replace crumbling sections with more durable materials to retain the same dimensions and visual effect. Some of his interpretations and choice of room names have been questioned by other scholars, but on the whole most visitors appreciate the reconstruction as an enhancement of their sense of the palace.

There is a great deal to explore at Knossos; we found a detailed guide, available at the site or in shops everywhere around, useful. Greek mythology refers to Knossos as "the Labyrinth," and it is just that! The maze of passageways, stairs, courtyards, and rooms is fun to explore; count on getting lost more than once. It takes some time for the intricacy of the palace to become apparent; after three hours in a rather limited space we were still discovering new chambers and running into dead ends as we tried to move from one area to another. The sense of a labyrinth grows and remains, and the Theseus-Ariadne-Daedalus archetypes come alive here as mythic representations of human bewilderment and ingenuity. Mythology indicates that Minos coerced Athens into supplying seven maidens and seven young men every nine years. Placed in the labyrinth, these hapless individuals were extinguished by the Minotaur, except for Theseus, who escaped with the help of Ariadne. Theseus killed the Minotaur and became King of Athens. As you nourish your imagination in the setting of these stories, don't forget to look carefully at what is before you. With your guide in hand, don't miss the wall paintings scattered throughout the site, the royal apartments, rows of pithoi (large clay jars for storing wine, oil, corn, and other items) in storerooms, pillar crypts, the throne room, workshops, and a theater.

After touring Knossos from one end to the other, you can stop somewhere for a picnic, as we overheard one young man proposing to his girl "in an olive grove, with the afternoon to while away," go to one of the many tavernas frequented by tourists, or find a taverna where local people are enjoying themselves and stop to sample their fare. We found one on a busy crossroads that looked just right, and it was. There were several handsome men in their seventies, with handlebar mustaches and twinkling eyes, talking to each other and to their grandchildren, who wandered in, and watching the university students who stopped for a Coke or lunch in between classes. Students grouped together at several tables, comparing class notes, with lots of extraneous conversation. One boy bounced out of his seat when he saw his pretty girl getting off a bus and almost stopped traffic as he rushed to meet her. As one car screeched around the corner "burning rubber" not once but twice on his return trip, the old men rolled their eyes and the students hardly noticed. Several teachers came down the steps from the university, the women in dresses and stockings, the men in jackets, all carrying briefcases, while the students wore western jeans ubiquitous throughout Greece.

Another excursion will take you out of Iraklion south, following signs to **Mires,** through a pleasant valley with vineyards, surrounded by hills with olive trees and some cypresses, onto a windy road with lovely mountain scenery. You will pass many people working in the vineyards while their donkeys wait patiently in the road, as well as men driving three-wheeled carts with the engine exposed in front. Women in scarves ride along with groceries in milk crates and there are also some cyclists and hikers.

Gortys is signed after **Agio Deka;** you will see the ruins of a church that had a chapel with paintings, flowers, and freshly lit candles when we were there. There are pieces of statues lying on the ground, a theater to see, and the famous stones containing the Law Code of Gortys. These large blocks are guarded by fencing, but you can see the letters. Take time to look at the knarled olive trunks and listen to the chirping of the birds in this rural setting.

Follow signs to **Phaistos (Festos),** which has another palace built by Minos. Life existed there in Neolithic times, as established by the excavation of artifacts beneath the floors of this Minoan palace. The setting of Phaistos on a hilltop between the sea and the mountains is peaceful and serene, with wonderful views of the ***Lasithi Mountains, Mount Dikti,*** Mount Ida, and the ***Bay of Messara;*** the king's chamber perches on the edge of the hill overlooking the pines to the snows of the mountain. Because the site is archaeologically "pure" (i.e., unreconstructed), a detailed guide helps you to identify major features of the palace as you wander through the ruins. There is an old palace as well as a new palace to sort out. In 1908 the Phaistos Disc was found; this 7-inch terracotta disc has a unique pattern of pictographs arranged in circular fashion leading to the center. Scholars date this piece at around 1600 B.C.; you can see it in the Iraklion Museum.

From Phaistos, follow signs to **Matala,** a beach village overhung by cliffs full of circular caves. As you near the southern coast, you will think you are in Arizona, with the same desert vegetation and dry soil on barren hills. Once a fishing village, Matala is now definitely a tourist trap, but worth a trip to see the caves. They have been inhabited by various people, including the Germans during World War II, as they kept watch for English boats, and the hippies of the last generation, when Matala was an "in" place for wandering youths. The caves are now fenced off against habitation, but you can visit them during the day. We did see clothes hanging outside some of the more remote caves, which suggests some transient population. Rock faces extend on both sides of the village, creating a horseshoe effect, with the beach in the middle. Nubile, topless nymphs were enjoying the clear aqua water and the sunny day on the beach when we were there.

You can either take the same road back to Iraklion (remember that a road traveled in the opposite direction is just like a new road for scenery), or you can retrace your route to Phaistos and then head northwest through some remarkable scenery to Rethimnon and then back to Iraklion on the coast road to complete a circuit.

Another pleasant route will take you to **Agios Nikolaos,** the capital of Lassithi, located on the *Gulf of Mirabella.* This charming town has a cosmopolitan flair; one can spend time sitting in the tavernas by the harbor people-watching, and boat-watching. We were fascinated by the crew of one fishing boat, endlessly sorting a gigantic net with the aid of a special fisherman's winch. The net had corks all along one edge and weights on the other; one can imagine the frustration of finding a figure-eight twist in it while bobbing around out at sea (just like packing a spinnaker on a sailboat—the idea is to make sure it emerges without a twist). The harbor area contains a small lake that is about 200 feet deep. In 1907 a channel was dredged to connect it to the sea; you can walk across the channel on a small bridge. Visit the church, *Agios Nikolaos,* to see fine ninth-century frescoes.

Head north from Agio Nikolaos, past a number of large hotels (Minos Beach has a nice buffet lunch), along a coastal drive with good views to **Elounta,** 11 kilometers away. From here you can take a boat to visit **Spinalonga,** a deserted island covered with ruins. One of the fortresses on the island dates from the 16th century. It was built by Greeks and originally named Olous; a Venetian fortress was built on that site in 1579. Then the Turks moved in for several centuries, until it finally became a leper colony; a local told us how the arrival of the lepers frightened the Turks and hastened their departure. People still living there tell many stories about the way people were committed to the island, some with only minor skin problems that were not really leprosy. One boy who was rescued by his father by boat at night later became a physician and still lives on Crete. The leper colony was disbanded in 1952, and the closest town on the shore gave the order to burn all buildings on Spinalonga. Today, those who visit the ruins will see a theater square, cemetery, mosaic work in some buildings, and cisterns. You can rent a paddleboat or swim over to the island; just don't try it in any kind of wind. We took a break from camping and spent the night directly across from Spinalonga. The setting is beautiful, with the later afternoon sun playing on the ruins across the water, and eerie in the early morning, with no activity in the settlement.

Driving east from Agio Nikolaos you will come upon a nice beach located just before the Istron Bay Hotel. The road continues to rise, with views of varied rock formations; there are a number of laybys for picture-taking or a picnic. The view ahead was of very dark, steep, barren mountains as you approach the ruins of *Gournia,* another ancient site worth visiting. When we were there, a sirocco was blowing from North Africa at 40–50 mph. Even rocks were blowing along the road and the sea below was white with spume.

If you drive south from Agio Nikolaos following signs for **Kritsa,** you will arrive at *Panhagia Kera,* a Byzantine church with beautiful frescoes. Each one tells a Biblical story and the faces are most expressive, especially the eyes. Although some sections have disappeared, the colors are brilliant in the remaining frescoes. Drive on a short distance to Kritsa, a town renowned for linen shops. You can buy rugs, table linen, pillow shams, Greek bags, blouses, and dresses.

Agios Nikolaos is, like Iraklion, a port of departure for other Greek islands. The ferry to Santorini, the *Cyclades,* is not noted for being on time; in fact, we were given three different sailing times and, on the day of departure, when we finally arrived on the quay at 10:30 p.m. the ferry was not there, nor was the agent. People began to arrive in little groups, mostly backpackers, as well as a number of trucks and one other car. At about 11:45 some lights appeared at the harbor entrance; the ferry steamed straight toward the quay, rounded up bow out, dropped an anchor, and backed down with lowered ramp. When we finally boarded at midnight we found an old-fashioned salon with reclining seats, asphalt floor, a long wooden bar, and two semicircular sofas inhabited most of the night by a group of men making coffee on a Gaz camping stove, while they talked and argued with gusto. We stretched out to sleep as best we could, and awoke in the morning to find a young seaman swabbing the floor around us.

SANTORINI (THIRA) As you approach Santorini from the south, the majestic rocky cliffs of the Akrotiri peninsula appear in shades of green, red, black, and white, a contrast to the whitewashed buildings in villages high up on the cliffs. Volcanic in origin, Santorini not only has very fertile soil but very different light qualities and hues. The colors in the rock vary in changing light throughout the day. Car ferries land at the "new" dock at the base of the cliff; to reach the plateau on top, you drive up the face of the cliff on a hairpin-turn road. Buses come down, hurtling around corners, while newcomers gingerly drive up with white knuckles. On the way up and down from the top, the view of the filled crater *(the Caldera)* is magnificent; you can see the outlines of the original island and the new volcanic islands that emerged in the center of the crater. When you reach the top, the road to **Thira** is rather poor, with deep holes on the side of the black top. The view from the cliffside town of Thira, looking out over the circular caldera, woke us up to the dramatic history of Santorini, which is associated with the legend of Atlantis. Plato wrote about Atlantis in two of his dialogues, "Timaeus" and "Critias," as a kingdom with two islands; some scholars identify the larger island with Crete and the smaller with Santorini.

The dramatic geological history of the island meshes with the disappearance of the legendary Atlantis. It is eerie to think about the living volcano that remained dormant for many years while Cycladic civilization developed and flourished during the period of Minoan civilization on Crete. Then, between 1500 and 1450 B.C., gigantic volcanic eruptions totally shattered life on the island; an earthquake precipitated volcanic action and the center of the island sank into the sea. The massiveness of the forces involved, probably after an earthquake introduced sea water into volcanic magma and created steam, can be measured by the size of the center caldera that you see today. It contains 32 square miles of water and is so deep that no ship can anchor in it; the three islands that curve around its outer walls are remnants of the original island. Seismic waves estimated at 200 feet in height (four times the size of the Krakatoa tsunumi) destroyed other cities including Knossos, Chani, and Gournia on Crete, 60 miles to the south, to name but a few. Some scholars associate this cataclysm in the center of the eastern Mediterranean with Biblical events recorded in the Old Testament. The remaining islands of the original Santorini are modern Thira, which is the largest, and horseshoe shaped; **Thirassia,** which is northeast of Thira; and **Aspronisi,** which is in the middle of the horseshoe opening to the Aegean Sea.

There are three more volcanic islands in the center of the caldera: **Palia Kameni** (old island that emerged in 197 B.C.), **Nea Kameni** (new island that emerged in 1701–1711), and **Mikri Kameni** (small burned island). You can take a boat trip to climb and overlook the tumbled chunks of uneroded lava on Nea Kameni. As you walk up from the shore you will surely wonder about the wisps of steam sometimes visible from this immense volcanic slag heap. Cinders are piled in contorted shapes and there are a number of craterlike depressions rather than the enormous steep and deep pit found at Mount Vesuvius in Italy. Terror at the lip of the crater on Vesuvius is real because there would be no retrieval for anyone who slipped in; at Nea Kameni one could climb up easily. If you go, be sure to wear hiking boots or stout shoes; people in sandals found the terrain difficult because the "clinkers" are awkward to walk on and the volcanic grit can fill shoes as well as sandals. Boots with socks were perfect for clomping along thinking about the wonder of this place instead of abraded feet.

We had one of those frustrating moments that occasionally overtake all travelers at Nea Kameni; the kind that is upsetting at the time but humorous afterward. After taking many pictures from the top we started back, camera bouncing over one shoulder, until we wanted to take more photos. At that point we realized that the little round black release button was missing and the camera would not function without it. We spent the rest of our time walking back slowly, retracing our steps with eyes scanning the black volcanic ash for the little round, essential black piece. Needless to say, like the needle in the haystack, we did not find it. With great restraint we resisted day-spoiling "why didn't yous" and eventually found a workable replacement for the release in Athens. In retrospect, this episode of looking for a black button on black lava strikes us as one of the most ridiculous moments of the trip.

After Nea Kameni, the next stop on the boat trip through the caldera is Thirassia, where you can take a donkey ride up to the village or relax in one of the tavernas on the shore. We chose Jimmies's, where we had fish just hours from the sea, squid, and a very tasty deep-fried vegetable, all enjoyed with Santorini wine. We found out from Jimmie's wife that the large stone wharves once supported the industry of mining porcelain from the cliff above.

Exploring the town of Thira itself can fill another afternoon and evening. The little winding streets, with whitewashed buildings jutting out at all angles, are a photographer's dream; in sunlight the white stucco set against brilliant blue domes is dazzling. From the cliffside the sea stretches out beyond the volcanic circle; within the circle you will see cruise ships and fishing boats moving about because none can anchor in this bottomless harbor. The cruise ships move slowly as they discharge passengers, off for a shopping spree, into motor launches. Yachts moor at the docks, which must be difficult in such an exposed spot when the wind is coming from the west. You will hear the jingle of bells as the donkeys amble up the 800 or so steps from the dock to the town, each with a tourist as passenger. (There is also a cablecar for a swift ride to the top.) Santorini shops contain the full range of souvenirs, rugs, linens, clothing, wine, and sundries. It is easy (and fun) to get lost in town because you can always reorient yourself by the sea. Restaurants and bars abound in layers, with entrances from the top leading down to each terrace. For a great way to relax, sit in the sun listening to classical music and sipping something at Franco's, have moussaka and a Greek salad at Zorba's, or a fine meal of lobster or sea breem at Kastro's (among any number of other possibilities).

Take an excursion to *Akrotiri,* located southwest of Thira almost on the end of the horseshoe. Just beyond the present town of Akrotiri you will find the ruins of the ancient town, which was covered by a thick blanket of volcanic ash in the 15th century B.C. volcanic explosion. In 1967 Professor Marinatos began excavating the site; some of the most beautiful frescoes in all of Greece were discovered and are now on display in the National Archaeological Museum in Athens. We found this site, completely covered by a gigantic tin shed, just as fascinating as Pompeii and far less commercialized; the excavations are still in progress, and tours through them are led by the archaeologists doing the work.

Akrotiri was an important town in Cycladean civilization, contemporaneous with Minoan civilization in Crete and possibly closely related to it through seafaring. A visit confirms your sense of apocalypse; the town buried in pumice, like Pompeii, is quite intact: Life simply stopped all at once on the day of doom. The houses are unusually large, indicating a prosperous trading community that could afford the room and the luxury of marvelous frescoes decorating the living quarters on second and third floors. One archaeological hypothesis attributes that evident prosperity to Akrotiri's location midway between the Greek mainland and the Near East, which gave it special significance and sophistication. According to this hypothesis, the Thirians were the seagoing arm of Minoan civilization, using ships as long as 120 feet. Akrotiri is a few yards from a good but exposed beach and has no harbor, but as long as boats were pulled up on beaches (a practice lasting at least 2000 years more), the city could have prospered as an important port and commercial center. (One of the frescoes showing many ships supports this theory.)

There are a number of beaches on Santorini; one is at **Perissa**—if you have not seen black sand before, you can here, and one end is bounded by a huge slab of volcanic rock. We found the strip of tavernas rather junky here; the beach is nice but not the adjoining beach community.

On the way back to Thira you can stop for lunch in a taverna, Faros (not far from the ferry road), with a great view over the caldera. It is run by a family, and their fish soup is a specialty. We were there on a festival day when they featured special foods and a live bousouki ensemble. We hope you will be lucky enough to happen on special moments of celebration in Greece. Sometimes we were just in the right place at the right time and other times we deliberately searched out some interesting festival. On this same day we spent in the modern village of Akrotiri, people were dressed up, dancing and singing in the tavernas and watching a procession; we could have joined in at any number of times and places.

One eventually has to leave Santorini, sad as that is. We drove down the hairpin turns to the dock, (not really that bad with a 10% grade) enjoying great views of the cliffs. The ferry has an interesting procedure for docking. It drops an anchor, then backs around to the pier. On this day the seamanship involved was delicate because of a strong crosswind with considerable chop, but the maneuver was performed casually and precisely. We were off for a sea tour past **Ios** and **Naxos**, then landed in **Paros**.

PAROS Is the place to go if you want a quiet vacation away from the clutter and noise of city life. This oval-shaped island in the Cyclades contains 81 square miles of rolling, mostly treeless hills, sandy beaches, and picturesque villages. Its quiet pastoral elegance is refreshing, and there is much to do. You can spend days lazing on a beach and swimming in aqua proper or spend some hours windsurfing, cycling or driving through the mountains or wandering through the maze of narrow streets in a village, photographing whitewashed Cycladic houses, or visiting archaeological sites, museums, and churches. Some of the villages are as intricate as Minoan labyrinths, yet the whole impression is one of order rather than chaos, of simplicity and a kind of organic rather than mechanical directness. Paros seems to have its own natural and beautiful form, and the unpretentious villages, mounted on small hilltops or sited beside small harbors, add to the symmetry of the whole. And the countryside is bucolic in the best sense of that word; like the villages, it suggests harmony and proportion rather than the drama and struggle of the Santorini landscape. If you happen to be in Paros during July or August there is an added decoration: the *Valley of Petaloudes* will be inhabited by thousands of colorful butterflies.

Evidence of life on Paros dates from 9000 B.C. Farming, fishing, and marble products sustained the life of the villages in early times. Maritime trade sent marble figurines and vases from Paros all over the ancient world. Beautiful white marble from Paros found its way into the monuments of nearby Delos, and sculptors have used Parian marble throughout the ages—Praxiteles, an artisan in the sixth century B.C.; Thrasyboulos, who created a gold and ivory statue of Asklepios found at Epidavros; and Skopas, who designed the Mausoleum of Halicarnassos; and, in modern times, the sculptors of Napoleon's tomb. The marble quarries on Paros no longer provide blocks for sculptors because world demand for marble has decreased and Italian quarries (e.g., Carrara) can supply marble less expensively. Now, you will see rough marble in stone fences and marble chips in road construction on Paros.

The ferries land at **Parikia**, a town built on the ruins of an ancient port. The tourist office is adjacent to the dock, in a windmill. You can get a map of the island there, as well as information on accommodations and sightseeing. Although local hoteliers will try to convince you to stay right in town when they meet the incoming ferries, we recommend the quieter pleasures of good hotels in villages like **Naoussa** and **Marpissa**. If you do not have ferry tickets for your next stop, you might want to check the schedule for the island of your choice in one of the travel agencies across the street from the pier. Service varies according to the season, and the day as well; passengers without cars have more possibilities than those committed to car ferries. Parikia has lots of coffee bars and tavernas where you can while away time and still see the ferry coming around the point in plenty of time.

In Parikia, the *Panaghia Ekatontapyliani,* or Katapoliana Church, is both architecturally interesting and also wreathed in legend. Some scholars claim that the name means "church of the hundred gates" or "doors"; in fact, it is claimed that 99 have been found but the 100th will only be discovered when Constantinople is returned to the Christians by the Turks. Believe what you will, the church is worth a visit.

A sixth century B.C. Doric temple probably contributed the columns. There is a cruciform font in the baptistry used for complete immersion during baptism. Although the original building was designed by Isidore of Miletus in the sixth century A.D., there have been a number of restorations since that time. Look for a figure across the courtyard depicting Isadore and Ignatius, the builder. Jealousy over their individual contribution to this beautiful structure caused them to fight on the rooftop until both fell to their deaths. Forever cast in stone, Isidore pulls his beard and Ignatius holds his aching head. There is a painting of Saint Theoktisti; her hand lies in a box in the church. She was captured by pirates, escaped, and lived for 30 years on Paros; found by a hunter and brought the communion bread she requested, she passed away. It is claimed that he cut off her hand as a good luck token but was held until he had returned it to her body. Her footprint is hidden under a wooden cover; visitors can remove their shoes and place a foot into hers for good luck.

The **Archaeological Museum** in Parikia features a 3-foot-long marble tablet on which is written part of the Parian Chronicle, found in 1897, that records history from long before Homer to 264 B.C. The scribe wrote little about political and military matters of the day, and more about cultural events and persons involved in the arts. A much larger section found in 1627 resides in the Ashmolean Museum in Oxford, England. The Parikia museum also holds a number of Parian marble sculptures, including a winged Victory, a medusa with snakes, and a lion and calf relief. There is a statue of Archilochos, a famous lyric poet born on Paros, in the courtyard. He is known for the creation of iambic pentameter; prior to this, Greek poetry used epic hexameter and the elegiac meter. Archilochus made such good use of this quick rhythm in his satiric verses that Hadrian called his work "raging iambics."

From Parikia, take the road to Naoussa for a day of beaching (perhaps at **Kolimbithres,** with its wind-sculpted rocks and sandy coves). This attractive port is full of fishing boats with their nets strung out, providing authentic background for photographers. It is also fun to get lost in the network of crooked but immaculately clean streets with whitewashed houses, shops, and tavernas. We stopped in one restaurant where we were invited to look at and smell the aroma of the various foods available; we found it so hard to choose among them that we tried some of each, with local wine adding the perfect touch.

During the summer of 1984 Demetrius U. Schilardi, curator of the Delfi Museum, found a 2600-year-old temple to Athena on Paros. This site is located below an earlier Mycenean structure overlooking Naoussa. The temple is about 32 by 16 feet and built of gray stone mined on Paros. Excavation is in process at this time.

Continuing the drive down the east side of the island, past waving green grass, low shrubs, small pines, spring flowers, and stone walls made partly with marble, we spotted a monastery on a hill just as we began to get views of the sea and of nearby Naxos. A man carrying a plastic bag of fish waved. The Greek people are very friendly and wave at visitors with a smile we always return. **Pisso Livadi** has a lovely sand beach with swings for children. Boats were tied up at a pier and tavernas were ready to serve thirsty travelers. **Logara Bay** features a windsurfing school on its sandy beach. If you want to see another lovely beach town with many private villas, continue on to Marpissa; otherwise, retrace your steps a little and head inland toward **Lefkai,** on a "half-made" road of marble chips that should be smooth by the time you arrive. This village is in one of the few green areas of the island and has a pleasant, shaded woods for walking and picnicking adjoining it. This drive through the hills is pleasant and rural; we noticed paths for mule transportation meandering around and over old stone bridges. To return to Parikia, continue past **Kostas,** by a marble quarry, then beside cuts through the hill that form the new road, where you can see the white marble with red earth coloring the surface. There is much more to see on the southern and western shores of this peaceful island if you have time for a longer stay.

You will not want to leave the islands on Greece, but if you must, start by taking the ferry to **Siros** and through the strait between **Kithnos** and **Kea** to Piraeaus. Then from Piraeaus, head toward Korinthos for another glimpse of the canal mentioned earlier. The drive along the south shore of the Gulf of Korinthos is very interesting, with one view after another of mountains that have suffered wind erosion and resemble the Bad Lands in America. Continue on this good road until you reach Patras. The ferry from Patras to **Brindisi,** Italy, takes 17 hours, a time to catch up on reading ahead for the next leg of your trip and to sleep.

Italy

BRINDISI is an important seaport for those traveling from Greece to Italy; it has served as a center for maritime activity from Greece, the Levant, and the Far East since Roman times. After declining in the Middle Ages, Brindisi regained trade when the Suez Canal opened in 1869. You may recall that the "India Mail" from Jules Verne's *Around the World in 80 Days* sailed from Brindisi after the Suez Canal was opened. Walk west on the *Regina Margherita* seaside promenade until you come to the 52 steps leading up to a terrace where one of two terminal columns of the *Appian Way* remains. The marble capital on top depicts Jove, Neptune, Pallas, Mars, and eight tritons. The remaining column was probably constructed in the second century A.D.; its companion was destroyed during an earthquake in the 16th century. Nearby, Virgil died, in a house marked with an inscription on the ruins. The *cathedral,* built in the 12th century, destroyed by an earthquake, and rebuilt in 1743, stands in *Piazza Duomo;* the apse dates from the earlier building. The *Palazzo Balsamo,* built in the 14th century, has a loggetta with Gothic arches superimposed over Romanesque arches. You may have seen the Knights Templar in London; its mate is here in Brindisi, a reminder of the English knights who embarked from this spot for Jerusalem. The *Marinaio d'Italia,* or the monument to the Sailor of Italy, stands in the form of a giant rudder, 174 feet high. Its form is unmistakable, dominating the harbor and the skyline, and there is a fine view of the city and the sea from the top.

Heading north from Brindisi, you can choose to take the highway, S379, which is a traffic-laden route along the coast and rather dull, or take S7 to **Taranto,** along parts of the Appian Way, or take S16 for a pleasant rural drive through orchards and olive groves, past the fascinating *trulli,* and in or around hill towns with panoramic scenery. If you choose the latter route, as we did, head for **S. Vito dei Normanni,** where you will begin to see conical houses that look as if they might be inhabited by the Seven Dwarfs. Called trulli, these dry-wall structures are made of gray flat stones placed in a circular, domed pattern. Some of the roofs have symbols painted on them, such as a cross, and a carved decoration on the very top as well. (The museum in **Alberobello** has posters defining each symbol.)

The next town, **Carovigno,** has a 15th-century castle that was built by Raymond del Balza Orsini, Lord of Taranto, to defend the inhabitants from marauding pirates and the Turks. A 65-foot tower was built on the seaward side to protect the town against maritime attacks. Nearby, the *Belvedere Sanctuary* is in a deep grotto with tunnels leading to the altar and a crypt. Pilgrimages are made here at Easter and during August. **Ostuni,** the next town, was originally a Messapian city, as verified by artifacts that were uncovered in the Necropolis. The *cathedral,* built between 1470 and 1495, has lovely rose windows and an elaborate facade. From the next town, **Cisternino,** with its Oriental houses and hanging balconies, there is a view of the Valle d'Itria, with a number of trulli. Continue on to **Locorotondo** and turn right on S172, following signs for **Selva di Fasano,** which is a lovely wooded oasis of estates, villas, and a number of pleasant hotels and resorts. The area is full of large trees, cool and green on a hot day, and the whole of the woods is spread across a hilltop hundreds of meters above the coastal plain; it is quite obviously a summer retreat from the heat of the plain below for the well-to-do residents of southeastern Italy. **Fasano,** below, is a picturesque old town to wander through, and there are a number of holiday seaside resorts along the coast, including **Torre Canne Terme,** which also boasts chlorine sulphur and bromine salt springs. **Savelletri** has a serene harbor made for photographers and contemplatives.

Back on the main track again, retrace your route through Locorotondo to **Alberobello,** where you can wander through a trulli district in the town; the hillside of the old town is an extensive natural museum of this strange but efficient form of architecture, even to the church towers. If you are not put off by the superficial trappings of tourism (Alberobello has discovered the value of its unusual heritage), you will want to spend several hours wandering through the fairyland streets of this town. Stop in the tourist office in the Piazza de Popolo for a map.

Continue on S604 through **Noci** and **Gioia d. Colle,** then take S171 across the Bari–Brindisi highway to **Altamura,** which has a bypass, and S96 to **Gravina** and the mountains beyond (look right after the town for a view from the bridge of a river ravine with rocks ravaged by erosion), heading toward **Potenza.** The trip up through the hills provides lovely views of the valley, with shades of green, the wind patterns blowing through the grasses, and, in the spring, red poppies surrounded by many varieties of yellow, white, pink, and purple blooms, overhung by thistle and Mediterranean pines with their accompanying shadows. Driving a road that winds through blowing wild flowers is a good omen for what follows. As you head northwest across the instep of the Italian boot, the landscape changes constantly at just the right tempo to avoid boredom—from low, rolling hills to open plain to high, large hills green with waving grain to wooded mountains and stark, high rock ridges, a symphony for the eyes.

When you reach **Oppido Lucano,** you will have climbed to 670 meters above sea level. We noticed a great deal of new construction in many of the hill towns, some probably as a result of the earthquake in 1980. Keep your camera ready for shots of hill towns and the adjacent rural countryside; this section of road is windy, with new views around each bend. Potenza, which overlooks the *Basento Valley,* was very heavily damaged by the 1980 earthquake and is practically a new city. After Potenza, where you join the S407 headed for **Salerno,** there are views ahead of higher mountains, then a gorge with unusually shaped rocks and an apparently deserted town at the top, eerie with black holes for windows, no shutters open or closed, and no sign of life at all—probably another relic of the great earthquake. A number of tunnels take you through a particularly wild section where the mountains are steep, with evidence of slides, netting to hold back the nearly vertical slopes, and some roofs over the road to protect cars from falling rock. Soon you will meet the autostrada and continue past **Eboli** (setting for the novel *Christ Stopped at Eboli*) to the exit for **Battipaglia,** where you will see signs for **Paestum.**

PAESTUM, originally Poseidonia, is located about 20 miles south of Salerno. It was an ancient Greek seaport city, dating back to the sixth century B.C., which fell into ruin because of an outbreak of malaria. The temples that remain are built of fine yellow limestone, with massive pillars in contrast with the green vegetation that has grown up around them. The *Temple of Neptune,* perhaps misnamed because it was probably dedicated to Hera (Juno), has 14 columns lining the sides; 6 are across the ends of a massive structure 200 feet long. The *Basilica* is the oldest temple in Paestum and it was also dedicated to Hera; it has 50 fluted Doric columns. The **Temple of Ceres** consists of 34 columns still standing, and contains a sacrificial altar. The **Archaeological Museum** houses the contents of Greek tombs, including paintings

South of Paestum lies one of the most beautiful sections of the Tyrrhenian coast. Having lived in this section of Campagnia for several months almost 20 years ago, with repeat visits to relive those days nostalgically, we dream of our next trip there from 4000 miles away. Much as we liked this sylvan countryside in the seemingly timeless south as it was—then untouched by tourism—it *is* there for visitors to enjoy. There are accommodations in all price ranges and more than enough peace and serenity for all. You can visit a smaller and quieter version of Paestum if you drive south along the coast road (S267) past **Acciaroli, Pioppi,** and **Marina de Casalvelino** to **Marina de Ascea. Scavi di Velia,** or **Elea,** is a site we have visited several times and we find it a perfect place to observe and enjoy an ancient town, untrampled by hordes of tour groups. Founded in 585 B.C. by the Focei of Asia Minor, it was famous for a school of philosophy called *Eleatica.* Excavated sections include part of the perimeter walls, a gate from the third century B.C. of Roman construction overlaid on Greek, basement foundations of the temple on the Acropolis from the fifth century B.C., a medieval tower, and a museum.

AMALFI DRIVE Back on the road heading north again, take time to enjoy the Amalfi Drive just beyond **Salerno,** site of Allied landings in southern Italy during September 1943. This cliff-edge road follows the southern perimeter of mountainous coastline ringing the *Sorrento Peninsula;* it is one of the most breathtaking roads anywhere in Europe.

The mountainside, with its vineyards and villages tilted toward the vertical, and the narrow, curvy, hairpin turns so far above the sea make the drive appealing and frightening. If you have a choice, avoid taking this magnificent drive on weekends and holidays when it may be full of traffic. We spent a great deal of time at each narrow turn one Easter weekend while tour buses maneuvered back and forth, trying to pass. This encounter was repeated over and over until one bus driver would either give up and back up, along with all the traffic behind him, or get out and wave his arms, with additional theatrics from drivers of nearby cars or pedestrians, until a compromise was reached. In any case, each spot was lovelier than the last. The rugged rocks, gorges plunging to the sea, hillsides sprinkled with orange and lemon trees, flowers everywhere, and people picnicking on a beautiful day defined the essence of an Italian holiday.

There are a number of nearly vertical towns along the coastal slope, including **Vietri** (famous for pottery, if you have room to carry it back), **Maiori, Ravello** (drive up to the piazza for an overview of the whole coast), **Amalfi, Minore, Maggiore, Vettica, Praiano,** and **Positano.**

The Sorrento Peninsula is high on a cliff overlooking the Tyrrhenian Sea; it divides the Gulf of Naples from the Gulf of Salerno. It is an ideal spot for both doers and sitters: there is much to visit and much to enjoy in the warm sun on this spectacularly beautiful peninsula.

CAPRI Just off the end of the peninsula lies the Isle of Capri, a paradise discovered by ancient Romans. It can be reached by boat from Sorrento for a day trip. You will not want to leave, however. Capri is composed of two gigantic rock masses with a cleft in the middle. Much of the coastline is high, jagged, and completely inaccessible by boat. In between these pinnacles of rock there are grottos and a startingly blue sea. The vegetation is lush and prolific. We enjoyed spending most of our time on the island taking walks through the areas that are wildest, particularly the coastline south of the village of Capri. (You can buy a little guide in the village with these walks clearly marked.) We have found that the walks often take longer than we plan, possibly because we pause so frequently to look down the cliffs to the surf below. You can also go into the *Blue Grotto* by boat when the sea is calm. We also recommend taking the bus to **Anacapri** and riding the chairlift up to the summit of *Monte Solaro,* where the view encompasses the island, the Sorrento peninsula, and the whole of the Gulf of Naples, including the city and Mount Vesuvius beyond.

From Sorrento, follow the road along the northwestern side of the peninsula (S145) through **Vico Equense** and **Castellammare di Stabia** to **Torre Annunziata,** then follow the signs to **Pompei.**

POMPEI, founded in the fifth century B.C., was covered by the eruption of Vesuvius in A.D. 79. Pliny described the scene: a strong earthquake in the morning, followed by smoke and a shower of cinder that covered the ground 3 feet deep. Some fled, some stayed indoors; then a second rain of molten lava and cinders covered the town. In 1748, during the reign of Charles of Borbon, excavation was undertaken. The streets have high curbs with stepping-stones across at the corners (with gaps for chariot wheels, which have left ruts). The buildings are made of brick with marble and plaster overlaid. The center of life in Pompei was the *Forum,* a square paved with marble flagstones. On it, the *Temple of Jupiter* was the most important place of worship; the *Basilica* was used for judicial and business affairs. There are two theaters, one large and one small, a gymnasium, and public baths. The houses and villas reflect many styles: the *House of Vettis* has well preserved frescoes and an Etruscan garden with statues; the *Tragic Poet's House* has a mosaic of a dog tied with a chain; the *Lucrezio Frontone House* contains mythological paintings; the *House of the Large Fountain* has lovely mosaic wall decorations; the *House of Venus in the Shell* is named after a mosaic depicting Venus sailing in the shell, escorted by two Amoretti; *Loreio Tiburtino's House* has more mythological paintings, a stream with waterfall, fountains, and statues in the garden; and the *Villa of Mysteries* contains a freize that may depict the initiation rites of one of the Dionysian cults that flourished in Pompei. The *Antiquarium* displays items that have been uncovered, including human and animal bodies preserved by lava. After you have explored the city, you can drive and then walk up to the crater of Vesuvius to see where it all began. There are two roads up the mountain: the one on the north side is paved and less precipitous. The rim overlooking the crater is narrow and will probably pump some adrenaline into your system.

From Pompei, take A2 around the edges of **Napoli** toward **Roma**, unless you have the time and inclination to stop at the ruins of ancient *Ercolano (Herculaneum),* the other seaside town destroyed by the eruption of Vesuvius in A.D. 79; to reach it, drive along the coast road (S18) from Torre Annunziata toward Naples. For those who wish to stop in **Caserta** (north of Naples), there is a huge palace (1200 rooms) built in 1752 to bolster the grandeur of Charles III, the Borbon king. It has been called the Versailles of the Kingdom of Naples. The accompanying park contains ponds, fountains, and a 256-foot-high waterfall. An English garden, planned for Maria-Carolina of Austria (the sister of Marie Antoinette), was completed in 1782.

Further on along A2, you will see signs for the *Abbey of Monte Cassino.* The abbey, destroyed four times, was reconstructed after World War II, when it was the site of one of the longest and most bitter battles of the Italian campaign because it guarded the crucial road to Roma. In spite of repeated destruction, there is a museum to visit that contains many of the riches of this abbey; it is historically important as the founding place of the Benedictine Order in A.D. 529 and it maintained its power and influence throughout the Middle Ages. Both St. Benedict and St. Scholastica lie in the basilica under the high altar. The view from the abbey takes in the lovely *Liri Valley.*

This section of the autostrada approaching Roma from the south provides beautiful mountain scenery, although the road itself is somewhat like a racetrack. Impatient drivers tailgate, blinking their lights as if they were off to an emergency. Trucks swing out to pass slowly, causing lines of cars driving bumper to bumper to form behind them. The road is not relaxing to drive, but neither are the streets of Roma.

Roma

Roma is large enough and complex enough to overwhelm the visitor. Driving is almost always frustrating and can be terrifying, and pedestrians take their lives in their hands when they set foot into a street. We found crossing the broad circular street around the Coliseum to be a real game of chance (even worse than trying to drive around the Arc de Triomphe in Paris). The noise, traffic, pollution, and the squalor of some sections can be depressing but should not make you skip the historic and artistic treasures of Roma. We have appreciated the city more by camping in outlying calm, peaceful settings to restore our battered senses. And we quickly learned *not* to drive during the four daily rush hours.

According to legend, Romulus (one of the twin sons of Mars, who were suckled by a she-wolf until a shepherd found them) traced the walls of the city in 753 B.C. and forbade anyone to cross the line. His twin brother, Remus, violated the injunction and was killed. (A live female wolf kept in a cage at the steps of **Capitoline Hill** perpetuates the legend.) However, there was probably a Stone-Age settlement on the site long before Romulus and Remus. Before the Roman Republic, an Etruscan king, Servius Tullius, believed in democratic government but was overthrown. Some of the art of the Etruscan period can be seen in the **Etruscan Museum** in the **Villa Giulia.** In 509 B.C. the Roman Republic was established, ruled by the Senate and Consuls. After 390 B.C., when the Gauls invaded and sacked Roma, she was ravaged again periodically. The Republic was replaced by the early Empire under Octavius, under the title of Augustus Caesar, from 27 B.C. until Nero burned most of Roma in A.D. 64. Marcus Aurelius later reunified the Empire and had many buildings erected that are still standing in Roma. The later Empire continued from A.D. 283 to 476, before it was overwhelmed by barbarian invasions and diminishing resources. Gradually, pagan buildings in Roma were converted to Christian uses; even the **Pantheon** was consecrated in 609. The Holy Roman Empire was founded in A.D. 962 by Otto I, former King of Saxony, leading to centuries in which Christian Rome was the center of church and state, but the modern political unification of Italy as a nation had to wait until the 19th century. Throughout all these vicissitudes, Roma has remained the symbolic center of Christianity and much of western civilization.

The **Roman Forum,** located between the **Piazza Campidoglio** and the **Palatine,** was once the center of Roman life during the Republic. Excavations during the 19th and 20th centuries have uncovered temples, prisons, an arch, and many other buildings. The Palatine is a continuation of excavated ruins, including gardens, houses, and a palace. The **Coliseum,** opened in A.D. 80, takes its name from the "colossal" statue of Nero that stood there; here gladiators fought and Christians were thrown to the lions in early forms of public entertainment. The Pantheon, started in 27 B.C. by Agrippa, has an impressive dome and represents the accommodation of classical Roma to the needs of the Holy Roman Empire.

Vatican City, the smallest state in the world, is located on a hill west of the Tiber River and is separated from Roma by a wall. Since 1929 it has been an independent state, having its own coins, newspaper, postage stamps, and radio station. The population is about 1000; about 500 of these are soldiers dressed in uniforms designed by Michelangelo. **St. Peter's,** begun in A.D. 319, is the largest church in the world. As you stand in the square you will be in an ellipse formed by two semicircles of Doric columns extending out as arms of the church. The dome, created by Michelangelo, is supported by four gigantic pillars. You can climb up into the dome, or take an elevator, for a panoramic view of Roma. In the first chapel on the right you will see Michaelangelo's *Pieta,* sculpted when he was 22 years old. It is now protected against vandalism by reinforced glass. The **Vatican Museum** is housed in a series of palaces and contains the largest collection of art treasures in the world. The **Sistine Chapel** may be the climax of your stay in Roma. Michelangelo's *Last Judgment,* on the end wall, and his frescoes on the ceiling cannot be adequately described; they must be seen.

The other delights of medieval and Renaissance Roma are too numerous to detail here. Those who want to explore the city in depth should plan to stay for five to seven days.

From Rome, you can take another section of the autostrada (A1) to **Firenze,** or you can choose to follow a more interesting route through some of the oldest and most powerful of the self-contained hill towns that controlled the interior of Italy from the 12th through the 14th centuries. If you choose the scenic route, start on the A1 north, another narrow road clogged with trucks, but leave it for the S3 at signs for **Terni;** this four-lane highway is newer and a much better road, with ever-changing mountain views and lots of hill towns to spot. The Umbrian countryside is a painter's study in green and brown, with varying shades in the dark green forests, spring green deciduous trees, vineyards, crops, and rounded mountains in large lumps and humps. Many of the hill towns are walled, enclosing beautiful winding streets and ancient buildings. Some contain art treasures that are not to be seen anywhere else. If you have time, you may want to visit **Narni, Amelia, Acquasparta, Orvieto,** or **Spoleto.**

TODI By luck, we landed in the lovely little town of Todi, located just off S3, because we decided to end a long driving day before reaching our planned destination. It was one of the best choices we have fallen into! To enter Todi you drive up a very steep, curving road through rural countryside to the town gate, then up an even steeper road inside the town, turning several times and continuing up the narrow street to the **basilica** and the piazza. The town lies 411 meters above sea level. Inside the **cathedral** there is a particularly exquisite rose window; below the window, Ferrau of Faenza painted a mural covering the entire wall. His *Universal Judgment* was probably patterned after the creativity of Michelangelo; the figures have expressive faces, and their bodies and positions are very realistic. Outside the cathedral, in the **People's Square,** you can spot the 13th-century **Captain's Palace,** which contains two large arcades or vaults *(voltoni)* where the town crossbow archers stayed. Nearby, the **People's Palace** dates back to 1213. The **Prior's Palace** was the residence of the mayors, vicars, and governors who ruled Todi.

There is a statue of Garibaldi in the square bearing his name. The **Temple of St. Fortunatus** contains the remains of the poet Jacopone; the walnut choir contains 58 stalls and covers the central apse. The statue in the middle is that of St. Fortunatus. The church of **Santa Maria Della Consolazione** is shaped like a Greek cross, with a large dome. On the outside you will see the Bramante style of architecture called rhythmic bay, characterized by alternating windows, pilasters, and niches, with triangular tops in between curved tops. Just inside is the wooden statue of Pope Martin I, with a silver toe. There are statues of the 12 apostles, copies of the originals in bronze, which were lost. In addition to this fine collection of churches and palaces, Todi has many narrow, winding streets for you to explore, and its open hilltop setting makes it a pleasant town to spend time in.

As we drove by more hill towns we thought about the concept of walls, so necessary in ancient and medieval times for the safety of the inhabitants. The word *suburb* derives from those living outside and below the walls, often in hovels, unprotected from maurading groups. Ironically, now as our cities decay and we need more protection in them than outside, the preferred residence is often in the suburbs. The dangerous encounter with an anonymous stranger is more likely to occur within than without the walls, as modern cities struggle to maintain minimal order and safety.

ASSISI Beyond Todi, continue on toward **Perugia** to the signs for Assisi, a lovely town visible from afar because it is spread over a hillside and dominated by a huge basilica and monastery. This is the town of Saint Francis, born in 1181, perhaps the most Christlike of saints, who devoted his life to befriending birds and animals, preaching the joys of a peaceful life serving others, writing poetry and songs for God, and other charitable works. The **Basilica of St. Francis** consists of two superimposed churches that have a common apse. The upper and lower basilicas are very different in style, but both are rich in frescoes by such painters as Simone Martini, Cimabue, and Giotto. In the lower basilica, the tomb of Orsini, a Gothic structure, lies behind the altar in the left transept; frescoes by Lorenzetti are on the vaults in this area. The tomb of St. Francis lies below, down many marble steps. The upper basilica contains lovely glass windows from the 13th and 14th centuries, and there are paintings and frescoes adorning all of the walls. Be sure to see the 28 panels that represent scenes from St. Francis' life, created by Giotto.

At the other end of town, **Saint Clare's Church** (Santa Chiara) has a white-and-pink striped facade. The rose window is exquisite. The crucifix that inspired St. Francis is in the Sacrament's Chapel; his tunic and other garments may be seen there as well. A nun with a black veil covering her head and face will give you a little card with a picture of the crucifix and a prayer on it. You can drop coins in the box as an offering. Walk down the steps to the crypt, where you will find another black-robed nun willing to read a description of St. Clare in the language of your choice and hand you a card with a print of the tomb and a prayer. Behind her lies the body of St. Clare, the bones blackened through the ages, wearing a black habit with a floral wreath around her head. The startling effect of the whole scene is tastefully and respectfully arranged.

As with most hill towns, Assisi is a walking town; take time to explore the little streets and views of the countryside. Then follow S75 past the outskirts of Perugia to *Lago Trasimeno,* a pleasant spot where you can spend time taking a steamer around the lake and relaxing. It has not always been so placid: in 217 B.C. it was the site of a major battle in which the Carthaginian Hannibal defeated the Roman Consul Flaminius and killed 16,000 of his troops.

At this point you are leaving Umbria and entering Tuscany, another region of green rolling hills, more walled hill towns, monasteries, and slopes full of vineyards and olive groves. We thought to ourselves, "Does the world really need so many olives?" We have seen olive groves all over Yugoslavia, Greece, and Italy; pretty as they are, one wonders if other basic foods might better replace some of those silvery trees.

SIENA S326 will take you to Siena, famous for a wild horse race, the *Palio delle Contrade,* held in the *Piazza del Campo* every July 2 and August 16. The Piazza del Campo looks like a giant scallop shell and is elaborately paved with red brick and white stone in patterns. Contestants and officials all wear medieval costumes, and participants are allowed to lash each other as well as the horses. The *Duomo* is located on the tallest hill of the three Siena is built on. It was begun in 1065 and completed during the 14th century, and has unique paving done by a number of artists over a period of two centuries. The *Cathedral Museum* contains the *Maesta of Duccio* as well as *The Three Graces.*

From Siena, take S2 to Firenze (Florence), for many the epitome of Italian cities.

FIRENZE grew from an Etruscan village into a city flourishing with trade guilds by the 11th century. In the 13th century the Guelphs appeared as supporters of Rome's popes against emperors who tried to gain power. Florence grew and prospered, led by shrewd and honest bankers who became influential all over Europe. The Medici regime gave splendor to the city through the arts for three centuries. The Italian Renaissance was born in Florence, through the sculpture and painting of Michelangelo, da Vinci, Rossellino, Bartolommeo, Botticelli, Ghiberti, Donatello, Pisano, Cellini, Giotto, Masaccio, Fra Angelico, and Lippi, and the writing of Dante, Machiavelli, Petrarch, and Boccaccio. A number of central books in western culture are associated with Florence. Among them are Dante's *The Divine Comedy;* Machiavelli's *The Prince;* and, more recently, Henry James's *Portrait of a Lady*. In 1944 Hitler's troops blew up all the bridges in Florence except the **Ponte Vecchio** (Old Bridge) as they retreated northward during the Italian campaign. In 1966 a flood swept through the city, covering treasures with mud; people all over the world contributed money and time in an effort to salvage them.

We have always enjoyed leaving something to see for our next trip to Florence, selecting what we want to do very carefully and savoring the experience. You may want to orient yourself first by studying maps and then by enjoying the panoramic view from the **Piazzale Michelangelo,** located on a hill above the city. The center of this remarkable city is small enough to be surveyed by eye and comfortably explored on foot. You will want to dispose of your car on the outskirts because the center of the city is congested and has very little parking.

Piazza Del Duomo (Cathedral Square) contains the **Cathedral of Santa Maris del Fiore,** begun in 1296 and finished in 1434. The spectacular exterior is covered with variegated white, green, and red marble; in comparison, the Gothic interior seems stark, bare, and enormous. You can climb up to the inner gallery of the dome for a view of the cathedral nave and outside onto the top of the dome for a panoramic view of Florence. The stained-glass windows were made from the work of Donatello, Uccello, and Ghiberti. In the first chapel in the north transept you can see the unfinished pieta, which Michelangelo worked on at the age of 80. And underneath the cathedral the ruins of an older 10th-century cathedral have recently been opened. Giotto designed the accompanying 269-foot **campanile** in the 14th century. There are 414 steps to the top, which offers another panoramic view. Facing the front of the Duomo is the **Battistero,** with huge gilt doors famous all over the world. The south door contains the work of Andrea Pisano done in 1330 and is Gothic in style; the north door, done by Lorenzo Ghiberti from 1403 to 1424, depicts the life of Christ; the east door, also by Ghiberti, illustrates scenes from the Old Testament. This door, said by Michelangelo to be worthy of the Gate to Paradise, lost five panels during the 1966 flood; all have since been found and restored. Inside the Battistero there is a 13th-century mosaic covering the ceiling (which can be lit if you request it).

Piazza Della Signoria is an open-air sculpture gallery containing "Perseus Holding the Head of Medusa" by Cellini; "Judith and Holofernes" by Donatello; a copy of "David" by Michelangelo; "Neptune" and "Hercules" and "Cacus" by Bandinelli. The **Palazzo Vecchio** (Old Palace) contains paintings and sculptures, the apartment of Eleanor of Toledo, wife of Cosimo I, a Medici, and the town hall. The **Uffizi Museum,** in a Renaissance palace, is the richest museum in Italy and one of the finest in the world. You will have to choose what you would like to see among the superb collections. The **Pitti Palace and Gallery** on the other side of the Ponte Vecchio houses more priceless art treasures. The **Boboli Gardens,** a beautiful example of Italian terraced gardens, are just outside the Pitti Palace. Admirers of Michelangelo (and readers of Irving Stone's *The Agony and the Ecstacy*) may want to continue searching for more of Michelangelo's work in the **Medici Chapel,** where you will see the figures of "Dawn," "Dusk," "Night," and "Day," or in the **Accademia Gallery,** with the original statue of David. There are many, many more museums, churches, and statues to see if you have the desire and the stamina. You will want to stroll slowly across the Ponte Vecchio bridge with its shops, and the **Mercanto Centrale** is an experience for shoppers who like to bargain for sweaters, leather goods, and straw pieces.

Leave Firenze on the A11, a newer and wider section of the autostrada, heading west for **Pisa.**

PISA, founded as a Greek port (although the coast is now 6 miles away), is the home of the **Leaning Tower,** a campanile with the top 14 feet off the vertical because of a slip of land during construction. You can climb 294 steps to the top for a fine view (the guardrails at the top leave a lot to be desired for the not-so-brave); if you do climb try *not* to go up just before the hour, because the bells will reverberate in your head. Galileo used the cathedral to study the pendulum, and the leaning tower to work on laws of gravity and the acceleration of falling bodies. The **Duomo** was built in marble of alternating colors; inside, the pulpit, shaped as a polygon, contains a series of pillars with statues depicting the Virtues.

Continue on up the Ligurian coast on A12 or S1 with stops at enchanting places like **Lerici, La Spezia, Rapallo, Santa Margherita Ligure,** and **Portofino.** We loved Lerici 20 years ago, with its picturesque fishing scene in the mornings and peaceful evenings for walking along the harbor. Rapallo is one of the many elegant resort areas along this rugged coastline blessed with a mild climate and lush foliage. One of the highlights of a trip a few years ago was driving up the mountain to the shrine of the **Madonna de Montallegro** (you can also get there by funicular). This church, built in 1557, is known for the mystery of the picture of the passing of the Virgin, which disappeared and then reappeared in its place; it is kept in the high altar. There are other treasures there including a pieta by Luca Cambiaso and an apparizione by Nicolo Barabino. Many votive offerings line the walls; they are fascinating to read as they reveal the lifeblood of the community. We were especially interested in the many momentos of sailing ships offered in thanks for a safe voyage, often worked on during lonely hours at sea by the men of Rapallo. The view from this church, over the Gulf of Rapallo, is magnificent.

Santa Margherita Ligure, just beyond Rapallo on the Portofino peninsula, is a beautiful resort town with a harbor chock full of gorgeous yachts. This place has attracted royal families, actors and actresses, politicians, and corporate executives since the early 1900s. In 1951 one of the preliminary conferences preceding the forming of the Common Market was held here.

Portofino, located on a lovely bay near the tip of the Portofino promontory, was once a quiet fishing village but is now an internationally known resort. You can climb up **Mount Portofino** or walk out to the lighthouse for a marvelous view of the Italian Riviera and the French Riviera, to the west. You can also take boats or footpaths from Portofino to other, more remote fishing villages along this aesthetically delightful coast.

As we continued along on the way to Genoa, we went through innumerable tunnels. The man who submitted the budget for this road must have been brave, indeed. At Genoa you have a choice to make, depending on the next leg of your trip. If you are heading for France you can continue along the riviera autostrada (A10) through Monte Carlo, Nice, and Cannes. If Switzerland is your next objective, there are several routes heading north through the various passes and tunnels—Mont Blanc, San Bernardo, Simplon, San Gottardo, or San Bernardino. If you are continuing through Italy, take A7 to Milano and the Italian lake region.

We would be inclined to visit the Italian lakes and settle in for a time, omitting the hassle of sightseeing in large cities. The lakes of Lombardy are unbelievably beautiful, with snowcapped mountains reflected in deep blue water, lemon trees planted amidst villas, promenades where you can sit and sip coffee or have an Italian ice, gardens everywhere, sailboats on the lakes, and warm sunshine even in winter. **Lago Maggiore** is 40 miles long and contains the **Borromean Islands.** The most famous of these, **Isola Bella** (Beautiful Island), looks like a wedding cake with its tiers and terracing. **Stresa,** a town on the western shore, was once a fishing village and is now an international resort. You will want to take a boat trip to enjoy the full variety and beauty of the lake. To the east beyond **Lago di Lugano,** a narrow mountain lake with handsome villas on the north shore, is **Lago di Como,** set between towering mountains to the east and west. It is 30 miles long and divides into two legs at its southern end; because roads are narrow and slow, it is best to see the lake by boat. Much farther to the east, **Lago di Garda,** the largest lake in Italy, is 32 miles long and 11 miles wide, with lowlands in the south and a beautifully engineered lakeside road at the more mountainous northern end. The climate is warmer there because the lake is sheltered from cold north winds by the mountains. To supplement the natural beauty of the Italian lakes, there are castles, cathedrals, and museums all over the region.

MILANO, today a progressive and volatile commercial city, still holds some of the treasures of the past, including the "Last Supper," located in the **Cenacolo Vinciano,** next door to **Santa Maria delle Grazie.** The **Duomo,** located in the center of Milan, is one of the largest cathedrals in the world. It is built in the shape of a Latin cross and is a wonderful maze of spires, gables, and sculpture; you can walk up onto the roof for a closer look at the statues. The renowned opera house, **La Scala,** built in 1779, has an enormous chandelier suspended from the frescoed ceiling, as well as a museum.

From Milano, the A4 will take you by the major cities of the Po valley—**Bergamo, Brescia, Verona, Vicenza,** and **Padova** (Padua)—any of which are worth exploring if you have the time. A4 will continue to Venezia, where you can choose accommodation on *Punta Sabbioni* (to the east) or the *Lido* (to the southeast), where there are fine beaches and ferry service to Venezia, or park your car in **Mestre** (some danger of vandalism for unattended cars with luggage exposed inside) if you plan to stay in Venezia itself.

FRANCE—THE SOUTH AND THE WEST

Paris to Avignon	727 kilometers
Avignon to Arles	39 kilometers
Arles to Carcassone	226 kilometers
Carcassone to Souillac	259 kilometers
Souillac to Tours	359 kilometers
Tours to Quimper	382 kilometers
Quimper to St. Malo	283 kilometers
St. Malo to Mont-St.-Michel	52 kilometers
Mont-St.-Michel to Coutances	78 kilometers
Coutances to Cherbourg	75 kilometers
Cherbourg to Omaha Beach	73 kilometers
Omaha Beach to Bayeux	19 kilometers
Bayeux to Paris	273 kilometers

From Paris: (Provence) Avignon, Apt, Arles; (Dordogne) Rocamadour, Souillac, Sarlat, les Eyzies; (Loire) Chenonceaux, Monthou-sur-Cher, Chambord, Vouvray; (Brittany) Pont l'Abbe, Pte. du Raz, Pte. de Penhir, St. Malo, Mont-St.-Michel; (Normandy) Coutances, Cotentin Peninsula, Cherbourg, Pointe du Hoc, Omaha Beach, Bayeux; to Paris.

    This trip includes a selection of varied, exciting landscape matched with five historically significant regions in southern and western France: Provence, the Dordogne, the Loire, Brittany, and Normandy. It makes no pretence of including major cities, although it begins and ends in Paris for convenience. Although we enjoy *the* city, we have come to feel that there are more discoveries for us lying in wait in the provinces, and so we have begun to explore the riches of the countryside of France with continuing delight and amazement. Americans tend to think of France as a small country, about the size of Texas, but geologically it contains almost everything one can find in the 3000-mile span across the Amer-

ENGLAND
Calais
Dunkerque
BELGIUM
ENGLISH CHANNEL
Cherbourg
Dieppe
Omaha Beach
Bayeux
Carteret
le Havre
Carentan
Rouen
Coutances
Caen
Brest
Morlaix
St-Malo
Pointe de Penhir
Avranches
Mont-St-Michel
St-Brieuc
Paris
Douarnenez
Quimper
Concarneau
Rennes
Pointe de Penmarche
Fontainebleau
Pointe du Raz
Angers
St. Gemmes
Blois
Tours
Chambord
Nantes
Saumur
Chenonceaux
Dijon
FRANCE
Poitiers
N
ATLANTIC OCEAN
Limoges
Angouleme
Lyon
Perigueux
Sarlat
Souillac
Rocamadour
Montauban
Albi
Gordes
Avignon
Apt
Nimes
Cavaillon
St. Remy
Arles
Aix
Carcassonne
SPAIN
MEDITERRANEAN SEA

ican continent; the only difference is one of scale—the changes in topography come faster, but they are no less distinct in character. To push the analogy, within a small span one can enjoy the Alpine regions (Rockies), the valleys of the Dordogne and Loire (Hudson and Mississippi), the beaches of Normandy (Virginia and North Carolina), deserts near the sea in Aude (California), and the rugged coast of Brittany (Maine). And all of this is within a day's drive of Paris on France's efficient system of autoroutes.

We have carefully picked a tiny sampling from the innumerable possibilities for you to visit in the southern and western provinces. You can follow this route to get the flavor of the special features of these very diverse regions, with more than enough left over to whet your appetite for future trips. We have suggested a circular route that you can join at many different points. Or you can choose to concentrate on a smaller section, with in-depth exploration as your goal. If you are connecting with routes in adjoining countries, you can do so with ease. We were lucky enough to live and travel in each area with local inhabitants, thereby receiving the benefit of their knowledge, which we are passing on to you.

Paris is a good place to start and a likely airport for you to fly into unless you are driving from another country. Our section on Paris is brief because we expect that you will want to buy a detailed guide of the city and explore it by pursuing your own interests.

Paris

The Parisii, a tribe of Celts, built a fortress in the middle of the Seine on what is now called *Ile de la Cite*. The town spread through the surrounding forest, and by the 12th century Paris was a center of western culture. The *Sorbonne* was founded in 1253. In succeeding centuries the city walls were extended, buildings and monuments rose, Napoleon brought back art treasures from his conquests, and the *Louvre* developed. French art, literature, and science made Paris the intellectual capital of Europe.

You can not hope to "see" Paris in a matter of days, but you can enjoy enough to make you want to return. Take a bus tour of the city and then go to the areas you are especially interested in on foot. Or take a tour on the Seine by boat. Or orient yourself with a bird's-eye view from the top of the *Eiffel Tower*. Then ramble as you wish through a section of the city, enjoying its pleasures—shops, sidewalk cafes, galleries, book stores, fine restaurants—slowly. The Metro is the quickest and cheapest way to get from one section of the city to another. *Notre-Dame,* an enormous gray stone Gothic cathedral on Ile de la Cite, was started in 1163. From across the Seine the size, pinnacles, gargoyles, and flying buttresses are most impressive. As you approach the west facade you will see a number of sculptures on the doorways, including the Last Judgment in the center with a figure of Christ in triumph. Above the north door is a series of niches containing the Kings of Judah (28 statues). The rose window, begun in 1230, is 31½ feet in diameter and served as a model for similar windows in other cathedrals. Inside, the light from the rose window illuminates statues and the lovely carving on the choir screen. Climb the 252 steps to the Grande Gallerie and 80 more up to the South Tower for a sweeping view of Paris. Nearby **Sainte Chapelle** also has beautiful stained-glass windows and mosaic work. The **Conciergerie,** once a medieval palace, served as a prison during the Revolution. Marie Antoinette, Robespierre, Madame du Barry, and Andre Chenier waited there before they went to the guillotine.

The **Right Bank** of the city refers to the expensive and fashionable section north of the Seine. Walking from east to west, begin at the Louvre, probably the most famous museum in the world, where you can see "Venus de Milo," "Winged Victory," "Mona Lisa," and more paintings, sculpture, and art objects than you can assimilate in a week. The **Tuileries Gardens,** developed in the 16th century for Catherine de Medici, who wanted an Italian Renaissance garden, are decorated with pools and sculptures. Rectangular in shape, they border the Seine and cover 60 acres of central Paris. The **Jeu de Paume** is a Louvre annex containing Impressionist paintings, and the **Orangerie** hangs the work of post-Impressionists and has special exhibitions. Next you will come to the **Place de la Concorde,** one of the largest and the most impressive squares in the world. Along with fountains and an obelisk, the square once held the guillotine. On your left you will see the **Petit Palais,** containing art collections, and the **Grand Palais,** a large exhibition building. Continue on the **Champs Elysees** to **Arc de Triomphe,** the largest arch in the world, where 12 avenues meet in the center of the star. The grave of the unknown soldier is in the center, with a flame burning day and night. The arch is decorated with a sequence of sculptures depicting the glory of France. Climb the 280 steps to the top for a fine view of Paris. To the north **Montmartre,** once a village for artists and writers, now is a tourist mecca. Its hill is crowned by the basilica of **Sacre Coeur,** a large white Romanesque/Byzantine structure that dazzles the eye.

The **Left Bank,** south of the Seine, is more student-oriented, cheaper, and has a Bohemian atmosphere. The **University of Paris,** the **Sorbonne,** is located in the **Latin Quarter. St. Julien le Pauvre,** the university's first chapel, is now a Greek Orthodox church. **St. Severin** is a beautiful late Gothic church with impressive stained-glass windows. The **Pantheon** is the burial spot of Victor Hugo, Rousseau, Voltaire, and Zola. **Hotel de Cluny,** a mansion built by the Abbots of Cluny, is now a museum of medieval art objects that features rare tapestries. The **Palais du Luxembourg,** built for Marie de Medici in 1620, is now the meeting place of the French Parliament, and the adjoining **Jardin du**

Luxembourg is a park containing many sculptures and monuments. The *Hotel des Invalides* contains the tomb of Napoleon surrounded by oversized columns and figures; his statue is 8½ feet tall, which is 3 feet 4 inches taller than he really was. Farther west is the *Tour Eiffel,* built by Gustave Eiffel in 1889 for the World's Fair. Although considered too "modern" and only temporary when it was built, it is still there for flocks of visitors to enjoy. Brief excursions outside the city proper will bring you to the overwhelming palace of *Versailles,* the grand chateau at *Fontainebleau,* or the more modest chateau at *Chantilly;* all are surrounded by formal gardens, and the last two adjoin extensive forest tracts that originally were hunting preserves.

Provence

From Paris, take the Autoroute du Soleil (E1) to **Avignon,** a good base for touring Provence. Provence was controlled by the Romans for a long time; the original tribes were the Gauls, and so the culture became known as Gallo-Roman. The land in the south of France is shaped like a giant theater: Picture the stage stretching to its widest as it meets the sea and the steps narrowing as they meet the mountains to the north. There is a triangular section on each side: the Rhone delta and the Camargue, containing a wildlife preserve and rice fields to the west and the mountains to the east. Provence is a fascinating land of varied contours, ranging from picturesque villages high up on craggy outcroppings of rock to gorges and canyons with water cascading down in cool spouts to fishing harbors along the Mediterranean. Colors are vivid, with fields of lavender grown for sachet and perfume, red poppies waving in all their glory, the spring green color of grapevines, and the silvery green of olive leaves; the red clay of the earth is striking as well. Van Gogh painted vineyards, olive groves, and cypresses, with lemons and the sun adding bright yellow to enliven landscapes with stippled brush effects. The mistral, a wild wind that rages through the region, causes destruction and an eerie sense of tension among the inhabitants. Many of the country homes were built facing toward the east to minimize the force of the mistral.

AVIGNON *Pont St. Benezet* is the ruined bridge of the song, "Pont d'Avignon," which you probably sang during childhood. The legend behind the song is that of a young shepherd, Benezet, who heard a voice from heaven telling him to build a bridge across the Rhone River at Avignon. An angel guided him to the Bishop of Avignon, who asked him to lift a heavy stone that a group of men together could not lift. Benezet was suddenly possessed with the power to do so, and he placed it on the river bank as the first stone in the foundation for the bridge. The people who were watching became so excited that they raised 5000 gold scudi to pay for the construction, and men volunteered to work on the bridge, forming a "Bridge Brotherhood." The bridge was begun in 1177 and finished in 1185; it is 900 meters long with 22 arches. Today you can see the four remaining arches and the chapel of *St. Nicholas* on one of the piers.

Le Palais des Papes was built during the pontificates of three of seven popes who reigned from Avignon. This gigantic feudal castle/fortress contains an area of over 15,000 square meters. From the outside, look up at the high walls with very narrow windows that make the palace almost invulnerable to attack. Inside, the structure is composed of two buildings: the Old Palace, constructed by Benedict XII between 1334 and 1342, and the New Palace, built between 1342 and 1352 for Clement VI. During the French Revolution furnishings, statues, and sculpture were destroyed; in 1810 the palace was turned into a barracks, and finally the city took over the restoration in 1969. Some of the frescoes were burned in the fire of 1413, but others remain almost intact. Don't miss the Room of the Deer on the third floor, which is painted with woodland scenes of hunting, falconry, and fishing, as well as of children playing. The Pope's Bedroom contains tempera paintings of birds on a blue background.

From Avignon, follow N100 to signs for *Fontaine de Vaucluse,* one of the natural wonders of France. Park your car and walk up to the head of the gushing River Sorgue as it emerges from below ground into a scenic pool backed by a cliff and resplendent with the reflections of surrounding trees, then cascades down over the rocks with great force. A warm day will seem cooler as you hear the water, see its white/aqua color, and stroll under giant shade trees. The flow of water can reach 200 cubic meters per second at its height in the spring. During the middle of the sixth century, St. Veran, then the Archbishop of Cavaillon, got rid of a monster, Couloubre, there. Future bishops of Cavaillon built a castle, now in ruins, which you can walk up to in 15 minutes. Look on the left bank of the spring for a hill, *Vache d'or,* which resembles a cow's head. It is said that there is gold hidden in the hill, guarded by a spirit who bellows at anyone trying to steal it, creating an uproar that resounds back and forth against the rocks and inside the mountain.

Petrarch lived here between 1337 and 1353 with the Bishop of Cavaillon, Phillipe de Cabasso. He wrote of his beloved Laura, whom he loved for 21 years, until she was stricken during the Black Death of 1348. There is a column marking the fifth centenary of his birth on the path leading to the fountain.

Next, follow signs to **Gordes,** a picturesque hill town located above the Imergue Valley. The *castle* contains a very interesting gallery of the work of Impressionist Victor Vasarely; there are three floors of exhibits, some in cases that rotate at the press of a button. We enjoyed a relaxed lunch in the central square and watched the world go by sitting in the shade across the road from the castle. Near Gordes you can visit the

Village of Bories; bories are stone structures with dome-shaped roofs that are similar to the trulli in southern Italy. This village is now a museum consisting of over 20 bories.

Continue on to **Roussillon,** a painter's town in shades of red and ocher in buildings as well as in the soil. Walk up to the highest point in town, where you will see a plaque, sitting like a round table, marked with the distances to many other places of interest. Laurence Wylie's *A Village in the Vaucluse* was set here. To continue this excursion for the eye in a landscape designed for aesthetic pleasure, take D104 to **Goult,** which has gray overtones in its buildings; you will also find a nice view of the ocher cliffs of Roussillon from Goult.

N100 will take you next to **Apt,** known for its crystallized and conserved lavender, truffles, and fruit. Located in the Cavaillon Valley, Apt has a pleasant riverfront and attractive shopping streets. There is a legend that the body of St. Anne, mother of the Virgin, came to Apt. ***Ancienne Cathedral Ste-Anne*** has a lovely stained-glass window of St. Anne, the Virgin, and Jesus. The ***Archaeological Museum*** has sarcophagi from Roman times; you can go underground to see part of the Roman arena there.

D943 south from Apt to **Cadenet** takes you through the ***Luberon Range*** on a winding road that is worth the time it takes to drive it. This gorge affords views of spectacular natural beauty at its finest. From Cadenet, take D973 to **Cavaillon,** D99 to **St. Remy-de-Provence,** and D5 through **les Baux-de-Provence,** where there are fantastic rock formations. Here there is a hill town, partly uninhabited and partly crowded with souvenir shops, as well as a castle to visit, with a fine view of the ***Val d'Enfer,* Arles,** and the Camargue from the top. Down below there are several excellent hotels with renowned restaurants. D17 will take you on to Arles.

ARLES is dominated by its elliptical ***arena,*** one of the oldest built in the Roman world. It is also one of the largest: 136 meters long and 107 meters high. There was once a third story that was topped by posts to hold a giant marquee. Down in the center, look for the taller-than-usual wall below the lower seats, designed to protect spectators from wild beasts. Sometimes a wooden floor was added for better vision; the sockets for the supporting beams are still there. Over the centuries, pieces of the arena were carted off to be used in construction, and at one point 200 houses and a church were contained inside the arena. Today bullfights are held there. The ***theater*** once held seats for 7000 spectators and was covered by a marquee. Much of the stone was taken for other buildings, but two tall pillars remain behind the stage. During the summer, various performing arts are scheduled there, returning the theater to its original function.

Vincent Van Gogh arrived in Arles in 1888 to begin his series of vivid color still lifes and landscapes. "Sunflowers" and the familiar

Langlois drawbridge were painted here. Paul Gauguin came later that year, but sadly, the two quarreled and Van Gogh cut off his own ear, then committed himself to an asylum at St. Remy-de-Provence.

The *Church of St. Trophime* is one of the most beautiful in Arles. In Romanesque and Gothic styles, it contains Aubusson tapestries, paintings, Christian sarcophagi, sculpture, and a deservedly famous cloister. The *Museon Arlaten* was developed with Nobel-Prize money received in 1904 by Frederic Mistral. Earlier he had founded the Felibrige society, created to revive the Provencal language, as well as traditional customs, folklore, and history of the area. There are 33 rooms to explore, including a reconstruction of the interior of a house in the Camargue. Models are dressed in traditional costume to enhance this scene.

From Arles, N113 will take you to **Nimes**, A9 to **Narbonne**, and A61 to **Carcassonne**. Carcassonne is an enchanting place out of a fairy tale with its turrets towering above sturdy walls; the town is set on a rise so you can see it as you approach. We came in at night, anticipation mounting as we viewed it from the highway, with the towers backlit, and climbed in through the gates, twisting and turning through the lamplight on narrow streets until we found a hotel open off season. The hotel was built into the massive town wall itself; we climbed a well-worn circular staircase in a tower up to our room. Exploring Carcassonne can be fascinating as you find stone blocks dating from Gallo-Roman times, cubic stones from the Visigoths, and rough sandstone masses from ducal times. During the Wars of Religion, people took these various stones to use in the construction of new buildings. In 1844 plans were begun to restore this medieval treasure. Prosper Merimee, the composer of the libretto of "Carmen" as well as the Inspector General of Historic Monuments, awarded the honor of restoration to Eugene Viollet-le-Duc. His work raised some eyebrows; authenticity to historical fact was questioned. However, the end result is very pleasing and you can feel the medieval atmosphere in this romantic city.

An alternate route to reach the Dordogne takes you through **Millau**, an interesting area filled with caves and grottoes, plane trees, and vineyards. The mountains rise in folds, with their sedimentary rock forming natural cliffs or stark manmade slices where the road has been cut through. Wire nets keep the rock from falling on the road and there are many places where you can stop for a picnic or to appreciate the view. As you approach Millau, you can look down on the old town huddled in the center, with newer buildings spread out around it. There are two rivers with bridges converging on Millau; the road descends, curving back and forth many times in switchbacks. Driving out on the other side, an electrified railroad, with its steel hoops, parallels the road. It is interesting to think of the engineering hours spent to construct electrified railroads, bridges, canals, tunnels, and roads through sheer rock; we take these conveniences for granted.

Dordogne

The Dordogne River glides, slides, tumbles, and cascades between high cliffs, past shingle beaches, through fields of maize and tobacco, orchards of walnuts, beside villages and chateaux high on the cliffs. It is a region for canoeing, kyacking, cycling, and walking. The Dordogne is very appealing as a vacation area for those who seek a pastoral retreat that is quiet, with lush, green foliage and a river that never loses its charm. Nothing is too grand or awesome for human scale, nothing too small to arouse interest and make the eye move over a rural world created in perfect proportions. Here, even more than in Provence, one wants to be a landscape painter. Even the prehistoric men who discovered this land and moved into its caves painted on the walls that gave them shelter.

To get to the Dordogne from Carcassonne, take E49 to **Montauban** and EB3/N20 to one of two scenic drives to **Rocamadour.** You will see D39 first, then D673. which is a slightly better road, but with more undulating distance to cover. Rocamadour is a site for pilgrimages; some climb the 216 steps from the village to the ecclesiastical city at the top, kneeling on each step. In 1166 the body of a man thought to be Zaccheus was found in a grave in a chapel there. After the body was moved to a tomb near the altar, miracles began to happen; pilgrims heard about the miracles and came to honor the statue of the Virgin. As donations poured in, several churches and an abbey were built around the little chapel; over the years the temptation of the presence of rich treasures prompted looting and vandalism. During the Wars of Religion the area was almost completely destroyed. In the 19th century reconstruction began and the pilgrims returned. The ***Miraculous Chapel of Our Lady of Rocamadour (Chapelle Miraculeuse)*** contains a statue of the Black Virgin and Child; there is also a bell hanging from the roof that rings when a miracle is about to happen.

We drove southeast on N140 toward **Gramat** and found a lovely chateau to stay in for a break from camping. Chateau de Roumegouse is set in an estate with lovely, tall trees, gardens, and walks to enjoy. The house has been renovated and open as a luxury hotel for the past 20 years. Dinner was a gourmet treat; dishes were served with perfection down to the last elegant touch. There is something very romantic about actually living in a chateau that has witnessed so many lives, some of which are the substance of its secret history.

Next, follow signs to ***Grottes de Lacave,*** which is 9 kilometers from Rocamadour on the south bank of the Dordogne River. There is a little electric railway and a lift down to the caves. The colorful stalagmites and stalactites in an array of shapes are reflected in the pools and rivers running underground.

Continue on D43 to **Souillac,** where there is a 12th-century church, *Eglise Abbatiale,* and a bas relief of Isaiah, who is poised in motion with his hands gesturing. There are beasts, monsters, and saints sculpted on a facade that was originally placed outside the door; it was moved inside for protection from the elements.

Take D703 and D704 to **Sarlat** and its maze of medieval passageways. The *Rue de la Republique* or *La Traverse* divides the town in two; we suggest parking and beginning your tour on the east side. The *Boetie House* was the birthplace of Etienne de La Boetie, a poet and friend of Michel de Montaigne, famous essayist of the 16th century. Montaigne wrote "On Friendship" following the death of Boetie at age 33 in 1563. This lovely Renaissance house has carved stone windowframes reminiscent of Florentine architecture. The 12th-century *cathedral* was built by Benedictine monks; the *Bishop's Palace* adjoining has an interesting 16th-century loggia on the upper floor. Nearby is the 17th-century *town hall,* its square the site of the Saturday morning market. During the summer the market area is alive with theatrical productions.

D47 will take you to *les Eyzies-de-Tayac,* often called "the capital of prehistory." Around the turn of the century, cave paintings were discovered here, followed by the excavation of weapons of Cro-Magnon man. The *Musee National de Prehistoire* features a sculpture of Cro-Magnon man by Paul Darde created in 1930. Inside, there is a fascinating collection of artifacts, displays, reconstructions of prehistoric skeletons, and reproductions of cave paintings. There are a number of caves open to visitors: *Grottes de Font de Gaume* contains drawings in color of bison, deer, mammoths, and other animals hunted at that time. In high season it is not easy to get tickets: only 20 visitors are admitted at any one time; protection of these priceless drawings is first, tourism second. *Grotte des Combarelles* consists of two cave tunnels with engravings of animals. The first cave to be found is *La Mouthe,* which has paintings of bison and horses.

As you leave the Dordogne region, take D47 and D170 to **Perigueux,** where three Byzantine domes are visible from the highway. Drive D939 to **Angouleme,** N10 to **Poitiers,** A10 to **Tours,** and N76 to **Chenonceaux.**

Loire

The Loire Valley is a fairyland filled with magic palaces to visit. Some of the chateaux are enormous; many are medieval fortresses, others are ostentatious pleasure palaces pure and simple; the memories of these retreats for kings are hidden in the walls, if only walls could talk! Intrigue and scandal stir up the imagination as you walk through the pages of history. The chateaux offer a rare opportunity to see with your own eyes the elegance and splendor of aristocratic life in former centuries. You can easily visit the larger, tourist-laden chateaux, but we hope you will also find one of the less well-known chateaux, which, for us, had a more special, personal atmosphere; we were lucky to discover and stay in the home/chateau of a marquis that has a fascinating history. Take a trip down some of the enchanting smaller roads and into quiet villages in search of your chateau—it's fun!

The Loire is a wide, quiet river beginning in the Massif Central, flowing through Orleans, and past the orchards, vineyards (try some of the local white wines), and gardens of the Touradine, and slowly widening as it passes through Blois, Tours, Saumur, Angers, Nantes, and out into the sea estuary. Fishermen enjoy the variety of fish in the rivers and streams in the valley, and hunters find wildlife plentiful: This has always been a valley friendly to man.

If you want to read about the area before you go, you might try: Marcel Proust, *Jean Santeuil;* Emile Zola, *Earth;* Honore de Balzac, *Eugenie Grandet;* or Charles Peguy, *Jeanne d'Arc.*

Although it is not easy to pick a favorite Loire castle, one cannot go wrong visiting **Chenonceau,** which is said to be the most popular (after Fontainebleau) in all of France. We find the setting of Chenonceau very appealing because its beauty is reflected in the waters of the River Cher. You may have seen pictures of this magnificent building atop stone arches over the river, with formal gardens adjacent—green foliage and blue water and sky contrasting with the white stone. It is elegant and beautiful. The approach along a wide boulevard of plane trees builds up anticipation for the treasures ahead.

Also known as the "Chateau of Six Women," Chenonceau was developed through the influence of six women who lived there over a 400-year period. The first woman was Katherine Briconnet, who was involved in the chateau's placement on the site and the design of the interior. Diane de Poitiers, mistress of King Henri II, received Chenonceau as a gift from the king in 1547. She was responsible for the lovely formal garden as well as a bridge from the castle to the bank of the River Cher. Guy des Carroys designed the Italian garden for her, and she delighted in receiving presents of rose bushes, fruit trees, white mulberry trees (for silk worms), and various exotic fruits and vegetables. This red-haired beauty was hated by Queen Catherine de Medici, who turned Diane out after the king died. Catherine added a park and a gallery on the bridge; she also gave fetes there, including the first display of fireworks in France. Louise of Lorraine housed nuns in the attic rooms; they had a drawbridge that they could pull up at night to isolate themselves from the outside world. In the 18th century, Madame Dupin attracted a following of intellectual visitors including Voltaire, Montesquieu, and Jean-Jacques Rousseau (who was once her son's tutor). Madame Dupin was respected and loved by the villagers, and perhaps the feeling they had for her was responsible for the lack of damage to Chenonceau during the French Revolution. In the 19th century, Madame Pelouze devoted herself to restoring the castle. Pick up a brochure in the language you prefer as you buy your ticket; the rooms are listed in order wth an explanation of the contents of each. The furnishings, paintings, and Flemish tapestries are treasures indeed.

If you are interested in following in our footsteps to discover a charming, less well-known chateau, come along! From Chenonceaux, continue east on either side of the River Cher to **Montrichard,** follow signs to **Monthou-sur-Cher,** then signs to *Chateau du Gue-Pean.* This chateau is set in the woods, away from the hustle and bustle of either tourists or townspeople. The building is rectangular, built around a courtyard with a pool and crowned by a tower on each of the four corners; three have funnel-shaped roofs and the fourth is shaped like a bell.

We were met at the door by le Marquis de Keguelin de Rozieres, a man in his seventies, who is a descendent of the Counts of Apremont, who have resided at the chateau since 1676. Soon we were esconsed in a tower room with an unbelievably high ceiling and a canopied bed, redolent in the rich memories of the past. After the visitors had departed at the end of the day, the guard rope was removed from each of the rooms. We had drinks in the king's bedroom, containing an immense stone fireplace, lovely furnishings, family photos, and a four-poster bed with a red and gold bedspread and curtains that was slept in by King Francois I! Dinner was served in the dining room on a Louis XVI table set with silver candelabra and the family flatwear and china. Portraits of some of the female members of the family covered the walls, as well as several Flemish tapestries. Both rooms were filled with art treasures and memorabilia from the rich past of the chateau and the family, one that has played an important part in French history, early and late. Early it was involved in the maneuverings between France and England during the reign of Henry VIII of England; later the marquis himself was one of the key leaders of the French Resistance during World War II; among other things, he organized the rebellion of Paris as Allied troops approached. His message to Ike on August 24, 1944 contributed to the decision that led Allied troops into Paris rather than bypassing it to chase German troops elsewhere. We learned more about the marquis and the history of his family the next morning when we toured the chateau. The library has especially interesting exhibits of significant memorabilia. He was awarded a special medal for his work in the Resistance and after the war was chosen by De Gaulle to represent France in Washington. The family has had equally illustrious friends and royal connections. There are letters and autographs from Byron, Victor Hugo, Napoleon Bonaparte, General de Gaulle, Alexander Dumas, Jean Cocteau, and Georges Sand as well as royal patrons in the 16th and 17th centuries. We had been curious about rumors of ghosts, of treasure buried beneath the Great Towers, of scandal and intrigue between the royal families in the 16th century; if you go, ask about Mary Tudor and her lover, Brandon, Duke of Suffolk, as well as Francois I and Louis XII. At one point in time Mary, King Louis XII's widow, was asked to leave by Francois I; instead she defiantly married Brandon in the chapel at Chateau du Gue-Pean. You can walk through history as you see the various rooms in this chateau; climb up one of the towers for a fine view of the wooded countryside.

From Chateau du Gue-Pean, follow signs through **Contres, Cheverny,** and **Bracieux** to **Chambord.** *Chambord,* the largest and most ostentatious of the chateaux, was built by Francois I as a hunting lodge in 1519. It is hard to believe that this 440-room palace was used as a retreat for hunting and entertaining; it seems the height of extravagance. Just keeping the 365 fireplaces supplied with wood must have taken many francs. Chambord is set in a large deer park that is now also a wildlife preserve. As you approach, you will be struck by the immense scale of the building, with its towers, turrets, dormers, and chimneys in a potpourri of design. Grand though it is, the impression is not of the castle of your dreams; a weekend might be fun but you "wouldn't want to live there." In any event, it is impressive.

The "keep" or main structure was developed by Leonardo da Vinci; on each level there is a Greek cross with apartments around it. You can't miss the famous double-ramp spiral staircase, which ascends from the first floor to the roof, in the middle of the Greek crosses. You can go up or down on one ramp never meeting people you can see on the other ramp; it must have been a tantalizing arrangement in those days of intrigue and seduction. Francois I built this castle with firm resolve, even when he did not have enough money to pay the ransom for his sons, languishing in captivity in Spain; he forced French citizens to give up their silver for the cause. Henri II, his son, was responsible for building the chapel. Louis XII favored it for riding and hunting, using the prized field hunting dogs kept there by the royal family. Louis XIV was in residence when Moliere presented his *Bourgeois Gentilhomme* for the first time in 1670. During the Revolution, the palace was attacked and the furniture ruined. Napoleon gave Chambord to Marshal Berthier in 1809; it was sold in 1821 at a public sale to the Duc de Bordeaux. In 1930 Chambord began to be restored as a national estate project. Today the grounds and first floors have been refurbished with tapestries, paintings, and lovely period furniture; some of the pieces are the originals from the chateau. The second floor houses a collection of hunting weapons and paintings, tapestries, and engravings relevant to the hunt. Be sure to take time to walk around the terrace, a favorite spot for royalty and guests to watch tournaments, fetes, and the return of the hunt. You can climb up inside a "lantern" staircase for a higher view if you wish.

From Chambord, follow signs to **Blois,** then N152 to **Amboise,** site of another major chateau, and **Vouvray,** an excellent stop for wine tasting and purchasing. We have been drinking Vouvray ever since tasting it there many years ago. Continue on the river road past Tours; you will see a number of caves, similar to troglodyte houses, carved into the hills. The road continues on the top of a raised dike, erected against flooding. There is also a bicycle path along the pleasant river road and a number of villages.

Continue on N152 to **Langeais** and **Saumur,** where there are famous chateaux, then follow D952 and D4 to **St. Gemmes,** on the outskirts of **Angers,** D411 and D102 around Angers to the entrance for A11 to **Nantes.** From Nantes, where you will leave the Loire and head for Brittany, take N165 to **Concarneau.**

Brittany

Brittany has a wild, sea-smashed coastline that we find very beautiful and exhilarating. The rocks are sawtoothed and strong-looking; the sand beaches provide a sharp contrast, with their soft, shifting surface. The fishing harbors and seaside resorts are pleasantly colorful and for the most part not unreasonably cluttered with tourists. Some of the people wear their Breton dress every day and most do on Sunday when they attend church. There is an aura of mystery about the landscape; the Druids were here and left menhirs (single upright stones) and dolmens (burial chambers) for visitors to ponder over. The villages, like those in Cornwall, to which they are closely related, seem not to have changed in hundreds of years.

Although there is much to see and do in **Quiberon** and the islands off the southwestern coast of Brittany, if you have the time, for a shorter tour we suggest starting at Concarneau. Concarneau is the second largest fishing harbor in France, a popular seaside resort, and is situated on an island within granite walls and ramparts. The old town itself, *Villa Close,* dating from the 14th century, can best be seen from a walk around the ramparts. You will also see the inner harbor, where fishing boats are moored, and the outer harbor, teeming with pleasure boats. There are several museums related to fishing and marine life to visit. If you are there on the right weekend in August, you will see the Fete des Filets Bleus, which features folk dancing by costumed Bretons. You can watch the fishing trawlers going in and out, as well as the spirited unloading at the fish auction between midnight and dawn.

From Concarneau, drive D44 to **Fouesnant, Benodet,** and **Pont-l'Abbe.** Take D785 to the *Penmarche Point* region; this area makes a fine base for enjoying Brittany. We stayed in **Le Guilvinec,** a lovely fishing village chosen by some of our English friends as their vacation retreat after they had explored Brittany for many years. Our "window on the world" overlooked the quay, where we found the activity of the fishermen constantly interesting to watch. One evening we counted 122 fishing boats, ranging from large trawlers to smaller lobster and crab boats. The rigs included huge winches used to wind up heavy nets and iron "doors" (stowed on each side of the boat when in port), which are used to open the seine nets when working at sea. There are crab and lobster pots stacked along the quay, and nets are laid out to dry and be repaired.

If you are there in the late afternoon, you will see a flurry of intense activity beginning sometime after 4:30, when the first boats come in at full speed, tie up at the quay, and unload plastic boxes of wriggling fish and langostine onto carts that are then run into the auction in the buildings adjacent to the quay. Often the fishermen who get in first receive the highest price for their fish; only if the catch of the day has been small will the price rise more at the end of the sale. The fishermen take a gamble, but from the intense work involved in getting their fish in first, we would gather that is the likeliest time to make the most money. This whole scene of the late-afternoon race to market could be from the twenties or even the end of the 19th century—apart from the diesels, of course: order in the midst of an appearance of confusion. The period of intense activity is brief—90 minutes at most—and natural, a part of the rhythm of the fishermen's long day, and totally without artifice. It must be frustrating for the fishermen to have to work around curious tourists, who peer down into their boats and stand in the way as they are moving heavy loads onto carts. These spectators are unloaded from buses provided by canny operators who know when they have something authentic: The passengers come to watch honest, old-fashioned work, something of a rarity in this era of computerized production and automated machinery. Hard work is there to be seen, if those who watch have an eye for it and some knowledge of how seine nets and lobster pots are handled. And the stamp of hard work is imprinted on the town as a whole—visible in plain houses and the lack of fancy shops or tourist traps. The houses in Guilvinec, as in many of the other local villages, are plain white with black roofs. They have painted doors and shutters, either brick or cement blocks around the windows for decoration, and some arched doorways. One further touchstone of the life of the town is the workmen's habit of leaving worn-out gear anywhere and everywhere; near the local boatyard we counted the skeletons of a dozen old fishing boats abandoned in the tidal mud, and old timbers, lines, and nets were left everywhere along the quayside. Guilvinec was too busy working to worry about its appearance.

COASTAL EXCURIONS Continue on out the Penmarch Peninsula past **St. Pierre** to the *Eckmuhl Lighthouse,* which is 65 meters high. If you climb to the top of the tower you will see Raz Point, Concarneau, and the coastline in between, reputedly the scene of Tristan and Iseult's final moments. From the lighthouse, continue along the coast to **St. Guenole** to visit the *Finistere Prehistoric Museum,* which houses artifacts from the Stone Age to the Gallo-Roman Era (including a dolmen). Across the road is a lovely sand beach, *Pors-Carn,* with dunes and a view across the bay. We saw some people sand sailing, on rollers, when we were there. Or drive a little farther north to reach **Point de la Torche,** which also has a lovely beach. A few kilometers north, the *Chapelle de Notre Dame de Tronoen* has the oldest calvary in France. ("Calvaries" are granite monuments depicting Christ on the Cross created by village stonemasons between the 15th and 17th centuries, sometimes to ward off the plague and often to give thanks for being spared.) This calvary depicts the Visitation, the Nativity, the Magi, the Last Judgment, and the Last Supper. Unfortunately, lichen and erosion have taken their toll on the expression on the figures.

Continue through **Ploneour, Plovan** (notice the church with modern stained-glass windows), and **Plozevet** to **Audierne.** Audierne is a fishing port and a sizable town, with a large harbor containing pleasure boats as well as fishing craft. Houses there are white and of three to four stories, with dormer windows; the windows have shutters, wrought iron at the bottom, and stone decoration around them. From Audierne, take D784 to *Pointe du Raz,* where you have to park your car in a lot and walk out to the end. Unfortunately, commercialism has arrived here in the form of souvenir stands and bars, similar to those at Land's End in Cornwall, England. The view is worth it, but we disliked the crowds. If you want to avoid the nonsense, you can turn onto a number of little roads before you reach the parking lot, and enjoy the serenity of a sea view unencumbered by tourists or claptrap. We parked near an abandoned bunker in what appeared to be an earlier fortification of some kind.

Continue along a scenic road signed to *Pointe de Van,* then take D7 toward **Douarnenez,** with forays out to any number of scenic spots along the coast, as you have time. At Douarnenez, take D107 to **Plonevez–Porzay,** then D63 and D47 to **Ste. Marie-du-Menez-Hom,** D887 to **Crozon,** and D8 to *Pointe de Penhir;* continue your scenic drive on D355 around *Espagnols Point,* D355 back to Crozon, D887 and D791 past **Menez-Hom** (one of the best places for a panoramic view of the surrounding coastline and area) to the corniche road heading toward **Le Faou.**

If you want still more of this magnificent coastal scenery, you can take a third peninsular excursion as follows: N165 through **Brest** (large and industrial), D789 and D85 to **St-Mathieu Point.** Continue on D85 to **le Conquet,** D28 to **Breles,** D27 around the coast to **Penfoul,** and follow signs to **Tremazan,** which will take you along a beautiful coastal road. Follow signs to **Kersaint,** then D168 to **Ploudalmezeau,** D28 to **Lannilis** and **le Folgoet** and D770 inland (south) toward **Landenncau** until you reach N12, where you head east toward **Morlaix, Guingamp,** and **St-Brieuc.** Then take D786 to **le Val-Andre,** D786 to **Erquy,** D34 to **Cap Frehel,** return to D786, and head toward **Dinard,** crossing the bridge on D168, then turning left to N13 to **St-Malo.**

Alternatively, you can come across northern Brittany on major highways such as N12 and N176, then take N137 north to St-Malo. If you are farther south in Brittany, you may want to cross on N164, then drive north to **Dinan** and then on to St-Malo.

ST-MALO, devastated during 1944, has now been reconstructed so that the old town looks just as it did during medieval times. The ramparts are the original 12th-century structure and the best place to start your tour. Begin at *St-Vincent Gate,* then proceed to *Bastion St-Louis, Bastion St-Phillippe, Tour Bidouane,* and back to St-Vincent. You will have views of the isthmus joining the old town to the mainland, the harbor, shipowners' houses, the Emerald Coast and islands, and the *National Fort.* There is a lot of river and sea traffic to identify, as well as enjoying the crashing waves along the seawall. There are signs warning you that if you are not aware of high tide and walk out to an island, you may be stuck on that island for six hours. Take time to explore some of the little winding streets in town; shopping here is enjoyable. *St-Vincent Cathedral* contains stained-glass windows by Jean Le Moal and Max Ingrand. St-Malo had a reputation for privateering, and Duquay-Trouin, a privateer from the 17th century, is buried in one of the chapels. Jacques Cartier, who sailed to Newfoundland and Labrador (but found the St. Lawrence River instead) in 1534 to search for gold, lies in another chapel here.

From St-Malo, you can either take the scenic route along the coast, D201 (D155 and D797 to D976) to **Mont-St-Michel** or N137, D4, and N176 to D976.

MONT-SAINT-MICHEL is a vision materialized. Seeing this immense abbey rising out of the sea inspires awe and wonder, to say the least. As you get closer, you will see that there is a cathedral surrounded by a monastery, with the town below, all enclosed by towers and ramparts. At low tide the shifting sandbanks surround it; some of them are quicksand. There is a 14-meter difference between low and high tide and the sea rises very rapidly. The Mount itself is a block of granite that rises 170 meters above the sand; although at the mercy of the sea, this hard rock withstands the battering of the elements.

Dating back to the eighth century, the abbey was painstakingly constructed through the ages with granite brought from elsewhere and inched slowly up to the top. The Mount was used as a refuge for people needing security, although some of those became thieves who made raids in the adjoining neighborhoods. Pilgrims came bearing gifts of money and land. Some well-known people chose to retire there in peace and quiet, and scholars came to live and work there. Now it is anything but quiet; as you enter the gate you are confronted with crowds and souvenir shops. We climbed up as quickly as possible to where the crowd thinned so we could let some of the feeling of this enormous place seep into us. Rather than follow a prescribed route we chose to climb at will, eventually reaching the monastery at the top. Visitors must go into the church with a guided tour provided in several languages; this limits the number of persons inside at one time. Don't miss the cloister, with its carved arcades and a courtyard garden looking out over spaces of sky and sand. The proportions of the view suggest silence and infinity. There are a number of halls to tour, as well as gardens and museums, which we chose to skip so we could instead enjoy the feeling of this ethereal place as a whole.

From Mont-St-Michel, take D275 and D75 to **Pontaubault** and Normandy.

Normandy

Oh, to be in Normandy in May when the apple orchards are in full bloom! We were lucky enough to be there then; the long walks and drives through the countryside will be remembered as sprays of blossoms set against spring green foliage and grasses. You can also taste it in the hard *cidre* that is either *doux* (sweet) or *brut* (dry) or in Calvados apple brandy. Stendahl called Normandy an "ocean of green"; with less flattery, Flaubert referred to it as a "dish of raw sorrel." But taste is just as important as sight here because Normandy provides many of France's dairy products; you haven't lived until you have tasted the heavy cream with fruit, cereal, and desserts.

Vikings who arrived in the tenth century in their slender, pointed ships (called drakkars or snekkars) gave the name "Northmen" or "Normans" to this region. It is divided into five *departements:* the **Eure** and **Seine-Maritime** are linked together to form Upper Normandy; **Calvados, Manche,** and **Orne** comprise Lower Normandy. The coastal area begins at **Le Treport** and continues for 375 miles westward to Mont-St-Michel. The **Alabaster Coast,** which is similar to the white cliffs of Dover across the English channel, are the farthest east; then, moving westward, comes the **Floral Coast,** a popular resort area, and the **Mother-of-Pearl Coast,** with its Invasion Beaches, and then finally the **Cotentin Peninsula** fringed with cliffs, dwindling to sandy beaches all the way west to Mont-St-Michel.

We have chosen a route along much of the coastal region, with forays inland for special places to visit. We were drawn both to the coast and the countryside, to beaches and to farmland villages, to churches and abbeys bulging with memories of the past, and to the site of the invasions of 1944, poignant with remembrances of those who fought and died there for the freedom of France and Europe.

If you are coming to Normandy from Mont-St-Michel, take D275, D75, and D43 to Pontaubault, then N175 from Pontaubault to **Avranches,** D104 around the city, D7 north to **Lengronne,** and D13 west to **Brehal.** Take D20 north to **Hauteville-Plage,** where there are sand dunes, a lovely sand beach, and a small area of summer homes. There are many pleasant little villages along the coast from **Granville** to **Coutainville.** D44 leads inland from Coutainville to **Coutances,** where there is a cathedral dating back to the original nave built by Geoffroy de Montbray in 1056. Don't miss the octagonal lantern tower called "the lead." There is a statue of Our Lady of Coutances in the central chapel. The Romanesque towers were "enveloped" or made stronger to support the needle-like spires. A short distance away you will find the public gardens; the view from the terrace overlooks the Bulsard Valley, which contains an aquaduct from the 13th century.

For a coastal trip along the Cotentin Peninsula, continue from Coutances on D2 to **Lessay,** D900 to **La Haye,** and D903 to **Carteret,** a seaside resort and a great center for hiking. The rocky promontory has a splendid view and the beach is small but attractive. Continue on D904 northward on a rather bumpy road enhanced by pleasant farms with lots of flowerpots on windowsills to complement the view. At **les Pieux** the road becomes smooth again; you will have a view of *Cap de Flamenville* and the sea. Continue on D904 a few kilometers to **Benoitville;** soon after the town, take D37 north, then D318 to **Biville,** where the road becomes narrow. You will pass a church with pottery flowers on the graves. Head onto D118, which is a winding, one-lane road leading to the sea and dunes. This is a good spot to park for a picnic, swim, or hike. D237 will take you along the coast to **Vauville,** and D318 to **Beaumont.** D403 will lead you on a steep (18% grade) paved road to **Herquemolin.** You can park in the parking lot or drive up a little farther and park on the only flat spot as the road turns inland for a marvelous sea view of the Channel Islands and the rocks below. Continuing on D901 will unfortunately bring you to a most unattractive power plant with huge cranes, mammoth buildings, and much activity—a real blot on this otherwise remote and lovely landscape. Turn left on D202 to *Nez de Jobourg,* a cliff area with another view. Walk out along the *Nez de Voidres* for a view of huge waves. Then take D901 to **Cherbourg.**

Although Cherbourg had been popular with traders during the Bronze Age, it did not become a naval center until the 19th century. Attempts were made in the 17th century to construct harbor facilities, but they were washed away by the sea; the city became a major port in 1853. Cherbourg played an important role during the Allied invasion in 1944 as a landing location for heavy equipment and supplies. The *Museum of War and Liberation* is located on top of the cliff overlooking the harbor at *Fort du Roule.* The Room of Maps is a highlight for those who would like to study the sequence of military events during the battle of Normandy. The Armoury contains clothing, arms, and flags; these are originals that have preserved. The museum also contains scale models of landings, photographs, models of equipment, and documents.

Emmanuel-Liais Park and the *Natural History Museum* located near the home of Emmanuel-Liais, are worth a visit. As an astronomer and a naturalist, he collected tropical plants in his garden; the Gulf Stream provides the warmth for their survival.

From Cherbourg, N13 will take you through **Valognes** to **Carentan,** an important dairy capital. You will see the octagonal spire of the belfry of *Notre-Dame Church,* which dates back to the 12th century. Continue on through **Isigny,** another dairy center specializing in butter production. From Isigny, take D514 to **Grandcampmaisy,** a resort area, and follow the signs for *Pointe du Hoc.*

Visiting this site five days before the 40th anniversary of D-Day, as we did, arouses strong but conflicting emotions. As we looked out over the wide panorama of beach and sea, with only a few peaceful sailboats tacking slowly in the sunlight, we tried to imagine that day: June 6, 1944: the bustling, crashing, frenzied activity of vessels unloading men and equipment onto a narrow strip of beach, and then the Rangers struggling to climb the cliff. We knew from our 10 weeks of living in south Devon, where the practice for the landing took place, what had preceded that ordeal. The Channel crossing was not calm, and many of the men were seasick. At 4:30 a.m. British assault landing craft arrived with 225 men from the U.S. 2nd Ranger Battalion. As they looked up at the cliffs of Pointe du Hoc, one said, "My God, they are up there waiting for us."

As that initial force hit the beach, the enemy opened fire, and 15 Rangers were killed wading through the waves and running across the narrow beach to the base of the cliffs. Lieutenant Colonel James Earl Rudder, a rancher and former football coach from Brady, Texas, headed with his group to climb the 100-foot-high cliffs and capture the guns at Pointe du Hoc. This assault was rather like assaults on fortified castles in ancient times, with rocks and stone walls to scale. Eighteen U.S. bombers confused the enemy by dropping bombs on them minutes before the Rangers began to climb up. The Rangers used rocket-fired equipment to anchor ladders to the top, then began to climb. Of the 225 Rangers, many were picked off by the enemy on the way up or as they faced each other, eye to eye, at the top, but 90 reached the top alive. Ironically, when they reached the gun emplacements that were the objective of the whole operation, they found them empty; the large guns had been moved back by the enemy in anticipation of invasion. Later the guns were located some distance from shore; had their location been known they could have been taken without such a tragic loss of life.

Pointe du Hoc remains as it was when the Rangers left it; bunkers were mostly destroyed, crater holes are everywhere, and there is one bunker you can walk into to look out through the gun slot down the cliff toward the now peaceful sea. There is a sign warning visitors about unexploded mines; you must keep to the paths in that area, even now. A stone monument placed in memory of the brave men who fought there is the only addition to the landscape.

Eight miles east, the men who fought and died lie in the *Normandy American Cemetery* above *Omaha Beach:* 9386 American war dead are buried here; 14,000 others who were originally buried there have been returned home at the request of their next of kin. The headstones are of white Italian marble, marked by a Star of David for those of Jewish faith and a Latin Cross for all others. There is a long series of pools with a loggia at each end. The southern loggia contains several large maps depicting the landings, naval support for them, and air operations on that day. The bronze statue, "The Spirit of American Youth," stands 22 feet high on the platform. The chapel has a lovely mosaic ceiling, with an altar made of gold and black "Grand Antique" marble from the Pyrenees. As you look out over Omaha Beach spread below the cemetery, filled with soft, fine sand, you may begin to feel the anguish of the day. Men landed behind the beaches from three Airborne Divisions as the Allied Naval forces assaulted Omaha Beach with heavy equipment at 6:30 a.m. The enemy had prepared continuous mine fields in the water and on the beach; their fortifications were connected by tunnels and enhanced by machine guns in trenches. It must have taken a great deal of courage to jump into waist-deep water (if they were lucky) and wade ashore knowing the danger of mines and feeling the whizzing bullets from the cliffs above. Yet they persevered, in spite of horrendous losses, slowly opening up one avenue after another for their buddies to follow. By 2:00 p.m. the Allies had weakened the enemy's fortifications enough to move inland to the highway by the entrance to the cemetery.

We lived in Normandy for a short time and were beginning to sense the trauma of this beautiful area as we heard about the lives of the people who lived in the once-peaceful little villages and farms during the war. One farm we visited was occupied by SS soldiers who were housed with the French family acting as camouflage. The soldiers published bulletins on the state of the battle and posted them on the door until a visiting Frenchman read the current notice and said, "Not good news." The bulletins were no longer posted. Most families were required to house one German soldier; one young soldier lived with the family of a baker who rose early in the morning to prepare his bread. The soldier was a late sleeper, and after he was consistently late to report in the morning, his commandant decided to transfer him to Russia; the young man was found later that day by the baker, dead by his own hand. This part of Normandy had not experienced battle on their land since the days of William the Conqueror. It must have been very difficult for the people to decide whether to stay in their homes or flee to some other place, which might be even more hazardous. Each choice had its unavoidable risks. The photographs appearing in the local papers during this memorial time showed entire cities, towns, and villages flattened by bombardment, with terrible loss of life. Yet it is peaceful now as one strolls along the hedgerows alive with flowers and gazes at cows munching in the meadows while listening to cuckoos sounding in the still air.

From Omaha Beach, take D6 to **Bayeux,** where treasures await you. The *Bayeux Tapestry,* an exquisite work of art, is unique in the world.

Scholars feel that this lengthy, embroidered chronicle was commissioned by Bishop Odon of Conteville and was created by the Saxon School of Embroidery in England over a 10-year period. The wool yarn in vivid red, blue, green, gray, black, and yellow is amazingly well preserved. The story, fashioned almost like a cartoon strip, relates the conquest of England by Duke William of Normandy. In addition to the large central narrative strip you will see a border running at the top and bottom that features scenes of rural life at that time. The design was made with intelligence and humor; there are hidden surprises to intrigue visitors. (By the way, if you are confused by the characters, remember that the English wear mustaches and the Normans do not.)

Bayeux is one of the best examples of a well-preserved historic town anywhere. It will be pleasant for you to walk through the streets, enjoying the architecture and ambience for a day. Don't miss the **cathedral,** with its Gothic spires on top of Romanesque towers. The tapestry was originally designed to be displayed there. Look for the story of Thomas Becket's murder in the south transept; there are a number of chapels, the treasury, and the crypt to visit. The **Baron-Gerard Museum** is housed nearby in the old bishopric, with a collection including porcelain and ceramics on the ground floor, paintings and tapestries one flight up.

From Bayeux, take N13 through **Caen** directly to Paris to complete this tour.

THE IBERIAN PENINSULA

Perpignan to Barcelona	177 kilometers
Barcelona to Valencia	336 kilometers
Valencia to Murcia	278 kilometers
Murcia to Motril	332 kilometers
Motril to Malaga	106 kilometers
Motril to Granada	70 kilometers
Granada to Bailen to Cordoba	247 kilometers
Cordoba to Sevilla	138 kilometers
Sevilla to Lagos	279 kilometers
Lagos to Lisboa	268 kilometers
Lisboa to Madrid	633 kilometers
Madrid to Santander	394 kilometers

Are there really "castles in Spain"? If this is your first visit to the Iberian Peninsula, you can test the truth of the old phrase just by looking up. Around the next turn you might see a castle perched on a craggy peak. For castle aficionados this is *the* country: Not only can you see them from below, you can also explore many of them from the inside. Looking down on the countryside from the ramparts is exhilarating, particularly if you have earned the view by climbing up many worn stone steps to get to it.

Looking up is a useful habit in Spain. The upward glance may reveal a hillscape spread with white houses and red roofs and church spires, or, in closer focus, cathedral gargoyles, flowers hanging from balconies several stories up, with people leaning elbows on iron grillwork to watch the world go by below. You can find unusual frames for your camera to record by looking for the juxtaposition of a distant tower through the opening of a narrow climbing street or a Moorish archway. The photographer with a stiff neck is no joke; you may want to photograph some of the ornate ceilings in palaces, castles, and cathedrals. In any case, you will want to take time to enjoy these upward visions.

Spain is sometimes referred to as a "miniature continent" because the terrain includes everything from rugged mountains (sierra means

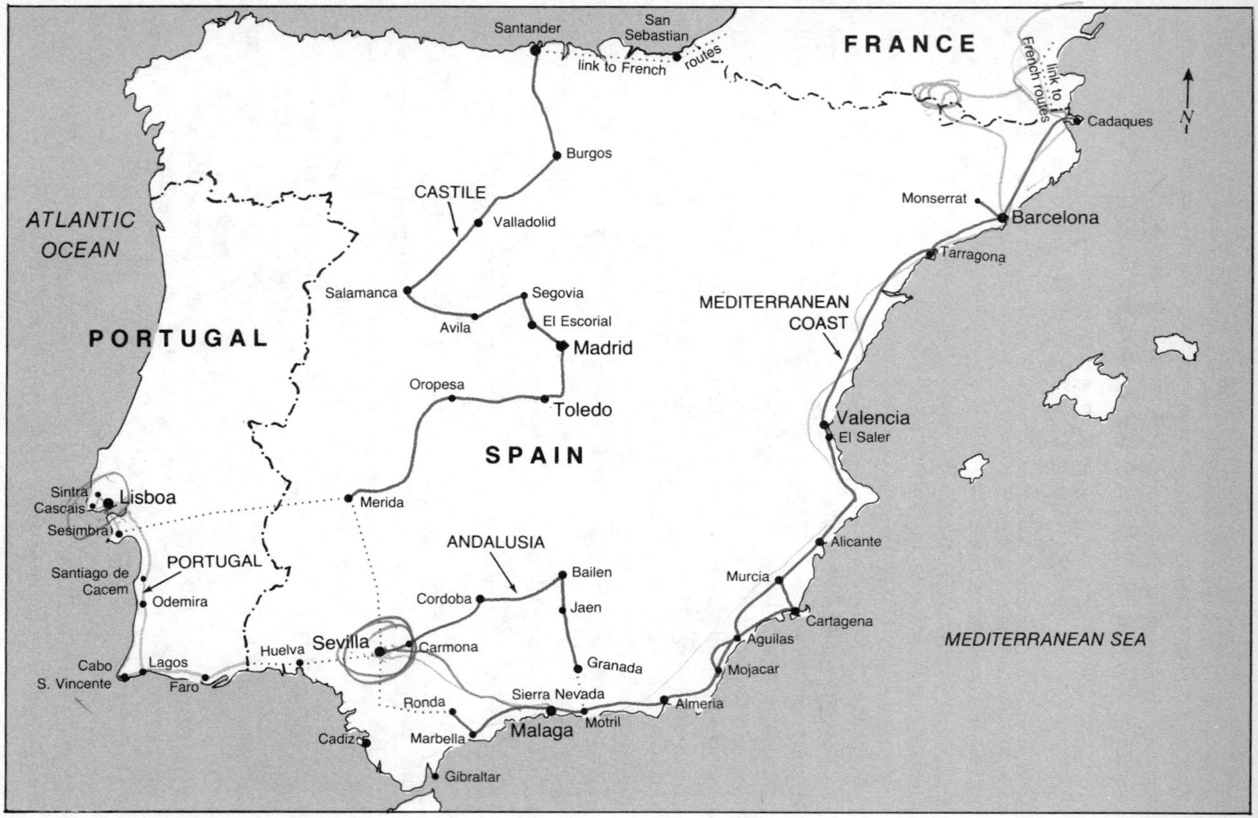

FRANCE
N
Santander
San Sebastian
link to French routes
link to French routes
Cadaques
Burgos
CASTILE
Valladolid
Monserrat
Barcelona
Tarragona
ATLANTIC OCEAN
Salamanca
Segovia
Avila
El Escorial
Madrid
PORTUGAL
MEDITERRANEAN COAST
Oropesa
Toledo
Valencia
El Saler
SPAIN
Sintra
Lisboa
Cascais
Merida
Sesimbra
ANDALUSIA
Alicante
Santiago de Cacem
PORTUGAL
Odemira
Bailen
Murcia
Cordoba
Jaen
Cartagena
Sevilla
Carmona
Huelva
Aguilas
MEDITERRANEAN SEA
Granada
Cabo S. Vincente
Lagos
Faro
Mojacar
Sierra Nevada
Ronda
Almeria
Motril
Malaga
Cadiz
Marbella
Gibraltar

"sawtoothed"), forests, vast plains, and fertile valleys to sandy beaches and coastal headlands. You can change from one to the other within a matter of hours, ski and sunbathe all in the same day. The variety of contour provides infinitely changing landscape, striking contrasts.

And does the rain *really* fall mainly on the plain? Actually, this large area, called the Mesata, does not receive much rain at all. Local inhabitants are always wishing for rain to control the dust as well as provide water for cities and countryside. Flora and fauna change from desert to forest varieties as you travel around Spain. The northern region, from Catalonia to Galicia, is humid, with an abundance of lush plant growth. The southern section, as well as much of the central plain, is so arid that little vegetation will grow without irrigation. The eastern and southern coasts, as well as the Andalusian plain, have a mild Mediterranean climate; winter does not exist in these regions. And the sea plays a major role in the life of Spain, with a coastline of 4000 kilometers circling around the whole peninsula to meet the barrier of the Pyrenees.

A number of mountain ranges march through Spain: the Pyrenees separate Spain from France; the Cantabrian Cordillera links with the western end of the Pyrenees; the Iberian Cordillera runs southeast from the Cantabrian range; the Central Cordillera, made up of several smaller mountain ranges, interrupts the plain; and the peninsula ends with the highest range, the Sierra Nevada, in the southeast, and the Sierra Morena, in the southwest. In Europe, Spain is second only to Switzerland in mountainous terrain.

Marked regional differences exist in the customs, foods, wines, dialects, and folklore. These rich traditions are visible in festivals, dancing, and crafts. You will probably want to return home with a selection of Spanish jewelry, ceramics, lace, or leather mementos. Each region claims its own cultural contribution to Spanish theater, music, art, and literature.

The Spanish people are very fond of quoting proverbs; one writer states that they are one of the richest treasures in the culture of collections. The variety of topics is endless. For example, from a collection from 1508, Sevilla:

Camino de Santiago, tanto anda el cojo como el sano. (On the road to Santiago, the lame walks as far as the healthy man.)

La una mano lava a la otra, y las dos al rostro. (One hand washes the other, and both of them the face.)

Dos amigos de una bolsa, el uno canta y el otro llora. (Two friends with one purse, the one sings and the other weeps.)

Buey suelto, bien se lame. (An untied ox cares for himself well.)

From Zaragoza, 1549:

Mas vale estar sola, que mal acompanada. (Better to be alone than in bad company.)

Mas vale medir y remedir, que cortar y arrepentir. (Better to measure and measure again than to cut and repent.)
Zaragoza, la harta; Valencia, la bella; Barcelona, la rica. (Zaragoza the abundant; Valencia the beautiful; Barcelona the rich.)

From Salamanca, 1555:
Aceite, vino y amigo, antiguo. (Oil, wine, and friends, old.)
De la mano a la boca se pierde la sopa. (From the hand to the mouth the soup is lost.)
Al que tiene mujer hermosa, o castillo en frontera, o vina en carretera, nunca la falta guerra. (He who has a beautiful wife, a castle on the border, or a vineyard on the highway never lacks problems.)

The record of life in Spain dates back 25,000 years; paintings in the Altamira caves near Santander belong to this period. Phoenicians and Greeks arrived to join the Iberians in the 11th century B.C. Their culture blended with the Iberian; the "Lady of Elche" is one of the sculptures that survives from this period. Each successive wave of newcomers from the north, east, and south profoundly influenced the character of Spanish life. Celts invaded from central Europe, then Carthaginians and Romans arrived in the second and third centuries B.C. (Ampurias, a Greek colony that you can explore, is near Gerona.) There are many Roman structures in Spain—houses, fortifications, temples, theaters, aqueducts—including those in **Segovia, Badajoz, Caceres,** and **Merida.**

In the fifth and sixth centuries A.D. the Visigoths ruled; you will see their sculpture and buildings in Merida, **Toledo, Asturias, Cordoba, Oviedo,** and **Zamora.** When the Moors came in the eighth century, the Christians fled to the north; not surprisingly, the delicate nuances of Moorish architecture are concentrated in Andalusia, particularly in cities like Cordoba, **Sevilla,** and especially **Granada,** with its fairyland Alhambra, but also in a few more northerly outposts of Moorish culture like Toledo. In 1492 the Catholic monarchs, Ferdinand and Isabella, finally drove the Moors out of Granada just as Columbus was stumbling on a new continent to the west. The year is a true watershed in Spanish history because it marks two events that led to the peak of Spanish power in the world. Spain became unified politically, religiously, and territorially, and she became rich through her conquests in the New World. Monuments from this pinnacle of opulence abound all over Spain—Romanesque architecture, later Gothic, then Mudejar. Gothic cathedrals were built in Oviedo, **Palencia, Pamplona, Barcelona, Gerona, Cuenca,** and Sevilla. You can see Mudejar buildings in Sevilla, Segovia, **Teruel,** and Toledo. During the 16th century the Renaissance and Baroque styles became popular in Spain. The massive *Escorial,* a monastery and palace near Madrid, was built in Renaissance style, as well as monuments in Toledo, Granada, **Valladolid,** and many other cities and towns. Later, Baroque cathedrals were built in **Valencia, Murcia,** and **Cadiz,** and the royal palaces around Madrid are in that style.

During the 19th century Spanish unity and power began to disintegrate due to repeated disputes surrounding the Carlist succession to the throne, and many of her colonies, like Cuba and the Philippines, were lost in the Spanish-American War. In 1936 Franco led a rebellion from the military garrison in Morocco. Civil war from 1936–1939 consisted of mass slaughters and other violent reprisals. Franco took over, establishing order by execution. Spain was devastated politically and economically. Recently Spain has been concentrating on modernizing and unifying a country that has not fully outgrown the heritage of a nation divided by a bloody and bitter civil war, though the country is now peaceful and prosperous.

WHERE TO STAY IN SPAIN AND PORTUGAL

Accommodation of all kinds is plentiful in Spain and Portugal. In fact, more villas, holiday apartments, and hotels are being built than some of the beach areas can tolerate. You can get great bargains by traveling off season.

Campgrounds abound in the coastal areas, and some of them are situated right on or overlooking the sea. Turn to "Europe under Canvas" for a sampling of reliable sites; you will see signs for many others along the road. If you come upon a particularly convenient or attractive site and wish to camp outside an official campground, you may do so with the permission of the owner. Or you can seek the advice of the local police. The information provided by the Spanish Tourist Office states that "no more than three tents or caravans may be set up together outside camp sites for more than three days, nor may the number of campers exceed ten." You must have a Camping Carnet to do this; it is helpful to have one anyway, because third-party insurance is included. In established sites you can leave the carnet (rather than your passport) in the campground office until you pay your bill; we prefer to keep our passports with us because they are also needed for cashing traveler's checks.

A rather special way to travel in Spain involves the **paradores,** hotels operated by the government. At this writing, there are 88 paradores in renovated castles, palaces, monasteries, and convents, as well as some built recently in vacation areas, particularly beaches or mountains. They offer comfortable rooms with bath and meals in buildings of great historical interest. The Spanish Tourist Office will send you a complete list; you can make reservations ahead for any you plan to use. During the high season many of them are booked six months in advance, but at other times you may be able to just drop in. Even if you don't want to stay in a parador, you can visit the interesting ones or eat a meal in them. **Pousadas** in Portugal are similar to paradores in Spain.

We have found that the combination of parador nights and camping offers us the best of both worlds. We used paradores when we knew we would be arriving late after a long day of driving. When camping, we planned to arrive at a reasonable time in the late afternoon so we could make camp, cook dinner, relax, and spend the next day or two enjoying the area.

The Mediterranean Coast of Spain

From the French border: Figueras, Llansa, Cadaques, Roses, Ampurias, Barcelona, Monserrat, Sitges, Tarragona, Valencia, El Saler, Alicante, Cartagena, Aguilas, Mojacar, Almeria, Motril, Malaga, Marbella, Ronda
(7–14 days, 1232 kilometers)

This itinerary takes you along the coast of Spain, from the French border to Marbella, through five coastal regions: the Costa Brava, from the French border to Blanes; the Costa Dorada, south to Tortosa; the Costa Del Azahar, south to Denia; the Costa Blanca, south to Almeria; and the Costa del Sol, west to Gibraltar. Each of these coasts has a distinctive character.

The **Costa Brava** (wild coast) has mountains, rugged rocks, and cliffs, softened somewhat by pine trees that march down to meet the blue sea. Coves and short, sandy beaches are interspersed with craggy cliffs. There are Greek ruins to visit and the fascination of Salvador Dali is captured both in the scenery of Cadaques and a museum in Figueras.

The **Costa Dorada** (golden coast) has long beaches and peaceful coves. Tarragona was a favorite vacation spot for Emperor Hadrian and also for Augustus; Roman ruins include an aqueduct.

The **Costa Del Azahar** (orange blossom coast), has long, sandy beaches. Valencia is famous for its delicious oranges and also as the stronghold of the legendary El Cid, who died there in A.D. 1099.

The **Costa Blanca,** noted for its sandy beaches, is one of the warmest areas in Spain, with a temperate climate in winter. Due to poor road conditions in some sections, tourist development has not proceeded very rapidly here; this means fewer concrete monstrosities cluttering up the coastline.

The southernmost **Costa Del Sol** is noted for a series of towns and villages offering watersports, golf, and tennis, as well as ample opportunity for basking in the sun. The towns and villages along this coast vary greatly in their sophistication and commitment to tourism, with those east of Malaga, in general, preserving more of their original character. Part of the area is close enough to Granada for a side trip to the Alhambra, or for an excursion to the mountain fastness of Ronda.

Although most of these coasts are crowded with tourists in summer, you can find real bargains in winter in all types of accommodation. People from many countries are enticed by package tours all along the Mediterranean. In many flats and villas, empty in winter, prices are greatly reduced; hotel prices are lowered and campgrounds are spacious, with few people around to suggest congestion. You can camp year-round in the south of Spain, barring a real cold snap. The English escape the nasty westerly gales of Britain by spending several months in their caravans along the south coast. It is also a pleasure to drive along narrow, winding coast roads during the off season without fighting bottleneck traffic.

If you are in a hurry to get to the south, you can drive the autopista from the French border to Alicante, where it stops, with forays inland and to the sea on secondary roads. Or, if you have more leisure, you can follow coastal roads that wind around and reveal some of the most surprising scenery found anywhere, a combination of wide seascape and barren mountains. Special signs indicate roads that will provide exceptional views.

The count of kilometers on this route is based on the total distance from the French border to Marbella; kilometers for your chosen side trips should be added. Days are figured on the minimum number required for pleasurable touring, with a suggested maximum for those who continue to move rather than settle in a single place.

Catalonia

The province of Catalonia is a good place to begin a tour of Spain. It lies within a triangle between the Mediterranean Sea, the French border, and the province of Aragon to the west. It encompasses part of the Pyrenees, the precipitous Costa Brava, the flatter, sandy stretches of the Costa Dorada, and the industrial and cultural center of Barcelona. Catalans have a rich historical background; since the sixth century B.C. the area has been invaded by Greeks, Carthaginians, Romans, and Arabs. The Catalans variegated cultural identity is preserved in many ways, such as in the Sardana, a dance that originated in sun worship. You may see this dance on Sundays or during festivals. Read George Orwell's *Homage to Catalonia* for a view of life there during the Spanish Civil War.

The Catalan dialect, though banned by Franco for more than 30 years, is still often used more than Castilian Spanish today. You may find that some road signs use the Catalan dialect, so that, for example, "Figueras" is "Figueres," "Ampurias" is "Empuries," and "Gerona" is "Girona."

COSTA BRAVA From the border, take A7 to **Figueras** and follow signs to the center to visit the *Salvador Dali Museum,* opened in 1974. This museum is both amusing and amazing, with one unusual painting after another. The absurd is mixed with fantasy into something one has to see to believe.

From Figueras, look for signs to **Llansa** (or Llanca), a beautiful village right on the sea. The winding road along the coast from Llansa to **El Port de la Selvais** is well paved and two-lanes wide, with views of blue water around every bend. If you're there on a wild day, there will be white caps and blowing spray. This little fishing village retains its ancient character despite the addition of white, red-roofed villas for summer vacationers. The coarse sand beach has shallow water that makes it safe for children.

For a magnificent drive through coastal mountains, follow GE613, which cuts across the peninsula and is a very rough road indeed. You will survive—it lasts for only 8 kilometers—as you look over sheer drops while driving in second gear at under 40 kilometers per hour. To be sure, there are lovely views for the passenger.

Eventually you will come to GE614, which is a good road leading to **Cadaques.** This old fishing port, made fashionable by the presence of an artist's colony, has a harbor loaded with sailing yachts and fishing boats, small beaches, and several hotels and bars around a shaded square. To the right is another harbor with smaller boats pulled up on the beach, including one resting up in a gnarled tree when we were there, and swings for children. Take one of the narrow, steep roads going up for a view from the top. Many painters and writers live and work in Cadaques, including Salvador Dali. There is a church in the old section with a Baroque altarpiece.

Retrace your steps on GE614 to **Rosas,** where there are ruins of a medieval fortress and a citadel built in the shape of a pentagon. You will see majestic cliffs above; go up to **Super Rosas** for the view.

Follow signs for **Ampurias** (Empuries), which is located two kilometers before you reach **La Escala.** This is one of the most interesting archaeological sites in Spain. In the sixth century, Phoenicians settled there and called their colony Emporion; a "new town," Neapolis, was built a hundred years later. You can see the remains of a basilica, several temples, cisterns, the town gate, marketplace, and a number of streets. Visit the museum to see diagrams and models of the excavation; there are also two third-century pagan sarcophagi and a small mosaic. Up the hill you will see the partially excavated Roman colony, which contains two villas with gardens and mosaic floors, and there is an amphitheater beyond.

COSTA DORADA Continue on down A7 to **Barcelona,** the second largest city in Spain. It has an ambience less distinctively Spanish than many other cities; perhaps it is more sophisticated and cosmopolitan because of the influence of its near neighbor, France, and its commercial role as one of the major seaports of the Mediterranean. Barcelona has some exciting modern architecture in the structures of Antonio Gaudi, a Catalan native who lived and worked in the city (1852–1926). His **Templo de la Sagrada Familia,** a cathedral, was started in 1882 by public gifts but was never completed because he did not leave plans before his untimely death. He was killed by a trolley as he was standing in front of the church collecting money for the construction. (He would not accept funds from either the state or the Church, but depended upon individual gifts.) The finished part includes eight spires rising to over 300 feet; four more were to have been built so the spires could stand as symbols of the 12 apostles. His style is marked by curves, asymmetrical lines, fantasy, and a touch of surrealism. **Guell Park** was originally designed as an expensive residential section but became a park instead when financial problems arose. Colored benches with curves, giant lizards, unusual pillars, and a mosaic are there to be enjoyed, and there is a marvelous view of the city on a clear day.

Pablo Picasso came to Barcelona when he was 14 years old. His "blue period," from 1901 to 1904, coincided with his years in Barcelona. The **Picasso Museum,** including works from every phase of his life but concentrating on his pre-surrealist period, contains most of his work that is displayed in Spain.

In the center of the old town you will find the **Barrio Gotica** (Gothic quarter). Although many of the buildings date from the 13th century, there is evidence of Roman occupation as well. The 13th-century cathedral is one of the largest Gothic structures in the country. Before you leave, stroll down the **Ramblas,** a wide promenade displaying flower stalls, cafes, restaurants, stores, and bird sellers.

Take time to enjoy **Montjuich,** where you will find **Pueblo Espanol,** a Spanish village containing buildings selected to portray the architecture and daily life of Spain. Regional artisans work on their crafts there. (Visiting this village before touring Spain can be useful because typical buildings from every region are laid out before you.) Also visit the museum of Catalonian art *(Museo de Arte de Cataluna)* and the archaeological museum *(Museo Arqueologica).*

One of Spain's most impressive natural sites and shrines is **Monserrat.** The mountain itself is part of a sawtoothed range that you can't help but see from miles away along the autopista. There is a monastery and a basilica up there amidst enormous spires of jagged rock. The atmosphere on top is almost more than eye or mind can comprehend—the gigantic masses of rock, some shaped like fingers stretching upward, some appearing to be overbalanced and hovering, towering above the solid, somewhat ponderous basilica itself. This is truly a beautiful place for a shrine.

To get to it from the autopista, take N11 toward **Manresa** and Monserrat, then bear right onto C1411 until you come to the bridge for the *Aereo Funicular.* Ride up in the cablecar, which climbs rapidly toward the steep, rocky crags, and in about ten minutes you will have risen over 4000 feet. (Alternatively, you can drive to the monastery by one of two circuitous roads offering magnificent views by following signs from either **Monistrol** or, farther north, Manresa.) Up on top, get a map from the information booth.

In such a place, one would expect many legends, such as the belief that St. Peter placed a carving of the Virgin in a cave up there. The story continues that a strange light hovered over the cave and drew shepherds to it. The bishop was summoned to remove the Black Virgin, and as his procession moved along, a mysterious force caused them to stop on the site of the present monastery. Although that monastery was destroyed by the French in 1811, the Black Virgin (or Madonna) survived.

When you arrive at the top, walk through the basilica after entering from the courtyard, where there are fine angles for viewing the facade, by the right-hand door. You will pass a number of chapels before you climb the stairs to see the *Black Madonna*, placed on a throne high above the altar. She is in a niche domed by beautiful Venetian mosaic work. Nine silver lamps stand for Monserrat and the eight Catalonian dioceses. Many pilgrims have made their way to this spot, and their pilgrimages are reflected in two alabaster candlesticks. Ancient paintings do not show the Madonna as black originally; some art historians believe that she has gradually become black over the centuries. She is enclosed in glass and holds a wooden ball in her hand for pilgrims to kiss. Her child is on her lap. There are also stained-glass windows, murals, paintings, and sculpture to admire inside the basilica.

Outside, the mountain is framed by many arches, all with different perspectives. (Don't forget your camera on this trip.) There are a number of hikes to even higher caves and hermitages for the active and curious visitor, each with its own magnificent set of views; the more sedentary can reach some of these by aerial tramway. You may feel as Goethe did: "nowhere but in his own Monserrat will a man find happiness and peace." (One caution: We are told that Monserrat can become quite crowded in high season, so if you are traveling at that time, it might be wise to choose a weekday or a weekend early morning for your visit.)

While in the region surrounding Barcelona, you may want to take a trip to **Sitges,** an attractive coastal town south of the city, with a palm-shaded promenade beside a sandy beach. One landmark is the church found at the end of the promenade, and there are several museums to visit: *Cau Ferrat,* which features ceramics, paintings, and forged-iron work, and *Mariciel de Mar,* which contains paintings by El Greco, Utrillo, and Rusinol.

Farther down the coast is **Tarragona,** a medieval city also rich in preserved Roman monuments. You can see 600 yards of the Roman wall still standing in the upper part of the city. The *Archaeological Museum* contains a collection of mosaics, including the Head of Medusa. Walk on the promenade, the *Paseo Arqueological,* through gardens between the Roman walls and those built by the British during the War of Succession in 1707. You will find the cathedral, which is both Romanesque and Gothic in construction, in the center of the upper town. The **Paleo-Christian Museum** contains tombs from the third century, a collection of mosaics, ivory, and pottery. The **Roman aqueduct,** also called the Devil's Bridge, has two rows of arches and is 400 feet long. For further background on Tarragona, read Rose Macauley's *Fabled Shore.*

The Levant

The Levant, or East, includes the provinces of Castellon, Valencia, Alicante, Murcia, and Albacete. The climate is mild and the soil is dry. However, with irrigation, fruit, vegetables, and flowers are grown in abundance here. (The Spanish word *huertas* means "large garden.") South of Valencia you will see rice fields in an area called **La Albufera,** where there is also a lake of the same name.

Various peoples inhabited the area, including Palaeolithic man, Phoenicians, Carthaginians, Romans, Visigoths, and Arabs. Because so many different cultures were brought to the area, various dialects are spoken, but there is not a special language here as there is in Catalonia. Many of the festivals held in the region feature giant figures called *fallas* that satirize various aspects of society and that are burned in huge bonfires at the end of the celebration. Valencia celebrates Las Fallas during the week before March 19th each year.

COSTA DEL AZAHAR As you enter the Levant from Catalonia, continue south on the autopista (with forays off route to beach towns as your time and inclination direct) until you come to **Valencia.** Although this city is industrialized, the center is attractive. The *cathedral* has an octagonal Gothic tower, called the Miguelete, which is actually unfinished. However, you can climb up to its roof for a view of the city and the sea. Count the belfries while you are up there—Victor Hugo once reached 300. The cathedral is a mixture of Romanesque, Gothic, and Baroque. In the *Chapel of the Holy Grail* there is a gold and agate chalice that according to legend, was used by Christ at the Last Supper. Searched for by Galahad, Lancelot, Parsifal, and Lohengrin, the chalice was presented to this cathedral in the 15th century.

The *Paleontological Museum* is housed in what was once a medieval granary. To the east of it you will find the *Church of San Esteban:* The Cid's daughters were married there. Rodrigo Diaz, an 11th-century warrior called El Cid, became legendary through the recording of his exploits in ballads and epic poems by Corneille and Guillen de Castro. El Cid died in Valencia in 1099; his body was positioned on his horse by his wife, Ximena, and taken through the opposing troops to Burgos to be buried. While in Valencia, take time to visit the *Grao* (old port) with your camera in hand.

You may want to make a side trip to *El Saler,* the Albufera area with rice fields and seaside resorts; it contains camping areas with a wide range of facilities along fine sand beaches backed by dunes. Stop along the road to buy a long net bag of Valencia oranges, which are large and easy to peel because of their thick skin. The orange groves are protected by fences made of reeds, either standing bound together or woven horizontally into a hedge. There were a number of cyclists along this flat stretch when we were there.

To rejoin A7 south of the Albufera take N332 at **Cullera.** Continue on A7, even though there is a gap in the autopista from **Jeresa,** near **Gandia,** to **Ondara.** For a pleasant side trip to three capes *(San Antonio, San Martin,* and *Moraira),* take Route N332 until you see a sign for **Denia.** Turn toward the sea then turn right at the next junction, driving along the coastal road until you see the castle of Denia. This pleasant town is a fishing and port center as well as a vacation site. A little farther along you will find **Javea,** an attractive town with two beaches and a modern church that looks like a ship's hull. In **Calpe,** you can see *Penon de Ifach,* which looks like the Rock of Gibraltar.

If you are heading from Valencia to **Alicante** without side trips, you will still have to put up with the break in the autopista from Jeresa at exit 60 to exit 62. Then you will have clear sailing to just north of Alicante, where the autopista—unfortunately—stops. (Even those who are not particularly fond of superhighways will come to regret the end of this one as they plod southward.)

COSTA BLANCA Alicante, the capital of the province, is also a thriving seaport and a resort center. It is said that the father of Hannibal, Hamilcar Barca, built the first fort in town. The spot is now occupied by the *Castle of Santa Barbara.* This fortress, sitting on *Mount Benacantil,* affords a fine view of the city. As you walk along the palm-shaded promenade, the *Esplanada de Espana,* you will feel the sensation of waves under your feet on the interesting marble pavement. (The town of **Monovar** provided this marble, as well as that for the Supreme Court Building in Washington, DC.)

Take time to walk along the *Rambla Mendez Nunez,* where you will pass many shops and outdoor cafes, eventually reaching the narrower streets of the old town. If you are fortunate enough to be in Alicante during the right week in June, you may catch the festival, the Fallas of San Juan. Large effigies depict local or national events satirically. Each district in the city fashions a display and also provides a Fiesta Queen, one of whom is chosen to rule over the fiesta. The week is crammed with parades, fireworks, dancing, and nightly celebrations. It ends with all of the effigies in bonfires.

From Alicante, take N340 through **Elche,** where 100,000 palms were once planted by Phoenicians. *Priest Grove* contains the enormous Imperial Palm, which has a number of trunks growing out of the original one. The garden is a pleasant place, with pools, fountains, and paths winding through various displays of plants. A replica of the statue, "The Lady of Elche," stands in Priest's Grove as well. (The original is in the Prado Museum in Madrid.) Palms are cut to be used on Palm Sunday and as charms against lightning.

Continue on N340 through cotton fields planted under trees in the orchards. The road is straight and flat, as good as you will find for two-laned roads in Spain. The area around **Orihuela** provides interesting views, with lemon groves marching up to craggy, barren mountains, and with cactus beginning to appear in this region as well. On the approach to **Monteagudo** you will see what first appears to be a huge cross on the mountain; as you come closer, you will discover that it is a figure of Christ towering above a monastery. **Murcia** has a towering cathedral to visit. The *Museo Salzillo* is interesting, with its collection of figures carried in the Holy Week procession.

From Murcia, you can plunge straight on down 340 to **Almeria** if you are in a hurry to get to the Costa del Sol, but we recommend a side trip to one of the least-developed rural sections of the coast. Follow the signs for **Cartagena,** but don't be deceived by them: the road to Cartagena to the south and Madrid to the north are both signed as autopista. You will find that the autopista to the south lasts for only 300 meters before receding into ordinary, two-lane N301. This road starts out with an attractive, undemanding pass over the *Sierra de Carrascoy,* then flattens out over a high plateau. There are many areas with posted speed limits of 60 kilometers, then 40, and sometimes even a crawling 20, which is not easy to maintain. Be sure to check your gas gauge before beginning this section. You will continue to drive over desolate, rolling and folding dry mountains. There is not much activity up there, but plowed fields in fruit orchards indicate some life; we saw one herd of black goats with a lonely shepherd. As you leave the plateau and start down toward the coast, you will see a number of *rampares,* dry washes that must be raging torrents during storms. Eventually, you will see a sparkling view of the ocean, and you may be surprised to find a city at the end of this desolate descent. Cartagena, founded by the Carthaginians, was a Roman naval port; it is now the site of a submarine school and naval base, as well as a busy commercial center. Sir Francis Drake sailed into the harbor in 1585 and sailed out again after confiscating the harbor guns, in one of his more audacious raids.

From Cartagena, take a secondary road signed N332 & 442 toward **Puerto de Mazarron,** which lies on a shingle beach surrounded by rocky coastline and palm trees. This would be a pleasant place to stop, and it has an abundance of camping sites and apartments to rent. However, we had mixed reactions when we noticed the number of cranes at work on new high-rise buildings, a first sign of the overdevelopment that has spoiled many sections of originally beautiful Spanish coastline. Continue on N332/342 toward **Aguilas,** past fields of clear polyurethane greenhouses covering lemon groves. As you drive up the rather desolate pass, you will find interesting rock formations along a road that appears to have been designed by a meandering donkey. It winds forward and backward around rocks and over one-lane bridges; 40 kilometers an hour is the maximum comfortable speed. There are few houses or people up there, except for an occasional family sitting outside in the late afternoon sun; it is hard to believe that inhabitants and vacationers use such a road to get anywhere.

The trip from Puerto de Mazarron to Aguilas takes one hour to drive. As you descend from the mountains to the town, watch carefully for a series of dips in the road that become washes when it rains; the first one you hit could rattle you around if you are flying high. Just west of Aguilas along the beach road there are a number of fine sites for caravans (but no facilities).

Soon after the next town, **San Juan de los Terreros,** there is a fork in the road that we missed the first time through, ending up in **Los Lobos,** where the road becomes even more primitive. We retraced our route and rejoined the road by the sea at **El Pozo del Esparto.** The correct road is signed **Garrucha,** then **Mojacar.** This stretch from Aguilas to Mojacar is absolutely spectacular, with the sea smashing against rocky outcroppings between beaches. It takes an hour to drive. You may find, as we have, that vows not to drive mountain passes or winding coast roads with sheer drops into the sea at night are not always possible to keep. In this case, we had no idea that the route we had chosen would take such a long time and perhaps had dallied too long earlier in the day. And the final stretch along the coast, where a new road was under construction, contained some interesting surprises at night, including a deep wash beyond Garrucha, where the road simply appeared to end amongst huge piles of gravel. Yet the area we have just described is naturally beautiful and well worth the extra time and struggle with slow, winding roads if you plan carefully. If you do end up in the mountains at dusk, you will be rewarded with an amazing array of brilliant pink tints silhouetting the mountains. On the other hand, you might find it just as pleasant to watch that sunset from your destination.

Mojacar is visible from a long way off because its white Moorish houses are perched on a steep hill. Driving the narrow streets at the top requires dexterity; it is really a walking town. For a number of decades inhabitants moved away from Mojacar—Walt Disney was twelve years old when his family moved to California—but the population is now on the upswing again, supported by tourism that is still low-key and, we thought, undisturbing. You might want to join the groups of inhabitants and visitors enjoying a sunny morning in the town square, having a drink and just relaxing. Mojacar is one of the few coast towns where you run no danger of feeling overwhelmed by high-rise tourist blocks.

From Mojacar, take secondary AL151 & 150 to rejoin the N340, and continue toward Almeria. As you drive toward **Sorbas** you will see doors leading into caves high up in the cliffs. Houses are perched on top; a river bed, dry when we were there, lies at the bottom. Near the middle of the long stretch of mostly barren mountains between Sorbas and Almeria, movie buffs may recognize the setting for many Hollywood films, including *The Centurions, Lawrence of Arabia,* and *Patton,* which were filmed near **Tabernas.** Nearby, at a spot on the map labeled with the anomalous "Mini Hollywood," is a movie set, **Yucca City,** set in an area of eroding, barren, dry mountains with unexpected moonlike shapes and angles. The sedimentary rock tilts and folds in all directions.

As you come down from this parched moonscape to rejoin the sea at Almeria, you reenter a lush world. Aldous Huxley wrote about Almeria, "You have the sun for a lover, Oh, fortunate earth." There the sun is said to shine for 3000 hours every year. Phoenicians and Carthaginians originally settled Almeria. Later, pirates monopolized the harbor as a springboard for their raids up and down the coasts of Spain. Then the Moors moved in for several hundred years. One of the best examples of a Moorish fortification in Spain is the **Alcazaba,** which dominates the city. Within it are three walled areas, including one containing the ruins of a mosque; the fortress has been restored, and during August, music and art festivals are held there. At the seafront, we enjoyed walking on the pleasant promenade under neatly trimmed palms. People were strolling in Sunday clothes or sitting at outdoor bars having a drink. There are a lot of fishing boats pulled up on the beach.

The road out of Almeria is cut from the cliffs and lies right next to the sea. There are a number of laybys where you can pull over and enjoy a picnic lunch. N340 continues through flat country totally filled with polyurethan greenhouses. The atmosphere is rural: We noticed a group of women washing clothes in a large trough that ran in front of their houses; a number of men were leading donkeys carrying loads of reeds on the highway. At **Torre,** the road climbs again and is bumpy but has beautiful views. There are many rocky promontories from which to view the next one jutting out into the sea.

COSTA DEL SOL The Costa Del Sol has a gentle Mediterranean climate with not much variation during the year. Many tourists head for one of the towns along its beaches. Near the Sierra Nevada range, the beaches are rugged where the mountains overlook the sea; farther to the west, the beaches are low and sandy. The vegetation is subtropical with a wide variety of plants. People come to enjoy the sun and to engage in all types of sports including fishing, rowing, sailing, waterskiing, swimming, tennis, golf, riding, and hunting. There are festivals in each town, especially during Holy Week. Bullfights attract some visitors, a full repertoire in music and dance others.

Along this coast, each town has its particular virtues. **Castell de Ferro** is a pleasant town; it has a beach with coarse sand. **Torrenueva** has the longest beach in the immediate area. **Motril** has several beaches, and you will see sugar cane growing in field after field there. **Salobrena** is an attractive town perched on rock; it has a walled section and a castle. At this writing, there is a fair amount of road construction in progress; it is sorely needed to provide more easily negotiated curves and a slow lane for uphill trucks.

The surface of the road improves at **Almunecar,** which has a *Roman aqueduct,* the *Monje Tower,* and the *Palacious Cave.* There are several beaches here, some with fine sand, others with shingle and sand. Off the main coast road, still N340, there are a number of side roads leading to beautiful views; we took one signed *Miradore de Cerro Gorda.* (For the convenience of the tourist, these roads, mostly sections of the old, slow, coast road carved into the side of the cliff, which is now being replaced by faster road running through rock cuts, are marked with special signs.) There are several places to stop for photographs or for lunch on the Miradore de Cerro Gorda, and the scenery is dramatic, with villas perched here and there on improbable sites, their terraces at the edge of sheer drops into the sea. Each turn offers another surprise in the general spectacle—ruins of a martello tower, a rockslide on part of the road, even the now familiar gigantic steer billboards on a hilltop.

Farther down the coast, **Nerja** is a heavily but pleasantly developed town mixing new with old—villas for sale, golf, and tennis, with flowers hanging over ancient walls, and Roman ruins nearby. Here the coast road becomes flat. **Lagos** is a charming little hamlet where we saw villagers—mostly fishermen and their families—sitting in the sun watching a strange world go by; we wondered what they thought of tourists and city people with enough money to buy the expensive villas nearby. **Torre del Mar** is a village that has high-rise apartments right next to ancient village houses. The town seems cosmopolitan in the shopping area; however, a few blocks away, we saw farmers plowing with donkeys in between large, modern villas. Contrasts between two worlds are almost overwhelming.

Malaga is considered the center of the Costa Del Sol. It has a fortress, archaeological remains, an international airport, a castle, a museum, and beaches. While driving in Malaga, we saw a goatherd with a large herd in the parking lot of a group of high-rise apartments, an indication of the two lives of this city. **Marbella** has a collection of lovely villas, gardens everywhere, and a long, sandy beach. The old village is set back from the water and is still partly walled.

From Marbella, a side trip to **Ronda** is well worth the drive. Take C339 from **San Pedro de Alcantara** up to the town, which sits on a plateau at the edge of a gorge, divided from intruders by a 525-foot-deep ravine—enough to daunt most aggressors. Juan Ramon Jimenez wrote of it: "Ronda, alta y honda, rotunda, profunda, redona y alta" ("Ronda, high and deep, rotund, profound, round and high"). The name *Ronda* comes from the horseshoe shape of its natural contour. You can walk over the "old bridge," *Puente Viaie,* built in the 17th century, then walk through the town and return over the "new bridge," **Puente Nueve,** built in the 18th century. A lower, third bridge was built by the Moors, who occupied the town for centuries. You can visit the **Collegiate of Santa Maria de la Encarnacion la Mayor,** which dates back to Roman days, but was converted into a mosque. The bullring, **Plaza de Toros,** is an important building in the life of the town. Francisco Romero, a local man, is considered to be the originator of the art of bullfighting in Spain; he also founded the Ronda school of bullfighting. In 1726, he was the first man to dismount from his horse and challenge the bull on foot. To get a firmer sense of the meaning and drama of this peculiarly Spanish passion, you might want to read Ernest Hemingway's *Death in the Afternoon* or *The Sun Also Rises.*

At the cliff edge in Ronda we were joined for a walk by a local guide striding along in his corduroy suit and flat Spanish hat, swinging a walking stick. He gave us all sorts of information in Spanish, including some about the Austrian poet, Rainer Maria Rilke, whose statue looks out over the ravine from the garden of the Hotel Reine Victoria, where he stayed. Rilke once said that as he looked into the chasm he could discern the light and darkness in himself.

Ronda is the conclusion of this long survey of the Mediterranean coast of Spain. There are a number of ways of getting to the heartland of the south, Andalusia. You can head for **Granada** either by returning to the coast at Marbella, driving east to Malaga, north on N331 to **Antequera** and then east on N321 & 342 to Granada, or by taking C339 north to **Algodonales,** then N342 east through **Olvera** and **Campillos** to the Antequera area and on to Granada. If you want to start your discovery of Andalusia at Sevilla, take C339 northwest from Ronda until it joins C343, then on to **Los Cabezas de San Juan,** where you can pick up the autopista (A4) to Sevilla. The first part of this route is fairly slow, with driving speeds often decreasing from 60 to 40 or 20 km/hr. The views are some of the nicest in Spain—a desolate area inhabited by poor Spaniards who may not have a telephone but do have TV, judging by the aerials, and whose subsistence comes from sheep and olives amidst a landscape of magnificent views. This is as good a way as any to begin to appreciate the distinctive qualities of Andalusia.

Andalusia

From Granada: Sierra Nevada, Jaen, Cordoba, Carmona, Sevilla (7–14 days, 385 kilometers)

This itinerary begins in Granada, a city of distinctive beauty and architecture—a fascinating combination of the beauties of nature and art. Some travelers feel that if you can see only one city in Spain, let it be Granada. The **Sierra Nevada** range, which is located 30 kilometers from

Granada, is the highest in Spain. You can ski there from November to May, hike during the warmer months, and enjoy remarkable views year-round.

Jaen is located at the foot of the *Sierra de Jabalcuz.* Long ago, it was the crossroads between Castile and Andalusia, so the Moors called it *Geen* (caravan route). The *cathedral* is a compound of Gothic, Renaissance, and Baroque architecture, and there are other churches, mansions, and a castle to visit.

Cordoba, located on the Madrid–Cadiz national highway, one of the oldest cities in Spain, is best known for its enormous mosque, *La Mezquita.* The nearby Alcazar (fortress) has been renovated as a museum and is used for concerts. *Calleja de las Flores* (Street of the Flowers) is only one of the many attractive walks you can take in the old Moorish quarter; there are courtyards lush with flowers to peek into.

Carmona dates back into the Neolithic Age and has prehistoric sites to visit, as well as Roman gates, walls, and the *Necropolis,* a burial area containing hundreds of tombs.

Sevilla, a city of many moods, is a seaport, a large commercial center, a home of the arts, flowers, and flamenco. It is famous for the *Giralda,* a Moorish tower with a Christian superstructure, and its massive *cathedral* is the third largest in the world.

The kilometers calculated for this route cover the distance from Granada to Jaen, Cordoba, Carmona, and Sevilla. Days are estimated on the basis of the minimum and maximum number needed to enjoy all of these cities.

The boundaries of Andalusia are the Mediterranean, the Atlantic, the Sierra Morena mountains, and Portugal. Its eight provinces are Almeria, Granada, Malaga, Cadiz, Huelva, Sevilla, Cordoba, and Jaen. Although the Romans arrived first, this area has retained more of the Moorish influence than anywhere else in Spain. The Moors arrived in **Tarifa** in A.D. 710 and began conquering one kingdom after another until Granada collapsed in 1492. Sevilla, Cordoba, and Granada all contain exquisite monuments in Moorish style.

Andalusia is also the land of great enthusiasm for fiestas, bullfights, and flamenco. All of its towns and cities have special festivals, as do many in other parts of Spain. However, with the warmest weather in the country available, Andalusia has celebrations during the winter months as well as the traditional spring Holy Week and summer times. The bullfight is especially popular in Seville and Ronda; some aficionados say that it originated in Ronda and was developed and codified into a highly specific art there by the Romero family, among others.

Flamenco dancing can get into your blood—if you find yourself caught up in the rhythm and beauty of this lovely art form. Changes in tempo range through a spectrum of moods and can be so exhilarating that you want to join the dancers; it can also be deeply expressive of somber moods. The traditional dress has a flounced skirt that fits the waist smoothly, with ruffles at the shoulder. It sometimes has a train and may be worn with a fringed shawl. The men wear fitted suits with jackets, boots with heels, and traditional flat Spanish hats. The mannered gestures of the dancers give one a visual presentation of the mood of the music; they are accompanied by guitars and cantors. You may feel like shouting *Ole* with the rest of the crowd.

Granada

You are likely to find yourself caught in the spell of Granada. The poet Francisco de Icaza wrote of a beggar to capture this feeling: "Give him alms, woman, for there is nothing in life, nothing, so sad as to be blind in Granada." The visual beauty of the **Moorish Palace** in the **Alhambra** is magnificent in itself. You may find it overwhelming when your ears pick up the sounds of fountains and waterfalls interspersed with the sound of bells. And, as you walk through the Alhambra's many gardens, you will become aware of the aromatic scents of jasmine, rose, myrtle, eucalyptus, and orange. Granada is a city for walking, listening, looking, and inhaling sweet and spicy scents.

Ibn Ahmar, prince of an Arab tribe, established his kingdom in Granada in 1238. For several hundred years after that Granada flourished as a cultural center and gathering spot for world-renowned artisans. During this period the Christian kingdoms to the north were becoming more powerful, and when Ibn Ahmar died in 1275, Granada was the last Moorish kingdom to survive. Ferdinand and Isabella married in 1479, uniting the kingdoms of Castile and Aragon; they went on to conquer other less powerful kingdoms and solidify their hegemony.

In Granada, the ruling monarch fell in love with Zoraya, a beautiful young girl. His Queen, Aicha, then deposed her husband and placed their son, Boabdil, on the throne. Boabdil tried to defend his kingdom but was forced, in 1492, to surrender the keys to the city and go into exile. There is a spot on the Motril–Granada road called **Suspiro del Moro** (the Moor's Sigh), where Boabdil, grief-stricken that he would never see his beloved Alhambra and Granada again, shed tears. His mother rebuked him, "You weep like a woman for what you could not hold as a man." The Christians had completed their conquest of Spain.

If you see nothing else in this part of Spain, don't miss the Alhambra, a series of palaces, gardens, courtyards, fountains, and a fortress—remains of the history just related. Alhambra means "the red castle," named so because of the red color of the clay used in its construction. As a background for your visit, read Washington Irving's *Tales of the Alhambra* for tales of its inhabitants and personal glimpses of his own life there; while on a ceremonial visit, Irving had been invited by the governor of the Alhambra to stay in his private apartments and did so. Irving describes his accommodations, the services provided by the family who lived there maintaining the palace, and incidents occurring while he was there. He also relates wonderful legends about the various rooms, towers, gardens, and the people who lived there. The book contains romantic engravings by David Roberts, another visitor who loved the Alhambra and the people of Granada.

At some point in your drive up to the parking lot of the Alhambra, you probably will be accosted by gypsy women who will try to throw a red or white carnation into your car and then grab your hand to tell your fortune. They are bold enough to walk right in front of your car; if you would rather not get involved you will need to be quite firm; they are not easily daunted.

Be sure to read about the various parts of the Alhambra before you go to visit; it is too complex to appreciate fully without some preparation. When you buy your ticket you will find a map on the back and four detachable stubs for each of the four sections inside. We found the addition of a detailed guide helpful. Comfortable walking shoes will help because some of the paths are muddy; the stone steps inside the Alcazar are worn and the risers quite high. You will find innumerable natural frames for photographs between the tall cypresses and shrubs, through arches and ornate windowframes. Many of your shots will probably include the beautiful Sierra Nevada mountains in the distance.

We spent several hours taking photographs inside the Moorish palaces. The rooms contain exquisite, fragile-looking walls, arches, ceilings, and decorations. We were amused by an American student who told us, while we were focusing our camera, that there were prettier rooms ahead. Each room does seem more exquisite than the last, and they are all quite different. On subsequent visits we discovered entirely new perspectives for enjoying a number of them. For example, when you are in the Hall of the Abencerrajes, walk up the steps to a small round pool, kneel down, and voila—you will see the reflection of the opposite wall in the water (it makes a nice photograph). Then hold a pair of sunglasses over the little pool and you will see the ceiling reflected in them. Avid photographers should watch for series of arches and may, as we did, develop stiff necks from photographing all of the marvelous ceilings. Of course, many of the windows provide interesting frames for landscape shots of the surrounding city and distant mountains outside the Alhambra.

The guards watch for people who get involved in the architecture or who seem to be very interested in any of the rooms and will offer tips on photographic angles. They will also take you to see the baths. Follow along through gardens and into darkened corridors until you come to the elaborate system of baths; the guide will describe the luxurious life experienced by those who were pampered there. Perfume wafted from jars placed in alcoves besides each bath, and maidens stood by to wait on them. (Guides expect a tip after this side trip.)

But whatever else you do within the walls of the Alhambra, don't hurry; allow some time for the simple but vanishing pleasure of contemplation as your eyes rest on the reflections of a facade in a pool, the ranked order of a formal garden, or the mural designs suggesting continuity rather than beginnings and endings. And if you have time, come back for another look at another time of day or in different weather. You will not be disappointed.

Another section of the Alhambra, the **Generalife,** was a retreat for the Moorish kings, a palace built overlooking the city. Walls and terraces were constructed in definite patterns, with flat, gray stones standing on edge to form fluting and round, white stones placed in the middle. Gardens were developed on several levels; they are lush with flowers, shrubs, and hedges of cypress trimmed in various shapes. The sound of fountains splashing and water flowing into pools is everywhere. Water cascades down three flights of steps along the handrails, sending up spray where it bounces forcefully. And there are views of the city from every angle as you walk through the apartments in the Generalife.

By chance, we wandered into another section of the Alhambra, the **Palacio de Carlos V,** when a Spanish crew was filming "Christopher Columbus." Actors resplendent in brilliantly colored costumes were relaxing in the sun during a break in filming. We peeked over the balcony from above until they actually began filming. In between shots, the director controlled the large group of actors milling around the circular arena with a bullhorn as they assembled under numbered placards. The mob roared during the scene, then fell back into apparent disorder until the next take was ready, in perfect contrast with the almost severe symmetry of the Palacio itself.

Take time to wander aimlessly through the gardens, full of fountains and foliage, in all sections of the Alhambra. The fountain of Charles V contains symbols of the rivers that flow through the area: the Beiro, the Darro, and the Genil, as well as symbols of the Golden Fleece and the coat of arms of the Mendoze family. Many people, speaking a variety of tongues, stroll or sit on benches enjoying the sunshine, yet, in such a sizable area, it does not seem crowded.

The **Alcazaba,** built in the ninth century, is the oldest part of the Alhambra. Walk up to the Torre de la Vela, a large watchtower, for a panoramic view of the city. The Cross of Reconquest was placed there when Ferdinand and Isabella entered the city in 1492.

Within the grounds of the Alhambra you will find the Parador Nacional de San Francisco in a Franciscan convent that was constructed around a Moorish palace. The bodies of Isabella and Ferdinand were buried in the crypt until they were taken to the **Royal Chapel (Capilla Real)** of the cathedral in Granada in 1521. If you have not seen a parador in Spain, here is one that has an interesting history, has been beautifully renovated, and is in a choice location. You can go in for lunch or a drink or just to look around. The dining room is dramatic, with giant purple paintings, purple seats and backs on the wrought-iron chairs, white tiled floor, and heavy white woven draperies. We can recommend the Hors d'oeuvre Parador, which consists of 18 different foods served in small oval dishes; the selection is different every time. Most of the paradores in Spain serve this for lunch, and other regional food specialties are also available. The lounges and galleries in San Francisco are decorated with Spanish antiques, portraits, and engravings. The bedrooms are comfortable, with twin beds, private white tiled bath, and garden views from the windows. This parador is more expensive than any of the others, but for a one-night break from camping or other inexpensive accommodation, we think it's worth it.

We recommend parking your car when you visit the city of Granada. It is difficult to navigate and to park in the narrow, twisting lanes of the older sections; in our efforts to find the Chapel Royal we bumped into the university and were lucky enough to find a spot on the small square there. As we wandered into some of the university courtyards, we noticed a large crowd of students gathered around a group of performers dressed in red and black with white ruffled shirts. They soon began singing Andalusian folk songs, and the students joined in, swaying with the music. If you keep your eyes open and wander around aimlessly in a city like Granada, you are likely to stumble on a moving experience like this.

The Chapel Royal is not open all day; check the hours or allow enough time to return. (At this writing it is open from 11 a.m.–1 p.m. and 4–7 p.m.) It was built as a mausoleum for Ferdinand and Isabella, who are buried in a crypt, along with other members of the royal family. You can see also the sword of Ferdinand, the crown and scepter of Isabella, and a collection of medieval Flemish paintings.

Take time to visit the area of the city called **Albaicin,** along the right bank of the Darro. This ancient Moorish quarter, though falling into some decay, is fun to wander through. Climb one of the steep alleys, peering into courtyards and doorways whenever you can. Be careful, though—the footing is uneven along the bed of stone, which slopes toward a center trough that carries waste water thrown out by the tenants. Continue driving through narrow lanes in the upper reaches of the Albaicin until you reach **San Nicholas Church,** where you will find a piazza with benches and a fine view of the Alhambra and the city. Local inhabitants relax in the sun—reading newspapers, playing with dogs, or watching young children ride their bicycles. When we were there a little girl, sitting on her balcony and swinging her legs between the wrought-iron bars, was singing a counting song. Neighbors called up to her and chatted with someone who called out a greeting from within her home. No matter what this community might think of tourists, it was obviously at ease with itself.

Before you leave, turn around toward your left as you face the Alhambra and see the gypsy caves on the next hillside **(Sacramonte)** behind the ruins of Moorish city walls. Some gypsies still live up there, ready and waiting to snag stray tourists (or even prearranged busloads of them) into watching flamenco dancing, accompanied by rotten red wine, leading to a finale of outstretched palms. The experience is not completely "authentic"; we have heard that some of the "inhabitants" spend a few hours there during the day before returning to their homes in the city.

SIERRA NEVADAS If you have time, take a side trip to the Sierra Nevadas, the highest range in Spain, only a 45-minute trip on GR420 from Granada; you will climb up 7500 feet in 28 kilometers. *Sol y Nieve*, the southernmost winter sports site in Europe, is a new "purpose-built" resort (a coinage of the British to describe the postwar efforts of alpine entrepreneurs—sleek, modern apartment blocks organized around a base of chairlifts, gondolas, and cablecars). Skiiers can try a variety of long, interesting runs (no treeline to interfere with off-piste skiing here), and hikers can climb to the top of *Veleta,* one of the highest peaks in Spain, on a day trip in warm weather. There is a wealth of enjoyment here for sports enthusiasts, photographers, and vacationers of all persuasions.

JAEN From Granada, take N323 north to Jaen, where olive trees dominate the countryside. The *cathedral* is a combination of Gothic, Renaissance, and Baroque architecture dating back to 1500. The *museum* contains treasures that include the veil used by St. Veronica to wipe the face of Jesus Christ. (This relic is kept locked away and is only shown at two brief times on Fridays.)

CORDOBA (CORDOVA) Continue on N323 to **Bailen** and then turn west onto NIV (E25) to Cordoba. Cordoba is one of the oldest of Spanish cities, dating back to 152 B.C., when it was a Roman municipality. From the 8th to the 11th century, Cordoba was the capital of Moslem Spain. Saint Ferdinand conquered the city in 1236; 200 years later Isabella had two interviews with Columbus there and decided during the second to support his voyage of discovery.

The courtyard of the *mosque* is filled with orange trees. Head for the tower in the outer wall for a view of the city; the steps have risers that are about 12 inches high, so wear comfortable shoes. When you enter the mosque your eyes will need time to adjust; it is quite dark inside. This amazing building is composed of red and white supporting columns, pillaged from a variety of buildings as far away as France and Carthage. There were originally 1096 pillars; when the *cathedral* was built inside the Mosque, only 860 were left. That is a story in itself— nowhere else has a cathedral been built inside a mosque. Charles V sadly observed that Christian churchmen had built what could have been built anywhere else, but had destroyed something that was unique in the world.

Part of the charm of Cordoba can be discovered by wandering in the narrow streets around the mosque. Be sure to peek into any open courtyard gates; the interior patios have been decorated with flowering plants, ceramic tiles, and fountains. On our way through this section, we came upon an organ grinder merrily playing as his sad-eyed donkey stood patiently. Walk a block toward the river from the mosque to see the **Roman bridge** before you leave the area. And visit the **Alcazar de los Reyes Christianos,** built by Alfonso XI in the 14th century. It is located around the corner from the entrance to the mosque, and contains a concert hall with Roman mosaics embedded in the walls. A large Roman marble sarcophagus sits in the hall, with a relief of an open door, perhaps symbolic of life everlasting.

Cordoba was the birthplace of a number of famous citizens. Lucius Annaeus Seneca, who lived from 4 B.C. to A.D. 65, is considered by some scholars to have been the most influential of all Spaniards. He was not only a philosopher, but also a poet, playwright, and orator; his political stature led him to serve as consul of Rome. Seneca taught Nero as a child and later became his counselor, but, ironically, was commanded to commit suicide by the same Nero. Many Spaniards, as well as people around the world, live by the stoic principles of Seneca's philosophy.

Luis de Argote y Gongora, 1561–1627, was a Spanish poet who was the master of the culterana style. This style is based on the theory that the reader's interest is aroused through figures of speech. The frequent use of metaphor, hyperbole, and rearrangements of Spanish word order were typical of the culterana style.

Moses Maimonides, 1135–1204, was a physician as well as a philosopher. As a writer and orator, he promoted principles that are now considered norms of Judaism; his *Guide to the Perplexed* explains religious theory rationally. His statue, by the sculptor Pablo Yusti, sits in the Jew's Quarter in Cordoba.

If you can arrange to be in Cordoba in late May, you can enjoy the fair of Our Lady of Salvation. Bullfights, plays, flamenco dancing and singing, competitions, and exhibitions take place, the most notable of the latter being the parade of horses and riders. Cervantes wrote that Cordoba was "the mother city of the best horses in the world." Men ride wearing dark, tightly fitting suits, boots, short jackets trimmed with braid, ruffled shirts, sashes, and the typical flat Cordoban hat. Women ride sidesaddle, wearing brightly colored dresses with flounced skirts and silk shawls gracefully wrapped around them.

CARMONA Continue west on NIV (E25) to Carmona. King Fernando III originated the saying on the coat of arms of Carmona: "Like the morning star at dawn, thus shines Carmona in Andalucia." Surrounded completely by fortified walls, this charming town has narrow streets with white row houses. Enter through an ancient gate and wind around the streets to a square where you can park your car; Carmona is a town to explore on foot. There are a number of churches to visit, some with Mudejar towers. The parador Alcazar del Rey Don Pedro was constructed on the site of the ruins of the Alcazar de Arriba. This Moorish fortress was used as a residence by King Pedro I; later it was used by the Catholic Monarchs as they were in the process of conquering Granada. It is one of our favorites because it has a feeling of antiquity along with modern conveniences. There is an interior courtyard filled with plants, a fountain, and chairs and tables for relaxing. The dining room has an interesting vaulted ceiling, with leaded-glass hanging light fixtures, and overlooks a terrace. The bedrooms have walls of white stucco with blue tiles framing the headboards, comfortable leather chairs, and offer distant views of the lower countryside from the windows.

The **Roman necropolis** was discovered and excavated in 1881 by George Bonsor. Amidst cypress trees, hundreds of burial chambers were cut into the stone. There are frescoes remaining on some tombs; others have carved family emblems. The Elephant tomb is large, containing several rooms and the statue of an elephant. The Servilia tomb is a colonnaded temple with vaulted chambers.

SEVILLA Continue on NIV (E25) to Sevilla. There aren't many signs leading to historic sites in Sevilla until you are right on top of them. As in other large cities, cars drive rapidly and honk if you hesitate. Try to study the map before you enter Sevilla so you will have some idea which way to turn in a crisis; if in doubt, just keep cool and head in the general direction of the *cathedral* spire. We suggest parking your car wherever you see a parking sign as you approach the cathedral. Although there are a limited number of parking spaces adjacent to the cathedral, they are usually filled; people seem to double-park and then sit in their cars hoping for a spot to open up. There are traffic wardens in abundance, who give out sternly worded tickets, but most of them are ignored or discarded. One warden, who made us move, told us that thieves would be attracted by the bags sitting on our backseat and one might smash a window in the car to get to them; we have been told by Spanish friends who lived in the Sevilla area for years that thievery is totally out of control there, more than anywhere else in Spain.

Sevilla has been enriched by all of the many civilizations it has nurtured during the past 2000 years. After the city was founded by Iberians or Phoenicians, the Romans conquered her in 205 B.C. The Visigoths settled and controlled the city until the Moors arrived in A.D. 712. King Fernando III reconquered Sevilla from the Moors; King Pedro the Cruel continued the monarchy, and the son of Ferdinand and Isabella, Juan, was born there. With the discovery of America in 1492, Sevilla became prosperous as the mercantile center of the New World. Many explorers set out from Sevilla, including Amerigo Vespucci and Magellan.

The massive Gothic cathedral in Sevilla is the third largest in the world. (St. Peter's in Rome and St. Paul's in London are larger.) Inside you will move through a panoply of beautiful stained-glass windows revealed by the changing perspectives of Gothic arches. The altarpiece is absolutely magnificent; it took many years for the best craftsmen of that day to carve the stone figures. Take the time to look through the gratings of the multitude of chapels lining the outer cathedral walls; they contain paintings, sculpture, and a remarkable series of stained-glass windows, including one from the 13th century. More paintings are displayed in two galleries, and adjacent rooms contain cases of relics from a number of saints—crosses, chalices, and other religious symbols. Near the center of the cathedral, the coffin of Christopher Columbus is carried by four giant figures who represent Aragon, Castile, Navarre, and Leon. Although his coffin rested originally in the cathedral in Havana, it was sent to Sevilla after Cuba became independent of Spain. Don't forget to climb the **Giralda,** a 322-foot tower next to the cathedral. Tote your camera up with you for some fine shots of the city.

Guides hover between the cathedral and the **Juderia** (the Jewish Quarter), hoping to lure tourists into a "special"—and obviously necessary—tour; it is not always a bad idea to snap at this bait if you don't mind getting hooked for an hour and can tolerate the guide's idea of what will interest you, but don't forget to set the price first unless you want a full-scale squabble later. The guide will probably show you the plaque dedicated to Maria, the inspiration for Carmen, and the house that Washington Irving lived in, but you might also be able to extract historical commentary on notable Spaniards who have lived and worked in the area.

Cultural tradition in Sevilla is rich and fascinating. Miguel de Cervantes spent his early years in Sevilla; he was imprisoned in the **Carcel Real (Royal Prison)** in the late-16th century because of arrears during his period as tax collector. (At that time, any official in arrears was flung in jail.) The episode was fortunate for Spanish literature because Cervantes began to write *Don Quixote* while he was incarcerated.

Music—particularly opera—has always flourished in Sevilla, just as it has in southern Italy. A number of the world's best-loved operas are set in Sevilla, featuring such protagonists as the wild and passionate Carmen, Don Juan, archetype of lovers, and Figaro, barber, guitar player, and master schemer, a character type inherited from Greek and Roman comedy. The gardens, palaces, and streets of Sevilla have also been romanticized in versions of *Don Juan* by Mozart and Strauss, *The Favorite, The Duke of Alba,* and *Dona Maria de Padilla* by Donizetti, *The Barber of Seville* by Rossini, *The Marriage of Figaro* by Mozart, *Alphonso and Estrella* by Schubert, and *Carmen* by Bizet.

If you fancy a vision of Carmen lounging by the door of the tobacco factory, you can visit the 18th-century factory, now a building owned by the university. In the 19th century, 10,000 female *cigarerras* were employed there.

If you can be in Sevilla for Holy Week, by all means do so. The religious significance of the week is taken seriously, with 50,000 people involved in processions that may last for hours; they wear heavy robes and carry the penetential cross or candles, and some go barefoot. When you arrive buy a copy of *Seville in Colour,* which is sold in bookstores and at newsstands. It describes the daily events and suggests the best places for watching processions. James Michener's *Iberia, Volume One,* describes Holy Week in greater detail. During April and May, there are colorful festivals, with parades of horses ridden by girls in Andalusian dress, bullfights, and Sevillana dancing. Booths are set up for entertainment; wine flows freely.

At this point you have reached the end of the Andalusian itinerary. If you wish to return to Granada, take N334 to Antequera, then N342 to Granada.

If you are going to Portugal, take A49 through **Huelva** to the border on the Rio Guadiana. The last section of this "national" highway is the worst we found in Spain, rough and full of holes, almost as if no one cared about getting to Portugal. At the border you must take the ferry unless you are willing to drive a ridiculous distance north on tertiary roads to **Rosal de la Frontera.** From Sevilla, you can also choose to take a side trip to Ronda by driving south to **Jerez** and east through **Arcos de la Frontera** and **Villamartin,** a beautiful and fascinating drive through increasingly desolate mountain terrain.

Portugal

From the border at Punta de San Antonio: Tavira, Olhao, Faro, Albufeira, Lagos, Sagres, Cabo San Vicente, Santiago do Cacem, Lisboa, Palmela, Setubal, Sesimbra, Estoril, Cascais, Cabo da Roca, Sintra, Queluz
(7–14 days, 557 kilometers)

The distances on this itinerary measure a coastal tour of the southern half of Portugal from the Spanish border at **Punta de San Antonio** west to **Cabo San Vicente** and north to **Lisboa.** (Alternatively, you can fly to Faro or Lisboa and rent a car there to tour Portugal.) The number of days you will wish to spend on this itinerary, which includes the lovely beaches of the Algarve and the enticements of a major metropolitan center, depends upon your sense of pacing and the number of side trips you take. Even those in a hurry should allow a week, and travelers with a preference for more leisurely exploration will find two more comfortable. If you get hooked on Portugal, as many do, you might even want a third week to head farther north to **Coimbra, Porto,** and the mountain ranges inland.

Portugal is located in the utmost southwestern corner of Europe; it is squeezed between the Atlantic Ocean and Spain. Unlike some coastal strips in Spain, it has not yet been overdeveloped by the tourist industry; there is room to breathe, even in much of the popular Algarve region along the south coast. The sun always seems to shine in this gentle climate, with mild winters and warm summers. Washed by the remnants of the Gulf Stream, its 500 miles of beaches provide a mecca for watersports, including swimming, sailing, fishing, rowing, waterskiing, surfing, and skindiving. Ashore, golf, tennis, riding, and shooting are also popular. Color and contrast range from blue sea to beaches of soft, golden sand, green plains and olive trees, wheat fields and cork trees with their brown peeled trunks, mountain peaks with snow, and purple vineyards. The wild beauty of the western cliffs culminating in the massive promontory at Cabo San Vicente contrasts with long sandy beaches in the east.

The three provinces included in this itinerary offer a variety of landscape. The **Algarve** received its name from the Arabic *El-Gharb*, (west); this area was the most westerly conquered by the Arabs. It extends from the Spanish border to Cabo San Vicente. The Algarve blooms year-round, with a variety of flowers, orchards, and crops; the coastline to the west of Faro is rugged with high cliffs, and that to the east is sandy with long offshore sand spits. The **Alentejo,** north of the Algarve, makes up a third of the land in Portugal and contains a wide variety of rural landscape ranging from relatively flat plains and rolling wooded hills to dry mountain ranges; in some sections there is not much vegetation except for cork trees and olive groves. **Estremadura,** deriving its name from the fact that it was once the southernmost area conquered by the Moors, encompasses Lisboa and extends northward up the coast. Pine trees, olive groves, orchards, and fields of wheat grow inland, while fishing villages and resorts are located along the coast.

The coastal areas were settled during the Paleolithic Era; later, Phoenicians and Greeks arrived. The Lusitanians moved into southern Portugal, building fortifications on hilltops. The Romans ruled next, then the Visigoths, and finally the Moors invaded in 711. In 1139 Afonso Henriques became king, and the Moors were finally driven out of Portugal with the conquest of Faro in 1249.

Prince Henry, the Navigator, began Portugal's period of world discovery in the early 15th century by founding a school of navigation at Sagres, leading to the extraordinary voyages of Bartolomeu Dias, Vasco da Gama, Christopher Columbus, and Fernao de Magalhaes (Magellan). As a result of these voyages and its colonies throughout the world, Portugal was extremely powerful until she was taken over by Spain in 1580. In 1654 she regained her independence, but agreed to allow Britain predominance, and the Napoleonic Wars further eroded her power through the interference of Spain, England, and France. In 1910 the Republic was formed, with separation of church and state following. A former professor of economics at Coimbra University, Dr. Salazar, joined the cabinet in 1928 as finance minister. He became prime minister in 1932 and ruled the country as a dictatorship for many years. He suffered brain damage in 1968 when his deck chair collapsed; Marcelo Caetano resumed the dictatorship. In 1974 the dictatorship was overthrown; free elections have been held since 1976.

Portugal is a land of dancing and singing. There are festivals with colorful regional costume, accordians, triangles, and bagpipes. Fado is a well-developed type of folk song, originating in 18th-century seamen's ballads. These melodies are sad and nostalgic, expressing feelings about the ways of destiny or lost happiness. Religious festivals, or *Romarias,* honor a patron saint; they can last for several days. Candles play an important part in the ceremony, as do fireworks. Folk dancing usually follows the religious ceremony.

The conventions of bullfighting in Portugal are very different from those in Spain. In Portugal, mounted contenders dressed in 18th-century style in embroidered coats, tricorn hats, and boots with silver spurs provoke the bulls, which have their horns covered. Bulls are not killed.

Algarve

This itinerary begins in the Algarve. From the border, drive west on N125 to **Tavira**, where there is a castle, the ***Castro dos Mouros.*** Tavira is noted as the tuna fish capital of the Algarve. ***Tavira Island*** is 2 kilometers from the town, with sheltered beaches on the landward side, exposed beaches on the sea side.

Continue on to **Olhao**, a fishing village with Moorish flair in its whitewashed "cubist" houses. Climb the belfry of the church, ***Nossa Senhora Do Rosario,*** for a view of the town. Ferries chug to **Armona**, a long, sandy island with beautiful beaches; or you can ride farther on the ferry to reach the island of **Culatra** for more excellent beaches.

The next stop is **Faro**, capital of the Algarve and a commercial center. Industry there includes plastic and building supplies, cork factories, marble works, food processing, and fishing plants. Faro has an airport and a ferry terminal. Faro beach, ***Praia,*** is very popular with tourists; it may be reached across a bridge from the mainland. One church, ***Igreja do Carmo,*** contains a chapel that is decorated with an estimated 1250 skulls and bones dug up from the Carmo cemetery in the 19th century—a macabre touch, to say the least.

Although snow does not normally fall in this area, a Moorish ruler long ago tried to simulate the snow that his Scandinavian bride missed. He planted a forest of almond trees and, sure enough, their white blossoms roused his queen from her melancholy. A local poet, Candido Guerreiro, was fond of writing about moonlight on the Algarve almond blossoms.

A major resort area west of Faro, **Albufeira**, has strangely shaped cliffs, the ***Ponta da Baleeira.*** There are other beaches to the west and to the east of Albufeira, as well as one reached through a tunnel from the town. An open-air market stretches through the streets.

Continue on N125 past **Portimao,** a busy industrial fishing port, to **Praia da Rocha,** which has a sand beach and rock formations. There is a 16th-century fort at one end of town, *Fortaleza de Santa Catarina.*

The next town to the west, **Lagos,** is a very pleasant place to spend a few days; it is one of our favorites. An ancient Roman town with the original name of Lacobriga, Lagos still retains some of its original Roman wall. It was a flourishing trading port during Moorish times.

Henry the Navigator used the governor's palace as his headquarters. (This building, as well as much of the town, was destroyed during the earthquake of 1755.) Prince Henry, the son of King Joao I, made a name for himself during an expedition to North Africa to crush the Moors in 1415; his father conferred the title of Duke of Viseu upon him when he returned. At the age of 21, Henry moved to this area of the Algarve in order to be near the "end of the world," where he proceeded to develop new navigational concepts. His crews sailed into the blue from this spot. An interesting wavelike pavement is set into a plaza under the statue of Prince Henry, who sits with a sextant in his hand.

Don't miss the only church that survived the earthquake, *Igreja de Santo Antonio;* the gilt and carved interior features cherubs, warriors, and angels. The *Museu Regional de Lagos* contains Roman mosaics, the original charter of Lagos from 1504, religious vestments, and folk costumes.

Lagos is a good base for side trips to **Sagres** and **Cabo San Vicente.** Sagres itself is just one street and a square. However, you have come to see the site of the School of Navigation and Cape St. Vincent. Watch for signs to the *Sacred promontory,* where there is a fort, once the setting for Prince Henry's school. Established in 1421, this school collected the most knowledgeable scholars, geographers, astronomers, and cartographers to develop a new navigational theory. By introducing celestial navigation as the best way of determining latitude, and improving the sextant and astrolabe to do it, the school made contributions to world exploration unequaled until the refinement of the chronometer in the late-18th century. The school was also devoted to training young Portuguese seamen, who were to remain the best and most adventurous in the world for more than a century. Look at the paving of the parade ground to see the large compass rose that was used in instruction.

Our favorite spot in the Algarve is Cabo San Vicente—a place to perch on the 300-foot-high cliffs with a picnic lunch, watching long Atlantic rollers approach the rocks and smash into them with unbelievable force. We sat on rocks a safe distance away from the edge, aghast at fishermen, standing right next to the sheer drop on the adjoining cliff, who were casually dangling their long fishing lines over the edge. We think you will probably shoot a whole roll of film here, as we did; each wave looks bigger than the last. When you manage to tear yourself away from the fascination of the view, walk into the lighthouse grounds and around to the right for a new perspective from the terrace. You can see some of the 200 ships that round the cape into the Mediterranean every day. It is also fun to watch the fishing boats down under the cliffs as they rise and fall with ease in the large, long swells created by 3000 miles of open water to the west.

The entire Cape Sagre/Cape St. Vincent area was once the lair of Sir Francis Drake, that swashbuckling Devonshire privateer and world circumnavigator who later led the British fleet in defeating the Spanish Armada; here he lay in wait for ships coming from the South Atlantic and Mediterranean toward Lisboa. He captured a ship that had on board most of the seasoned barrel hoops and staves from the continent. In an age when water, food, and gunpowder were all carried in barrels, this was a minor catastrophe; casks could be built, but it took time to season the staves and hoops. Drake related that the bonfire he built "burned right merrilie."

St. Vincent was a 4th-century Spanish priest killed by the Roman governor. His body rested at the Sacred Promontory until the 12th century, when his bones were transferred by ship to Lisboa. Legend describes the journey as one accompanied by ravens, who then settled near his final resting place. You can see two ravens and a sailing ship on the seal of Lisboa.

To reach Lisboa from Lagos, drive on N120 to **Odemira.** Along the way you will see many cork trees stripped of their bark. A local inhabitant told us that it takes about four years for each tree to grow new bark. This lush green area of southwestern Portugal has some towns and a few houses scattered about the countryside, but it is very thinly populated and noticeably "rural" in the sense that also applies to Andalusia in Spain and Campagnia in Italy. We drove past a gypsy camp with a number of tepeelike buildings covered with plastic and branches; farther along, we saw two carts loaded with young gypsy families. There are a number of windmills perched on hillsides or in open fields, none of which seemed to be working. We saw women trudging home from a village with wheelbarrows full of shopping or bags on their heads; women here do a lot of hard, physical work and look much older than they are. We did not see any women drivers in this part of Portugal, but a number of men use motorcycles for transportation rather than sport. At night people on the roads do not seem to wear reflectorized garments—whether walking, bicycling, or riding a motorcycle—which will cause you some anxiety. As you enjoy this lovely section of the country, watch for signs near Odemira and stay on N120, not N393, which is a secondary road that takes much longer.

Santiago de Cacem is a pleasant hill town north of Odemira and east of **Sines.** (Avoid the latter unless you are prepared to see rapid industrialization wrecking a lovely old port town.) There is a castle, a municipal museum, and nearby, the Roman ruins, *Mirobriga*. We stopped in the Posada San Tiago, an old mansion, for lunch. Pousadas, meaning "places of rest," like the paradores in Spain, are state-owned hotels in historic buildings such as castles and convents.

N120 becomes E52, then is joined by N5. When you reach N10, turn left toward **Setubal** and pick up the motorway, E4, into Lisboa.

Lisboa (Lisbon)

Lisboa (Lisbon) has one of the most beautiful sites in the world; its orientation is irrevocably toward the surrounding sea—historically through the voyages of discovery, commercially as a major deepwater port, and visually through prospects of the estuary from the many monuments you will visit. With more to explore than you can possibly fit into several days, it would be easy to spend a week or two here. We suggest that you buy a detailed guide of the city in order to pick out the sites that interest you most.

Lisboa was probably founded by the Phoenicians in 1200 B.C. According to one legend, it was Ulysses who founded the city—a notion that appeals to the literary imagination, since its original name was "olyssipo." In any case, the Greeks, and then the Carthaginians, conquered the city; in 205 B.C. the Romans arrived, developing Lisboa into an important provincial town within the network of their empire. The Visigoths invaded next, followed by the Moors in A.D. 714; Lisboa became a thriving city with active trading in the Moslem world. In 1147 King Afonso I wrested control from the Arabs, and Lisboa was named capital of Portugal in 1255. During the 15th and 16th centuries, following Vasco da Gama's voyage to the Indies, Lisboa became one of the richest cities in the world, and Portugal the greatest maritime power. The scene of traders buying and selling large quantities of gold, silver, ivory, jewels, spices, and silks must have been something to behold. The market for precious metals and minerals continued into the 18th century, when gold and diamonds were brought from Brazil.

On the morning of November 1, 1755, the Great Earthquake roared through Lisboa, flattening most of the city. At this moment, on All Saints' Day, the churches were crowded, with thousands of candles flickering at altars. The earth shook three times, buildings collapsed, candles fell and spread their flames to wooden saints, crucifixes, and walls. People sought escape in the River Tagus, but that too rose, in seeming vengeance, as a giant tidal wave that swept through the city. The Tagus rose and roared through twice more; fires raged throughout the city, lasting for five days. It is estimated that 40,000 died and 17,000 buildings were destroyed. The Marquis of Pombal directed the cleanup of the city from his coach, where he lived for the first week. He ordered vessels that were not destroyed to give up their cargoes for the support of survivors; buildings were demolished, the dead buried, and looters hanged. Then he planned the reconstruction of the city. You can read a fascinating account of the earthquake and its aftermath in Voltaire's *Candide.*

As you enter Lisboa, you will probably cross on the bridge built in 1966 as the Salazar Bridge, now called **Ponte 25 de Abril,** named for the 1974 revolution. This bridge has the longest single span in Europe: 1103 meters. The overall length is 2278 meters and it stands 70 meters above the water. Near the bridge on the southern shore, across the harbor from Lisboa, is an immense statue, "Cristo Rei" (Christ in Majesty). Although 28 meters high, it is a "small" replica of one in Rio de Janeiro.

Drive up the hill to the **St. Jeronimos Chapel,** located in the park north of the Monastery of Jeronimos, where you will have a view down to the river, waterfront, and the **Tower of Belem.** The tower was originally built in the water; the river altered its course years ago, and now the tower is on the edge of the river. Constructed from 1515 to 1520, during the reign of King Manuel, it is the one completely Manueline building left in the city; other similar buildings were adapted to new styles or reconstructed in the original. The architect, Francisco de Arruda, used Moorish lines with the addition of Manuel's emblem of the globe and a cross. This five-storied tower, with rounded sentry boxes on the corners, was used as a prison in the 19th century; it has a whispering gallery inside.

The **Museu da Marinha** contains exhibits on all maritime subjects; especially interesting are two 18th-century ceremonial barges, one of which was used during a visit of Queen Elizabeth II. The museum includes a gift shop that sells books, maps, and a marvelous nautical board game. The **Gulbenkian Planetarium** is in the same building.

The **Mosteiro dos Jeronimous** is one of the treasures of Manueline architecture. King Manuel began the building in 1502, and riches from the voyages of Vasco da Gama were poured into this monument. Look particularly at the entrance to the church, where a statue of Prince Henry the Navigator is placed on a pedestal above the arch.

Down on the waterfront again, you can't miss the **Padrao dos Descobrimentos** (**Monument to Discoveries**). In the shape of a ship's bow, it was erected in 1960 to mark the 500th anniversary of the death of Prince Henry the Navigator. The prince points the way to a group of people including King Manuel, carrying a sphere, and Camoes, carrying *The Lusiads.*

We suggest two day tours into the region surrounding the city that may easily be taken from Lisboa. The first circles west and north from Lisboa to Estoril, Cascais, Cabo da Roca, Sintra, Queluz, and back to Lisboa. Start by driving west from Lisboa, following signs to **Estoril** on N6. Estoril is an internationally famous resort with a casino, horse racing, regattas, and festivals, It has also been the home of deposed European kings. You will pass **Carcavelas,** where there is a fortress, then **Cascais,** which would be worth a longer stay. Cascais has an interesting museum, a castle, and many large mansions on the west and north side of town. Continuing along the coast road, there are laybys where you can pull over to watch the long Atlantic rollers and have a view of the lighthouse. This part of the coast is rugged, and the sea is powerful because it sweeps across 3000 miles of ocean. Swimming can be extremely dangerous when high surf creates a strong undertow.

Drive on to **Cabo da Roca,** a cape with a lighthouse, the westernmost point of continental Europe. THE LAND ENDS AND THE SEA BEGINS is inscribed on a stone at the tip of the point. You can buy an elaborate signed and sealed certificate here if you wish, establishing beyond doubt that you have gone as far west as you can without the help of the great navigators.

Colares is a pleasant village in the next valley north along the coast; roses bloom over garden walls there, and you will begin to catch glimpses of the castle at **Sintra,** which can be seen for miles away perched up on a hill. This lovely town attracts many visitors with its cool, green, wooded surroundings, created by a belt of precipitation on the leeward side of the coastal mountains. Kings of Portugal have come to Sintra as a favorite summer residence. Byron was in residence in 1805 and began "Childe Harold" amid the "horrid crags, the cork trees and mountain moss, sunken glen, the vine on high and willow branches below," with the "tender azure of the unruffled deep" not far away. Sintra would be a pleasant place to spend several days if you need respite from constant movement.

Continue circling back toward Lisboa through the town of **Queluz,** which has a royal palace reminiscent of Versailles. Indeed, Queen Maria visited Versailles during her childhood, when she was affianced to Louis XV. This rococo palace, in pink and white, stretches its wings around a series of gardens, Especially worth noticing are the queen's dressing room, the hunting room, and the throne room. Here, in 1792, Queen Maria lay in a darkened room enduring visions of herself burning in "Hell's own fires" and went mad.

The second tour circles south and east from Lisboa, to Palmela, Setubal, and Sesimbra. Drive to **Palmela** on E4. This hill town huddles under a large castle, now the Pousada Do Castelo Palmela. Inside, the rooms are elegantly appointed, with large green plants, chandeliers, groupings of comfortable chairs on oriental rugs, and Spanish antiques. From bedroom windows you can see the white houses of Lisboa to the north and the Serra da Arrabida and the sand of Troia to the south. Eucalyptus perfumes the air and pines please the eye with a deep, rich green. Palmela Castle was the headquarters of the Military Order of Santiago, allowed to settle in Portugal by Afonso Henriques, the first king of Portugal, who had captured the castle in 1147. The Monks of Palmela, who lived in the monastery, were also knights of the castle; the emblem of the Order of Santiago de Espada is a cross in the shape of a sword, which must have required some elaborate theological justification. The medieval fortification was constructed for defense by archers; there are round turrets as well as square towers. The later, outer walls were designed to be defended with firearms and consist of walls with ramparts in a polygon shape. The earthquake of 1755 damaged Palmela Castle, but it was restored in 1940. You can walk around the ramparts and up into the tower for views of the countryside.

Next, drive to **Setubal,** which is an industrial center with a busy port. Thriving shipyards and a sardine fishing fleet are major industries in Setubal. For the tourist there is a castle, museums, churches, and the old town to visit. From Setubal, drive out along the lovely corniche road to **Figuernina,** where there is a sand beach with parking along the road. Just beyond **Galopos** there are several laybys for a picnic with a view. At **Creiro** there is another beautiful sand beach. Then the road swings inland and the setting becomes pleasantly rural in a way you will have come to expect in Portugal. There is a castle at **Santana,** before the road winds down the mountain to **Sesimbra.** This picturesque fishing-village-cum-resort has a lovely sand beach where local men straighten their nylon fishing lines by pulling them around a pole set some distance away. There are short strings attached to the long lines, each with its set of hooks. You can pick up an informative booklet, *Portuguese Line Fishing,* from the information office right on the beach. This is a great place to camp; ask about local campsites at the same office. From Sesimbra, follow signs to Lisboa, which will lead you back to E4 and the marvelous new bridge over the Tagus.

This side trip ends the Portuguese itinerary. If you are returning to Spain, drive east on N4 (E4) to the border near **Badajoz.** Remember that it is not easy to exchange escudos for pesetas once you have left Portugal, and that you can exchange them at the border only if you arrive during normal working hours. If you carry them into Spain or other European countries, you will find it extremely difficult to get them converted into other currencies.

Castile

From Lisboa: Merida, Oropesa, Toledo, Madrid, El Escorial, Segovia, Avila, Salamanca, Valladoid, Burgos, Santander (14–21 days, 1273 kilometers)

This itinerary begins in Lisboa if you are continuing from the Portuguese itinerary; it moves eastward up onto the Spanish plateau through Merida and Oropesa to Toledo. Alternatively, you can fly to Madrid, establish a base there, and take day trips to the cities and towns in the area. Or you can spend some time in Madrid, a day or two in Toledo, and then head north out of Castile along the route we have suggested to Santander, where you will find ferry service to England or to the French border just east of San Sebastian.

The drive from Lisboa to Merida takes about four hours. **Merida,** in the province of Estremadura, is perhaps the best-preserved Roman city in Spain; there are many Roman monuments to visit in this city dating from 25 B.C.

Toledo is even more spectacular than you might have imagined it to be, spreading over a hill and surrounded by a ravine and the River Tagus. The cathedral stands out against the sky and the treasures inside are well worth a visit. Architectural delights and hillside vistas make the narrow streets fun to explore.

Madrid is located in the exact center of Spain. As the capital, it is a busy city with streaming traffic, yet there are squares, broad avenues, statues, and fountains for strollers to enjoy. Madrid has the Prado, one of the finest art museums in the world, where your feet will give out before you have seen enough of the collection.

El Escorial, northwest of Madrid in the foothills of the Guadarrama Mountains, is a gigantic palace and convent. It was planned and built by Philip II as what we would now call a politician's retreat, a place where he could live as a monk and still rule his country and much of the western world.

Segovia has a Roman aqueduct that still operates, a cathedral, and a number of mansions in the old town. Nearby **Avila** has the best-preserved medieval walls in Spain, with 90 towers around the ramparts.

Salamanca is a magnificent and largely unspoiled university town (at least at the southern end) built of golden sandstone; there are palaces and two cathedrals to visit. **Valladolid** is also a university city, and has other buildings of interest because the Spanish monarchs lived there between the 12th and 17th centuries.

Heading north out of Castile, **Burgos** is located on a windswept plateau, with the Rio Arlanzon flowing through its center. El Cid, who lived there in the 11th century, provided the city with a wealth of legends.

Santander, often a place to get to in a hurry to catch the ferry to England, is also a pleasant resort. This city, on the Cantabrian coast, has long sand beaches. Prehistoric caves with extraordinary paintings have been found nearby, and many artifacts are displayed in the *Santander Prehistory Museum.*

Castile is divided into two parts: *New Castile* and *Old Castile.* New Castile is made up of the provinces of Cuenca, Ciudad Real, Guadalajara, Madrid, and Toledo. Most of the region is an immense, dry plain. The Toledo Mountains separate the paths of the two rivers that flow through, the Tagus and the Guadiana. The word *Castile* comes from *castillos* or castles, which were built as fortresses against raids by either Christians or Moslems. And this is the land of Don Quixote, who roamed around looking for adventures with his faithful squire, Sancho Panza.

Old Castile contains the provinces of Avila, Burgos, Logrono, Segovia, Soria, Palencia, and Valladolid. The central plateau, the Meseta, is a barren grazing area that also produces wheat and rye. The Gredos and Guadarrama mountain ranges extend across the region from southwest to northeast.

MERIDA You feel you are in Roman times when you visit the ruins in Merida. These are not just outlines exposed in the earth but structures several stories high and remarkably well preserved. The ***theater,*** built by Agrippa in 24 B.C., is at least four stories high with columns and some sculptures intact on the proscenium. The amphitheater is almost perfectly intact, with many rows of seats in a semicircle facing the proscenium, reached by entrances at various levels. Cypress stand majestically behind the theater as a perfect frame. The ***arena*** dates from the first century B.C. and has protective cornices to shield *persona importanta* from wild beasts. Chariot races were run around the track, and sometimes the center was flooded for mock sea battles. As we sat on those ancient seats, enjoying the sun, we noticed little purple flowers growing between the rows—pleasant scents and sights on a beautiful day that have not changed in two millennia. Near both the theater and the arena, the foundations of the ***Roman house*** still enclose visible mosaic work.

There are extensive ruins adjacent to the monument fence; we also noticed unconcerned children playing soccer on a field amid unprotected ruins that are 2000 years old. The Roman bridge in Merida, ***Puente Romano,*** has 82 arches; gypsies sometimes camp under it. There are also two Roman ***aqueducts,*** the San Lazaro and the Los Milagros. Water from them flows into two lakes, the Cornalvo and the Proserpina, which serve as a resort area for the city.

From Merida, take NV toward Madrid. This is an easy, straight, level, two-lane road with mountains on either side to the north and south. The road goes over a small mountain pass, then abruptly comes upon a nuclear power plant at **Almaraz.** We can recommend a lunch stop in **Oropesa** at the Parador Virrey Toledo. This very popular parador, almost as difficult to book into as San Francisco in Granada, was crowded for Sunday lunch. Virrey Toledo is a castle-cum-palace built in 1366 and rebuilt in 1402 in Gothic-Mudejar style. It stands on a hill with a lovely view of the countryside. The lounges are filled with paintings, wooden chests, old tables and cupboards, and comfortable chairs, and there's a fireplace in the bar.

From Oropesa, continue on to **Talavera de la Reina,** where you will be tempted to buy ceramics in many factory stores. NV will take you to the turnoff for Toledo on N403.

TOLEDO Toledo is one of our two favorite cities in Spain; it vies with Granada for first place. Cossio wrote: "Toledo is the city which presents the most complete and characteristic ensemble of all that the genuinely Spanish land and civilization have ever been. It is the most perfect epitome, the most brilliant and evocative summary, of Spain's history. So, a traveller who can only spend a single day in Spain ought, without hesitating, to spend it seeing Toledo." That pretty well sums up the thoughts of many travelers, who find the city an unforgettable one.

We suggest parking your car and walking in Toledo because the streets are narrow, tortuous, and full of cul-de-sacs that will trap unwary drivers; the same features provide pleasure for those on foot, who also have access to many narrow lanes and steps. Follow the signs into the city past a lot for bus parking, and farther up the hill you will find a parking lot on the edge of the bluff leading down to the river. There are small garages in the preceding block if you don't mind leaving your keys so cars blocking each other can be juggled. We chose the lot out in the open and locked up, even though Toledo does not share Sevilla's reputation for thievery.

One of the remarkable sights of Toledo is the **cathedral**, especially from an adjoining hilltop. It is lighted several nights a week, depending upon the season. The building is massive and the 300-foot spire dominates the town, but you cannot see much of the outside of the cathedral from the street because it is surrounded by other buildings. Enter through the Puerta de Mollete, next to the main tower, where you can buy tickets for various chapels and the treasure chamber; although the cathedral proper is open all day, the other sections have shorter visiting hours. The stained-glass windows date from the 15th and 16th centuries; don't miss the rose windows over the south and north doors. The **Treasure** is located at the foot of the great tower, in the Tower Chapel. The collection includes the monstrance, a masterpiece of gold and silver work by Enrique de Arfe in the 16th century. It is 2½ meters high, weighs 200 kilos, and has 5000 parts. During the feast of Corpus Christi, in late May or early June, the monstrance is carried through the streets. The town is decorated with tapestries and bunting; flowers and thyme in the decorations perfume the air. After you have looked at the many other treasures and relics in this chapel, turn your eyes upward to the ceiling, which was constructed from wood and stucco in Moorish style. It is formed into stalactites and stalagmites, borrowing the natural formations found in grottoes and caves.

There are over 20 chapels to visit. Be sure to look at the Mudejar doorway of the **chapter house**, which is exquisite. The **sacristy** contains a gallery of paintings, many by El Greco. Look for "El Expolio" and 13 paintings of the 12 apostles and Christ. There are also paintings by Goya, Titian, and Van Dyck here. Visit the **choir**, where there are two rows of carved walnut choir stalls. One level depicts Old Testament figures, the other scenes from the conquest of Granada. The choir contains two organs, one in Baroque and one in Neoclassical style. The larchwood altarpiece, or retable, is large; it extends to the ceiling. The story of the New Testament is told here. You will also see a hat dangling near the main altar. At one time cardinals were buried in a spot of their choosing, with their hats hanging above them.

El Greco, Domenico Teotocopulos, was born in Crete but lived in Toledo for much of his life until his death in 1614. His paintings are full of rich color and violent movement, often with supernatural emphasis. You can visit the house he lived in, which contains a museum of his paintings; the "View and Plan of Toledo" is here; the other original panorama of Toledo is in the Metropolitan Museum in New York. The church of **San Tome** has an annex in which you will find another of El Greco's masterpieces, "The Burial of the Count of Orgaz." This painting is based on the life of the Conde de Orgaz, a man who protected the needy and the poor. During his funeral in San Tome, Saint Augustine and Saint Stephen miraculously appeared, lifted up his body, and laid it in the tomb. El Greco took two years to paint this work; each of the faces in the group surrounding the count is a portrait of a well known figure from the 16th century. The person who is fifth from the left end of the group is supposed to be El Greco himself, and the little boy in the bottom left is his son, Jorge Manuel. The signature of the artist and the date of the completed work can be found in a handkerchief in the little boy's pocket.

Near the church of San Tome lived the architect who built the bridge of **San Martin.** According to legend, Juan, the builder, realized that he had made a serious mistake in construction and that the bridge would collapse when the scaffolding was removed. He knew that his prestige and respect would vanish if that happened. As he became more despondent, his wife planned to solve this problem. One night she left the house, went to the foot of the bridge, and set fire to the framework supporting it. Her husband was able to rebuild the bridge into the solid structure you see today. In gratitude to his wife, he carved her portrait on the main arch of the bridge.

There are many more churches, museums, a palace, and the **alcazar** to visit in Toledo. We suggest that you buy a detailed guide such as *This is Toledo* so you can choose what you would most like to visit. Do take time for the simple pleasure of wandering through the streets. You may also want to do some shopping for the specialties of Toledo: damascene jewelry, swords, and trays.

Before you leave the Toledo area you may want to visit the region to the southeast called **La Mancha,** domain of the wanderings of Cervantes's Don Quixote and Sancho Panza. Windmills, reminding you of one of the don's most fanciful encounters, are all around, and the village of **El Toboso** is supposed to be the home of his heroine, Dulcinea. This parody of the romances of chivalry is a delight to reread.

From Toledo, take N401 to Madrid.

Madrid

Friends who have spent a number of years living and teaching in Madrid feel that Castile is the most interesting part of Spain, both historically and culturally, because it has dominated the rest. The region containing Madrid and its satellites—older cities such as Toledo, Segovia, Avila, and Salamanca—sits in the center of the Spanish plateau, isolated by mountains and distance from the commercialism and sometimes unrestrained tourism of the coasts; it is the political center of the country and lays claim, as does Andalusia, to one of the central strands in Spanish culture: the Catholic heritage.

Madrid looks the part of a capital city, with broad, tree-lined avenues, many statues, circles built around elaborate fountains, and a generous supply of massive buildings that visually remind one of the role of central governments in European history. Madrid reminds us of Paris in these respects. But there is another, less ponderous side to the city: Take time to wander through the old town, **La Ciudad Antigua,** with its alleys, steps, and narrow streets. You can park your car in a garage under the **Plaza Mayor,** once the center of old Madrid. This arcaded square has been the setting for religious observances, dramas, bullfights, festivals, and a tournament held in 1623 to honor King Charles I of England.

Right around the corner, at Cuchilleros 17, you will find Botins, one of Hemingway's favorite restaurants. You will feel you have been here before if you've enjoyed *The Sun Also Rises* and *Death in the Afternoon;* suckling pig is a house specialty. Down the street is another restaurant frequented by Hemingway, Casa Paco, at Puerta Ceprada 11, where you can stand in the bar for a drink or have their famous steak dinner upstairs. The steak is very tender and is served on a plate so hot that you can cook a rare piece a little more right there if you wish.

The **Royal Palace,** begun in 1737, was the residence of the royal family for many years. King Juan Carlos does not reside there now, but it is still used for state ceremonies and banquets. State guests now stay in the former royal apartments. There is a lot to see in the ornately furnished apartments, as well as a library, royal pharmacy, armory, and carriage museum.

People who live in Madrid have been known to furnish their apartments with treasures found in the **Rastro,** a giant flea market selling antiques, paintings, animals, clothing, and anything else you can think of. It's just as much fun to wander around looking and enjoying the scene as it is to participate.

If you are a museum aficionado, you will love Madrid. A favorite with many visitors is **Museo Lazaro Galdiano,** which is housed in the home of Jose Lazaro Galdiano. There are five floors of treasures including a portrait by Leonardo da Vinci on the ground floor. You can see the original sculpture, "La Dama de Elche," which you may remember from a visit to Elche, in the south of Spain, in the *Museo Arqueologico*. A replica of the Altamira caves is here also; because they are often closed, this is a chance to see the prehistoric paintings. *Museo del Ejercito* displays armor, arms, trophies, and a sword that once belonged to El Cid. *Museo Taurino,* which details the history of bullfighting, is located next to the *Las Ventas Bullring,* the largest one in Spain.

We've been saving the best for last—the *Prado Museum,* one of the finest in the entire world. Most of the works hung here were originally in private collections—notably that of the monarchy, from the 16th through the 19th centuries. The museum contains whole sections devoted to major Spanish artists such as El Greco, Velazquez, and Goya, Flemish paintings collected by the monarchy, and Italian and Dutch works commissioned by Charles V and Philip II.

Buy a guide when you begin your visit so you can plot your route to cover your own favorites amidst the endless rooms of this massive collection. Look for El Greco's "The Trinity," where you will recognize the influence of Michelangelo in the powerful bodies. The "Adoration of the Shepherds" portrays intense emotion on the faces of the figures, with an ethereal quality in the setting. It is not easy to choose a single favorite from the Velazquez collection: "The Surrender of Breda" transmits a silver quality with interesting use of light for emphasis. "Las Meninas" ("The Maids of Honour") focuses on the lovely little princess, Infanta Dona Margarita, and, through contrast, on the dwarf figure in the right foreground. "The Tipplers," featuring a benign version of the God of Wine, makes us smile with its air of relaxed festivity. "The Spinners" represents the comparison of the weaving of a young girl, Arachne, with that of Pallas Athene. Murillo's "The Immaculate Conception" places Mary in an ethereal setting with angels. Goya's "The Nude Maja" and "The Dressed Maja" may or may not have been modeled on the Duchess of Alba; Goya is supposed to have had a love affair with her. Raphael's "The Cardinal" has eyes that stare out, seeming to follow you across the room. There are a number of portraits by Titian, including his famous "Self Portrait." Bosch's "The Garden of Earthly Delights" is one to fascinate those who try to interpret it. Don't miss Rubens's "The Adoration of the Magi," gigantic and full of detail. And, and, and . . . there is no stopping until your feet are too weary and your eyes too bleary to assimilate more; we suggest that you pay the nominal admission fee again on another day, when you can bring the paintings the fresh perception they deserve.

The Prado is only one of many possibilities in a city loaded with cultural attractions. Check the schedule of the interesting modern performing arts center, *Centro Cultural De La Villa.* When we were there one of its several theaters presented a wonderful flamenco evening featuring Blanca Del Rey. She is a precise and flamboyant dancer, projecting emotion in every movement, especially in a fascinating bullfight where her constantly moving shawl created a visual tempo in the air. Her elaborate dresses were a panoply of forms and colors as she gracefully whipped her train around. She was accompanied by several male dancers, guitarists, and cantors. At the end of the performance the audience went wild, shouting *Ole* with great vigor and throwing flowers onto the stage, which she kissed and threw back. This was an evening we wouldn't have missed for anything, and you can also find a number of opportunities to see first-rate flamenco dancing in many Madrid nightclubs.

When you have had your fill of the big city, take A6 northwest until you see signs for *El Escorial,* a monastery, palace, and mausoleum. Philip II, like the pharaohs who built pyramids to memorialize themselves, created this immense building as a residence and as the tomb for his burial. The gray granite looks forbidding and cold from the outside; in fact, it is cold inside as well, at least in winter. Unless you choose to go with a private guide (they wait at the entrance), you will have to wait some minutes (not more than half an hour) for a scheduled tour to begin, but there is enough to see in this massive place to make a brief wait worthwhile. There are paintings and intricate tapestries throughout the palace. Some of them were designed from Goya's work, as well as the work of other Spanish artists; others are Flemish tapestries. Brussels tapestries are hung in the throne room. Philip's bedroom was located right next to the church so that he could go in whenever he wished; when he was very ill and dying he could watch the mass from his bed. Don't miss the retable in the church, which was designed by Herrera. Large pillars support a cupola that is 302 feet high. The *library* has books and manuscripts dating from the fifth century B.C. This collection is probably the most valuable in Spain.

After leaving this monument to the magnificence of Spain's past, take C600 to the *Valle de los Caidos (Valley of the Fallen)*, reached by a lovely road leading up through pines. The huge cross memorializing the agony of Spain in the thirties, is visible from a great distance, and a church has been built into the mountain there. Franco built the monument to commemorate the dead from both sides during the Civil War, but there is still bitter feeling about it among those who were alive during those dreadful times.

At this point you may want to make a side excursion to **Segovia**, a picturesque town located north of El Escorial. The Marquis of Lozoya described Segovia impressionistically: "The sharp arrowshafts of the poplars, which autumn decks out in pale gold, blend with the spires of the Alcazar, the soaring pinnacles of the Cathedral, the slender sculpted belfries of the churches, the towers of palaces. . . . The light makes an afternoon in Segovia a never-to-be-forgotten festival, especially in the late summer and early months of autumn. In the minutes just before sunset, the city as a whole seems to be set on fire. Sometimes, the towers are offset against a background of slate-grey clouds. It is then that the Segovian towers appear to be lit up from within, and continue to shine when all about them has been extinguished.''

Segovia reminds us of a ship, with the shape of the ***Alcazar*** forming the bow. The Alcazar looks like a Disney castle with its many slender spires and turrets. Walk on the ramparts for a view of the narrow, curving streets of the old town. Don't miss the ***Roman aqueduct,*** which is 800 meters long and rises 100 feet above the Plaza de Azoguejo at its highest point.

If you are continuing on to **Avila,** return to A6 and watch for a sign to Avila via N501. As we approached, we noticed an unusual collection of enormous rocks, with three or four piled on top of each other. Although a natural phenomenon in the hills surrounding the city, they are so strangely flattened that one speculates in the Stonehenge vein, wondering whether prehistoric man had anything to do with these striking formations. Avila itself, surrounded on three sides by hills and mountains, is completely walled. The walls, built from 1090 to 1099, are thought to be the best preserved in all of Europe. They average 12 meters in height and 3 meters in thickness, and their shape is hexagonal. There are 90 towers spaced along the walls, giving it a scalloped effect. Of the nine entrance gates, those of San Vicente and the Alcazar are among the oldest and most interesting.

The ***cathedral*** is both a church and a fortress. The apse, ***El Cimorro,*** is an enormous tower that forms part of the town walls. Inside, the choir stalls are from the Renaissance. Don't miss the tomb of Bishop Don Alfonso de Madrigal, or El Tostado, which is done in alabaster. Avila is noted as the birthplace of Saint Teresa, who worked for reform all her life. She founded 17 convents and gained many converts for the church. As one of the most influential figures in the Counter-Reformation, her letters, autobiography, and other mystical writings have been handed down through the centuries.

N501 will take you directly from Avila to **Salamanca,** located on the River Tormes. This university town, with its golden sandstone buildings, is a place we would like to live in some year. The atmosphere seems relaxed and warm, with students, faculty, and townspeople meeting as they cross the Plaza Mayor or in the cafes and bars around it. Anyone who is interested in taking courses at the university is welcome to do so, and the summer-term program is particularly appealing. The ***university library*** is approached through a Gothic entrance. It contains more than 50,000 volumes, bound in leather and parchment; ancient manuscripts and extemely valuable books are housed in a small room in the center. Take a look at the facade of the university from the Patio de Escuelas. Built at the beginning of the 16th century, it was designed and sculpted by gold and silver smiths. The ornate carving was done on three levels, with heads in scallop shells, impressive medallions, and pinnacles on top. On the lower end of the right-hand pilaster the frog on one of three skulls is famous among students, who rub him for good luck on examinations.

Salamanca was conquered in the third century B.C. by Hannibal. At the end of the siege his troops ransacked the city after forcing all of the inhabitants to leave. The men were not allowed to wear cloaks or to take their swords, but the crafty women hid their husbands' swords under their clothing.

In the eighth century the Moors arrived, staying for 300 years. In the 14th and 15th centuries Salamanca was divided by the wars between two prominent local families. During an argument over a game of pelota, the Manzano brothers killed two Monroy brothers. Their mother, Dona Maria, arranged to have the killers decapitated and the Manzano heads were placed on the Monroy tomb. As in any blood feud, such as that between the Capulets and Montagues in Verona, these retributions continued interminably, in this case until 1476.

There are two cathedrals to visit in Salamanca. The **Old Cathedral,** built in Romanesque style, was constructed in the 12th century. Look at the 53 tablets by Nicolas Florentino on the reredos of the main altar. In the center you will see the image of the Virgen de la Vega in copper, with Limoges enamels around the throne. The cupola, *Torre de Gallo,* shows Moorish influence.

The **New Cathedral,** begun in 1513, is in Gothic style. There is a legend that the Cristo de las Batallas, now located in the Sagrario Chapel, was carried by El Cid during his campaigns. It is also said that he later gave it to Bishop Don Jeronimo de Perigueux.

There is a particularly interesting house in Salamanca built by a knight of Santiago. As a memento of his homeland, Galicia, he had scallop shells sculpted into the walls; the **Casa de las Conchas** also has Isabeline windows and wrought-iron grillwork.

E3 will take you from Salamanca to **Valladolid,** another old university town and modern city. Once the capital of Spain, Valladolid was the home of the monarchy in Castile in the 15th century. Ferdinand and Isabella were married there in 1469, joining Castile and Aragon and thereby setting the stage for centuries of Spanish world power. In 1809 Napoleon also set up his headquarters in Valladolid, leading to the long and difficult Peninsular War.

San Gregorio College now houses the **National Sculpture Museum.** This fine collection includes three rooms containing the work of Alonso Berruguete, considered to be the most outstanding 16th-century Spanish sculptor. Many other artists are represented here. In Calle Miguel Iscar you can see the house Cervantes lived in. It contains furnishings of the period, some of which belonged to him. He spent the last years of his life there.

From Valladolid, continue on Route E3 to **Burgos,** the lair of El Cid. You may have seen the 1951 film, with Charlton Heston as the legendary knight. Although Rodrigo Diaz, "El Cid," was born 9 kilometers away in Vivar, Burgos claims this hero, and his body is buried in the cathedral with that of his wife, Ximena.

El Cid, a loyal supporter of Ferdinand the Great, was equally prepared to support his son, Sancho II. However, Sancho was mysteriously killed; there was some suspicion that Alfonso VI, his brother, was not entirely innocent. At that point, El Cid demanded an oath from Alfonso stating that he had not killed his brother. Annoyed at this suspicion, Alfonso banished El Cid from court. Later, following a reconciliation, El Cid supported the king and on his orders conquered Valencia in 1094. Although El Cid died in 1099, Ximena managed to hang onto Valencia for three more years. When defeat came she placed her husband's body in the saddle and rode through the lines to Burgos.

The "Poem of the Cid" (El Cantar de Mio Cid) was written by an anonymous minstrel, at a time when those alive could still remember him in all his glory. In this poem a warrior, banished by his king, leaves home to seek his fortune elsewhere. He felt "as if a nail was torn from his flesh" as he left his family. As he rode out of town, the people of Burgos dared not open their doors to wish him well because they feared retaliation from the king. One hundred knights accompanied him; he rode with his long beard tied up so that no one would be tempted to pull it. He captured the Count of Barcelona, who promptly went on a hunger strike. The poem contains a description of the trick that El Cid played on the money lenders when he needed money. Apparently, he filled a chest with sand, sealed it, and exchanged it for money, as if it contained treasures. Because they felt they could not doubt the word of a knight, they never opened it. This episode ended happily when he was eventually able to repay the money and reclaim the chest, with his honor still intact.

The **cathedral** in Burgos, begun in 1221, is the third largest in Spain. The walnut choir stalls depict biblical scenes and mythological symbols. There are 15 chapels to visit, some of them quite large. The **Capilla Del Santo Cristo** contains an image of Christ that is said to have human hair and nails; it is covered with either the hide of a water buffalo or human skin. The **Capilla de la Consolacion** resembles the "honeycomb" Moorish ceilings in Granada. Look for the **Papamoscas,** or Flycatcher Clock, which opens its mouth when the clock chimes the hour, and take time to visit the **Cloisters,** where you will see large figures sculpted from stone, clay, and wood. Besides Ferdinand and Isabella, the figures include representatives from each of the continents.

From Burgos, take N623 to **Santander.** If you are heading for the ferry to England, as we were, be sure to allow enough time to cross the mountains. In all honesty, we must say that we were not able to explore Santander because we almost missed the ferry; in fact, we heard that a number of cars and trucks did miss that sailing because of a blizzard in the mountains. We found that driving a two-lane road with some long, steep hills in blizzard conditions posed some unexpected problems, especially if that small mountain road is the main artery for truck traffic. Most cars could get through with ease, but when several trucks stop, slide, or otherwise jam the road, you, too, are stuck. In conversations with many people who drive these northern roads frequently, we discovered that the N623 is the best road to take from Burgos; the one steep section on this road, with switchback turns, is mercifully short. N611 from **Palencia** has a number of longer hills where trucks stall. The best way to go in really bad weather is the longer autopista from Burgos to **Bilboa,** then the coast road, N634, to Santander. Of course, if you are traveling in the warmer months, there will be no problem at all, but many who enjoy the temperate climate of southern Spain in the winter may be caught unawares when they head back to England by sea or France by road. If you are going to France, the autopista through Bilbao and **San Sebastian** to **Biarritz** is the fastest and best route in any season (unless you want to take a side trip on N240 to **Pamplona).**

We understand that Santander was devastated by a tornado in 1941; the *New Town* was built to include gardens and promenades by the sea, and was developed with buildings no more than four or five stories high. Santander is perhaps most famous for the prehistoric caves discovered in the area. The *Altmira Caves,* to the west along the coast, contain paintings of animals dating from around 12,000 B.C. (These caves are closed much of the time because of the deterioration of the paintings.) Modern Santander is a resort with three fine beaches in the area; you can also take a ferry to **Somo** and **Pedrena,** which have extensive sand dunes.

This is the conclusion of the itineraries we suggest as a means of exploring the delights of the Iberian peninsula, a region of extraordinary historic importance and continuing appeal to travelers of all persuasions—whether they are seeking sun, beaches, mountains, monuments, or just a fresh perspective on ways of living. We have, of course, left many fascinating regions untouched, such as Aragon and Galicia in Spain and the Beira Litoral and Beira Alta in Portugal, but what we have suggested is more than enough to fill the month or two that even the most lucky visitors may have to spend.

EUROPE UNDER CANVAS

CAMPSITE GUIDES We have not found it easy to buy European campground guides in the U.S. Call your local bookstore for help in ordering a guide, or write:

Complete Traveller
199 Madison Avenue
New York, NY 10016

Travellers Bookstore
22 East 52nd St.
New York, NY

Forsyth Travel Library
9154 West 57th St.
Box 2975
Shawnee Mission, KS 66201

Most of the national tourist offices put out a guide listing all approved campsites in the country. Some of them include a star system indicating the quality of services provided. You can get these by writing in advance, sometimes as you go through Customs, or in the local tourist offices as you travel.

Commercial guides list a variety of detail. Some of them list the kind of water available (ocean, lake, river); the nature of the beach (shingle, rock, sand); sun on the sites (shady or exposed); sports available on site or nearby; difficulty for caravans; ground (grassy, sandy, rocky); and one listed a column entitled "exceptional natural beauty." One guide also includes annotated comments sent in by travelers on specific campsites. Recommended guides include:

AA Camping and Caravanning in Europe. Published by the Automobile Association, Farnum House, Basingstoke, Hampshire, RG21 2EA England. This guide did not always have listings for areas we happened to need. The listings it does have include specific details on facilities and some prices.

Caravan Club Foreign Touring Handbook. Published by the Caravan Club, East Grinstead House, East Grinstead, West Sussex RH 19 1UA, England. An excellent guide with annotated comments by travelers. Only includes campsites that are known by its staff and members; therefore some areas are more fully covered than others. Some prices and some directions are given for finding the campgrounds. Membership fee.

RAC Guide to British and Continental Camping and Caravanning Sites. Published by Royal Automobile Club, 83–85 Pall Mall, London. Campground location is indicated on maps in the front of the book with numbers indicating where detailed information is found. This guide is 8½ x 11 inches, an awkward size to carry.

Handbook and Sites List. Published by Camping and Caravanning Club Ltd., 11 Lower Grosvenor Place, London, SW1. This guide lists sites in England only. There are helpful details and maps for some locations. They also maintain their own club sites. Membership fee.

Europa Camping and Caravaning. Published by Reise and Verkehrsverlag, Postfach 800830, Stuttgart, Germany. This guide includes a great deal of information about each campground. There are maps, information on ferries, currency exchange tables, and international price lists.

LOCATION Unless you have traveled the same route before, you should allow time to search for a campsite that is pleasant and has the amenities you would like. A description in a campsite guide will give you basic information about amenities, but the view may be different as seen from another pair of eyes. We have found that for a one-night stand we are comfortable rolling in anytime before dusk (often very late during Northern European summers) and picking a site without too much looking around. It is nice to have cleanliness and lack of noise from close neighbors, but we have survived cheerfully when conditions were dreadful, knowing that we would be somewhere else the next night.

We quickly learned which campsite guides were accurate and which we could not count on at all. At lunch or while driving, we would read the descriptions and pick out one or more campsites to investigate in the area we were aiming for. For a long stay we were quite fussy about the view, locale, and reasonable facilities. In some beautiful areas it was not difficult to find the perfect spot. In or near cities we found crowded conditions and often ended up altering our plans to head for more beautiful sites in the suburbs or the surrounding countryside.

DESIRABLE AMENITIES On the whole, campgrounds on the Continent tend to be well planned, with trees separating sites, spotlessly clean bathroom and shower facilities, generally pleasant surroundings, washing machines, swimming pools, and a well-stocked shop. In Britain we found many well-equipped campsites and a few quite primitive ones that were less costly and sometimes well worth it for an appealing lake or mountain view. The more primitive British campsites are generally old farms; often the bathrooms are built into barns and the sites themselves are on grass or meadow, complete with cows or sheep. In Scandinavia some of the campsites include little houses for cooking, washing dishes, and social gatherings.

SEASONS AND HOLIDAYS As with every other aspect of travel during a particularly busy holiday weekend, finding a campsite can be difficult. If possible, it is wise to book in advance. Otherwise plan to arrive in time to find a site before they are all gobbled up. We tried to stop by 3 or 4 p.m. when we thought it might be difficult to find a spot. Much of the summer is busy in Central Europe; we did not find this to be true in Scandinavia, except near ferries.

Most of our travel has been done off season (April through June, September, and October), which has some real advantages. We felt we could escape the tourist syndrome and all its attendant nonsense—higher prices, less interest on the part of people in places visited, more arrangements to make competing with other tourists. We did not encounter lines and waits at ferries, museums, restaurants, or castles. Sometimes we opened up campgrounds, and although we froze on some April nights when the temperature plummeted, it was worth it. Not being patient with crowds and lines, we prefer this leisurely and unharried kind of travel.

CHARGES Campground charges are set on various bases—the vehicle, tent or tents, dining canopy or tent extension, or number of campers. Some charge by the person, others charge by the size of each tent. For those with caravans, there is an additional charge for electrical hookup. Our entourage included one car, one large tent with extension, two small tents, and four persons. We paid anywhere from $1.05 to $9.17 per night, depending upon location and season. During a trip to Italy we paid a low of $2.40 in a gorgeous campsite on Lake Como not yet fully opened and a high of $9.17 a week later at Sorrento on Easter weekend. Most campsite guides list prices, but such listings are often out of date and may be inapplicable during the season in which you arrive. It is a good idea to check the posted prices at a campground when you arrive (including local taxes and extra fees) to be sure of the cost. But no matter what the specific cost at a site, remember that it is likely to be only 10% to 20% of what it would cost to put your party up in a pension or hotel for the night.

Campsite fees vary widely according to the amenities offered and the season of the year. Resort locations charge much higher fees because campers are a captive group when they choose to vacation there. We often camped off season and were usually charged less than the standard rate if we "opened" the campground. The manager often apologized for the hastily cleaned bathrooms and hoped we would enjoy our stay. Those that offered only the barest necessities did not charge very much, and often the superb view of a lakeside meadow or the fun of living within the grounds of a ruined castle made it all worthwhile. During holiday seasons (for example, Easter in Italy, Whitsun in England, August in France) resort area campgrounds were jammed with tourists who paid very high fees indeed. It didn't pay to shop around at such seasons in desirable resort areas because all decent camping areas were charging high fees. Some campgrounds offered a discount for those carrying "camping carnets."

CAMPGROUNDS These campgrounds are listed in their order of appearance in the itinerary; the list is a sampling of well-established campgrounds. National and local tourist offices have more complete, up-to-date lists available. Many small campgrounds advertise themselves only by a sign on the road.

Southwestern England

Fleet Farm Park, *Hayling Island* (Hampshire). Phone: (07016) 5850. Offers hot showers, swimming. Located on A3023 from Havant.

Goodwood, *Chichester* (Sussex). Offers hot showers, shop, shade, views of Sussex Downs. Turn off A286 at Singleton or Mid Lavant from A285.

Undercliff Riviera, *Isle of Wight*. Phone: (0983) 730268. Offers hot showers, beach, shade. Take A3055 to St. Catherine's Road, then turn right.

Appledurcombe, *Isle of Wight,* Phone: (0983) 852597. Offers hot showers, shop, swimming in the sea, swimming pool, shade. Drive 5 miles from Shanklin on A3021, turn left, then continue 2 miles.

Beaper Farm, *Ryde, Isle of Wight,* Phone: (0983) 72210. Offers hot showers, shop, beach, shade. Located 4 miles south of Ryde on A3055.

Manor Farm Camping, *Seaton* (Devon). Phone: (0297) 21524. Offers hot showers, shop, swimming, views over bay. Located 7 miles west of Lyme Regis on A3052.

Sun Park Soar, *Salcombe* (Devon). Phone: (0548) 561378. Offers hot showers, shop, swimming, view of sea. Drive 3¼ miles from Kingsbridge on A381, fork right through Malborough on Bolberry Road, turn south 1½ miles to Soar.

Killigarth Manor Estate, *Polperro* (Cornwall). Phone: (0503) 72216. Offers hot showers, shop, pool, beach, hill and terraced site with shade. Drive 4 miles from Looe on A387.

Silversands Holiday Park, *Kennack Sands,* Lizard (Cornwall). Phone: (0326) 290631. Offers hot showers, shop, shade. Take A3083, then B3293.

River Valley Caravan Park, Relubbus, *Penzance* (Cornwall). Phone: (073676) 3398. Offers hot showers, shop, beach, trout fishing. Located on B3280 3 miles northeast of Marazion.

Polmanter Farm Camping, Halsetown, *St. Ives* (Cornwall). Phone:

(0736) 795640. Offers hot showers, shop, beach. Take B3311 to Halsetown.

Penrose Farm, Goonhavern, *Truro* (Cornwall). Phone: (087257) 2287. Offers hot showers, shop, sites on meadow, beach. Turn off A30 to B3285. Site in 1½ miles.

The Headland, *Tintagel* (Cornwall). Phone: (08404) 239. Offers hot showers, swimming 500 meters, beach.

Putsborough Sands Caravan Site, Manor Farm, Putsborough, Georgeham, *Braunton* (Devon). Phone: (0271) 890231. Offers hot showers, shop, gentle slope, adjacent sandy beach, excellent surfing. Leave Braunton on B3231 to Croyde and Georgeham, follow signs to Putsborough and the sands, located 4 miles northwest of Braunton.

Mill Farm, Fiddington, *Bridgwater* (Somerset). Phone: (0278) 732286. Offers hot showers, shop, swimming pool, free boats, canoe hire. Drive 6¼ miles west of Bridgwater, turn north at Keenthorne Garage to Fiddington.

Newton Mill Touring Center, Newton St. Loe, *Bath* (Avon). Phone: (0225) 333909. Offers hot showers, shop, trout fishing. Take A4 from Bath to Globe Inn, turn onto B3110.

Bell Caravan and Camping Site, Lydeway, *Devizes* (Wiltshire). Phone: (038084) 230. Offers hot showers, shop. Located on edge of Salisbury Plain, 3½ miles southeast of Devizes on A342.

Stratford-upon-Avon Racecourse, *Stratford-upon-Avon* (Warwickshire). Camping Club of Great Britain site. Phone: (0789) 67949. Offers hot showers, shop 500 yards, near Anne Hathaway's Cottage. Located near A46 and A422 in Stratford.

Swinford Farm Campsite, *Swinford*, Oxon. Phone: (0865) 881368. Offers hot showers. On the River Thames. Take B4044, Oxford-Whitney Road, for 1 mile from Eynsham village.

Riverside Caravan and Camping Site, *Wallingford*. Phone: (0491) 35232. Offers hot showers. On the River Thames. Access is from A4130 on the north side of Wallingford.

Laleham Park Camping Site, Thameside, *Laleham* (Middlesex). Phone: Chertsey 64149. Offers hot showers. On towpath road. Take B376 from Staines High Street to Laleham village.

London-Crystal Palace, Caravan Harbour, Crystal Palace Parade, *London*. Caravan Club of Great Britain site. Phone: 01–778–7155. Offers hot showers, shops 5 minutes. Located on the foundations of the original Crystal Palace. Use a London map to find Crystal Palace Parade.

London-Abbey Wood, Cooperative Woods Caravan and Camping Site, Abbey Wood, *London*. Caravan Club of Great Britain site. Phone: 01–310–2233. Offers hot showers, shop, wooded area. Follow a map to the junction with Basildon Road, B213, turn right at Crumpsall Street; the site is signposted.

England Central, Wales, and the Lake District

See also *Southwestern Circuit*.
 The Bridge Inn, Dorrington, **Shrewsbury**. Phone: (074343) 209. Offers shade, shops ½ mile. Located 6 miles south of Shrewsbury on A49.
 Clwyd Holiday Camps, Brynmelyn Caravan and Camping Site, Llandderfel, **Bala** (Gwynedd). Phone: 06783212. Offers hot showers, shop, site on riverside, salmon and trout fishing. Take B4401 for 2½ miles west of Llandrillo, 5 miles east of Bala.
 Penybont Touring Park, Llangynog Road, **Bala** (Gwynedd). Phone: (0678) 520549. Offers hot showers, shop, beach 2000 yards. Located southeast of Bala on B4391, near Dee Bridge.
 Snowdonia National Forest Park Camp, **Beddgelert**. Offers hot showers, shop, shade, views. Located about ½ mile northwest of Beddgelert on A40085.
 Fallbarrow Park, Rayrigg Road, **Windermere**. Phone: (09662) 4428. Offers hot showers, shop, swimming, boating, fishing on lake. Turn south off A591 at small road. ½ mile on north side of Windermere village; site is on right 1½ miles.
 Coniston Hall, **Coniston** (Cumbria). Phone: (09664) 223. Offers hot showers, shop. Located by Coniston Water. Drive ¾ miles south of Coniston on A593.
 Park Coppice, **Coniston**. Caravan Club of Great Britain site. Phone: (09664) 555. Offers hot showers, shops 1.3 miles. Located on National Trust land to the west of Coniston Water; wooded site.
 Derwentwater, **Keswick**. Camping and Carvanning Club site. Phone: (0596) 72392. Offers hot showers, shop. Located on Derwentwater Lake, canoe hire. From A66, turn off onto A591, Keswick. At T-junction turn left to Keswick, at the bus station turn right for Borrowdale, fork right at Tithebarn Street Church, fork right after car park, first right after Rugby Club.
 Houghton Mill Park, Mill Street, Houghton, **Huntingdon**. Phone: (St. Ives) 62413. Offers hot showers, shop, adjacent to 17th-century watermill; a National Trust property. Take A1123, turn south through Houghton village to the mill.
 Great Shelford, **Cambridge**. Camping and Caravanning Club site. Phone: (0223) 841185. From Trumpington, turn right onto A1301 signposted Shelfords, ½ mile town sign Great Shelford, 100 yards, turn down lane between houses.
 Highfield Farm Camp Site, **Comberton** (near Cambridge). Phone: (022026) 2308. Offers hot showers, shop.

Scotland

Muirhouse Camping, Marine Drive, **Edinburgh.** Phone: 031 336 6874. Offers hot showers, shop, signposted on all main roads.

Dunnikier Park, **Kirkaldy** (Fife). Offers hot showers, shop, golf adjacent, shingle/sand beach 2 miles. Turn left off A92 at crossroads on A988, right in ¾ mile.

Garthdee Caravan Park, Garthdee Road, **Aberdeen.** Phone: (0224) 23456. Offers hot showers, shop, bowling, pitch and putt. Take A92 to Aberdeen, across Bridge of Dee, take minor road south at roundabout for ½ mile.

Peterhead Lido Camping, **Peterhead** (Aberdeenshire). Phone: 3358. Offers hot showers, shop, beach. Located on sea. Drive 2 miles south on A952.

Fraserburgh Kessock Road Municipal Camping, **Fraserburgh** (Aberdeenshire). Phone: 4557. Offers hot showers, shop, sand beach 100 yards. Turn right off A92 into Kessock Rd., site on left.

Milton of Fonab Caravan Site, **Pitlochry** (Perthshire). Phone: (0796) 2882. Offers hot showers, shop, fishing, views. From Pitlochry, take road over River Tummel; at T-junction turn left; site is opposite distillery.

Blair Castle Camping, **Blair Atholl,** Pitlochry (Perthshire). Phone: (Blair Atholl) 263. Offers hot showers, shop, pony treks, trout fishing. Site is on Blair Castle grounds. Drive on A9 past bridge over the River Tilt.

Glenmore Campsite, **Aviemore** (Inverness-shire). Phone: (Cairngorm) 271. Offers hot showers, shop, fishing, boating, skiing. Turn off A9 to B9152, in Aviemore to B970; site by Loch Morlich.

Dochfour Estate, Scaniport Camping and Caravan Site, **Scaniport** (Inverness-shire). Phone: 251. Offers hot showers, shop. Located on A862 4 miles south of Inverness.

Cruivend Caravan and Camping Site, **Beauly** (Inverness-shire). Phone: 2230. Offers hot showers, shop. Located on river. Turn left off A862 immediately after bridge over River Beauly.

Viewfield, **Breakish,** Isle of Skye. Phone: (Breakish) 433. Offers shop, swimming, boating, fishing. From Kyleakin, take A850 Portree Road for 6 miles; site on right at Breakish village.

Glen Nevis Caravan and Camping Site, **Glen Nevis, Fort William** (Inverness-shire). Phone (0397) 2191. Offers hot showers, shop. Located off A82 2 miles east of Fort William.

Glen Gallain Camping, **Oban** (Argyle). Phone: (Kilninver) 200. Offers hot showers, fishing, shingle/sand beach. Located 16 miles south of Oban on A816.

Witches Craig Camping and Caravanning Park, Blairlogie, *Stirling*. Phone: (0786) 4947. Offers hot showers, shop, beach. Located on A91 2 miles northeast of Stirling.

Scandinavia

DENMARK

Charlottenlund Strandpark, Strandvejen, *Charlottenlund, near Copenhagen*. Phone: (01) 62 36 88. Offers hot showers, shops 1 km, sand beach. Located on grounds of old castle. Take Copenhagen/Helsingor Coast Road. Site is on seaward side 2 km north of Tuborg factory.

Naerum Camping, Ravnebakken, *Naerum, near Copenhagen*. Phone: (02) 80 19 57. Offers hot showers, shop, popular site, woods. Take A3 (E4) motorway to north for 16 km, then west to Naerum, over bridge and sharp left.

SWEDEN

Sandskogens Campingplatz, *Ystad*. Phone (0411) 770 00. Offers hot showers, shop. On Baltic coast, shaded. Take M15 3 km east of Ystad.

Stenso Camping, 381 00 *Kalmar*. Phone: (0480) 207 33. Offers hot showers, shop, beach near site. Signposted from town center.

Ekerumsbadets Camping, *Borgholm, Oland*. Phone: (0485) 551 90. Offers hot showers, shop, shaded, sand/shingle beach. Located on Route 136 between Farjesaden and Borgholm.

Rosjons Campingplatz, *Sollentuna, near Stockholm*. Phone: (08) 35 34 75. Offers hot showers, shops 2 km, swimming in lake, laundry facilities, partly shaded. Take E3 north from Stockholm, signed Norrtalje. Pass Morby Centrum on left after 7 km. Take Sollentuna exit, turn left and follow 5 km. At second set of traffic lights with pylons adjacent, turn right onto small road, signed to site.

Bredangs Camping, *Skarholmen, near Stockholm*. Phone: (08) 97 70 71. Offers hot showers, sauna, beach 500 m, shop, underground to Stockholm. Take E3 to Bredang, then site is signed.

Orsandsbadens Camping, *Leksand*. Phone: (0247) 112 24. Offers hot showers, shop, swimming on Lake Seljan. Located 2 km north of Leksand.

Enabadets Camping, *Rattvik*. Phone: (0248) 11 606. Offers hot showers, shops, lake swimming, wooded. Located north of Rattvik.

NORWAY

Stubljan, Camping, Stubljan am See, *Oslo*. Phone: 28 62 35. Offers hot showers, shop, sand beach 100 m. Take E6, Goteburg/Oslo Road.

Skavanger Camping, *Kongsberg*. Phone: (034) 320 31. Offers hot showers, shop. From Kongsberg, take 8 to Geilo; site is on right after 1.5 km.

Kjornes Camping, *Sogndal*. Phone: (056) 821 00. Offers hot showers, shops 2 km, partly shaded, useful for ferries at Kaupanger. Site on edge of Sogndalsfjord, 2 km southeast of Sogndal.

Veganeset Camping, *Balestrand*. Offers hot showers, shop, swimming, views. Located 5 km northeast of Balestrand, adjacent to Dragsvik ferry.

Camping Kvanndal, *Kvanndal, near Bergen*. Phone: (055) 258 55. Offers hot showers, shops adjacent, swimming in fjord, ferry boats noisy but fun for children to watch. Signed in Kvanndal.

Ringoy Camping, Ringoy, *Kinsarvik*. Phone: 2708. Offers hot showers, shops adjacent, swimming in fjord on site, fishing, boating, free row boats. From Kinsarvik, take 7, first site on left.

Midttun Camping, Nesttun, near Bergen. Phone: (05) 273 180. Offers hot showers, shop, good base for Bergen. Take E68 from Nesttun for 1.5 km.

Camping Mosvagen, Rogaland, East Mosvagen, *Stavanger*. Phone: (045) 32 971. Offers hot showers, shop. Located 4 km southwest of Stavanger.

Skotterig Family Camping, Hovag, *Kristiansand*. Phone: 29665. Offers hot showers, shop, sand beach, fishing, boating on site. Take E18 signed Arendal from Kristiansand, then 401 on right.

DENMARK

Camping Blommehaven, Orneredeveg, *Hojbjerg, near Arhus*. Phone: (06) 27 02 07. Offers hot showers, shop, sand beach on site. Follow signs through Mareselisborg Forest.

Odense Kommunes Camping, Odensevej, *Odense*. Phone: (09) 11 47 02. Offers hot showers, shop, popular site. Located 4 km south of Odense.

The Low Countries, the Rhine, Bavaria, the Alps, and the Black Forest

HOLLAND

Het Amsterdamse Bos, Kleine Noordijk, *Aalsmeer, near Amsterdam*. Phone: (020) 416868. Offers hot showers, shop, shade, parklike setting; near airport. Site is 2 km west of Amstelveen, near Bovenkerk.

GERMANY

Campground Neckartal, *Heidelberg*. Phone: (06221) 802506. Offers hot showers, shop, shade, nice site on bank of River Neckar; some noise and interesting river traffic. 5 km from Heidelberg on B37 toward Neckargemund.

AUSTRIA

Camping Platz Reichenau, *Innsbruck*. Phone: (052 22) 4 62 52. Offers hot showers, shop, shade. Take motorway exit Innsbruck Ost, turn right onto Langer Weg, turn left before river.

SWITZERLAND

Pointe a la Bise, Route d' Hermance, *Vesenaz, near Geneve*. Phone: (022) 52 12 96. Offers hot showers, shop, swimming. Site is between Vesenaz and Bellerive.

Camping Unterbergiswil, *Meggan-Merlischacken, near Luzern*. Phone: (041) 371804. Offers hot showers, site on lake.

GERMANY

Bankenhof, *Tittisee-Neustadt*. Phone: (07652) 336. Offers hot showers, shop, swimming in lake adjacent. Turn right by lake 3 km from town.

Erholungsparadies Adam, *Buhl, near Baden-Baden*. Phone: (07223) 23194. Offers hot showers, shop, swimming pool, lake. Take motorway exit Buhl toward Lichtenau, 1 km.

Southeast Mediterranean

YUGOSLAVIA

AutoCamp Preluk, *Opatija*. Phone: (051) 617–913. Offers hot showers, shop. Located in natural cove of Preluk, on sea, 8 km from Rijeka, 3 km from Opatija.

Campground Adriatic, *Primosten*. Phone: (059) 70022. Offers hot showers, shop, shade; on sea. Site is north of Primosten and west of N2.

Campground Rozac, *Trogir*. Phone: (058) 73105. Offers hot showers, shop, shade attractive with pines and olives. Site is 2 km from Trogir on Ciovo Island, north of Split on the sea.

Auto Camp Lisicina, *Omis*. Phone: (058) 86 332. Offers hot showers; small; open all year.

Auto Camp Solitudo, *Dubrovnik*. Phone: (050) 20770. Offers hot showers, shop. Site is located on peninsula of Lapad; view.

GREECE

Condokali Beach Camping International, *Corfu*. Phone: (0661) 91 202. Offers hot showers, shop, sports fields, shaded, spacious. Site is 5 km north of Kerkira.

Corfu Camping, *Ipsos*. Phone: (0661) 93 246. Offers hot showers; orange grove; small, family operated; across road from sea; early rising roosters and turkeys.

Camping Apollon, *Delphi*. Phone: (0265) 82762. Offers hot showers, shop. Site is 1.5 km from Delphi, has view.

Delphi Camping, *Delphi*. Phone: (0265) 82363. Offers hot showers, shop, tennis courts, pool, skiing 25 km away.

Dafni Camping, *Dafni, Athens*. Phone: (021) 5811 563. Offers hot showers, shop. From Athens, turn left at lights by monastery.

Voulas Camping, *Voula, near Athens*. Phone: (021) 8952 712. Offers hot showers, shop; noisy aircraft. Site is on main Sounion–Athens road, on sea, 15 km south of Athens.

Kastraki Camping, Assini–Nauplia–Tolon area of *Peloponisos*. Phone: (0752) 59386. Offers hot showers, shade; S28 is nice corner lot on sea and river. Site is next to Assini ruins.

Malia Camping, *Crete*. Phone: (0897) 31461. Offers hot showers, shop; on sea. Site is 37 km east of Iraklion.

Camping Arkadia, Missiria–Rethimno area, *Crete*. Phone: (0831) 28694. Offers hot showers, shop, bamboo dividers, small sites; on sea.

Camp Elizabeth, *Crete*. Phone: (0831) 28694. Family run, neat; geraniums, olive grove; on sea, shade. Site is 3 km east of Missiria.

Camp Aghia Marina, Chanea, *Crete*. Phone: (0821) 48555. Offers hot showers, shop; pleasant with palms. Site is 8 km west of Chanea.

Camping Koula, Paroikia, *Paros*. Phone: (0284) 22081. Offers hot showers, shop; small, flat, shaded; across road from shingle beach.

Camping Naoussa, Naoussa, *Paros*. Phone: (0284) 51595. Offers hot showers; flat, open, no shade; beach near, view of bay, country setting.

Camping Kafkis, Marpissa, *Paros*. Phone: (0284) 41392. Site is on hillside, terraced, below monastery; view of sea and Naxos.

ITALY

Pineta Al Mare, Specchiolla, *Carovigno, near Brindisi*. Phone: (0831) 968057. Offers hot showers, shop; partly shaded in pines, sand beach across road. Site is 20 km northwest of Brindisi, east of S379.

Camping Pilone, *Marina di Ostuni*. Phone: (0831) 970775. Offers hot showers, shop, shade, beach. Site is northeast of Ostuni.

Intercamping Apollo, Via p. di Piemonte, *Paestum*. Phone: (0828) 811178. Offers hot showers, shop, sand beach; eucalyptus and pine trees.

Camping Esperia, *Marina di Ascea*. Phone: (0974) 971036. Offers hot showers, shop, shade, shingle beach. Site is 20 km northwest of Palinuro.

International Camping, Nube d'Argento, *Sorrento*. Phone: (081) 8781344. Offers hot showers, shop; terraced, pool, beach 300 meters; difficult access for caravans. Site is on outskirts of Sorrento.

Campground Villa Adriana, Tivoli, *Roma.* Phone: (0774) 329091. Offers hot showers, shop, shade, pool. Site is east of Roma on Roma–L'Aguila road.

Campground Fonte Maggio, *Assisi.* Phone: (075) 813636. Offers hot showers, shop, shade, pool; terraced, olive trees, view of countryside. Site is 1 km from Assisi on road to Ermo delle Carceri.

Campground Internazionale Certosa, *Firenze.* Phone: (055) 2020445. Offers hot showers, shop; terraced, part shade, on top of hill. Site is near Monastery of Certosa, exit 23.

Campground Panoramica, Fiesole, *Firenze.* Phone: (055) 599069. Offers hot showers, shop; narrow steep road, part shade. Site is 1 km north of Fiesole.

Campground Maralunga, *Lerici, La Spezia.* Phone: (0187) 966589. Offers hot showers, shop; shaded, on coast.

Camping Europa, Menaggio, *Como.* Phone: (0344) 31187. Offers hot showers, shop; partly shaded, on lake. Site is 30 km from Como, on west shore.

France

Camping Beausejour-les-Tasses, *St-Raphael.* Phone: (94) 950367. Offers hot showers, shop; hilly site in pine woods; swimming 400 meters. Site is 2 km east of town off N98.

Camping Chantecler, *Aix-en-Provence.* Phone: (42) 261298. Offers hot showers, shop; terraced site on hill; cabins, swimming. Exit motorway at Aix–Eston A8.

Les Chenes Verts (The Evergreen Oaks), *Calviac, Dordogne.* Phone: (16) 53592107. Offers hot showers, shop; shade, pool. Site is between Souillac and Sarlat on N704A.

Camping des Chateau, *Bracieux, Loire.* Phone: (16) 54464184. Offers hot showers, shop; large, flat, trees and pines; edge of pretty village. Site is 9 km from Chambord.

Parc de Fierbois, *Sainte-Catherine de Fierbois, Loire.* Phone: (47) 654335. Offers hot showers, shop, lake, pine trees, tennis, bungalows. Site is north of Ste-Maure off A10. Castel et Camping Site #185.

Grand Camping de la Plage, *Le Guilvinec, Penmarche, Brittany.* Phone: (98) 946190. Offers hot showers, shop; shade, on sea, sandy beach. Located between Guilvinec and Penmarche.

L'Etang de la Breche, *Varennes-sur-Loire.* Phone: (41) 512292. Offers hot showers, shop, shade, pool. Site is near Saumur. Castel et Camping Site #195.

La Ferme du Vieux-Chene, *Dol de Bretagne.* Phone: (99) 480955. Offers hot showers, shop, shade, pond for fishing, canoeing, tennis, chalets.

Chateau du Martragny, *Martragny, near Bayeux.* Phone: (31)

802140. Offers hot showers, shop, part shade, pool. Castel et Camping Site #185.

The Iberian Peninsula

THE MEDITERRANEAN COAST OF SPAIN

Campground Port de la Selva, *Port de la Selva*. Phone: (972) 38 72 87. Offers hot showers, supermarket, shade trees, swimming pool for children. Follow Llansa sign, then Port de la Selva sign, then turn right at sign for Cadaque. Site is 1 km on right.

Campground Cadaque, *Cadaque*. Phone: (972) 25 81 26. Offers hot showers, supermarket, beach. Turn left onto unmade road, approach road rough.

Playa Port de la Vall, *Port de la Selva*. Phone: (972) 58 71 86. Offers hot showers, shop; beach on site. Located 2 km northeast of Port de la Selva between the sea and coastal road.

Campground Tamarit, *Tarragona*. Phone: (977) 65 01 28. Offers hot showers, supermarket; shade trees in one section, a new section in a meadow with some trees; beach; located beneath the ruins of Tamarit Castle. Drive 8 km east of Tarragona on N340, turn right at km stone 249.

Campground El Saler, *El Saler*. Phone: (96) 3670411. Offers hot showers, supermarket, swimming pool, pine trees; sand beach 300 meters away.

Campground Palmeral, *Elche*. Phone: (965) 458066. Offers hot showers, supermarket, swimming pool; located in a palm forest. Well signposted.

Campground La Garrofa, *Almeria*. Phone: (951) 23 57 70. Offers hot showers, supermarket, shade trees, swimming.

Don Cactus, *Motril*. Phone: (958) 62 31 04. Offers hot showers, supermarket, beach. This campground is popular as a weekend retreat for families and tends to be crowded even in winter. Signposted from N340 between km stones 9/13.

Campground El Paraiso, *Almunecar*. Phone: (958) 63 02 30. Offers hot showers, supermarket, shade trees, swimming, automatic washing machine. Located east of Almunecar on N340.

ANDALUSIA

Campground Maria Eugenia, *Granada*. Phone: (958) 23 18 81. Offers hot showers, supermarket; fruit trees. Located 2 km northeast of Granada on N342.

Campground Sierra Nevada, *Granada*. Phone: (958) 23 25 04. Offers hot showers, supermarket, pool. Shaded; noisy at weekends. Located in Granada on the Jaen–Madrid road.

Campground Municipal del Turismo, **Cordoba.** Phone: (957) 27 050 48. Offers hot showers, supermarket, shade trees, pool. Located north of Cordoba toward Villaviciosa.

Camping Villsom, **Sevilla.** Phone: (954) 72 08 28. Offers hot showers, supermarket, palms and orange trees, pool. Located 12 km from Sevilla on N4.

PORTUGAL

Parque Orbitur, ***Quarteira, west of Faro.*** Phone: 6 52 38. Offers hot showers, supermarket, swimming, laundry facilities; terraced, located at the top of a hill west of Faro.

Parque de Turismo de Lagos, **Lagos.** Phone: 6 00 31. Offers hot showers, supermarket, shade trees; sites separated by hedges. Located southwest of Lagos center.

Parque Municipal de Campismo, **Sesimbra.** Phone: 2233 694. Offers hot showers, supermarket, swimming.

Parque Orbitur Areias, **Guincho.** Phone: (040) 285. Offers hot showers, supermarket, pine woods, beach.

Campground Lago de Proserpina, **Merida.** Phone: 30 20 91. Offers supermarket, shade, swimming. Located 5 km north of Merida.

CASTILE

Greco, **Toledo.** Phone: (925) 22 00 90. Offers hot showers, supermarket, pool. Located on terraces leading down to the Rio Tajo.

Campground Madrid, **Madrid.** Phone: (91) 2022835. Offers hot showers, supermarket, pool; terraced site on a hill. Located 7 km from Madrid on the Burgos road.

Campground Escorial, **El Escorial.** Phone: (91) 890 0821. Offers hot showers, supermarket, pool; mountain views. Located 49 km northwest of Madrid.

Don Quijote, **Salamanca.** Offers hot showers, supermarket, swimming. Located by River Tormes, east of Salamanca toward Aldealengua.

CAMPING EQUIPMENT

For a short trip you will be happier with the absolute minimum of equipment. Oddly enough, it seems to be true that the same equipment will also do for a longer trip. Through a process of trial and error, you can discover which items mean a lot to you while traveling under canvas and which are not used much, if at all. About half of the following items will probably be essential for you:

air mattresses or foam pads
asbestos mitts
breadboard
broom, small
can opener
chairs, folding
clothesline and pins
cook kit
corkscrew
corn tongs (for turning bacon)
dishcloth or sponge
dishpans
dishtowels
dishwashing liquid or soap bar
funnel
ground sheet
juice container
kettle
knives
lanterns and flashlights
mallet
matches
packsack for camping gear
paper towels
plastic bags

plates, cups, bowls
pump for air mattresses
rope
salt and pepper
scissors
scouring pads
shopping bag
silverware
sleeping bags (for appropriate temperature range)
string
stove
table, small
tablecloth, plastic
tent
tent stakes
tools (long-handled spoon, slotted spoon, pancake turner, soup ladle)
tools (hammer, pliers, wrenches, screwdrivers, knife, grommet kit, sewing kit)
trash bags
water jug
wax paper
wind shield for stove

Travelers who do not own camping equipment may prefer to rent it upon arrival in Europe. Many large camping stores in major cities offer this service. We chose to bring sleeping bags and air mattresses with us and bought the rest in England. Because camping has been very popular there for a long time, Europe offers a great variety of camping equipment; we enjoy shopping for just the right gear there. We were delighted to increase our collection of tents with a French tent that was light, easy to erect, dry, and very comfortable. We bought additional small two-person tents for each child to give them a little respite from togetherness. These tents weighed almost nothing and were dry and easy to manage; they also increased our capability for backpacking and mountain hiking. For those with very small children or those who prefer camping with more comforts and accessories, renting a small camping vehicle or tent trailer may be preferable. Or, if you want comfort all the way, you can rent and tow a caravan. On an earlier trip when our children were three and six years old, we bought a camper, which solved the tent problem except for one tent we had brought along to let the family spread out.

It is important to select just the right stove for your culinary pleasure. We have finally settled on two small, easily stored Gaz stoves that provide us with quick heat for a two-pot meal. Gaz butane refills are easily available anywhere in Europe. In the past we have used Optimus, Primus, and Svea, burning gas, white gas, and alcohol, respectively. Although all performed well, none was as convenient or fast as the small butane stove. Heavy, complicated two-burner liquid fuel stoves are usually not worth the space they take unless you are traveling with a camper or tent trailer.

The other assorted equipment you need is easily available in any camping store. We bought three large plastic boxes and a number of smaller ones to hold our dishes, utensils, and other gear. They stacked in one packsack, keeping everything orderly. When we made camp we would lay out the plastic boxes in the same order in the bell end of the tent extension. The entire family knew where every item could be found, no matter where we were. The other packsack held the two small plastic dishpans, then the cook kit with the kettle on top. All the other cooking necessaries fit around these items so the cook could unpack gear always knowing where things were, while others erected tents.

European campers carry lanterns that we felt were too bulky to take home with us. Instead, we bought a fluorescent light that hooked up to our car battery, and found that very bright, compact, and handy (it also doubled as an emergency vehicle light). In addition we had flashlights for each person and a battery-powered lantern for each tent.

Most European campgrounds do not furnish tables as American campgrounds do, so one must bring something to sit on. We could have gotten along very well with air mattresses to lounge on but did find little folding canvas sand chairs much easier on our backs (though they were hard to get up from). We also bought a small low folding table that came in very handy while we were cooking. It held a candle in a can at dusk, and later provided a flat surface for card games.

Camp housekeeping was not difficult once we had persuaded everyone to take off shoes before going into tents. During rainy weather we placed our Wellington boots (English rubber boots) carefully between the tent and the fly sheet with a plastic bag over the top to keep them dry. We had a ground sheet covering the area in front of the tent, and a little whiskbroom swept away any bits of dirt that otherwise would have been tracked into sleeping quarters. A camper's entire attitude and pleasure during a spell of bad weather can depend on having at least one clean, dry place to retreat to.

Many European tents are now sold with an "extension" that adds a "living room" to your tent in bad weather. We camped without one for a while in October, but after nine days of rain decided we needed an extension. We sewed together two nylon fly sheets to make an extension that, though not completely waterproof along the ridge, was quite an improvement over the open air and rain. It had two long zippers on each side so that the side away from the wind could be opened up and held with poles. One end zipped right onto our larger tent; the opposite end was made in a bell shape and contained our "kitchen area" with boxes all lined up on a ground sheet. The center area was large enough for five small chairs, the folding table, and a happy family playing games at night—out of the wet!

For a short trip abroad it makes sense to buy all your equipment at home to avoid the frustrations and delays of shopping after arrival. However, if you prefer to rent or buy equipment when you arrive, the Yellow Pages are a good place to begin. Camping stores abound all over Europe, and many of them rent equipment. Most of them stock a complete selection of anything you will need. Having compared prices in various camping stores throughout central England, we found the differences in the cost of cooking equipment and camping accessories insignificant. Tents are another matter, ranging from high-quality light mountain tents to elaborate, large framed tents with many "rooms"—both expensive purchases—to cheaper, less well-made discount versions. Buying a tent requires careful research in advance, but since many British, French, Italian, and Scandinavian tents are marketed in mountaineering and camping stores in America, you can set your requirements and do most of your homework before you go.

CAMP COOKING

Part of the fun of travel is the opportunity to taste special foods in each country. As we drove through Scandinavia, the sighting of another berry stand brought great joy to children and parents alike. Cloud berries, like their name, were out of this world! In Denmark we tried smorbrod (open-faced sandwiches with a variety of special toppings) a number of times and could easily assemble the ingredients to make our own. Indonesian food is very good and popular in the Netherlands because many Dutch people lived there before World War II and learned to cook these foods expertly. Of course, in both the Netherlands and Switzerland chocolate is superb, and Cadbury's provides a similar temptation in England. In Paris we have tried Alsatian cooking, with huge platters of sauerkraut and sausage topped with champagne, as well as more typical French cuisine. Italy offers an unimaginable variety of pasta dishes as well as special treats like veal with Marsala. Sauerbraten in Germany, apple strudel in Austria, raclette and fondue in Switzerland are all remembered with pleasure. In England we picked blackberries along the hedges in the fall and made beautiful fresh desserts, as well as enjoyed roast beef and Yorkshire pudding, plowman's lunches, and rum trifle for dessert.

Some of the pleasure associated with these special foods comes from eating in an atmosphere that is certainly authentic. Some of these foods and many others can be brought to the campsite and enjoyed there, like fish and chips taken straight from the shop wrapped in newspaper and enjoyed while piping hot. In seaport towns crab can be purchased cracked and ready to be eaten with a supply of paper napkins.

Camping allows people to "cater for themselves," which saves bundles of money. You can lay in a stock of canned goods in countries that have cheaper prices and use them with extra pleasure in more expensive neighboring countries. Perishable foods can be purchased en route either from supermarkets or from little shops wherever you happen to be. We usually purchased basic supplies from a supermarket where the prices were on the products, allowing us to muse a little with a list in hand. When purchasing for a trip, we estimated the number of meals we thought we would eat in camp, subtracting those we might eat out or bring in from local stores.

Many campgrounds have stores on the grounds. They are very handy for a forgotten item or two, but the supplies are usually limited and rather expensive. Often fresh bread, rolls, or croissants are available in the morning at the camp store, and we did indulge ourselves in these local luxuries. We also usually purchased milk there every morning so we could have it cold. Sometimes it was even delivered to the tent! In one area there was a farm on the grounds, and the fresh eggs we bought there all had double yolks and were giant size.

Usually we chose to eat out at lunch, while sightseeing. It is often more convenient, and far less expensive, to prepare dinners in the cozy atmosphere of your own campsite with a candle stuck in a can for a glow and perhaps a cup of sherry or local wine to warm the heart. Our children enjoyed selecting favorite foods from our stock of canned goods and acting as chef for the night. After dinner we had plenty of time to go for a walk, enjoy the view or a sunset, just loll around, and meet other campers to look over their collections of ingenious and practical camping gear.

LOCAL WINES AND BEERS Wines never taste as good as they do right where they are produced. We did a lot of our own wine tasting and came upon some fine local wines that are not exported—a real incentive to return! Beers that command a high price when imported into the United States are an affordable treat while in the country of origin. It is easy to become spoiled with Lowenbrau or Heinecken's available at a decent price. A special pleasure in Germany and England is sampling the draft beer. It is now possible to get a list of pubs serving totally natural beer (''real'' beer) in many areas of England.

COOKING BY COMPUTER Organizing a total food plan in advance certainly makes travel more enjoyable. ''Cooking by computer'' involves making up a set of index cards with a menu for one day, including recipes that are more involved than just opening cans, and a shopping list of ingredients. A separate card can list staples to keep on hand. When preparing for a trip just pull the cards for the menus you plan to use, add the staple card, and jot down the number of total items needed on your shopping list. Another card can list cooking utensils and equipment that need to be packed.

If that seems like a great deal of work, you can also ''cook by chart.'' Make columns for breakfast, lunch, dinner, and snacks across the top and list the days of the trip down the sheet. Then fill in the menus by day and add up the number of items needed for your shopping list.

We carry a very small notebook with foods listed by category, and enter new recipes as we go. Over the years we have collected some interesting combinations. We are always on the lookout for new products that do not need refrigeration, as well as an expanding collection of dehydrated and freeze-dried foods.

Packing the mound of cans and boxes for a long trip is not easy, but at least they decrease as the trip progresses. We use up the largest cans early in the trip and end up with a few boxes and packets of lighter foods.

During the day we carry a separate lunchbox with items like a small cutting board, knife, plastic tablecloth, napkins, thermos (or two) cups, jar of peanut butter, jelly, cheese, and meat spreads. Cartons can also be used to hold canned goods as long as the cans are in some kind of order so they all needn't be removed for a meal.

A sample list of nonperishable staples includes the following:

bouillon	marmalade
cereal, hot	pancake mix
cocoa	powdered milk
coffee	salad cream
crackers	salt and pepper
fruit-drink mix	sugar
honey	syrup
jelly	tea

Most European campgrounds do not permit open fires, which does away with "s'mores" (graham cracker, roasted marshmallow, and chocolate sandwich) from our days of camping as children, freshly caught fish cooked on a grill in canoe country, and other foods that taste particularly good cooked over a fire. When using a two-burner Coleman stove in the past we have enjoyed foods that can be cooked slowly without much trouble. However, the stoves that most of us will probably choose to use in Europe will be small and the fuel will be too expensive for the luxury of slow cooking. Therefore we lean heavily on canned goods, dehydrated and freeze-dried packets, and other foods that do not take long to heat. Foods that some of us think rather unexciting right out of a can taste better after a day spent exploring a new area and storing up memories. The addition of herbs, grated cheese, sauces, bouillon, or lemon juice can make ordinary canned food more palatable.

Appropriate beverages are served with meals. Juice accompanies breakfast with a choice of cocoa (and powdered or longlife milk), coffee, tea, or fresh milk; for lunch fruit juice, beer, or milk; for dinner wine, beer, fruit juice, or milk. Milk can be purchased daily everywhere or longlife milk can be carried.

Fruit is available for both lunch and dinner with occasional pastries, cookies, or other treat for dessert. We usually served vegetables for dinner because it was more convenient to pull out the sandwiches we had made in the morning for lunch on the road. Soup as a first course for dinner is relaxing while the rest of the dinner cooks. Then the soup pot can be filled with water and heated during the meal for dishwashing.

On days when a "rolling breakfast" is desirable to get going, there is canned juice, fruit, hard cheese, rolls, and other easily eaten food that can be served with no preparation. Car coffeepots are available that can be plugged into the cigarette lighter. By boiling water and supplying instant mixes, it is possible to stretch out breakfast over half the morning.

We chose not to carry anything that we did not consider easily transportable. For example, we did not carry cooking oil but instead used a little margarine in our Teflon pan. Except for fruit, which we purchased in markets frequently, we did not carry foods that bruised easily. We did buy fresh meat occasionally, when it happened to be convenient, but did not carry it. Traveling with a cooler, as we do in the United States, did not seem necessary.

DRIVING REGULATIONS

An international driving permit is desirable in a number of countries. Ask for an Italian translation of your driver's license if you are going to Italy. The international driving permit is available from automobile associations. For Spain, make arrangements to get a bail bond. If you have an accident there, you will be detained without one.

Your insurance company will issue you a green card, which indicates that your car is fully covered. Be sure to carry the registration with you. You will also need a sticker carrying the letters designated for the country of origin of the car. (GB for Britain, F for France, S for Sweden).

Some countries, including Yugoslavia, Greece, and Austria, require you to carry a first-aid-kit. Many countries insist on your having a warning triangle in your car.

Be aware of the practice of giving priority to the car on the right. In urban areas you must give way to anyone coming from the right, no matter how small the road is. However, in the countryside the major roads have priority. Roundabouts move counter-clockwise; persons entering from the right have priority. In some countries the opposite is true; those on the roundabout have priority by a special sign. Trams have priority in most cities. You may not pass when passengers are getting on or off. In some mountainous regions ascending cars have priority over descending cars. You must carry chains when driving in the winter in some locations. It is possible to rent them from a garage and return them to another designated garage.

Parking regulations vary. In some cities you need to buy vouchers from service stations, banks, or some shops. Parking dials or clocks to place inside your windshield are used in some areas. Some cities have blue zones where parking is limited to 1½ hours.

Tourist gas coupons purchased before you enter Italy will save you money. (Rental cars are not eligible for coupons.) You can buy a package covering the northern part of Italy or the southern part; we recommend buying the entire package if you will be traveling our route. You will use up the autostrada coupons rapidly. Take your car registration and passport with you to purchase them. Yugoslavia also offers gas coupons.

For travel in Spain you must carry spare bulbs for headlight, sidelight, and taillights. Check regulations in each country on when to use full, side, or dipped headlights.

When you write to national tourist offices for each country ask for a copy of their driving regulations. You can also get them at most borders when crossing into a country.

CONVERSION TABLES

Clothing Size	American	British	Continental
women's dresses, suits, and coats	8	30	36
	10	32	38
	12	34	40
	14	36	42
	16	38	44
	18	40	46
women's blouses, sweaters	34	36	42
	36	38	44
	38	40	46
	40	42	48
	42	44	50
	44	46	52
women's shoes	6	4½	36
	6½	5	37
	7	5½	38
	7½	6	38
	8	6½	38½
	8½	7	39
men's suits, sweaters, coats	34	34	44
	36	36	46
	38	38	48
	40	40	50
	42	42	52
	44	44	54
men's shirts	14	14	36
	14½	14½	37
	15	15	38
	15½	15½	39
	16	16	40
	16½	16½	41

Clothing Size	American	British	Continental
men's shoes	9	8½	43
	9½	9	43
	10	9½	44
	10½	10	44
	11	10½	45
	11½	11	45

Weights

ounce = 28.35 grams	1 gram = 0.04 ounce
pound = 0.45 kilogram	1 kilogram = 2.20 pounds
ton = 0.91 metric ton	1 metric ton = 1.10 tons

Liquid Measure

pint = 0.47 liter	1 liter = 2.11 pints
quart = 0.95 liter	1 liter = 1.06 quarts
gallon = 3.79 liters	1 liter = 0.26 gallon

Length

inch = 2.54 centimeters	1 centimeter = 0.39 inch
foot = 0.30 meter	1 meter = 3.28 feet
yard = 0.91 meter	1 meter = 1.09 yards
mile = 1.61 kilometers	1 kilometer = 0.62 mile

Distance

Kilometer to miles:
1 kilometer = .62 mile
10 kilometers = 6.20 miles
20 kilometers = 12.40 miles
30 kilometers = 18.60 miles
50 kilometers = 31.00 miles
75 kilometers = 46.50 miles
100 kilometers = 62.00 miles
Multiply by .6

Miles to kilometers:
1 mile = 1.6 kilometers
10 miles = 16.00 kilometers
20 miles = 32.00 kilometers
30 miles = 48.00 kilometers
50 miles = 80.00 kilometers
75 miles = 120.00 kilometers
100 miles = 160.00 kilometers
Multiply by 1.6

Gasoline

U.S. gallons:	to liters:
1	3.8
2	7.6
3	11.4
4	15.1
5	18.9
6	22.7
7	26.5
8	30.3
9	34.1
10	37.9

Temperature

To compute Fahrenheit: multiply Celsius by 1.8 and add 32.
To compute Celsius: subtract 32 from Fahrenheit and divide by 1.8.

Celsius		Fahrenheit
100	boiling point	212
90		194
80		176
70		158
60		140
50		122
40		104
37	normal body temp	98
30		86
20		68
10		50
5		41
0	freezing point	32

INDEX

Abbey Craig, Scotland, 51
Aberdeen, Scotland, 47–48
Absalom, Bishop, 56
Acciaroli, Italy, 120
accommodations, xxi
  bed-and-breakfast, xxii
  camping, xxi–xxii, 199–212
  chateaux, xxii–xxiii
  guest houses, xxii
  hostels, xxii
  National Trust inns, xxii–xxiii
  paradores, xxii–xxiii
  pensions, xxii
  pousadas, xxii–xxiii
Acharavi, Greece, 97
Acquasparta, Italy, 124
Acropolis, 100
Addison, Joseph, 24
Adlisuil, Switzerland, 81
Adventures of Harry Richmond, The (Meredith), 5
Aegean Islands, 105–106
Aegisthus, 103
Aeschylus, 102
Afonso, King, 184
Agamemnon, 102
Agio Deka, Greece, 109
Agios Nikolaos, Greece, 110
Agony and the Ecstacy, The (Stone), 128
Agrinion, Greece, 98
Agrippa, 123
Aguilas, Spain, 165
Ahmar, Ibn, 171
Aigle du Midi, 78
Akronafplia, Greece, 104
Akrotiri, Greece, 113
Alabaster Coast, France, 148
Albania, 96
Alberobello, Italy, 118
Alborg, Denmark, 66
Albufeira, Portugal, 181
Albufera, Spain, 164

Alcester, England, 36
Alentejo, Spain, 180
Alexander I, King of Scotland, 51
Alfonso VI, King, 196
Alfonso XI, King, 176
Algarve, Portugal, 179, 180, 181–184
Algodonales, Spain, 169
Alhambra, Spain, 171–174
Alicante, Spain, 164
  sights, 164
Alice's Adventures in Wonderland (Carroll), 24
Almaraz, Spain, 189
Almeria, Spain, 167
Almunecar, Spain, 168
  sights, 168
Altamira Caves, 193, 198
Altamura, Italy, 119
Amalfi Drive, Italy, 120–121
Ambleside, England, 39
Amboise, France, 143
Amelia, Italy, 124
Amfilohia, Greece, 98
Ampurias (Empuries), Spain, 160
Amstel River, Holland, 71
Amsterdam, Holland, 70–71
  sights, 71
Amymone, 104
Anafestus, Pauluciis, 87
Andalusia, Spain, 169–171
Andermatt, Switzerland, 77
Andersen, Hans Christian, 57
Angers, France, 141, 144
Angouleme, France, 140
Antequera, Spain, 169
Antonius, 105
Antwerpen, Belgium, 84
Apollo, 98
Appian Way, Italy, 118
Apt, France, 137
  sights, 137
Arahova, Greece, 99

225

226 Index

Arbroath, Scotland, 48
Archilochos, 116
Arcos de la Frontera, Spain, 179
Arden, Scotland, 51
Argos, Greece, 102
Arhus, Denmark, 66–67
   sights, 66–67
Ariadne, 108
Arlberg, Austria, 76–77
Arlberg Pass, 77
Arles, France, 137–138
   sights, 137–138
Armada, Spanish, 13
Armona, Portugal, 181
Arnhem, Holland, 72
Arnold, Matthew, 25
Around the World in 80 Days (Verne), 117
Arta, Greece, 98
Arthur, King, 18, 21, 26
Arundel, Sir John, 16–17, 18
Asclepius, 102, 115
Asine, Greece, 104
Aspern Papers, The (James), 89
Assisi, Italy, 125–126
   sights, 125–126
Athine (Athens), Greece, 99–102
   sights, 100–101
Atlantis, 112
Atreus, 103
Attalus, King, 101
Audierne, France, 146
Aurelius, Marcus, 123
Aurlands Fjord, Norway, 64
Austen, Jane, 7, 22
Austria, 75–77
Austrian State Tourist Department, xvi
Avebury Circle, England, 22–23
Aviemore, Scotland, 48–49
Avignon, France, 135–136
   sights, 136
Avila, Spain, 188, 195
   sights, 195
Avon, River, England, 35
Avranches, France, 148

Bacon, Francis, 42
Badajoz, Spain, 187
Baden-Baden, Germany, 82–83
   sights, 82–83
Baggensfjord, Sweden, 61
bail bond, Spain, xxiv
Bailen, Spain, 175
Bala, Wales, 36
Bala Cynwd, Pennsylvania, 36
Baldock, England, 43
Ballater, Scotland, 48

Balzac, Honore de, 141
Bandinelli, 127
Bannockburn, Scotland, 51
Barabino, Nicolo, 128
Barber of Seville (Rossini), 178
Barca, Hamilcar, 164
Barcelona, Spain, 160–161
   sights, 161
Barnstaple, England, 22
Basento Valley, Italy, 119
Basingstoke, England, 26
Basovizza, Yugoslavia, 89
Bath, England, 22
Battipaglia, Italy, 119
Bavaria, 75
Bayeux, France, 151–152
   sights, 151–152
Beaumont, France, 149
Beddgelert, Wales, 37
Beiro River, Spain, 173
Belgian Tourist Bureau, xvi
Bellerophon, 102
Benedict XII, Pope, 136
Benedictine Order, 122
Ben Nevis, Scotland, 50
Benodet, France, 144
Benoitville, France, 149
Bergamo, Italy, 130
Bergen, Norway, 65
   sights, 65
Bern, Switzerland, 78
Berruguete, Alonso, 196
Berthier, Marshal, 143
Betws-y-Coed, Wales, 37
Biarritz, France, 198
Bilbao, Spain, 197
Bingen, Germany, 74
Biokava Masef, Yugoslavia, 94
Biville, France, 149
Bjornson, Bjornstjerne, 65
Black Forest. *See* Schwarzwald.
Blackawton, England, 11
Blackmore Gate, England, 22
Blackmore, Richard, 13, 41
Blagaj, Yugoslavia, 94
Blanc, Mont, France, 78
Blois, France, 141, 143
Boabdil, 171
Bodensee, 81
Boetie, Etienne de la, 140
Bofel, Switzerland, 77
Bognor Regis, England, 5
Boleyn, Anne, 41
Bonivard, Francois, 78
Bonsor, George, 177
Bordeaux, Duc de, 143

Index

Borlange, Sweden, 62
Borromean Islands, Italy, 129
Borrowdale, England, 38
Boscastle, England, 21
Bosch, 193
Bosham, England, 6
Boswell, James, 32
Bourdzi, Greece, 104
Bournemouth, England, 7
Bourton-on-the-Water, England, 23
Brac, Yugoslavia, 93
Bracieux, France, 143
Braemar, Scotland, 48
Brahms, 82, 83
Brandon, Duke of Suffolk, 143
Braque, 72
brass rubbing, 4
Brehal, France, 148
Breles, France, 146
Brescia, Italy, 130
Brest, France, 146
Briconnet, Katherine, 141
"Brideshead Revisted," 25
Bridgewater, England, 22
Bridgnorth, England, 36
Brig, Switzerland, 77
Briksdalbre Glacier, Norway, 64
Brindisi, Italy, 117–118
  sights, 117–118
Bristol, England, 22
British Tourist Authority, xvi
Brittany, France, 144–148
Broadford, Scotland, 49
Bromsgrove, England, 36
Brooke, Lord, 35
Brown, Capability (Lancelot), 34
Bruges, Belgium, 84
Brunnen, Switzerland, 80
Bruxelles (Brussels), Belgium, 84
Budislavic, Ivan, 92
bullfighting, 170, 181, 193
Bulsard Valley, France, 149
Buna, Yugoslavia, 94
Burford, England, 23
Burgos, Spain, 188, 196–197
  sights, 197
Burns, Robert, 47
Byron, Lord, 42, 78, 102, 142, 186

Cabasso, Phillipe de, 136
Cabo da Roca, Portugal, 186
Cabo San Vicente, Portugal, 182–183
Cadaques, Spain, 160
Cadenet, France, 137
Cadnam, England, 7

Caen, France, 152
Caesar, Augustus, 123
Caetano, Marcelo, 180
Calpe, Spain, 164
calvaries, 146
Calvin, John, 78
Camargue, France, 135
Cambiaso, Luca, 128
Cambridge, England, 30, 40–42
  sights, 41–42
Camoes, 185
Campania, Italy, 120
Campillos, Spain, 169
camping, 199–219
  amenities, 200
  charges, 201
  cooking, 216–219
  equipment, 213–215
  guides, 199–200
  lists of sites, 202–212
  locations, 200
  seasons and holidays, 201
Cannes, France, 129
Cantabrian Cordillera, Spain, 155
Canterbury Tales, The (Chaucer), 25
Canute, King, 67
Cap Frehel, France, 146
Cape Wrath, Scotland, 49
Cap de Flamenville France, 149
Capel Curig, Wales, 37
Capri, Italy, 121
  sights, 121
car rental, lease, purchase, xxii, xxiii–xxiv
car shipment, xxiv
Caracalla, 82
caravan rental, xxv
Carcassonne, France, 138
Carcavelas, Portugal, 185
Carentan, France, 150
Carlyle, Thomas, 32, 54
Carmen (Bizet), 178
Carmona, Spain, 170, 176–177
Carovigno, Italy, 118
carnet, camping, xxvi
Carroll, Lewis, 24
Carroys, Guy des, 141
Cartagena, Spain, 165
Carteret, France, 149
Cary, Joyce, 24
Cascais, Portugal, 185
Caserta, Italy, 122
Castell de Ferro, Spain, 167
Castellammare di Stabia, Italy, 121
Castile, New, Spain, 188–189
Castile, Old, Spain, 188–189
Castro, Guillen de, 163

228 Index

Catalonia, Spain, 159–163
Cavaillon, Archbishop of, 136
Cavaillon Valley, France, 137
Cavendish, England, 42
Cavtat, Yugoslavia, 94
Cecil, William, 42
Celtic crosses, 14, 19
Celts, 45
Centrall Cordillera, Spain, 155
Cervantes, Miguel de, 178, 191, 196
Cetina, River, Yugoslavia, 93
Cezanne, 81
Chagall, Marc, 81
Chambord, France, 143
Chamonix, France, 78
Chantilly, France, 135
Charlemagne, 81, 87
Charles I, King of England, 6
Charles III, King of Naples, 122
Charles V, Holy Roman Emperor, 175
Charles, Prince of Wales, 31, 37
Charlie Is My Darling (Cary), 24
Chateau of Six Women. *See* Chenonceau.
Chaucer, 25, 32
Chenier, Andre, 134
Chenonceau, France, 140, 141
Cherbourg, France, 149, 150
  sights, 149
Cher, River, France, 141
Cherwell, River, England, 23
Chester, England, 38
Cheverny, France, 143
Chichester, England, 6
  sights, 6
"Childe Harold" (Byron), 98, 186
Children of Men (Phillpotts), 14
Children of the Mist (Phillpotts), 14
children, traveling with, xxxiv
Chillington, England, 11
Chipping Norton, England, 23, 35
Christowell: A Dartmoor Tale (Blackmore), 14
Chur, Switzerland, 77
Chysauster, England, 18
Cimabue, 125
Ciovo, Yugoslavia, 92
Cisternino, Italy, 118
Clement VI, Pope, 136
clothing list, xxvii
Clytemnestra, 103
Cockermouth, England, 39
Cocteau, Jean, 142
Colares, Portugal, 186
Coleridge, Samuel Taylor, 39
collecting, xxxiv

Cologne. *See* Koln.
Colwyn Bay, Wales, 38
Como, Lago di, Italy, 129
"Companion to the Guide, A" (Warton), 24
Concarneau, France, 144
Coniston, England, 38
Conteville, Bishop Odon of, 152
Contres, France, 143
Copenhagen, Denmark, 56–57
  sights, 56–57
Cordoba, Spain, 170, 175–176
  sights, 175–176
Corfu. *See* Kerkira.
Corneille, 163
Cornwall, England, 14–21
Corpus Christi, Feast of, 190
Costa Blanca, Spain, 158, 164–167
Costa Brava, Spain, 158, 159–160
Costa Del Azahar, Spain, 158, 163–164
Costa Del Sol, Spain, 158, 167–169
Costa Dorada, Spain, 158, 160–163
Cotentin Peninsula, France, 148
Cotswolds, England, 23
Couch, Sir Arthur Quiller, 16
countdown list, xxxi
Countainville, France, 149
Coutances, France, 149
Cowes, England, 6, 7
credit cards, xix
Creiro, Portugal, 187
Cres, Yugoslavia, 90
Crete, Greece, 107–111
  sights, 107–109
Critias (Plato), 112
Cuillins, Scotland, 49
Culatra, Portugal, 181
Cullera, Spain, 164
Culloden, Scotland, 49
currency regulations, xx
customs, xxv
Cyclades Islands, 111–117

da Gama, Vasco, 180, 184, 185
da Vinci, Leonardo, 126, 143
Daedalus, 108
Dalarna, Sweden, 62
Dali, Salvador, 159–160
Dalmation Coast, Yugoslavia, 89
Danish Travel Office, xvi
Dante, 126
Darde, Paul, 140
Darro River, Spain, 173
Dartmoor National Park, England, 14

Dartmouth, England, 12–13
  sights, 12
Death in Venice (Mann), 89
Death in the Afternoon (Hemingway), 169
De Clinton, Geoffrey, 36
Degas, 81
De Hooch, 71
Delabole, England, 21
Delfi, Greece, 97–99
  sights, 98–99
Demeter, 98
Den Fynske Landsby, Denmark, 67
Den Haag, Holland, 72, 84
Denmark, 56–58, 66–67
Devon, England, 7–14
Devon, Earl of, 8
Diana, Princess of Wales, 31
Dias, Bartolomeu, 180
Diaz, Rodrigo, *See* El Cid.
Dickens, Charles, 13, 21, 22, 32
Dinan, France, 147
Dinard, France, 146
Dinaric Mountain Range, Yugoslavia, 89, 93
Dinkelsbuhl, Germany, 75
Diocletian, Emperor, 93
Divine Comedy, The (Dante), 126
Dodgson, Charles. *See* Lewis Carroll.
Dolgellau, Wales, 37
Don Juan, 178
Don Juan (Byron), 102
Don Quixote (Cervantes), 178, 189
Donatello, 126, 127
Donizetti, 178
Donne, John, 32
Dorchester, England, 7
Dordogne, France, 139–140
Dorking, England, 5
  sights, 5
Dornie, Scotland, 49
Dostoyevsky, 83
Douarnenez, France, 146
Doyle, Sir Arthur Conan, 14, 32
Drake, Sir Francis, 13, 165, 183
driving regulations, 220–221
Dryden, John, 42
du Barry, Madame, 134
Dubricius, 26
Dubrovnik, Yugoslavia, 94–95
  sights, 95
Dumas, Alexander, 142
du Maurier, Daphne, 16
Dundee, Scotland, 48
Dunster, England, 22

Dupin, Madame, 141
Dyrehaven, Denmark, 57

Eagle of the Ninth (Sutcliffe), 26
Earth (Zola), 141
East Allington, England, 11
Eboli, Italy, 119
Edinburgh, Scotland, 46–47
  sights, 46–47
Edward I, King of England, 37
Egoist, The (Meredith), 5
Eiffel, Gustave, 135
Elche, Spain, 164–165
  sights, 164–165
El Cid, 163, 193, 196–197
Elea, Italy, 120
Eleanor of Toledo, 127
Elefsis, Greece, 99, 105
El Escorial, Spain, 188, 194
El Greco, 107, 162, 190, 191, 193
Elizabeth I, Queen of England, 42
Elizabeth II, Queen of Great Britain, 31, 34
Elounta, Greece, 110
El Port de la Selvais, Spain, 160
El Saler, Spain, 164
Elsinore. *See* Helsingor.
El Tobosco, Spain, 191
Ely, England, 30, 40, 42
emergencies, xxxii
Emma (Austen), 5
Empuries. *See* Ampurias.
Enkoping, Sweden, 62
Enkhuizen, Holland, 73
  sights, 73
Ennerdale, England, 38
Epidaurum. *See* Cavtat.
Epidavros, Greece, 104–105
  sights, 105
Episkepsis, Greece, 97
Ercolano, Italy, 122
Erithre, Greece, 99
Erquy, France, 146
Eskdale Pass, England, 38
Espangnols Point, France, 146
Estoril, Portugal, 185
Estremadura, Spain, 180
Ethelfleda, 35
Eugenie Grandet (Balzac), 141
Euripides, 102
Evans, Sir Arthur, 108
Exeter, England, 7, 13
  sights, 13
Exmoor, England, 13
expenses, estimating, xix

Index

Fabled Shore (Macauley), 163
fado, 181
Faenza, Ferrau of, 124
Fagernes, Norway, 64
Falmouth, England, 16–17
  sights, 16
Far from the Madding Crowd (Hardy), 7
Faro, Portugal, 181
  sights, 181
Fasano, Italy, 118
Feldkirch, Switzerland, 77
Felsenegg, Switzerland, 81
Ferdinand, King of Aragon, 171, 173, 196
Ferdinand the Great, King, 196
Fernando III, King, 176, 177
Festos, Greece, 109
Ffestiniog, Wales, 37
Fielding, Henry, 22, 32
Figueras, Spain, 159–160
Figuernina, Portugal, 187
Finnish National Travel Office, xvi
Firenze (Florence), Italy, 126–128
  sights, 127–128
Fishbourne, England, 6
Flam, Norway, 64
flamenco dancing, 170–171, 175, 193
Flaminius, 126
Flaubert, Gustave, 148
flight, getting bumped from, xxxiii
Florentino, Nicolas, 196
Floyen, Norway, 65
Fodele, Greece, 107
Fontaine de Vaucluse, France, 136
Fontainebleau, France, 135
Forster, E. M., 42
Fort William, Scotland, 50
Fortescue, Sir Edmund, 9
Fouesnant, France, 144
Fowey, England, 16
Fowles, John, 7, 13, 19, 98
Fox, John, 24
Fraddon, England, 20
Francois I, King of France, 142, 143
Frank, Anne, 71
Franz I, Emperor of Austria, 76
Frederick III, King of Denmark, 56
Freiburg, Germany, 82
French Government Tourist Office, xvi
French Lieutenant's Woman, The (Fowles), 7, 13
Frenchman's Creek (du Maurier), 16
Froude, James Anthony, 8
Fyn, Denmark, 67

Galaxidi, Greece, 98
Galileo, 128
Galopos, Portugal, 187
Galsworthy, John, 25
Gandia, Spain, 164
Garda, Lago di, Italy, 129
Garibaldi, 125
Garmisch-Partenkirchen, Germany, 75–76
  sights, 75
gas coupons, xx
Gaudi, Antonio, 160–161
Gaunt, John of, 36
Gea, 98
Geneve, Switzerland, 78–79
  sights, 78
Genil River, Spain, 173
Genoa, Italy, 129
Gent, Belgium, 84
German Tourist Information Office, xvi
Germany, 73–75, 82–83
Gersau, Switzerland, 80
Ghiberti, 126, 127
Giacometti, Augusto, 81
Giethoorn, Holland, 72
Gioia d. Colle, Italy, 119
Giotto, 125, 126, 127
Glencoe, Scotland, 50
Gloucester, Duke Humphrey of, 25
Goethe, 89, 162
Gol, Norway, 63
Gongora, Luis de Argote y, 176
Goonhilly Downs, England, 17
Gordes, France, 136
Gortys, Greece, 109
Gotland, Sweden, 59
Goult, France, 137
Gournia, Greece, 111
Goya, 190, 193
Gramat, France, 139
Granada, Spain, 169, 171–175
  sights, 173–174
Grandcampmaisy, France, 150
Granville, France, 149
Grasmere, England, 38
  sights, 38
Graves, Robert, 25
Gravina, Italy, 119
Great Gable, England, 38
Great Langdale, England, 38
Gredos Mountains, Spain, 189
Greece, 95–117
  ancient sites, 98–99, 100–101, 102, 103, 104, 105, 107–108, 109, 113
  ferries, 106, 111, 115
  National Tourist Office, xvi
Greppen, Switzerland, 80
Grieg, Edvard, 65
Guadarrama Mountains, Spain, 188

Guadiana, Rio, Spain, 179
Gudvangen, Norway, 64–65
Guerreiro, Candido, 181
Guide to the Perplexed, The (Maimonides), 176
Guingamp, France, 146
Gulval, England, 18
Gweek, England, 17

Haarlem, Holland, 72
Hadrian, 116
Hafelekar, Austria, 76
Hakluyt, Richard, 24
Hakluyt's Voyages (Hakluyt), 24
Hallsands Village, England, 10–11
Hals, Frans, 71
Halsingborg, Sweden, 58
Hamlet (Shakespeare), 57
Hammarskjold, Dag, 58
Hannibal, 126, 196
Hapsford, England, 38
Hardy, Thomas, 7, 21, 25
Harms, E. H., xxiv
Harrogate, England, 40
Haugesund, Norway, 65
Hauteville-Plage, France, 148
Hawker, R. S., 24
Hawkshead, England, 39
Hayling Island, England, 6
Hebrides, Scotland, 50–51
Heidi (Spyri), 77
Heidelberg, Germany, 74
  sights, 74
Heilbronn, Germany, 74
Heimskringla (Sturluson), 54
Helford River, England, 17
Helsingor (Elsinore), Denmark, 57
Helston, England, 18
Hemingway, Ernest, 169, 192
Henley, England, 24, 34
Henri II, King of France, 141
Henriques, Afonso, King of Portugal, 186
Henry VIII, King of England, 6, 9, 13, 16, 41
Henry the Navigator, Prince, 180, 182, 185
Hepworth, Barbara, 20
Heracles, 102
Herculaneum. *See* Ercolano.
Herquemolin, France, 149
Hesiod, 102
Heyerdahl, Thor, 63
Hirtshals, Denmark, 66
History of the Britains (Geoffrey of Monmouth), 21
Holland, 70–73
Holy Roman Empire, 123

Homage to Catalonia (Orwell), 159
Homer, 102, 104
Honefuss, Norway, 64
Hoorn, Holland, 73
Horse's Mouth, The (Cary), 24
Horsham, England, 5
hostels:
  American Youth Hostels, xxii
  Canadian Hosteling Association, xxii
  Youth Hostels Association (England), xxii
Hound of the Baskervilles, The (Doyle), 14
householding, xxix–xxxi
Housman, A. E., 42
Huelva, Spain, 179
Hugo, Victor, 134, 142, 163
Humphrey Clinker (Smollet), 22
Huntingdon, England, 40
Huxley, Aldous, 167
Hvar, Yugoslavia, 93
Hydra, 102

Iberia (Michener), 179
Iberian Cordillera, 155
Iberian Peninsula, 154–198
  accommodations, 157–158
Ibsen, Henrik, 63, 65
Icaza, Francisco de, 171
Idylls of the King (Tennyson), 21
Igls, Austria, 76
Ignatius, 116
Igoumenitsa, Greece, 97
Ij River, Holland, 71
Ilfracombe, England, 22
Immigrants, The (Moberg), 58
Inachus, 102
Innsbruck, Austria, 76
  sights, 76
insurance, xxvi
Interlaken, Switzerland, 78
Invergarry, Scotland, 50
Invermoriston, Scotland, 49
Inverness, Scotland, 49
Io, 102
Ioannina, Greece, 97
Ios, Greece, 114
Ipsos, Greece, 97
Iraklion, Greece, 107
Irish Tourist Office, xvi
Irving, Washington, 171, 178
Isabella, Queen of Castile. *See* Ferdinand, King of Aragon.
Isigny, France, 150
Isola Bella, Italy, 129
Italian Government Tourist Office, xvi
Italian Journey (Goethe), 89

232 Index

Italy, 87–89, 117–130
Itea, Greece, 98

Jaen, Spain, 170, 175
Jaeren, Norway, 66
Jamaica Inn (du Maurier), 16
James I and VI, King of England and Scotland, 51
James, Henry, 25, 42, 89, 127
Javea, Spain, 164
Jean Santeuil (Proust), 141
Jeanne d'Arc (Peguy), 141
Jenins, Switzerland, 77
Jeresa, Spain, 164
Jerez, Spain, 179
Jimenez, Juan Ramon, 168
John Caldigate (Trollope), 42
Johnson, Samuel, 32
Jones, Ken, 17
Jonkoping, Sweden, 59
Jonson, Ben, 32
Juan Carlos, King of Spain, 192
Jude the Obscure (Hardy), 25
Juliana, Queen of the Netherlands, 71

Kalakairinos, Minos, 108
Kalmar, Sweden, 58
Kamperhoek, Holland, 72
Karlstad, Sweden, 61
Kassiopi, Greece, 96
Kastel Riviera, Yugoslavia, 92–93
Kastracki Beach, Greece, 104
Katherine, Princess of Aragon, 42
Kaupanger, Norway, 64
Kea, Greece, 117
Kendal, England, 38
Kenilworth, England, 36
Kenilworth (Scott), 36
Kerkira (Corfu), Greece, 96
  sights, 96
Kersaint, France, 146
Keswick, England, 38
Ketelbrug, Holland, 72
Ketelhaven, Holland, 72
Kidderminster, England, 36
Kilchberg, Switzerland, 81
Kingsbridge, England, 7
Kinsarvik, Norway, 65
Kithnos, Greece, 117
Klampenborg, Denmark, 57
Knossos, Greece, 107–108
Knott Pass, England, 38
Knox, John, 47
Knute, King, 58
Koblenz, Germany, 73
Kolimbithres, Greece, 116

Koln (Cologne), Germany, 73–74
  sights, 74
Konstanz, Lake of. *See* Bodensee.
Korakiana, Greece, 97
Korcula, Yugoslavia, 93
Korinthos, Greece, 102
Korinthos, Gulf of, 117
Korsor, Denmark, 67
Kostas, Greece, 117
Kristiansand, Norway, 66
  sights, 66
Kristianstad, Sweden, 58
Kritsa, Greece, 111
Krk, Yugoslavia, 90
Kroken, Norway, 64
Kussnacht, Switzerland, 80
Kvanndal, Norway, 65
Kyle of Lochalsh, Scotland, 49
Kynance Cove, England, 18

La Albufera, Spain, 163
Ladby, Denmark, 67
Laerdal, Norway, 64
La Escala, Spain, 160
Lagerlof, Selma, 61
Lagos, Portugal, 182
  sights, 182
Lagos, Spain, 168
La Haye, France, 149
Lake District, England, 29, 38–40
La Mancha, Spain, 191
Lamb, Charles, 42
Lamorna, England, 19
Landenncau, France, 146
Land's End, England, 15, 19–20
Langdale Pikes, England, 38
Langeais, France, 144
Lannilis, France, 146
Lasithi Mountains, Greece, 109
La Spezia, Italy, 128
Lavenham, England, 42
law, encountering the, xxxiii
Lawrence, D. H., 20
Lazaro Goldiano, Jose, 192
Lech, Austria, 76
Lechlade, England, 23
Le Conquet, France, 146
Leeds, England, 40
Le Faou, France, 146
Lefkai, Greece, 117
Le Folgoet, France, 146
Le Guilvinec, France, 144
Leksand, Sweden, 62
Lelystad, Holland, 72
Leman, Lac, Switzerland, 78

Index 233

Lengronne, France, 148
Lenkovic, Ivan, 90
Leonora Christine, Princess of Denmark, 56
Lerici, Italy, 128
Les Baux-de-Provence, France, 137
Les Eyzies-de-Tayac, France, 140
Les Pieux, France, 149
Lessay, France, 149
Le Treport, France, 148
Le Val-Andre, France, 146
Levant, Spain, 163–169
Lewis, C. S., 24
Liapades, Greece, 97
Liddell, Alice, 24
Lidingo, Sweden, 61
Ligure, Italy, 128
Lincoln, England, 30, 40
Lion, The Witch and the Wardrobe, The (Lewis), 24
Liri Valley, Italy, 122
Lisboa, Portugal, 184–185
  sights, 185
Lisse, Holland, 72
Little Compton, England, 23
Lizard Point, England, 17
Ljusnarsberg, Sweden, 62
Llanberis, Wales, 37
Llandrillo, Wales, 36
Llangollen, Wales, 36
Llansa, Spain, 160
Llydaw, Wales, 37
Locke, John, 24
Locorotondo, Italy, 118
Loen, Norway, 64
Logara Bay, Greece, 117
Loire, France, 140–144
Lom, Norway, 64
Lombardy, Italy, 129
London, England, 30–33
  sights, 31–33
Longest Journey, The (Forster), 42
Looe, England, 15
Lorna Doone (Blackmore), 13
Lorraine, Louise of, 141
Los Cabezas de San Juan, Spain, 169
Louis XII, King of France, 143
Louis XIV, King of France, 143
Luberon Range, France, 137
Lugano, Lago di, Italy, 129
luggage, xxviii
Lund, Sweden, 58
  sights, 58
Lusiads, The (Camoes), 185
Luste Fjord, Norway, 64
Luxembourg, 83–84
Luxembourg Consulate General, xvi

Luzern, Switzerland, 79–80
  sights, 79–80
Lyme Regis, England, 7
Lymington, England, 7
Lyngby, Denmark, 57
Lyse Fjord, Norway, 66

Macauley, Rose, 42, 163
Macdonald, Flora, 50
Machiavelli, 126
Madrid, Spain, 187, 188, 192–194
  sights, 192–193
Magalhaes, Fernao de (Magellan), 177, 180
Maggiore, Italy, 120, 129
Magic Army, The (Thomas), 12
Maidenhead, England, 27, 34
Maienfeld, Switzerland, 77
Maimonides, Moses, 176
Mainz, Germany, 74
Maiori, Italy, 120
Makarska, Yugoslavia, 93
Malaga, Spain, 168
Malaren, Lake, Sweden, 59
Malmo, Sweden, 58
Manacle Point, England, 17
Mandra, Germany, 99
Mann, Thomas, 81, 89
Manresa, Spain, 161, 162
Manuel, King, 185
Marazion, England, 18
Marbella, Spain, 168
Margaret, Countess of Snowdon, 31, 34
Maria, Queen of Spain, 186
Maria-Carolina of Austria, 122
Maria Anna, Empress of Austria, 90
Maria Theresia, Empress of Austria, 76
Marie Antoinette, Queen of France, 82, 134
Marina de Ascea, Italy, 120
Marina de Casalvelino, Italy, 120
Marlborough, Duke of, 34
Marlowe, Christopher, 32, 41, 42
Marpissa, Greece, 115, 117
Marriage of Figaro, The (Mozart), 178
Martigny, Switzerland, 77
Martin I, Pope, 125
Martini, Simone, 125
Marvell, Andrew, 42
Mary Queen of Scots, 47
Mary (Tudor), Princess of England, 142
Matala, Greece, 109
Matisse, 81
Mayor of Casterbridge, The (Hardy), 7
medical problems, resolving, xxxiii
Medici, Catherine de, 41
Medici, Marie de, 134
Medusa, 102

234 Index

Meersburg, Germany, 82
  sights, 82
Menez-Hom, France, 146
Meredith, George, 5
Merida, Spain, 187, 189
  sights, 189
Merimee, Prosper, 138
Merlin and the Gleam (Tennyson), 21
Merry Wives of Windsor (Shakespeare), 34
Merwede Canal, Holland, 71
Messara, Bay of, Greece, 109
Messolongi, Greece, 98
Mestre, Italy, 130
Mestrovic, Ivan, 93
Metz, France, 83
Mevagissey, England, 16
Michelangelo, 123–124, 126, 127
Michener, James, 179
Mikine (Mycenae), Greece, 102–104
  sights, 103
Milano, Italy, 129–130
  sights, 129
Miletus, Isidore of, 116
Millau, France, 138
Milles, Carl, 61
Milne, A. A., 31
Milton, John, 42
Minore, Italy, 120
Minos, 108
Minotaur, 108
Mirabella, Gulf of, Greece, 110
Mires, Greece, 109
Mistral, Frederic, 138
Moberg, Vilhelm, 58
Mojacar, Spain, 166
Moliere, 143
Mondrian, 72
money, getting, xix
Monistrol, Spain, 162
Monmouth, Geoffrey of, 21, 25
Monovar, Spain, 164
Monserrat, Spain, 161
Montaigne, Michel de, 140
Montauban, France, 139
Montbray, Geoffrey de, 149
Monte Carlo, Monaco, 129
Monteagudo, Spain, 165
Monthou-sur-Cher, France, 141
Montrichard, France, 142
Mont-St-Michel, France, 18, 147–148
Moors, 88
Mora, Sweden, 62
Moraira, Cape, Spain, 164
Moray Firth, Scotland, 49
More, Sir Thomas, 24
Moresgaard, Denmark, 67

Moreton-in-Marsh, England, 23
Morlaix, France, 146
Mortimer, England, 26
Moscenicka Draga, Yugoslavia, 90
Mosel River, Germany, 73
Mostar, Yugoslavia, 94
  sights, 94
Motril, Spain, 167–168
Mount Dikti, Greece, 109
Mount Ida, Greece, 107, 109
Mount Pilatus, Switzerland, 79
Mount Ucka, Yugoslavia, 90
Mount Vesuvius, Italy, 112, 122
Mousehole, England, 19
Mozart, Wolfgang Amadeus, 75, 178
Muiderberg, Holland, 72
Mull, Scotland, 51
Munchen, Germany, 75
Murcia, Spain, 165
Murillo, 193
Mutters, Austria, 76
Mycenae. *See* Mikine.

Nacroy Fjord, Norway, 64
Nafpaktos, Greece, 98
Nafplion (Nauplia), Greece, 102, 104
Nantes, France, 141, 144
Naoussa, Greece, 115
Naples, Gulf of, Italy, 121
Napoleon, 133, 135, 142
Napoli, Italy, 122
Narbonne, France, 138
Narni, Italy, 124
national tourist offices, xvi
Naxos, Greece, 114
Nelson, Horatio, 6, 31
Neretva, River, Yugoslavia, 94
Nerja, Spain, 168
Nero, 123, 176
Ness, Loch, Scotland, 49
Netherlands National Tourist Office, xvi
Neumann, Balthasaar, 82
Neustadt, Germany, 82
Newman, J. H., 24
New Mill, England, 18
Niederhorn, Switzerland, 78
Nigardsbre, Norway, 64
Nimes, France, 138
Noci, Italy, 119
Nordkette Mountain Range, Austria, 76
Normandy, France, 148–152
  sights, 148–152
Normandy, Duke William of, 152
Norrkoping, Sweden, 59
North Sea Canal, 71
Northanger Abbey (Austen), 22

Index

Northleach, England, 23
Norway, 62–66
Norwegian National Tourist Office, xvi
Not Honour More (Cary), 24
Nyborg, Denmark, 67
Nyon, Switzerland, 78

Oban, Scotland, 50–51
Observations of the Faerie Queene of Spenser (Warton), 24
Octavius, 123
Odemira, Portugal, 183
Odense, Denmark, 57, 67
  sights, 67
Odysseus, 97
Oland, Sweden, 59
  sights, 59
Olhao, Portugal, 181
Olvera, Spain, 169
Omis, Yugoslavia, 93
Ondara, Spain, 164
Opatija, Yugoslavia, 90
Oppido Lucano, Italy, 119
Orestes, 103
Orihuela, Spain, 165
Orkney Islands, Scotland, 49
Oropesa, Spain, 189
Orrefors, Sweden, 58
Orsini, Raymond del Balza, 118
Orvieto, Italy, 124
Orwell, George, 159
Oslo, Norway, 62–63
  sights, 63
Ostuni, Italy, 118
Otto I, Holy Roman Emperor, 123
Oxford, England, 23–25, 29
  sights, 23–25
Oxford Book of English Verse (Quiller-Couch), 24
"Oxford in the Vacation" (Lamb), 42

packing, xxvii
Padova, Italy, 130
Paestum, Italy, 119–120
  sights, 119–120
Palencia, Spain, 198
Palmela, Portugal, 186
Pamplona, Spain, 198
Panormos, Greece, 107
paradores, 157, 173, 176, 189
Paris, France, 133–135
  sights, 133–135
Parnassus, Mount, Greece, 99
Paros, Greece, 114–117
  sights, 115–116
Participotius, Angelus, 87

Pasha, Ali, 98
passports, xxv
passports, loss of, xxxii
Patras, Greece, 102, 117
Patscherkofel, Austria, 76
Pavlova, Anna, 57
Pedrena, Spain, 198
Pedro I, King, 177
Pegasus, 102
Peguy, Charles, 141
Peloponnese, Greece, 102–105
Pelouze, Madame, 142
Pendennis (Thackeray), 13
Penfoul, France, 146
Penmarche Point, France, 144
Penrhyndeudraeth, Wales, 37
Pentland Firth, Scotland, 49
Penzance, England, 18
Pepin, King, 87
Pepys, Samuel, 42
Perigueux, France, 140
Perissa, Greece, 114
Perranporth, England, 20
Perseus, 102
Persuasion (Austen), 7, 22
Perugia, Italy, 125
Peterborough, England, 42
Petrarch, 126, 136
Phaistos. *See* Festos.
Philip II, King of Spain, 193
Phillpotts, Eden, 14
Picasso, Pablo, 72, 81, 161
Pickwick Papers (Dickens), 13, 22
Pillar Rock, England, 38
Pindar, 102
Pioppi, Italy, 120
Piraeaus, Greece, 105, 117
Pirgi, Greece, 96
Pisa, Italy, 128
  sights, 128
Pisano, Andrea, 126, 127
Pisso Livadi, Greece, 117
Pitlochry, Scotland, 48
Ploneour, France, 146
Plonevez-Porzay, France, 146
Ploudalmezeau, France, 146
Plovan, France, 146
Plozevet, France, 146
Plymouth, England, 11, 13
  sights, 13
Pocitelj, Yugoslavia, 94
Podgora, Yugoslavia, 94
Point de la Torche, France, 146
Point de Van, France, 146
Pointe de Penhir, France, 146
Pointe du Raz, France, 146

Poitiers, France, 140
Poitiers, Diane de, 141
Polo, Marco, 87
Polperro, England, 15–16
  sights, 16
Pombal, Marquis of, 184
Pompei, 121–122
  sights, 121, 122
"Pompei" (Hawker), 24
Pont l'Abbe, France, 144
Pont St. Benezet, France, 135
Pontaubault, France, 148
Poole, England, 7
Port Gaverne, England, 20
Portimao, Portugal, 182
Port Isaac, England, 20
Portofino, Italy, 128
Portrait of a Lady (James), 127
Portree, Scotland, 49
Portsmouth, England, 6
  sights, 6
Portugal, 19, 179–187
Portuguese Tourist Office, xvi
Poseidon, 97, 98, 100
Positano, Italy, 120
Potenza, Italy, 119
Potter, Beatrix, 39
pousadas, 157, 184, 186
Praia da Rocha, Portugal, 182
Praiano, Italy, 120
Prettejohn, Elizabeth, 11
Primosten, Yugoslavia, 91
Prince, The (Machiavelli), 126
"Prose Edda" (Sturluson), 54
Proust, Marcel, 141
Provence, France, 135–138
Puerto de Mazarron, Spain, 165
punting, 24, 30
Pyrenees Mountains, 155
Pythius, 98
Python, 98

Queluz, Portugal, 186
Quiberon, France, 144
Quiller Couch, Sir Arthur, 16, 24

Rab, Yugoslavia, 90
Randers, Denmark, 66
Rapallo, Italy, 128
Raphael, 193
Rattvik, Sweden, 62
Ravello, Italy, 120
"Ravenna" (Wilde), 24
Reading, England, 26
  sights, 26
Rebecca (du Maurier), 16

Rembrandt, 71
Remus, 123
Renoir, 81
Rethimnon, Greece, 107
Return of the Native, The (Hardy), 7
Revsnes, Norway, 64
Reynolds, Sir Joshua, 24
Rhine River, Germany, 73
Rhone Delta, France, 135
Rijeka, Yugoslavia, 90
Rilke, Rainer Maria, 169
Rival, The (Sheridan), 22
Robert the Bruce, King of Scotland, 51
Roberts, David, 172
Robespierre, 134
Rocamadour, France, 139
Rofels, Switzerland, 77
Roldal, Norway, 66
Roma, Italy, 122–124
  sights, 123–124
Romero, Francisco, 169
Romulus, 123
Ronda, Spain, 168–169
  sights, 168–169
Rosal de la Frontera, Spain, 179
Rosamond (Swinburne), 25
Rosas, Spain, 160
Rossini, 178
Rothenburg ob der Tauber, Germany, 74–75
Rotterdam, Holland, 73, 84
Rousseau, Jean-Jacques, 134, 141
Roussillon, France, 137
route and mileage chart, xviii
Royston, England, 43
Rubens, Peter Paul, 35, 41, 193
Rusinol, 162
Ruisdal, 71
Ruskin, John, 24, 39, 89

Saffron Walden, England, 42
Sage of Gosta Berling, The (Lagerlof), 61
Sagres, Portugal, 182
St. Agnes, England, 17
St. Andrews, Scotland, 47
St. Anton, Austria, 76
St. Austell, England, 16
  sights, 16
St-Brieuc, France, 146
St-Gemmes, France, 144
St. Guenole, France, 145
  sights, 145
St. Herbert's Island, England, 39
St. Ives, England, 20
  sights, 20
St. Juliot, England, 21

Index

St. Keverne, England, 18
St-Malo, France, 147
　sights, 147
St. Margen, Germany, 82
Ste. Marie-du-Menez-Hom, France, 146
St-Mathieu Point, France, 146
St. Michael's Mount, England, 18
St. Peter, Germany, 82
St. Pierre, France, 145
St. Remy-de-Provence, France, 137
S. Vito dei Normanni, Italy, 118
Salamanca, Spain, 188, 195–196
　sights, 196
Salazar, Dr., 180
Salcombe, England, 7, 8–10
　sights, 9–10
Salen, Sweden, 62
Salerno, Italy, 119
Salobrena, Spain, 168
Salona, Yugoslavia, 92
Saltsjobaden, Sweden, 61
Salzburg, Austria, 75
　sights, 75
Sand, Georges, 142
Sandhamn, Sweden, 61
San Pedro de Alcantara, Spain, 168
San Sebastian, Spain, 198
Santa Margherita Ligure, Italy, 128
Santana, Portugal, 187
Santander, Spain, 188, 197–198
Santiago de Cacem, Portugal, 183
Santorini, Greece, 111–114
　sights, 111–114
Sarlat, France, 140
　sights, 140
Saronic Gulf, Greece, 105
Sauda, Norway, 66
Saumur, France, 141, 144
Savelletri, Italy, 118
Sawrey, England, 39
Scafell Pike, England, 38
Scavi di Velia, Italy, 120
Scharnitz, Austria, 76
Scheveningen, Holland, 84
Schilardi, Demetrius, 116
School for Scandal, The (Sheridan), 22
Schubert, 178
Schwarzwald, Germany, 82
Scilly, Isles of, 19
Scott, Sir Walter, 36
Sechan, Charles, 83
Secret Woman, The (Phillpotts), 14
Seefeld, Austria, 76
Seegrube, Austria, 76
Segovia, Spain, 188, 194–195
　sights, 195

Seine River, France, 133
Selva di Fasano, Italy, 118
Seneca, Lucius Annaeus, 176
Senj, Yugoslavia, 90–91
　sights, 90
Sesimbra, Portugal, 187
Setubal, Portugal, 184, 187
Seurat, 72
Sevilla, Spain, 170, 177–180
　sights, 177–178
Shakespeare, William, 25, 35
Shaw, George Bernard, 32
Shelley, Percy Bysshe, 25, 39
Sherford, England, 11
Sheridan, Richard Brinsley, 22
Shipwreck (Fowles), 19
Shrewsbury, England, 36
Sibenik, Yugoslavia, 91
Siegfroid, Count of Ardennes, 84
Siena, Italy, 126
　sights, 126
Sierra de Carroscoy, Spain, 165
Sierra de Jabalcua, Spain, 170
Sierra Morena Mountains, Spain, 155
Sierra Nevada Mountains, Spain, 155, 169–170, 175
Silchester, England, 26
　sights, 26
Siljan, Lake, Sweden, 62
Sintra, Portugal, 186
Sion, Switzerland, 77
Siros, Greece, 117
Sisae, Greece, 107
Sitges, Spain, 162
Sitticus, Marcus, 75
Skare, Norway, 65
Skipton, England, 40
Skopas, 115
Skudeneshavn, Norway, 65
Skye, Isle of, Scotland, 49–50
Slapton Sands, England, 11
Sligachan, Scotland, 49
Smollet, Tobias, 22
Sogne Fjord, Norway, 64
Solin, Yugoslavia, 93
Somo, Spain, 198
"Song of the Western Men, The" (Hawker), 24
Sophocles, 102
Sorbas, Spain, 166
Sorgue, River, France, 136
Sorrento Peninsula, Italy, 120
Souillac, France, 140
Sounion, Greece, 101–102
　sights, 101
Southey, Robert, 39

Spain, 158–179, 187–198
Spakenburg, Holland, 72
Spanish Tourist Office, xvi
Spartilas, Greece, 96
Spean Bridge, Scotland, 50
Spectator papers (Addison), 24
Spinalonga, Greece, 110
Split, Yugoslavia, 93
  sights, 93
Spoleto, Italy, 124
Spyri, Johanna, 77
Sqourades, Greece, 96
Staffa, Scotland, 51
Stamford, England, 42
Staphorst, Holland, 72
Stavanger, Norway, 66
  sights, 66
Steen, 71
Stendahl, 148
Stephen, Leslie, 20
Stevenson, Robert Louis, 47
Stirling, Scotland, 51
Stockholm, Sweden, 59–61
  sights, 60–61
Stoke Fleming, England, 12
Stokenham, England, 11
Stone, Irving, 128
Stonehaven, Scotland, 48
Stones of Venice, The (Ruskin), 89
Stow-on-the-Wold, England, 23
Strasbourg, France, 83
Stratford-upon-Avon, England, 35
  sights, 35
Strauss, 178
Stresa, Italy, 129
Strete, England, 11, 12
Strinilas, Greece, 96
Stuart, Charles (Bonnie Prince Charlie), 47, 49, 50
Studley, England, 36
Sturluson, Snorri, 54
Styhead Pass, England, 38
Sulla, Roman general, 105
Sun Also Rises, The (Hemingway), 169
Super Rosas, Spain, 160
Sutcliffe, Rosemary, 26
Sweden, 58–61
Swedish National Travel Office, xvii
Swinburne, Algernon, 21, 25
Swindon, England, 23
Swiss National Tourist Office, xvii
Switzerland, 77–81

Tabernas, Spain, 167
Tagus River, Portugal, 184, 187
Talavera de la Reina, Spain, 189

Tale of Squirrel Nutkin, The (Potter), 39
Tales of the Alhambra (Irving), 171–172
Taranto, Italy, 118
Tarifa, Spain, 170
Tarragona, Spain, 162
  sights, 162–163
Tavira, Portugal, 181
  sights, 181
Tell, William, 80
Tennyson, Alfred, Lord, 8, 21, 42
Teotocopulos, Domenico. *See* El Greco.
Terni, Italy, 124
Tess of the D'Urbervilles (Hardy), 8
Thackeray, William Makepeace, 13, 32, 42
Thames River, England, 31
Themis, 98
Theodosius, Emperor, 105
thievery, xxvi
Thira. *See* Santorini.
Thive, Greece, 99
Thomas, Dylan, 25
Thomas, Leslie, 12
Thorne, England, 40
Thrasyboulos, 115
Thun, Switzerland, 78
Thyestes, 102
"Timaeus" (Plato), 112
Tintagel, England, 21
Tintoretto, 87, 88
Tiryns, Greece, 103, 104
Tisamenus, 103
Titian, 87, 88, 190, 193
Titisee, Germany, 82
Todi, Italy, 124–125
  sights, 124–125
Toledo, Spain, 188, 190–191
  sights, 190–191
Toledo Mountains, Spain, 188
Tolkien, J.R.R., 25
Tolon, Greece, 104
Tom Jones (Fielding), 22
Torcross, England, 11
Tormes River, Spain, 195
Torpoint, England, 15
Torquay, England, 11
Torre, Spain, 167
Torre Annunziata, Italy, 121, 122
Torre Canne Terme, Italy, 118
Torre del Mar, Spain, 168
Torrenueva, Spain, 167
To the Lighthouse (Woolf), 20
Toulouse-Lautrec, 81
Tours, France, 140, 141, 143
tourist information, xvi
Tragic Comedians, The (Meredith), 5
transportation, xxiii

Trasimeno, Lago, Italy, 126
travelers' checks, loss of, xxxiii
Trawsfynydd, Wales, 37
Trebarwith, England, 20
Tremazan, France, 146
Trevelyan, G. M., 42
Trewoofe, England, 19
Trieste, Italy, 89
Trogir, Yugoslavia, 92
  sights, 92
Trollope, Anthony, 42
Trumpington, England, 42
Tullius, Servius, 123
Tuscany, Italy, 126–128
Twain, Mark, 80
Tyndrum, Scotland, 51
Tyrol, Austria, 76

Uccello, 127
Uetliberg, Switzerland, 81
Ugborough, England, 8
Ullswater, England, 38, 39
Umbria, Italy, 124–126
Unto a Good Land (Moberg), 58
Uppsala, Sweden, 59, 61
Urk, Holland, 73
Utrecht, Holland, 71
Utrillo, 81, 162

Val d'Enfer, France, 137
Valencia, Spain, 163–164
  sights, 163, 164
Vallodolid, Spain, 189, 196
  sights, 196
Valle de los Caidos, Spain, 194
Valognes, France, 150
Van Dyck, 35, 71, 190
Van Gogh, Vincent, 71, 72, 135, 137–138
Vanern, Lake, Sweden, 62
Vanishing Cornwall (du Maurier), 16, 17
Varmland, Sweden, 61
Vasa, Gustavus, 58, 62
Vasarely, Victor, 136
Vatican City, Italy, 123–124
Vattern, Lake, Sweden, 59
Vauville, France, 149
Velazquez, 193
Veleta, Mount, Spain, 175
Venezia, Italy, 87–89
  sights, 87–89
Verbier, Switzerland, 77
Vermeer, 71
Verne, Jules, 117
Verona, Italy, 130
Veronese, 87, 88
Versailles, France, 135

Vespucci, Amerigo, 177
Vettica, Italy, 120
Vevey, Switzerland, 78
Vicenza, Italy, 130
Vico Equense, Italy, 121
Victoria, Queen of Great Britain, 7
Vietri, Italy, 120
Vigeland, Gustav, 63
Village in the Vauclusé, The (Wylie), 137
Villamartin, Spain, 179
Viollet-le-Duc, Eugene, 138
Virgil, 117
Vis, Yugoslavia, 93
Visby, Sweden, 59
Viste, Norway, 66
Vitznau, Switzerland, 80
Vivar, Spain, 196
Volendam, Holland, 73
Volosko, Yugoslavia, 90
Voltaire, 87, 134, 141
Voss, Norway, 65
Vouvray, France, 143

Wales, 36–38
Wallace, Sir William, 51
Wallingford, England, 27
Wareham, England, 7
Warminster, England, 22
Warton, Thomas, 24
Warwick, England, 35–36
Warwick, Earl of, 35
Wasdale Head, England, 38
Waugh, Evelyn, 25
Waverley (Scott), 51
Webb, Aston, 12
Weggis, Switzerland, 80
Wellington, Duke of, 26
Wheddon Cross, England, 22
Wight, Isle of, England, 6–7
Wild Strawberries, 62
Wilde, Oscar, 24, 32
William the Lion, King of Scotland, 51
Windermere, England, 38
Windsor, England, 34
Winnie the Pooh (Milne), 31
Wolsey, Cardinal, 23
Women in Love (Lawrence), 20
Wonderful World of Nils, The (Lagerlof), 61
Woolf, Virginia, 20, 33
Wordsworth, William, 38–39
Worthing, England, 5
Wren, Sir Christopher, 23, 41
Wylie, Laurence, 137
Wyrnose Pass, England, 38

Ximena, wife of El Cid, 163

Yeats, William B., 25
Yelverton, England, 13
York, England, 30, 40
Ystad, Sweden, 58
Yugoslav Tourist Office, xvii
Yugoslavia, 89–95
Yusti, Pablo, 176

Zadar, Yugoslavia, 91
  sights, 91
Zahringen, Dukes of, 78, 82
Zennor, England, 20
Zermatt, Switzerland, 77
Zola, Emile, 134, 141
Zuiderzee, Holland, 72
Zurich, Switzerland, 81
  sights, 81
Zurs, Austria, 76

The Foulkes on a hike in Sweden with two of their children, David and Carrie.

Patricia and Robert Foulke have spent four sabbatical years in Europe over the last twenty years, living in both southern Italy and England, and they have traveled and refined every itinerary in *Fielding's Motoring & Camping Europe*. Robert Foulke, who has a Ph.D. in English from the University of Minnesota, is a professor of English at Skidmore College and a former chairman of Skidmore's English department. Patricia Foulke, who has an M.A. in education from Trinity College, Hartford, CT, taught elementary-school grades, remedial reading, and special education classes for twenty years. Together, the Foulkes own and operate a sailing school on Lake George, New York, where they make their home.